Marketing Semiotics Research:

Consumption Trends, AI, and the Economics of Experience

Marianna Boero
University of Teramo, Italy

Rossana Piccolo
https://orcid.org/0009-0003-1637-4701
University of Teramo, Italy

IGI Global
Scientific Publishing
Publishing Tomorrow's Research Today

Vice President of Editorial	Melissa Wagner
Director of Acquisitions	Mikaela Felty
Director of Book Development	Jocelynn Hessler
Production Manager	Mike Brehm
Cover Design	Jose Rosado

Published in the United States of America by
IGI Global Scientific Publishing
701 East Chocolate Avenue
Hershey, PA, 17033, USA
Tel: 717-533-8845 | Fax: 717-533-7115
Website: https://www.igi-global.com E-mail: cust@igi-global.com

Library of Congress Cataloging-in-Publication Data

Names: Piccolo, Rossana, 1987- editor
http://id.loc.gov/rwo/agents/n2024063295 | Boero, Marianna editor
http://id.loc.gov/rwo/agents/no2017140658
Title: Marketing semiotics research : consumer trends, AI, and the economics of experience / edited by Rossana Piccolo, Marianna Boero.
Description: Hershey, PA : IGI Global Scientific Publishing, [2026] | Includes bibliographical references and index. | Summary: "The book aims to present the state of semiotic research in marketing, advertising, and consumption, while also providing direction for future research. It will focus on how social change is reflected in the consumption system, aiming to describe the reciprocal exchange between objects of study and methods of analysis"-- Provided by publisher.
Identifiers: LCCN 2024055178 (print) | LCCN 2024055179 (ebook) | ISBN 9798369380246 hardcover | ISBN 9798369380253 paperback | ISBN 9798369380260 ebook
Subjects: LCSH: Marketing research http://id.loc.gov/authorities/subjects/sh85081350 | Semiotics in advertising http://id.loc.gov/authorities/subjects/sh2008008080
Classification: LCC HF5415.2 .M3255 2025 (print) | LCC HF5415.2 (ebook) | DDC 658.8/3--dc23/eng/20250117
LC record available at https://lccn.loc.gov/2024055178
LC ebook record available at https://lccn.loc.gov/2024055179

British Cataloguing in Publication Data
A Cataloguing in Publication record for this book is available from the British Library.

Table of Contents

Detailed Table of Contents

The square of the axiology of consumption and the square of the advertising philosophies are two milestones within the semiotics of advertising. Developed around the mid-1980s by the French semiotician and consultant Jean-Marie Floch, they crossed the boundaries of applied semiotics and became part of the tools available to marketing researchers. The chapter aims to propose some developments of these two models, illustrating them and conducting both a theoretical review and an empirical investigation, focused on the Italian context. In this way, it will be possible to advance some integrative proposals – the mapping of narrative configurations and the square of declensions of the discursive genres – able to increase the heuristic power of the original typologies.

Nowadays brands are increasingly expected to adopt activist stances on political, social, and environmental issues. Popular examples include Patagonia's commitment toward the conservation and restoration of the natural environment and Nike's longstanding support for the Black community in the US, to name a few. These corporate efforts have come to be known as 'brand activism' and concern publicly stated positions on sensitive issues by means of advertising, public relations, and other media. Despite the increasing dissemination of activist marketing campaigns, however, brand activism remains underexplored from a semiotic standpoint. This chapter aims to fill this gap by proposing a new methodological tool merging semiotics and netnography to analyze both the narrative strategies used within activist commercials and consumers' reactions to these messages. Dove's 2024 'The Code' campaign will serve as a case study to illustrate this approach. Results will furnish interesting insights into the relationship between consumers, brands, and social issues.

Preface

In an era characterized by accelerated digital transformation, heightened consumer expectations, and the convergence of physical and virtual worlds, the role of semiotics in marketing has never been more critical. Semiotics offers a vital lens through which to understand how brands communicate, how consumers interpret messages, and how meaning is co-created across diverse platforms and cultural contexts.

This edited volume, *Marketing Semiotics Research: Consumer Trends, AI, and the Economics of Experience*, brings together emerging research and applied insights at the intersection of semiotics, consumer behavior, AI technologies, and experiential marketing. The book explores how meaning is constructed and navigated in complex omnichannel environments, how artificial intelligence enhances symbolic interpretation, and how semiotic tools can help marketers design emotionally resonant, culturally aware, and ethically sound brand experiences.

Our aim is to offer scholars, practitioners, and students a comprehensive overview of how semiotic theory and practice are being applied to real-world marketing challenges—from the evolution of advertising and phygital experiences to brand activism and storytelling on social media. The book also delves into emerging methodological approaches, such as the integration of netnography and AI analytics with semiotic analysis, to better understand contemporary consumer culture.

The diversity of geographic, academic, and professional backgrounds among our contributors ensures a rich and global perspective on the ever-evolving semiotic landscape of modern marketing. Whether you are a marketing strategist, a semiotician, a digital analyst, or a brand consultant, this collection invites you to explore how meaning drives engagement, innovation, and value in today's consumer economy.

CHAPTER OVERVIEW

Chapter 1: Semiotics of Omnichannel and Phygital Purchase Experiences

Paolo Odoardi & Antonio Laurino

This chapter proposes a semiotic framework to decode the phygital and omnichannel retail environment. By constructing a semiotic square, it categorizes consumers into four ideal types: Human touch lovers, Tech enthusiasts, Pragmatists, and Conservatives, each guiding CX design and innovation in hybrid purchase contexts.

Chapter 2: Digital-Physical Harmony: The Impact of Symbols on Phygital Consumers

Esma Ebru Sentürk

Here, semiotics is positioned as the glue that binds the digital and physical aspects of branding. The chapter explains how cohesive symbolic messaging fosters emotional and cognitive resonance among consumers navigating phygital spaces.

Chapter 3: The Role of Semiotics in Digital Marketing

Sarvesh Khaitan & Kartikeya Singh

Using qualitative interviews, this chapter investigates how consumers interpret visual signs and brand messages in digital media. It emphasizes the importance of culturally sensitive and symbol-rich communications in building brand identity and loyalty.

Chapter 4: AI, Semiotics, and Marketing

Naga Palakurti

This chapter explores how AI enhances semiotic interpretation by analyzing real-time consumer data. It shows how AI technologies like NLP and machine learning can be leveraged to design symbolically rich, emotionally resonant consumer interactions.

Chapter 5: Semiotics, Advertising, and Classification

Antonio Laurino

Building on Jean-Marie Floch's foundational models, this chapter introduces new tools, such as the square of discursive genres, for analyzing advertising narratives in the Italian market. It bridges theory with empirical insight, enriching semiotic analysis in localized contexts.

Chapter 6: Challenging Beauty Norms in the Digital Age

Alice Venturini

This case study on Dove's 2024 "The Code" campaign explores how brand activism can be semiotically decoded through a hybrid methodology combining netnography and narrative analysis. It sheds light on consumer-brand dynamics in socially charged messaging.

Chapter 7: Digital Marketing and Semiotics

Nilesh Anute et al.

This collaborative chapter explores the symbiotic relationship between digital marketing and semiotics, emphasizing how meaning is shaped in online ecosystems through visual, textual, and symbolic cues. It positions semiotics as central to brand success in digital spheres.

Chapter 8: A Semiotic Approach to Brand Storytelling in Social Media

Caterina Scianna

Focusing on visual storytelling as a key strategy in digital branding, this chapter shows how narrative and semiotic techniques create authenticity and emotional depth in social media campaigns. It reveals storytelling as both an art and science in the digital age.

Together, these chapters form a cohesive and forward-looking exploration of marketing semiotics in the 21st century, offering tools, frameworks, and case studies that illuminate how brands can communicate meaningfully in a rapidly shifting cultural and technological environment.

Edited by Marianna Boero and Rossana Piccolo

Introduction

In recent years, contacts between semiotics and marketing have become increasingly frequent and systematic. Marketing professionals are devoting greater attention to semiotic analysis tools, while semiotics itself is showing renewed interest in fields such as marketing, consumption, and advertising communication, thereby reinforcing its practical as well as theoretical relevance. The marketing world's interest in semiotics can be attributed to the latter's methodological rigor, which offers innovative insights into traditional social issues while also shedding light on new ones, such as consumer behavior theory and brand analysis. Conversely, semiotics is increasingly drawn to this realm of meaning-related challenges.

Moreover, the growing complexity of communication phenomena in contemporary post-industrial societies drives communication professionals and corporate research managers to seek new analytical tools to understand the mechanisms and evolution of today's consumption scenarios. As consumption phenomena become increasingly symbolic and cultural, the need for sophisticated analysis becomes more pressing (Bianchi 2005; Boero 2017).

Semiotic models offer marketing enhanced insights beyond those achievable with traditional methodologies, while their application in the social field challenges semioticians to refine their analytical categories (Rolle 2014). In this perspective, consumption reveals itself as a complex mechanism that appropriates existing situations, desires, or needs from the collective imagination and transforms them for specific communicative purposes. It translates them into narratives in which Subjects pursue diverse Objects embodying various social values. The semiotic analysis of advertising thus becomes a profound social investigation into the motivations underlying consumption, uncovering narrative constants and invariant patterns in the valorization of Objects by Subjects (Semprini 2003).

Notably, Jean-Marie Floch's work in the early 1990s, particularly in his books *Semiotics, Marketing, Communication* (1990) and *Visual Identities* (1995), gathered significant studies on this subject. In his essay *J'aime, j'aime, j'aime: Car Advertising and the System of Consumer Values*, Floch demonstrates the potential synergy between semiotics and marketing by applying generative semiotics tools to a corpus of automotive advertising texts. Central to these studies are the theoretical and analytical tools developed by Greimasian semiotics, such as the semiotic square, which makes it possible to reconstruct a typology of the possible forms through which advertising communication enhances the objects it promotes. This framework—an axiology of consumption values—remains today the foundation of numerous semiotic investigations of advertising. By offering "greater intelligibility, greater relevance, greater differentiation" (Floch 1990), the semiotic method reveals the hidden strategies underlying signs and serves as a strategic tool in various domains of brand communication: from analyzing an individual advertisement to examining broader campaigns, from monitoring communicative coherence to designing logos, packaging, and retail spaces.

This collaboration between marketing and semiotics was strengthened in subsequent years with the rise of sociosemiotics, a branch of semiotics that emphasizes its empirical and analytical vocation. Over time, the semiotic gaze has focused primarily on advertising and branding, and to a lesser extent on spaces of consumption and packaging. In this regard, Ceriani (2001, 2007), Bianchi (2005), and Bianchi and Ragonese (2013) have further developed Greimasian methods and tools for the analysis of advertising and marketing communication. Marrone (2007) extends these reflections to the semiotic study of the brand, advocating for a departure from schematic narrativity—often used in applied semiotics for advertising and marketing discourse—in favor of forms of subjectivity and experience more closely linked to affectivity, aesthetics, corporeality, and the sphere of forms of life and the rhythms of social transformation.

Another area of convergence between semiotics and marketing concerns packaging. Ventura (2022) highlights how product packaging has gradually evolved from a simple container into a complex semiotic object, capable of fulfilling multiple communicative, marketing, logistical, and hygienic functions. Packaging narrates the story of the product it contains, enhances it, and translates it, presenting itself as a continually renewed semiotic unit.

Recently, with the advent of digital technologies, semiotics has renewed its interest in marketing issues, particularly in relation to the growing prevalence of artificial intelligence (Boero and Greco 2023). Bianchi and Cosenza (2020) edited a volume on digital communication that compiles contributions exploring the dialogue between semiotics and digital marketing—from Search Engine Optimization (SEO) practices to new branding strategies in digital business communication. More recently, Cosenza (2024) proposed a theoretical-methodological approach that further bridges semiotics and digital marketing, introducing the concept of consultative semiotics and offering a reasoned checklist for designing digital marketing campaigns.

While semiotics increasingly examines the world of marketing, its objects of study, and its investigative methodologies, marketing and business communication likewise pay close attention to the descriptive language and analytical tools of semiotics. Examples include Ferraresi and Schmitt's (2007) work on consumer experience, Musso's (2005) study of brand communication, and Qualizza's (2006) research on consumption practices and new marketing trends, including local brands. As Oswald (2011) observes, the extent to which consumers recognize, internalize, and relate to brand meanings has a tangible impact on a firm's financial performance. Brand meaning is not merely an added value but a prerequisite for creating brand value. Managing brand equity therefore fundamentally entails managing brand meanings—that is, managing semiotics.

On this basis, the book aims to present the state of semiotic research in marketing, advertising, and consumption, while also providing directions for future research. It will examine how social change is reflected in the consumption system, aiming to describe the reciprocal exchange between objects of study and methods of analysis. The goal is to provide a comprehensive account of this dual movement, illustrating how semiotic and marketing methodologies mutually enrich each other and evolve in response to social transformation

This volume brings together a series of contributions that explore the intersection between semiotics and marketing, following the pioneering approach of Jean-Marie Floch, whose work demonstrated the strategic value of semiotic tools for understanding and shaping brand communication. Moving from Floch's contribution, the volume also draws on Laura Oswald's influential studies in *Marketing Semiotics*, which have emphasized the role of brand meaning as a driver of consumer engagement and a determinant of brand equity. The chapters address a wide range of themes, from the role of emotions in brand communication and experiential marketing strategies in the fashion industry to the evolution of Floch's classification models in the Italian advertising context. The focus extends to the semiotics of omnichannel and phygital purchase experiences, offering frameworks for customer experience design and innovation, and to emotional branding in emerging markets, examined through the mediation of digital marketing in contexts such as the Horn of Africa. The book also investigates the convergence of creativity and artificial intelligence, analyzing AI-driven marketing strategies and their capacity to produce emotional resonance, as well as case studies such as Dove's The Code campaign, which challenges beauty norms in the digital age. Other contributions examine brand storytelling on social media, emerging trends in advertising with fact-based evaluations of contemporary strategies, and the interplay between AI, emotional branding, and personalized consumer experiences. Several chapters focus on digital marketing and semiotics, mapping consumer trends, the economics of experience, and the role of semiotics in decoding AI-driven consumer interactions. Collectively, the volume positions marketing-oriented semiotics as a dynamic research field that not only interprets the symbolic dimension of consumption but also provides actionable frameworks for innovation in brand communication— reaffirming Floch's insight that semiotics is both an analytical lens and a strategic resource, and resonating with Oswald's argument that managing brand equity fundamentally means managing brand meaning.

One of the most innovative aspects of this volume lies in its truly international and interdisciplinary scope: it brings together contributions from scholars and practitioners affiliated with diverse research centers across the globe, each reflecting on a field in constant transformation. This diversity of perspectives allows for a rich and multifaceted dialogue, where theoretical insight meets applied practice. On one side, semiotics opens itself to marketing, expanding its analytical frameworks to engage with the dynamics of consumption, branding, and digital communication. On the other, marketing embraces the semiotic gaze, recognizing its potential to uncover the symbolic and cultural dimensions of consumer behavior and to guide strategic brand management. This reciprocal openness fosters a fertile ground for methodological innovation, enabling the co-evolution of both disciplines in response to shifting social, technological, and cultural contexts.

Future research directions in this interdisciplinary dialogue will likely intensify along several converging paths. As marketing increasingly operates in hybrid physical-digital environments and engages with highly fragmented, emotionally driven consumer publics, the semiotic approach will need to refine its tools for decoding complex, multi-platform narratives and fluid brand identities. Conversely, marketing will continue to benefit from the semiotic capacity to interpret cultural codes, consumer imaginaries, and the performative power of communication, translating these insights into more resonant and ethically responsible strategies. Emerging areas such as AI-driven personalization, immersive brand experiences, and the semiotics of sustainability offer fertile ground for collaborative inquiry, while the ongoing influence of cultural diversity and global market integration will demand context-sensitive frameworks. This evolving exchange between semiotics and marketing promises not only to enrich both disciplines theoretically and methodologically, but also to redefine their role in shaping consumer culture and market innovation.

Marianna Boero
University of Teramo, Italy

Rossana Piccolo
University of Teramo, Italy

REFERENCES

Beasley, R., & Danesi, M. (2002). *Persuasive Signs: The Semiotics of Advertising* (Vol. 4). Mouton De Gruyter. DOI: 10.1515/9783110888003

Bianchi, C. (2005). *Spot. Analisi semiotica dell'audiovisivo pubblicitario*. Carocci.

Bianchi, C., & Cosenza, G. (2020) (eds.), Semiotica e digital marketing, Aracne, Rome.

Bianchi, C., & Ragonese, R. (2013). *L'annuncio stampa*. Carocci.

Boero, M., & Greco, C. (2023). "Semiotics, Artificial Intelligence, ChatGpt. Research Lines, Analytical Perspectives and Potential Application", Filosofi(e). *Semiotiche*, *10*(1), 2023.

Ceriani, G. (2001). *Marketing moving: l'approccio semiotico. Analizzare il mix di comunicazione, gestirne gli effetti di senso*. Franco Angeli Milan.

Ceriani, G. (2007). *Hot spots e sfere di cristallo. Semiotica della tendenza e ricerca strategica*. Franco Angeli.

Codeluppi, V. (2020). "Semiotica e pubblicità: Il problema della marca", Filosofi(e). *Semiotiche*, *7*(1), 2020.

Cosenza, G. (2024). *Semiotica per campagne di digital marketing. Alcune proposte operative*. Ocula.

Eco, U. (1968). *La struttura assente. Introduzione alla ricerca semiologica*. Bompiani.

Fabris, G. (2008). *Societing: il marketing nella società postmoderna*. Egea.

Ferraresi, M., & Schmitt, B. H. (2007). *Marketing esperienziale. Come sviluppare l'esperienza di consumo*. FrancoAngeli.

Floch, J. M. (1990). *Sémiotique, marketing et communication. Sous les signes, les stratégies*. Puf.

Flux, n. 25, vol 29, 2024

Greimas, A. J., & Courtés, J. (1979). *Sèmiotique. Dictionnaire raisonné de la théorie du langage*. Hachette.

Landowski, E. (1989). *La société réfléchie. Essais de socio-sémiotique*. Seuil.

Lombardi, M. (Ed.). (2001). *Il dolce tuono*. FrancoAngeli.

Marrone, G. (2007). *Il discorso di marca. Modelli semiotici per il branding*. Laterza.

Musso, P. (2005). *I nuovi territori della marca. Percorsi di senso, discorsi, azioni*. Franco Angeli.

Oswald, L. (2011). *Marketing Semiotics: Signs*. Strategies, and Brand Value.

Paris, O. (2020). "Costruire un mito: Marche, prodotti e la rappresentazione dell'italianità nel mondo", Filosofi(e). *Semiotiche*, *7*(1), 2020.

Polesana, M. A. (2019). *Pubblicità e valori. Nuovi consumi e nuovi messaggi per una società che cambia*. FrancoAngeli.

Pozzato, M. P. (2001). *Semiotica del testo. Metodi, autori, esempi*. Carocci.

Qualizza, G. (2006). *I nuovi luoghi del consumo: percorsi, esplorazioni, progetti*. Edizioni Goliardiche.

Rolle, L. (2014). *Semiotica in pratica*. FrancoAngeli.

Semprini, A. (2003). *Lo sguardo sociosemiotico. Comunicazione, marche, media, pubblicità*. FrancoAngeli.

Traini, S. (2018), "The slow pace of change in advertising New family types in advertisements for people carriers", Ocula, www.ocula.it

Ventura Bordenca, I. (2022). *Food packaging. Narrazioni semiotiche e branding alimentare*. Franco Angeli.

Chapter 1
Semiotics of Omnichannel and Phygital Purchase Experiences:
A Framework for CX Design and Innovation

Paolo Odoardi
https://orcid.org/0009-0008-2194-383X
Università Telematica Internazionale Uninettuno, Italy & Università della Repubblica di San Marino, San Marino

Antonio Laurino
https://orcid.org/0009-0006-8544-4525
Università di Bologna - Alma Mater Studiorum, Italy & Università della Repubblica di San Marino, San Marino

ABSTRACT

This chapter explores the transformative impact of omnichannel and phygital experiences in modern retail, emphasizing their implications for customer experience (CX) design and innovation. The rise of retail innovations, such as click and collect, endless aisle, AR/VR-enabled stores, virtual try-ons and metaverse commerce, necessitates a deeper understanding of how consumers navigate these hybrid physical-digital shopping landscapes. Employing a semiotic approach, the research leverages the semiotic square as a heuristic tool to analyze the interplay between various purchase modalities, revealing the underlying values guiding and shaping consumer behavior. Through the definition of a phygital and omnichannel

DOI: 10.4018/979-8-3693-8024-6.ch001

semiotic square, the study identifies four ideal consumer types: Human touch lovers, Tech enthusiasts, Pragmatists and Conservatives. The article provides a framework for interpreting complex omnichannel dynamics and a tool to align touchpoints, designing coherent, impactful customer experiences.

The rise of e-commerce has been a transformative force in the retail industry. Fueled by advancements in technology and changing consumer behaviors, online shopping has experienced exponential growth in recent years. According to Statista, global retail e-commerce sales are projected to reach $8 trillion by 2027.[1] This remarkable growth can be attributed to several factors, including increased internet penetration, the convenience of online shopping, and the wider range of products available online.[2] E-commerce has ushered in a new era of consumer behavior, giving rise to the "digital native". This type of customer is characterized by their innate familiarity with technology, their preference for online shopping, and their expectation of seamless, personalized experiences. They are tech-savvy, often multitasking across multiple devices, and they value convenience and efficiency. As consumers increasingly embrace digital channels, e-commerce continues to reshape the retail landscape, forcing traditional retailers to adapt or risk falling behind. In the US market, e-commerce is becoming the most common sales channel in more and more categories. According to Boston Consulting Group 60% of retail innovation leaders are prioritizing investments in e-commerce.[3]

As a parallel trend, we are facing a shift driven by the proliferation of diverse digital touchpoints that redefine commerce and consumer experiences (Liu et al., 2018): we are undeniably in a post-web era. The traditional web, once the dominant digital landscape, has been supplanted by a multitude of interconnected technologies. These innovations blur the lines between the physical and digital realms, creating seamless and immersive shopping journeys (Mele & Russo-Spena, 2022). Consider the emergence of augmented reality (AR), which overlays digital information onto the physical world, enabling consumers to virtually try on clothes or visualize furniture in their homes. Similarly, virtual reality (VR) transports shoppers to virtual showrooms, offering unparalleled product exploration. Moreover, voice assistants like Amazon Alexa and Google Assistant empower consumers to make purchases through voice commands through empathic AI agents (Mari et al., 2024), while chatbots provide instant customer support and personalized product recommendations. Social commerce platforms (Turban et al., 2012) like Facebook, Instagram and TikTok have transformed social media into marketplaces, allowing users to discover and buy products directly within their feeds. Additionally, the Internet of Things (IoT) connects everyday objects to the internet, enabling smart homes and appliances to facilitate automated purchases.

These technological advancements, among many others, collectively usher in a new era of commerce, where the boundaries between online and offline shopping are increasingly blurred, and the consumer experience is elevated to unprecedented heights. What kinds of consumers inhabit and navigate this new and changing landscape? What sense-making dynamics contribute to the definition of these new customer experiences? Is a new age of "phygital natives" (Kotler et al., 2023, p. 25) coming? What is the role of consumer experience in omnichannel retailing? These issues need to be addressed from a broader view, namely digital humanities (and specifically semiotics), that goes beyond merely technical or economic aspects.

1. INTRODUCTION[4]

In this scenario, omnichannel marketing, characterized by the seamless integration of online and offline channels, has redefined how consumers interact with brands. From mobile apps and augmented reality in-store experiences to personalized online recommendations and click-and-collect services, these innovations are reshaping the traditional consumer journey. However, these advancements bring complexity, as they involve diverse touchpoints, technologies and consumer expectations, and the modern marketing landscape requires new tools to interpret, design, and predict consumer interactions across multiple channels. Semiotics, as the study of meaning-making processes, offers a powerful framework for decoding these complex interactions and crafting strategies that resonate with consumer needs and expectations.

In the omnichannel world, meaning emerges not only from individual touchpoints but also from the relationships between them. For instance, we can intuitively say that a "phygital" shopping experience combines the tangible trust of in-store interaction with the convenience of digital technologies. Through semiotics tools we can map the interplay between these elements, revealing underlying structures and patterns that contribute to consumer satisfaction or frustration. Our first goal is to build a semiotic map of omnichannel and phygital experiences which could offer a conceptual framework to identify and analyze key values and narrative structures that link multiple touchpoints into a cohesive customer journey, making the dynamics of omnichannel purchasing more intelligible. Secondly, by proposing our semiotic map, we could also provide marketers, designers, strategists, and, ultimately, brands with a design tool for interpreting omnichannel behaviors, predicting the success of new solutions and avoiding potential failures in customer experience design.

The semiotic methodology that will be applied will take its cue from the approach proposed by Jean-Marie Floch in one of his best-known semiotically oriented marketing consulting works: the analysis of travelers' routes in the Paris metro (Floch, 1990/2001, pp. 13-39). In particular, the theoretical tool that will be used, and put to the test, will be the semiotic square (Greimas & Courtés, 1979), understood as a useful and powerful tool for mapping a sector, fragmented and multidimensional, like the phygital one.

More specifically, we will proceed as follows: we will illustrate an exemplary case of the application of semiotics to the study of a marketing phenomenon: Jean-Marie Floch's famous analysis of the paths of travelers in the Paris metro (§ 2); we will propose an in-depth theoretical study of the semiotic square tool (§ 3); we will proceed to the elaboration of an omnichannel and phygital semiotic square, which will also lead us to delineate a typology of consumers (§ 4); we will apply the square to the broad and nuanced field of omnichannel, showing how this tool can help to bring clarity to a vastness of concrete phenomena, generally and indistinctly traced back to phygital (§ 5-9); we will give some indications for a possible use of the framework by designers and marketers for strategic and productive purposes (§ 10).

2. JEAN-MARIE FLOCH'S SEMIOTIC METHODOLOGY

Given our first goal to bring clarity on the intricate and dynamic landscape of omnichannel and phygital shopping experiences, we will employ a semiotic methodology that can shed light on the underlying meanings that shape consumer behavior in these multifaceted environments. Inspired by Jean-Marie Floch's seminal work on semiotic analysis of rail user behavior, we will adapt and extend his approach to examine the contemporary phenomenon of omnichannel and phygital consumption.

Jean-Marie Floch's work on developing a behavioral typology of railway users is found in his book *Semiotics, Marketing and Communication*. Floch uses semiotic analysis to understand the different ways in which people use public transportation: "How then does a traveller live his or her journey? And what are the different ways of doing it? As every RATP agent knows from experience, not to mention the rest of the staff of the transport authority in charge of development, clients have a whole range of behaviours" (Floch, 1990/2001, p. 13).

Floch's methodological approach, while drawing inspiration from ethnomethodology, is fundamentally rooted in semiotics. His research involved observing and documenting the behaviors of railway passengers, similar to ethnomethodological studies. However, the analytical framework he employed to interpret these observations was distinctly semiotic. By utilizing the semiotic square as a conceptual tool, Floch was able to identify and categorize the underlying meanings that shaped these behaviors. This semiotic lens allowed him to move beyond a mere description of observed actions and delve into the deeper semantic significance of passenger experiences:

> *From that point on, from the moment when the rereading of our indexing forms and notations confirmed the pertinence of a category pitting discontinuity*

against continuity, it became useful to pause and reflect on everything it might possibly offer. We knew that what the semiotician does at such a point is to project the category onto a semiotic square in order to set up the network of relations organizing the semantic microuniverse this category represents, and to identify the positions of the virtual meanings that such a network defines. (Floch, 1990/2001, p. 20)

Figure 1. Category projection onto a semiotic square

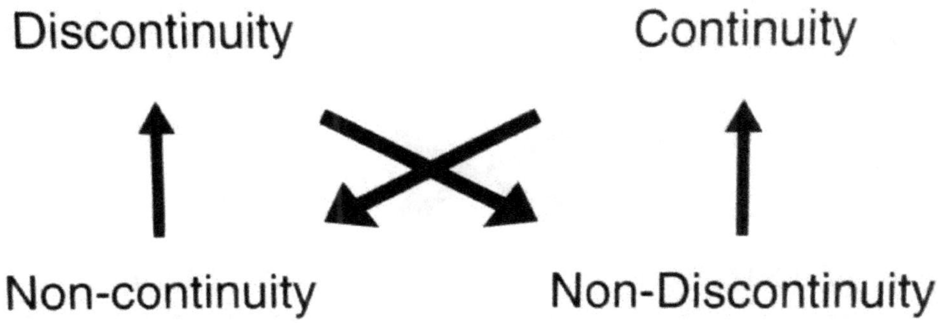

(Source: Floch, 2001, p. 20)

Beginning with this abstract categorization (Figure 1), Floch then proceeds to fill the four positions thus identified with meaning, starting with the assumption that "since each of these valorizations logically implies a valorizing subject, it is possible not only to interdefine four basic types of metro and RER traveller but also to develop a qualitative typology of these travellers. We shall designate the four as surveyors, professionals (or pros) as we have dubbed them, daydreamers and strollers" (Floch, 1990/2001, p. 24).

These four types of traveller, as a result of the deployment of a single conceptual category, are schematized as follows (Figure 2):

Figure 2. Qualitative typology of RER travellers

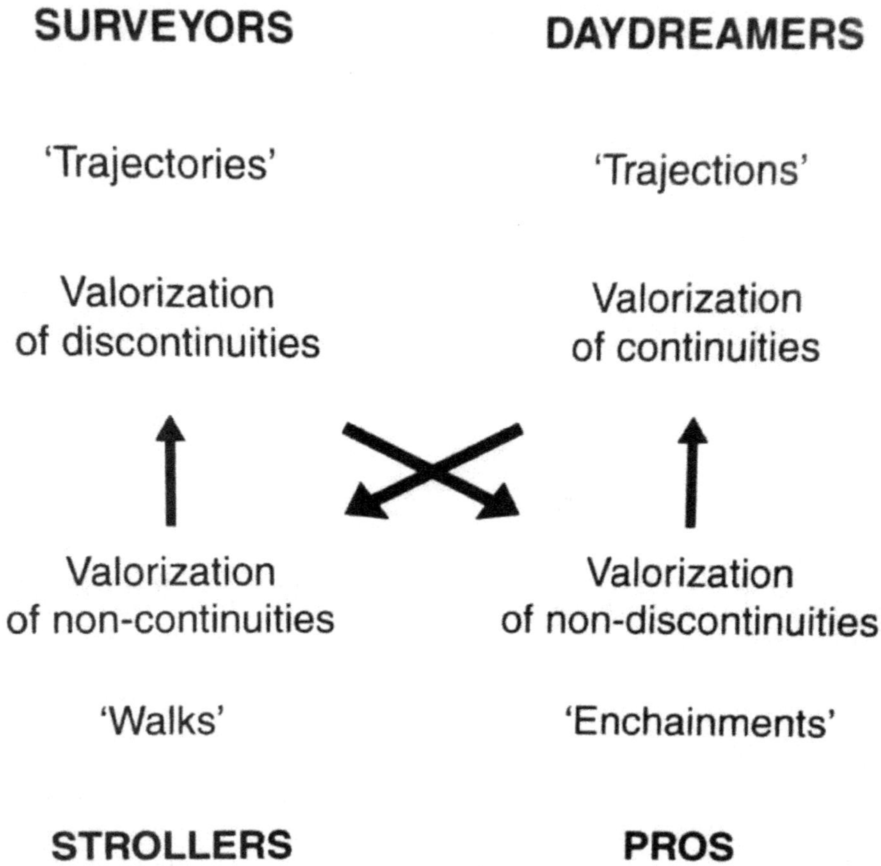

(Source: Floch, 2001, p. 25)

Let briefly explore these four distinct types of passengers:

- Surveyors: these passengers focus on efficiency and practicality, prioritizing the fastest and most direct route to their destination. They are primarily concerned with the functional aspects of the journey, such as timetables and connections.
- Daydreamers: these passengers are more interested in the experience of the journey itself, using it as an opportunity to relax, reflect, or simply escape from their daily routines. They may enjoy the scenery, the atmosphere of the train, or the opportunity to read or listen to music.
- Strollers: these passengers take a more leisurely approach to their journey, exploring the different options available to them and enjoying the freedom to

change their plans as they go. They may be interested in visiting different stations or towns along the way, or simply taking their time to enjoy the journey.

- Pros: these passengers are highly experienced travelers who are familiar with the railway system and know how to make the most of their journey. They may use the journey to work, socialize, or conduct business, and are often able to find ways to optimize their time and maximize their productivity.

Floch's semiotic methodology provides a rigorous framework for understanding and interpreting specific behavioral domains. By employing the semiotic square, researchers can delve into the underlying cultural codes and symbolic meanings that shape human actions. This analytical tool enables the identification of key oppositions and contradictions within a given context, shedding light on the complex interplay of signs and symbols that influence behavior.

However, the power of Floch's methodology extends beyond mere analysis. It serves as a generative tool for designing future experiences and predicting the potential impact of specific interventions. By understanding the existing semiotic landscape, researchers and practitioners can identify opportunities for innovation and develop strategies to shape desired behaviors. Floch's work underscores the importance of this productive and predictive dimension of semiotic analysis, emphasizing its central role in shaping strategic decision-making and innovation. Following the author: "One of the compelling questions was: 'Where and at what moment can one or must one intervene with respect to such and such a type of traveller?'" (Floch, 1990/2001, p. 14).

Through the application of the semiotic square, researchers can explore potential future scenarios and assess the likely outcomes of various interventions. By anticipating the symbolic and cultural implications of these interventions, organizations can make informed decisions that align with their strategic goals. Floch's methodology, therefore, offers a valuable tool for both understanding the past and shaping the future.

Building upon the foundational work and methodology of Jean-Marie Floch, this research aims to extend and adapt his framework to the contemporary landscape of omnichannel and phygital consumption. While we will not undertake a traditional ethnographic study, we will employ a semiotic approach to analyze the innovative elements within our chosen omnichannel case study. In fact, we follow a widespread use of the semiotic square as a tool to create semantic maps of semiotic behaviour with reference to a specific market or domain or area of application, as proposed in advertising (Floch, 1990, 1995, 2013; Laurino 2020a, 2020b), marketing (Ceriani, 2001), branding (Semprini, 1992; Marrone, 2007; Rossolatos, 2012, 2015) and in the social realm (Landowski 2006; Marrone 2001).

By adopting a phenomenological lens, we will explore the lived experiences of consumers within these complex and multifaceted environments. This broader semiotic perspective will enable us to gain a deeper narrative understanding of the consumer behaviors that shape the omnichannel and phygital experience.

3. A BRIEF THEORETICAL OVERVIEW ABOUT THE SEMIOTIC SQUARE

The semiotic square, a conceptual tool devised by the Lithuanian-French semiotician Algirdas Julien Greimas (1966, 1970, 1983; Greimas & Courtés, 1979), serves as a framework for analyzing and mapping the meaning within a specific cultural or discursive domain, often referred to as a microuniverse. It functions as an elementary structure of signification or as a topographical approach to the logical organization of a semantic universe. It operates by establishing an initial binary relationship between two terms, such as "good" and "evil" or "hot" and "cold". These terms, known as contraries, form the foundation of the square. From this initial opposition, two additional terms emerge: the contradictory which negates the first term, "not good", and the contradictory which negates the second term, "not evil". They are in a relationship of implication with the alternative term in the axes of contrariety. Therefore, it consists of four interconnected terms: two contraries, S1 and S2, and their respective negations, ~S1 and ~S2 (we will name these positions from #1 to #4 in the chapter). A standard schema of the tool is presented in Figure 3.

Figure 3. Greimas' semiotic square[5]

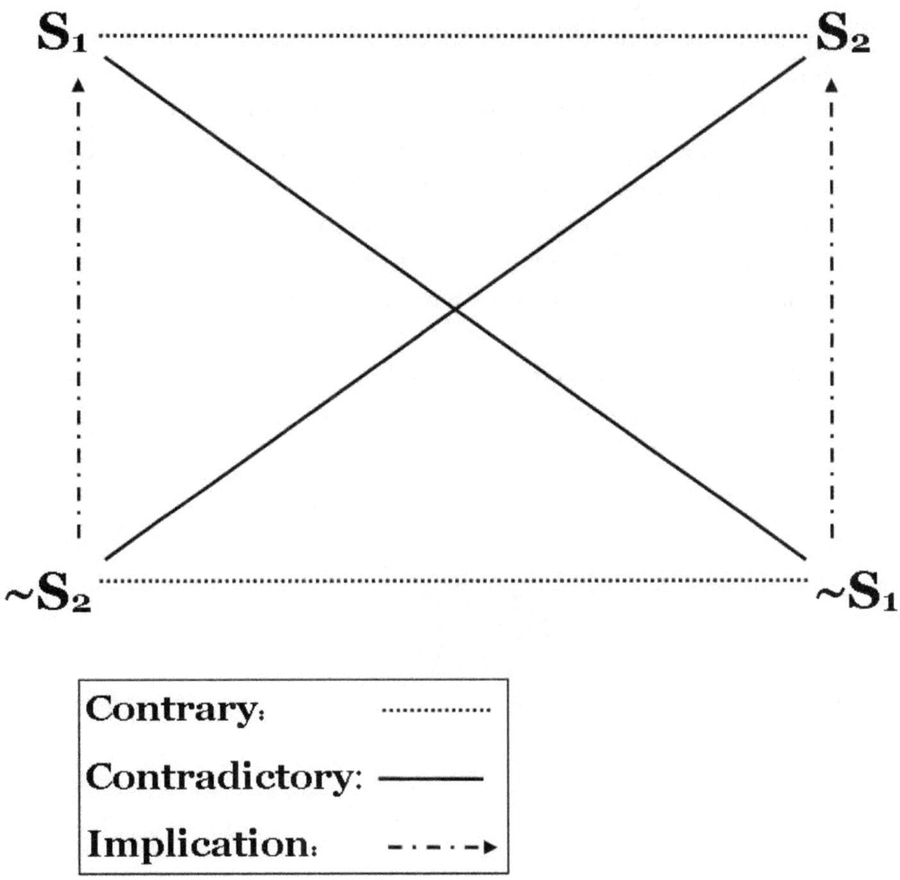

By mapping these terms onto a square, this model allows for a comprehensive exploration of the semantic relationships within a given context, revealing nuances and complexities that might otherwise remain hidden. In other words, by analyzing the relationships between these terms, the semiotic square allows for a deep understanding of the underlying meaning and value systems present within a specific cultural or discursive context. It serves as a powerful lens through which to examine the complex interplay of signs, texts, spaces, digital interfaces, revealing the intricate web of signification that constitutes our reality.

But the heuristic power of this tool does not end with the identification of the above four terms. In fact, it is possible to identify some additional terms, called metaterms or compound terms: they represent complex relationships and concepts that emerge from the interplay of the primary terms, by exploring their intersections and negations, allowing for a deeper exploration of meaning and signification.

- For instance, the "complex term" combines the initial opposition, S1 and S2, revealing a synthesis of the two contraries.
- Conversely, the "neutral term" represents the space outside the binary opposition, combining terms ~S1 and ~S2, the "subcontraries", so called because they are contrary terms located below the contraries.
- Positive and negative deixis refers to the relationship between a term and its contradictory term. It highlights the intensification of a term by affirming its semantic value and simultaneously negating the opposite value.

We will name these positions from #5 to #8 in the chapter; Figure 4 shows the full schema of the tool as considered in the present research.

Figure 4. Map of the semantic positions in the semiotic square

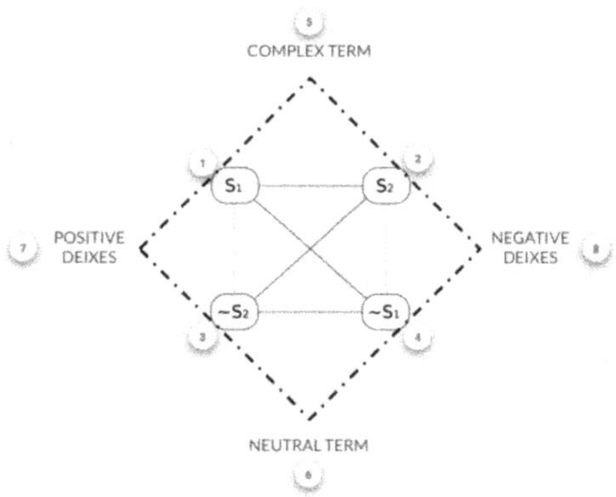

By examining these metaterms, we gain insights into the complexities of meaning and the dynamic nature of semiotic systems. To explain how these metaterms work, let's take, without going into further detail, a classic example (Figure 5), that of the semiotic square applied to the opposition between "masculine" and "feminine", as recently revised (Hébert, 2020).

Figure 5. An example of a semiotic square[6]

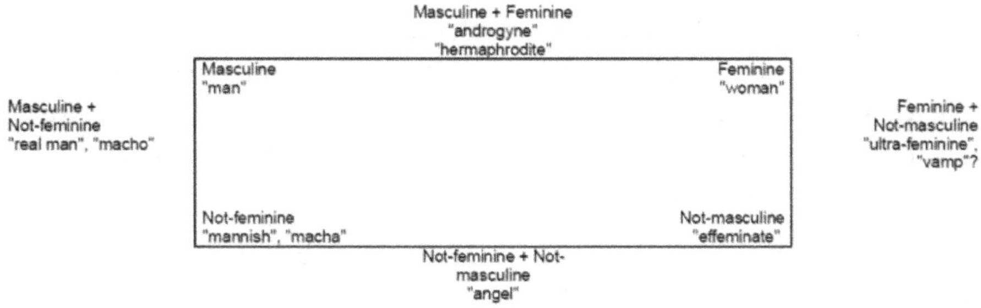

4. THE OMNICHANNEL AND PHYGITAL SEMIOTIC SQUARE

Following the work of Jean-Marie Floch, we sought a semantic category that could account for the two main ways of completing a purchase, in-store or online, asking: what dimension drives a consumer towards one modality or the other? In other words, the goal we set out is to investigate the values underlying a given purchase modality: in fact, regardless of the product – whether it is a luxury good or a commodity – the same purchase may occur differently depending on what the consumer enhances in the customer journey experience. A Gucci bag, for example, can be bought either in an exclusive boutique, where the customer is cuddled, or in a luxury online marketplace. The difference lies in the value attached to the mode of purchase, not in the value system of consumption. And here, of course, the reference is to another well-known Floch (1990) contribution, namely the axiology of consumption and the different forms of valorization of objects: pragmatic, utopian, critical, ludic and aesthetic. Consequently, our analysis of modal values soon focused on modal verbs, culminating in a semiotic square of modalities. Specifically, the choice fell on the opposition of "being able to be" versus "being able to do". On the one hand, "being able to be" means being able to be present, assisted, certain of the tangible characteristics of a product, typical of those who value contact with others, with the merchandise, and ultimately with the physical space, configuring itself also as being able to be there. "Being able to do", on the other hand, implies being able to choose, decide, save (time, money, energy), which characterizes the digital world, capable of multiplying possibilities and optimizing processes.

Each of the two terms of the category was then negated, obtaining "being able not to do" and "being able not to be". "Being able not to do" accounts for those who are motivated by what they can avoid: avoiding making online payments, waiting for product delivery, queuing at the checkout, having to deal with returns. But also the inability to do in times and places other than the here and now, in a particular sense of exclusivity, as in the case of purchasing limited-edition products during specific online events. Finally, "being able not to be" is realized in avoiding being in contact with people, being invited to try certain products by sales assistants, ultimately being a buyer in binding spaces, times, and places. The four terms thus obtained give rise to the following square (Figure 6):

Figure 6. The omnichannel & phygital semiotic square

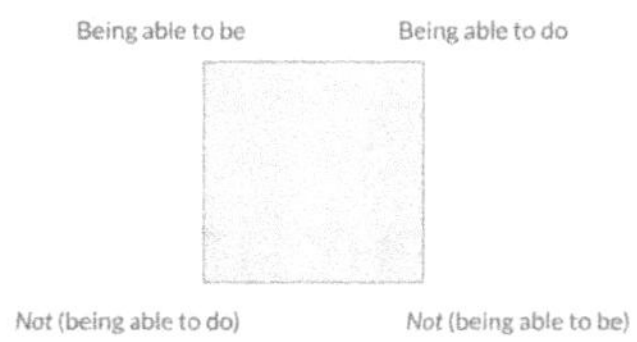

It is important to note that the negation of the two contrary terms is conFigured in all respects as a weakening, that is, the exclusion of some possibilities. The identified category, in fact, contains that full power which, in the two contradictories, is partially annulled. Hence the possible predilection of consumers for some specific, and therefore partial, aspects of the purchasing process.

Through this tool, it is possible to articulate four distinct and at the same time interdependent dimensions. Dimensions pursued by as many ideal-typical consumers, who together outline a typology, with the virtue of being formed by semantically inter-defined terms. This is, of course, an abstract categorization, which can benefit from the identification of four more concrete lexicalizations. Reviewing the literature searching for a widely understood vocabulary, we have chosen to use some labels, borrowing them from Moore (2014), which are in some ways arbitrary but have the merit of being sufficiently widespread among practitioners:

- Human touch lovers, corresponding to the consumers who value "being able to be"
- Tech enthusiasts, corresponding to the consumers who value "being able to do"
- Conservatives[7], corresponding to the consumers who value "not (being able to do)"

- Pragmatists, corresponding to the consumers who value "not (being able to be)"

Figure 7. The semiotic square of omnichannel & phygital personas

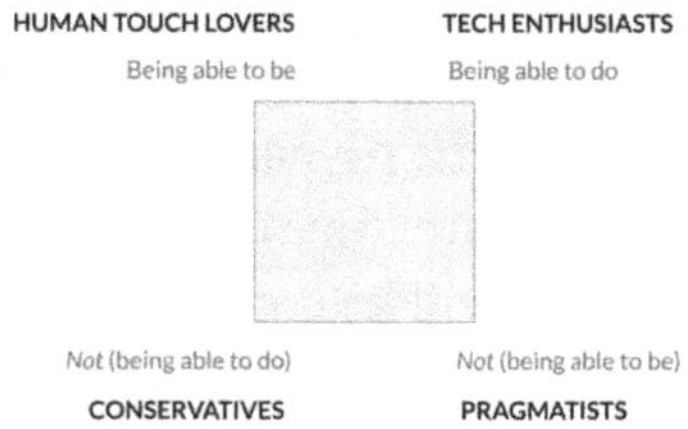

Let us proceed with a description of the four types (Figure 7), trying to give a narrative depth to each of them.

- Human touch lovers: consumers who tend to make a purchase process exclusively in the store; they feel the need to try the product, grasp its tangible, sensitive characteristics, likes to wear, and more generally, try the product; they seek interaction with shop assistants and need to be reassured. This predilection can turn into a rejection in the online purchasing mode for a wide spect of products, from clothing to travel experiences.
- Tech enthusiasts: consumers who have a euphoric and enthusiastic attitude toward all the possibilities that technology offers in the purchasing process. They are often among the first to try new ways and features offered by technology providers and are often among the first to experience them. They experience gratification in using dedicated brand apps, innovative payment tools, new business models in the sharing economy, interactions with AI-based customer care tools.
- Pragmatists: consumers who are ready to deny, in the form of contradiction, the benefits and values of buying in the presence in favor of a pragmatic and tactical benefit. These are the typical people who, even though they are in the store, are willing to leave the store without the desired product because they conclude the online purchase, either at that time or later, in exchange for economic or logistical benefits. For practical reasons and denies the spatial and temporal constraints of the in-store shopping experience and thus we label them as pragmatics.

- Conservatives: consumers who approach online shopping modes with curiosity and interest but partially denie the possibilities of digital because they do not fully trust some of the potential of digital, from the payment system to the certainty and speed of shipping to the reliability of customer service. In partially denying these purchasing potentials they return to more traditional modes and for this they can be labeled as conservatives.

Finally, it is important to note that, in semiotic literature, the square may be used on a semantic (static) level or a syntactic (dynamic) level, namely distinguished by the changes in position of each object over time (Greimas & Courtés, 1979). Considering the purpose of this research, it will be considered only on the semantic level, as the logical articulation of a given opposition, therefore being a topographical tool to map a specific semantic domain. The analyst is naturally the one who defines, depending on the objectives of analysis, what degree of coherence and homogeneity are adequate while using it as an analytical tool on the corpus.

Now that we have introduced the path-to-purchase typology and identified four ideal types, we can ask how they relate to the popular concept of the persona. Introduced by Alan Cooper (1999), in the field of interaction design, personas are:

> *composite archetypes based on behavior patterns uncovered during the course of our research, which we formalize for the purpose of informing the product design. By using personas, we can develop an understanding of our users' goals in specific contexts – a critical tool for ideating and validating design concepts [...] identifying the significant and meaningful patterns in user behavior and determining how these behaviors translate into archetypes that accurately represent the appropriate cross section of users. (Cooper et al., 2007, p. 62)*

While initially a design tool, the concept quickly diffused across disciplines, including marketing. Since we are dealing with the users from a narrative point of view, and are questioning the meanings of the behaviour, a fruitful dialogue with the semiotic sphere is also open, as in Cosenza (2014, 2020, 2024) and Grillo and Polidoro (2023). While our typology aligns with a personas model, key distinctions arise. Firstly, we isolate a specific facet of a character's motivational values. Secondly, and this is where the real difference lies, in our model they are defined not solely by their intrinsic values but also by their relative position within the typology. This approach fully grasps semiotics' understanding of value as both differential (defined by its relation to other values) and phenomenological (experienced subjectively).

5. MAKING SENSE OF OMNICHANNEL: CONTRADICTING THE DIGITAL EXPERIENCE

This paper posits that the semiotic square can serve as a valuable tool for understanding and managing the evolving landscape of omnichannel customer experiences. To test this hypothesis, we examine emerging omnichannel purchasing behaviors. By applying the semiotic square to these new modalities, we assess its efficacy in providing both greater intelligibility and actionable insights for marketers designing contemporary consumer experiences. This approach, on the path laid out by Batat (2022), is indeed part of a more general trend in media studies, shifting the axis of analysis from textuality to the more or less stable systems they belong to. The terms environment and ecology are commonly used to describe the integration of user, technology and media user flows, in the perspective of a true media ecology (Cecchi et al., 2018; Belluati & Tirocchi, 2023; Ugenti, 2016; Granata, 2015). The scenario that emerges from the semiotic analysis situates the experience of omnichannel interaction in the contemporary post-media sphere, where:

> *It is no longer possible to clearly define what is "medial" and what is not, nor can we define when we are in a medial situation and when we are out of it: rather, we are immersed in systems and environments of relationships and exchanges, ready to use the different resources that these environments make available to us in relation to the objectives that are proposed to us or that we propose to ourselves, and to assume roles and positions in accordance with what is implied by the use of these resources. (Eugeni, 2015, p. 28)*[8]

Given the goal of bringing order to a complex and nuanced scenario, we find it useful to start from the semantic positions opened by the two contradictors.

In the position of "not (being able to do)" (#3), we find, as mentioned, the magnification of what it is possible to avoid doing: for example, paying online, waiting for product delivery, standing in line at the checkout, having to deal with returns. All aspects valued by a specific type of consumer that we have defined as conservative.

In the scenario of the different "technical" solutions that can be adopted, Click and Collect can be traced back to this position. It is an omnichannel retail phenomenon that merges the convenience of online shopping with the immediacy of in-store pickup. Customers initiate their purchase journey online, selecting products and completing the transaction digitally. Subsequently, they collect their order from a designated physical location, often a brick-and-mortar store. Many leading brands in the western markets have begun offering this service, as documented in Figure 8 and 9, and in the US market, in-store pickup is projected to jump to $154 billion in retail sales by 2025.[9]

Figure 8. Decathlon's C&C program[10]

Figure 9. Sephora's C&C program[11]

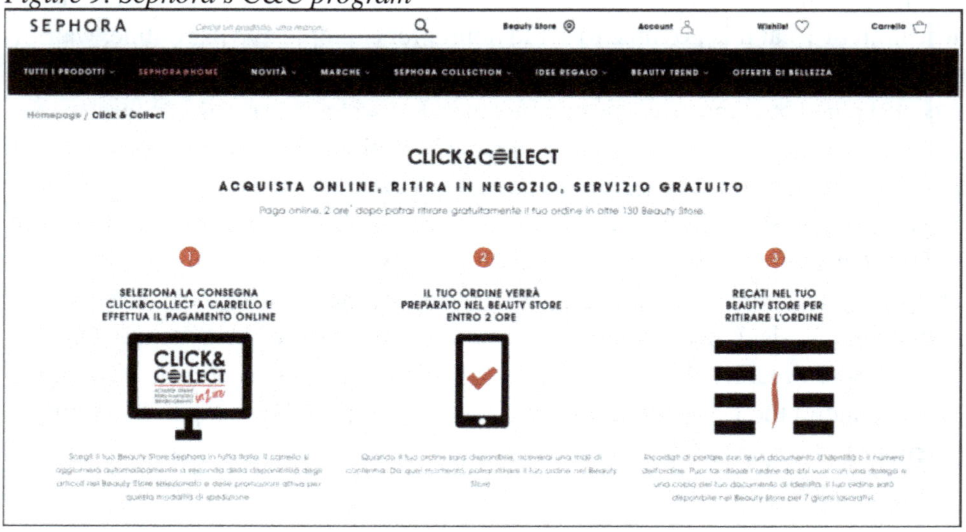

A brand might decide to target this type of consumer and then design a click-n-collect strategy based on the consumer's preference for this shopping mode. This means designing both the technology and the physical space to enable the choice of this specific customer journey that is responsive to this semantic choice of shopping method. In other words, the brand suggests an experience and interaction design that makes them effective in that semantic space. The technology makes it possible to design an experience which proposes a story to the potential customer to buy, and if this story is actually chosen by the potential customer, this leads to better interaction and, ultimately, to growth. What we are seeing today is that the look and feel of stores, the physical layout of stores, is also changing profoundly as a result of this new experience design. As a pioneering project in this area we can consider the Walmart redesign of its stores for the launch of Walmart Pickup, the service that enables users to order items online and pick those items up in any Walmart store (Figure 10).[12]

Figure 10. Walmart Pickup, external layout of the store[13]

6. MAKING SENSE OF OMNICHANNEL: CONTRADICTING THE PHYSICAL EXPERIENCE

If we move along the way of contradiction of our main category we can negate the “being able to be” pole, coming to a “not (being able to be)” (position #4). Here we find, as mentioned, the magnification of what it is possible to avoid being: for example, to be in contact with other people, to be invited to try on certain products by salespeople, ultimately to be buyers. All aspects valued by a specific type of consumer that we have defined as pragmatist.

In this semantic area we find interesting phenomena like endless aisle: a retail concept that transcends the physical limitations of brick-and-mortar stores. By seamlessly integrating digital technology into the in-store experience, retailers can offer customers access to an expansive, virtual inventory that extends far beyond what can be physically stocked on shelves (Figure 11, 12 and 13). This expanded product assortment empowers shoppers to explore a diverse range of options, discover new products, and make informed purchasing decisions. More specifically, an endless aisle is a digital portal, be it through tablets, kiosks or otherwise, into a retailer's entire inventory, accessible from their physical locations. The endless aisle fundamentally alters the traditional customer journey: instead of being restricted to the products available within the store's walls, customers can browse and purchase items from a virtually limitless catalog. This expanded choice empowers consumers to discover new items, compare options effortlessly, and make informed purchasing decisions. The motivation behind this shift lies in the desire for convenience, personalization and the thrill of exploration. Customers are drawn to the endless aisle's ability to cater to specific preferences, streamline the shopping process, and provide a unique, interactive experience that blurs the lines between online and offline retail. These are therefore consumers who are ready to deny certain aspects of buying in a physical store, such as being concretely in contact with the product and leaving the store with the item materially in their hands. All in the name of a greater benefit, in this case the possibility of choice, which defines them, in relation to the other types identified, as distinctly pragmatics.

Figure 11. Example of endless aisle experience[14]

Figure 12. Example of endless aisle experience[15]

Figure 13. Example of endless aisle experience[16]

Within the framework defined through the semiotic square of the omnichannel, interdefined semantic positions establish the contextual meaning of specific customer purchase behaviors. These positions emerge through opposition and relational dynamics with other customer behaviors. These semantic areas, while possessing distinct meanings, can accommodate a diverse range of customer journey typologies. This inherent diversity signifies that multiple behaviors can coexist within a single semantic area. This observation possesses significant implications. Firstly, it enhances analytical rigor by recognizing the nuanced variations within seemingly homogenous customer segments. Secondly, it empowers marketers with creative freedom. By understanding the underlying narrative sensibility of customers within a specific semantic area, marketers can envision and propose novel customer scenarios that resonate with their desires and expectations.

A prime example is the coexistence of the endless aisle proposition and showrooming behavior, both catering to the same underlying customer narrative sensibility. Showrooming describes the consumer practice of physically visiting a brick-and-mortar store to examine a product in person, often interacting with sales associates for information and assistance, and then subsequently purchasing the product online at a lower price from a competitor (Gensler et al., 2017). This behavior leverages the in-store experience as a valuable resource for product exploration and decision-making while capitalizing on the potential cost savings offered by online retailers. The purchaser path enabled by showrooming involves a multi-channel journey. Consumers initiate the process in the physical store, gathering crucial information and gaining firsthand experience with the product. They then transition to the online realm to compare prices, read reviews, and ultimately complete the purchase transaction. The primary motivation driving this behavior is the pursuit of the best possible deal. Consumers recognize the convenience and often lower prices available online, while simultaneously appreciating the value of the in-store experience for product evaluation and personalized assistance, demonstrating, therefore, in this case too – as in the previous one of the endless aisle – a marked pragmatic trait, which justifies the label pragmatists.

7. MAKING SENSE OF A SINGLE CHANNEL: LEVERAGING ON THE CONTRARIES

After shedding more light on some of the more hybrid and nuanced phenomena in the contemporary phygital landscape, let us return to the two original positions, in which we find the terms opposed to each other, and try to delve into their nature.

Let's start by taking a closer look at the "being able to do" position (#2), corresponding to the buyer persona of the tech enthusiast. Brands aiming to engage consumers who prefer this type of online shopping must transcend traditional e-commerce models, they can no longer be content with implementing traditional e-commerce. They must offer innovative solutions that leverage the being able to do modality, and increase the potential and possibilities of online shopping. By adopting innovative strategies that capitalize on the "do-it-yourself" paradigm, brands can expand the potential and possibilities of online retail, offering consumers enriched online shopping experiences.

One simple and recent example is the new payment method that goes under the label "Buy Now, Pay Later" (BNPL). It is a financial service that allows consumers to make purchases and pay for them in installments over a short period, often interest-free. This payment method has gained significant popularity, particularly among younger consumers, as it offers increased flexibility and convenience. When choosing BNPL, customers are motivated by several factors. Firstly, it enables them to make immediate purchases without the full upfront cost, making it easier to afford larger or more expensive items. Secondly, BNPL can help manage cash flow, as it spreads the cost of a purchase over time, reducing the financial burden of a single large expenditure. Additionally, BNPL can offer a sense of control and financial empowerment, allowing customers to make purchases based on their desired timeline and budget. The several possibilities – the being able to do – that is typical of the interaction with a financial intermediary is then easily made possible at the checkout stage, just choosing the option.

Moving on to take a closer look at the position of "being able to be" (#1), corresponding to the buyer persona of the "Human touch lover", one cannot fail to point out an obvious experiential character. In this regard, there are a number of studies that go under the label of experiential marketing. This perspective, as defined by Schmitt (1999), goes beyond traditional advertising by creating immersive brand experiences that engage consumers on a sensory, emotional and cognitive level. This approach recognizes that consumers are increasingly seeking unique and meaningful interactions. By leveraging interactive events, sensory engagements, personalized interactions and leveraging social media for sharing, experiential marketing aims to build strong emotional connections, foster brand loyalty and drive customer advocacy. According to Batat (2019), experiential marketing transcends traditional marketing tactics by focusing on creating unique and memorable customer journeys. Batat emphasizes the importance of designing experiences that resonate with consumers on an emotional and sensory level, fostering deeper connections and building lasting brand loyalty. Her framework, centered around the 7Es (Experience, Exchange, Extension, Emphasis, Empathy, Emotional touchpoints, Emic/Etic process), provides a comprehensive guide for businesses to design and deliver exceptional customer experiences across all touchpoints. This approach prioritizes consumer needs and preferences, creating personalized and meaningful interactions that go beyond simple transactions. The reasons explored by these authors, that reflect on, among other things, the experientialization of the point of sale, are the ones that drive store transformation projects and strategies. From a semantic point of view, therefore, they address a potential consumer moved by the mode of being able to be, as a preferred mode of purchase. Ultimately, it is the magnification of experiential and sensory elements that qualifies this pole and makes it diverge from its opposite.

8. MAKING SENSE OF PHYGITAL: INNOVATIVE RETAIL AND METAVERSE COMMERCE

These two poles – physical and digital, "being able to be" and "being able to do" – can be considered in stark opposition. Nonetheless, as we have previously illustrated, there exists, within the semiotic square model, the possibility of their coexistence, in a hybrid semantic position called "complex term" (#5). Dropping theoretical reflection into the concrete context, when a retailer offers an experience that includes traditional physical elements and digital elements that add further potential, from their coexistence comes a shopping experience that creates a combination greater than the mere sum of the parts. In this regard, we speak of "phygital", an expression that comes precisely from the fusion of the terms "physical" and "digital". While there are many definitions of "phygital" proposed in different fields, sectors and disciplines – for an up-to-date review see Mele et al., 2023 –, we can now also propose a semiotic one. From our perspective, then, phygital is that which reconciles and enables normally opposing and alternative modal possibilities.

In other words, it is the complex term that is the result of the fusion of a full "being able to be" and a full "being able to do". To this semantic metaterm position we can attribute two families of solutions:

- innovations that transform the point-of-sale space by incorporating AR/VR;
- innovations that transform digital spaces into interactive experiences.

Starting with the former, it is easy to note how various technological solutions are implemented in the traditional stores of major multinational companies (Stigliano & Kotler, 2018). For example, one brand that has extensively and constantly innovated its physical stores is Nike, starting from the "House of Innovation 000" flagship store.[17] Inside these kinds of innovative stores it is easy to find interactive screens, surfaces with multitouch functionality that enables employees and customers to experience Nike products in a whole new way. The installation exemplified in Figure 14 is comprised of product videos, league statistics and comparable shoe data. Availability in terms of size and colour can be detected in real time, using RFID technology in combination with 3D cameras, supporting user interaction.

Another example is the evolution of the H&M fitting room with smart mirrors.[18] In fitting rooms we can find some screens that recognize items brought in, offer personalized styling suggestions and allow customers to request additional items without leaving the fitting room (Figure 15). These advanced technological tools also allow for seamless payment options with faster checkout processes and personalized styling recommendations, tailored to individual customer preferences. All with the aim of creating a more engaging and personalized in-store shopping experience for customers.

In both cases we are therefore faced with a fully realized "being able to be", in terms of being in the shop, to which is added a "being able to do", declined in the various functionalities listed earlier. And, as mentioned, it is precisely this coexistence (with a full integration) that is expressed by the complex term.

Figure 14. Smart screen in Nike's Store[19]

Figure 15. H&M fitting room with smart mirrors[20]

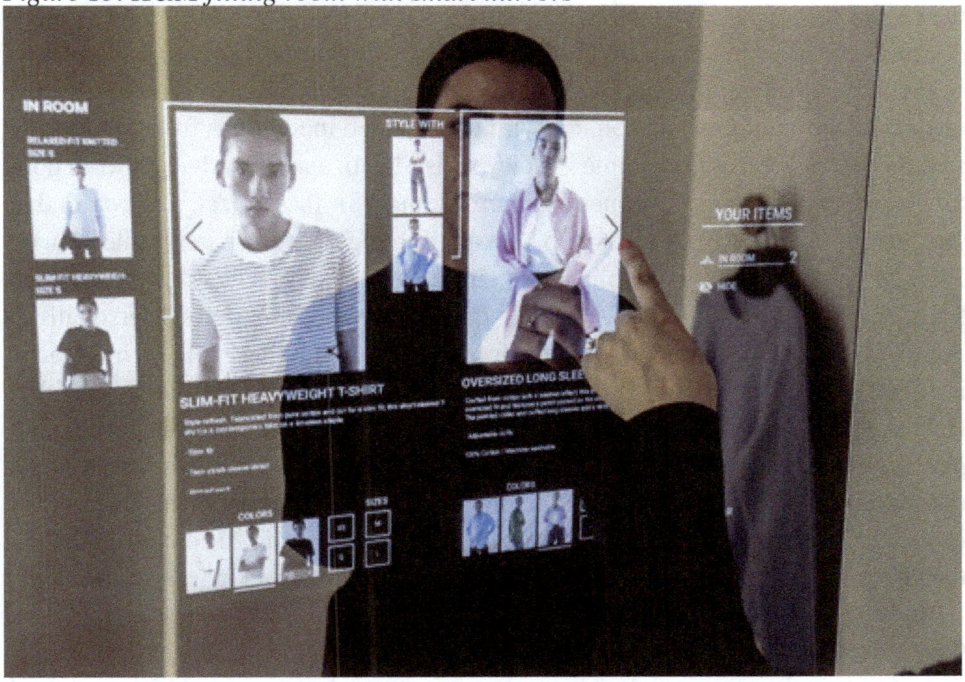

Turning to innovations that transform digital spaces into interactive experiences, the reference is to the recent and articulated phenomenon of the metaverse (Ball 2022). Characterized as a convergence of Web 2.0, Augmented Reality (AR) and Virtual Reality (VR), metaverse presents a novel e-commerce landscape. Metaverse commerce represents the convergence of virtual and physical retail, enabling consumers to explore, interact with and purchase products within immersive digital environments. This transformative experience extends beyond traditional online shopping, offering customers a multi-sensory journey where they can virtually try on clothes, test drive cars or even attend virtual fashion shows. The allure of metaverse commerce lies in its ability to cater to the evolving needs and desires of modern consumers.[21] By providing a sense of community, escapism and personalized experiences, the metaverse empowers individuals to express their unique identities and connect with like-minded individuals. This heightened engagement fosters a deeper emotional connection with brands, ultimately motivating consumers to choose this innovative purchasing pathway (Rane et al., 2023).

Numerous brands are currently exploring the potential of phygital experiences within the metaverse commerce domain. For example, Gucci has been a pioneer in exploring the metaverse, leveraging its digital presence to engage younger audiences and redefine luxury experiences. Gucci Town on Roblox (Figure 16) is a virtual space served as an early entry point, offering interactive games, mini-games and the ability to purchase virtual Gucci items for avatars. According to the brand "A digital destination on Roblox dedicated to those seeking the unexpected, Gucci Town is a place to discover more about the House and its heritage, as well as to express one's own individuality and connect with like-minded individuals from all over the world."[22] Another prime example is Macy's Mstylelab: an immersive platform built to reward loyal Macy's customers (Figure 17 and 18); the project was awarded at the 28th Annual Webby Awards[23]. While spotlighting their fresh new collection on 34th, Mstylelab invites the public into a virtual version of New York with a surreal twist, featuring in-experience shopping through iframe integration, personalized digital fabrics and customizable avatars powered by ReadyPlayerMe. A mention is needed for Nike's Metaverse initiatives, primarily exemplified by Nikeland within Roblox (Figure 19). By creating a virtual world where consumers can interact, play and customize their avatars, the brand leverages the Metaverse to transcend traditional marketing by offering engaging and interactive experiences that extend beyond traditional retail channels. Nearly 7 million people from 224 countries visited the environment in the year of lunch[24]. But the examples are now very numerous.

In these cases – and in similar cases – we are faced with a full can-do offered by the potential of digital to which is added a can-be that is the result of the simulation of physical space, with its sensations and perceptions, enabled by augmented virtual reality.

Figure 16. Gucci Town on Roblox[25]

Figure 17. Macy's Mstylelab[26]

Figure 18. Macy's Mstylelab[27]

Figure 19. Nikeland

(Source: Nike)

9. FURTHER SEMANTIC TERRITORIES TO EXPLORE

The possibility of identifying metaterms, as we have seen in the case of phygital, makes it possible to distinguish and thus shed light on hybrid and fuzzy phenomena. Referring to two further possibilities provided by the semiotic square, let us now consider the two deixis, composed of an original term, "being able to be" and "being able to do", and the opposite contradictory. In more detail, we find on the one hand full "being able to be" and "not (being able to do)", and on the other hand full "being able to do" and "not (being able to be)". Within the panorama of solutions and technologies under analysis, these two positions allow us to account for some peculiar phenomena.

In the left deixis composed of "being able to be" and "not (being able to do)" (position #7) can be usefully positioned the autonomous store, whose best-known occurrence is certainly Amazon Go (Figure 20 and 21). Amazon Go stores[28] represent a revolutionary concept in the retail industry, seamlessly blending the convenience of online shopping with the sensory experience of physical stores. Customers enter these stores, equipped with the Amazon app, and simply grab the items they desire. Advanced sensor technology tracks product selection, eliminating the need for traditional checkout lines. Payment is automatically processed upon exiting the store, linked to the customer's Amazon account. This shopping experience caters to time-conscious consumers who value efficiency and seek to minimize time spent on mundane tasks. It also appeals to those who appreciate the convenience of cashless transactions and the ability to quickly grab essential items without the hassle of queuing. By prioritizing speed, ease and a futuristic shopping environment, Amazon Go taps into the growing trend of prioritizing convenience and personalized experiences in retail (Varma et al., 2024). It is clear, then, that in this genre of solution a being able to be in the store and a being able not to do happily coexist. In particular, being able not to stand in the checkout line; which so much is leveraged – we would say enhanced – even within advertising campaigns.

Figure 20. Amazon Go store[29]

Figure 21. Amazon Go store[30]

Turning then to the right deixis, the one in which we find a full "being able to do" and a contextual affirmation of a "not (being able to be)" (position #8), it is possible to trace back to this position some augmented reality apps and features such as the virtual try on and the 3D planners.

The virtual try-on feature is a technological marvel found in many iOS and Android apps. This innovative tool empowers consumers to virtually "try on" products like clothing, accessories, offering a realistic preview before making a purchase (Figure 22). A great example of this is Sephora Virtual Artist (Figure 23), one of the most innovative mobile propositions, which uses AR technology to allow customers to try thousands of Sephora products directly from the mobile app, providing a highly interactive and personalized experience. By bridging the gap between the digital and physical realms, virtual try-on fosters a sense of confidence and assurance in the consumer's decision-making process. This technology mitigates the uncertainties associated with traditional online shopping, where sizing, fit and color accuracy can be challenging to assess. As a result, consumers are more likely to embrace this interactive and immersive shopping experience, ultimately leading to increased purchase intent and reduced return rates.

Figure 22. Example of virtual try-on[31]

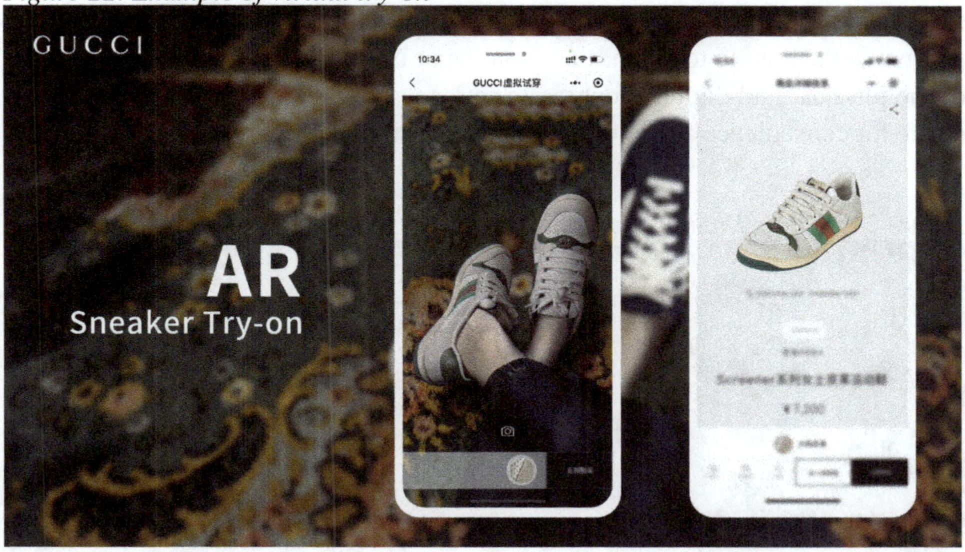

Figure 23. Sephora Virtual Artist[32]

As far as 3D planners are concerned, we cannot fail to mention IKEA's Kreativ app (Figure 24), a significant leap in the furniture retail industry. By allowing customers to virtually place IKEA furniture within their own spaces through augmented reality, the app addresses a fundamental consumer pain point: visualizing how a product will look and function in their specific environment. This innovative approach fosters a sense of ownership and confidence in purchasing decisions. The app streamlines the purchaser path, enabling customers to directly transition from visualizing the product in their space to purchasing it online or in-store. This seamless integration of the physical and digital shopping experience caters to the modern consumer's desire for convenience and control, ultimately driving sales and brand loyalty.

Figure 24. IKEA's Kreativ app[33]

Both of the solutions illustrated happily combine a "being able to do", specifically being able to do a trial, the result of the possibilities offered by digital, with a "being able not to be", specifically being able not to be physically in the store and in contact with the product.

In conclusion, a further possibility of categorization is offered to us by the last metaterm: the neutral term (position #6). This term combines the two contradictory terms, "not (being able to do)" and "not (being able to be)". In this complex semantic area, in which what one can not do and not be is valued by consumers, could be traced to what is defined as frictionless commerce. Frictionless commerce is a theoretical concept that describes the ideal state of digital commerce where all obstacles and barriers to purchase are eliminated, resulting in a seamless and effortless customer experience. It focuses on minimizing friction points throughout the entire customer journey, from initial product discovery to final checkout. This concept is driven by the desire to create a frictionless experience that is intuitive, efficient and personalized. This is, in essence, an area where what is not and need not be done is valued, and could be further and usefully investigated from a semiotic perspective.

10. CONCLUSION

Semiotics, by its very nature, investigates the generation and interpretation of meaning. It posits that meaning is inherently social and culturally constructed, and therefore, fundamentally intelligible. By conducting a rigorous analysis of the semantic values within a specific cultural or discursive context (a semantic microuniverse), semiotic inquiry assumes an inherently exploratory function. The application of the semiotic square, a heuristic device that systematically deconstructs a given semantic category, facilitates the creation of a comprehensive and nuanced map of the analyzed domain. This process of 'exploding' semantic categories allows for a systematic and rigorous understanding of the underlying structures and values that govern meaning-making within the chosen context.

As a first result of our research, we are now able to offer a clear semiotic mapping of the omnichannel domain, which is presented in the marketing literature in an ambiguous and disjointed manner, with much overlap and little clarity about the nature of the phenomena – as documented in Mele et al., 2023, with a dozen of parallel definition of phygital collected from the literature, where the label is used in connection with context, spaces, objects, applications, shopping experience, customer journey. We have demonstrated by means of examples our central hypothesis: the semiotic square offers a robust framework for analyzing the complexities of omnichannel consumer experiences. We are now able to distinguish several phenomena that are often conflated or confused, but which appear to be very different on a much more rigorous semantic level of analysis.

This research adopts a consumer-centric perspective, focusing on the unfolding of their shopping journey. Our focus diverges from existing scholarship on consumer values, such as Jean-Marie Floch's model (Floch, 1990), which elucidates how consumers imbue products with meaning and how these meanings influence purchase decisions. Buying luxury goods, for example, following utopian values, can therefore be, on the modal side, both a high tech experience or a totally physical and experiential one, depending on the modal values of a specific customer related to the customer journey chosen. The second result of our research is then to further differentiate the modal aspects of meaning making and to highlight this autonomous feature that is so important in today's omnichannel landscape.

Within the discourse of omnichannel – and this is the third claim that our analysis has proven – the emphasis unavoidably shifts from technological determinism towards consumer-centric experiential design. The terms "phygital" and "omnichannel" do not denote specific technologies, retail formats or digital touchpoints. Rather, they signify the orchestration of these elements to cultivate meaningful consumer experiences (Lemon & Verhoef, 2016). Then, the concept of omnichannel transcends technological platforms and physical spaces. It resides within the consumer's perception and engagement. A single product or service can assume diverse semantic meanings depending on the experiential context within which it is encountered. This underscores the primacy of consumer experience in shaping omnichannel success. Technologies serve as instrumental facilitators, enabling the configuration of sensory environments that resonate with the brand's desired brand identity and target audience's value systems. The effectiveness of an omnichannel strategy hinges on its ability to align with the consumer's existing value frameworks and cultural orientations.

The arguments made and the analytical tools developed lead us to address a critical question: how can brands and marketers use semiotics to make sense of the omnichannel world and create meaningful customer experiences? The answer is twofold, the proposed omnichannel and phygital semiotic square could be useful for marketers, brand strategist, designer and UX professionals:

- looking to design and plan innovative omnichannel and phygital experiences;
- seeking tools to manage and assess, namely align and give coherence to physical and digital touchpoints, in a cohesive design perspective.

Contemporary enterprises confronting the complexities of omnichannel strategies grapple with critical decisions regarding the introduction of new customer experiences and their orchestration. This research introduces an exploratory tool designed to assist brands in navigating this intricate landscape by discerning which experiences to facilitate and which to preclude. By introducing a semiotic framework tailored specifically to the omnichannel domain, it's possible to elucidate the underlying dynamics of consumer behavior across multiple touchpoints, and this empowers marketing professionals, designers and strategists with the necessary tools to foster innovative and impactful omnichannel experiences while mitigating the risks of costly missteps. This approach underscores the pivotal role of semiotics in the design process, this is our fourth claim. Semiotics, as a discipline concerned with the study of meaning-making, provides a powerful framework for crafting impactful media experiences (Eugeni, 2010). In the realm of design, meaning is not inherent but rather a construct. It is an entity that must be deliberately invented and strategically deployed. Semiotics, therefore, emerges as an indispensable tool for achieving this objective in this field. With this claim we follow a wide perspective developed in Zinna (2004), Deni and Proni (2008), Zingale (2009, 2012, 2020), Bianchi et al. (2010), Odoardi (2020, 2024).

Translating this conceptual framework into practical brand experience design necessitates a critical examination of target audiences. Each brand must meticulously define its ideal customer profile. This process involves constructing a comprehensive buyer persona, a fictional representation of the target customer, to guide the development and delivery of the buying journey. The proposed framework provides a valuable roadmap for brands navigating the complexities of contemporary consumer meaning making processes. By understanding the values and motivations that drive potential consumers, brands can effectively orient themselves and tailor their experiences accordingly. They can choose to be bound to a specific niche or to speak to a broader audience. Ultimately, the technological underpinnings of this framework empower brands to craft compelling purchase narratives that could or could not resonate with potential customers. The technology enables an experience design that proposes a purchase story to potential customers, and if this story is actually chosen by potential customers this leads to better interaction and ultimately to economic growth for the brand as well. We can then try, from a semiotic point of view, to predict a meaningful or meaningless interaction. At this point, it is useful to recall Umberto Eco's concept of the "model reader" (Eco, 1979), which emphasises the strategic role of the text in guiding interpretation. The text doesn't passively await interpretation; instead, it actively employs linguistic and structural strategies to steer the reader towards a specific understanding. Indeed, we translate this strategic concept to the media experience level. That is, we have in mind a broader user model, as in Cosenza (2015), the intended (and strategically defined) user of media experience design.

On the other hand, contemporary brands face the imperative of continuous assessment and evaluation across all customer touchpoints and the holistic purchase experience they engender (Keller & Swaminathan, 2019). The current data-rich environment, while offering unprecedented insights, presents the challenge of meaningful interpretation. Recognizing the dynamic nature of consumer values, preferences, and the competitive landscape, brands must prioritize the proactive management and ongoing monitoring of digital touchpoints. Semiotics emerges – this is our fifth and last claim – as a valuable framework for systematically analyzing, evaluating and comprehending the coherence and cohesion of the narrative proposal of the brand (Semprini, 1993; Ceriani, 2001; Marrone, 2007; Rolle, 2014; Rossolatos, 2015). This necessitates a deep understanding of the narrative meanings these touchpoints convey to consumers, enabling brands to maintain a competitive edge.

REFERENCES

Ball, M. (2022). *The metaverse: And how it will revolutionize everything*. Liveright.

Batat, W. (2019). *Experiential marketing: Consumer behavior, customer experience and the 7es*. Routledge. DOI: 10.4324/9781315232201

Batat, W. (2022). What does phygital really mean? A conceptual introduction to the phygital customer experience (PH-CX) framework. *Journal of Strategic Marketing*, *32*(8), 1220-1243. DOI: 10.1080/0965254X.2022.2059775

Bianchi, C., Montanari, F., & Zingale, S. (Eds.). (2010). *La semiotica e il progetto 2. Spazi, oggetti, interfacce*. Franco Angeli.

Ceriani, G. (2001). *Marketing moving: L'approccio semiotico. Analizzare il mix di comunicazione, gestirne gli effetti di senso*. Franco Angeli.

Cooper, A. (1999). *The inmates are running the asylum*. Sams. DOI: 10.1007/978-3-322-99786-9_1

Cooper, A., Reimann, R., & Cronin, D. (2007). *About face 3: The essentials of interaction design*. Wiley.

Cosenza, G. (2014). *Introduzione alla semiotica dei nuovi media*. Laterza.

Cosenza, G. (2020). Narrative semiotics, storytelling, and User Experience Design (UXD). *Lexia*, *33*, 51–71.

Cosenza, G. (2024). Semiotica per campagne di digital marketing. Alcune proposte operative. *Ocula*, *25*, 36–58.

Deni, M., & Proni, G. (Eds.). (2008). *La semiotica e il progetto. Design, comunicazione, marketing*. Franco Angeli.

Eco, U. (1979). *The role of the reader: Explorations in the semiotics of texts*. Indiana University Press. DOI: 10.2979/2846.0

Eugeni, R. (2010). *Semiotica dei media: le forme dell'esperienza*. Carocci.

Eugeni, R. (2015). *La condizione postmediale. Media, linguaggi e narrazioni*. La scuola.

Floch, J.-M. (1995). *Identités visuelles*. PUF.

Floch, J.-M. (2001). *Semiotics, marketing and communication: Behind the signs, the strategies* (Bodkin, R. O., Trans.). Palgrave. (Original work published 1990)

Gensler, S., Neslin, S. A., & Verhoef, P. C. (2017). The Showrooming Phenomenon: It's More than Just about Price. *Journal of Interactive Marketing*, *38*(1), 29-43. DOI: 10.1016/j.intmar.2017.01.003

Greimas, A. J. (1966). *Sémantique structurale*. Seuil.

Greimas, A. J. (1970). *Du sens I. Essais sémiotiques*. Seuil.

Greimas, A. J. (1983). *Du sens II. Essais sémiotiques*. Seuil.

Greimas, A. J., & Courtés, J. (1979). *Sémiotique. Dictionnaire raisonné de la théorie du langage*. Hachette.

Grillo, E., & Polidoro, P. (2023). Simulacri per progettare. Un punto di vista semiotico su archetipi e personas, *Filosofi(e) Semiotiche*, *10*(2), 66-75.

Hébert, L. (2020). *An introduction to applied semiotics: Tools for text and image analysis*. Routledge.

Keller, K. L., & Swaminathan, V. (2019). *Strategic brand management: Building, measuring, and managing brand equity*. Pearson.

Kotler, P., Kartajaya, H., & Setiawan, I. (2023). *Marketing 6.0: The future is immersive*. Wiley.

Landowski, E. (2006). Les interactions risquées. *Nouveaux actes sémiotiques, 101-102-103*.

Laurino, A. (2020a). Per una nuova assiologia del consumo. Una proposta di ampliamento, approfondimento e aggiornamento del modello flochiano, *Ocula*, 1-29.

Laurino, A. (2020b). Intorno al quadrato delle filosofie pubblicitarie. Per una sottoarticolazione di alcune delle categorie flochiane originarie, *Filosofi(e) Semiotiche*, *7*(1), 116-129.

Lemon, K. N., & Verhoef, P. C. (2016). Understanding customer experience throughout the customer journey. *Journal of Marketing*, *80*(6), 69-96. DOI: 10.1509/jm.15.0420

Liu, H., Lobschat, L., & Verhoef, P. (2018). Multichannel retailing: A review and research agenda. *Foundations and Trends in Marketing*, *12*(1), 1-79. DOI: 10.1561/1700000059

Mari, A., Mandelli, A., & Algesheimer, R. (2024). Empathic voice assistants: Enhancing consumer responses in voice commerce. *Journal of Business Research*, *175*, 114566. DOI: 10.1016/j.jbusres.2024.114566

Marrone, G. (2001). *Corpi sociali: processi comunicativi e semiotica del testo*. Einaudi.

Marrone, G. (2007). *Il discorso di marca. Modelli semiotici per il branding*. Laterza.

Mele, C., & Russo-Spena, T. (2022). The architecture of the phygital customer journey: A dynamic interplay between systems of insights and systems of engagement. *European Journal of Marketing*, *56*(1), 72–91. DOI: 10.1108/EJM-04-2019-0308

Mele, C., Spena, T. R., Marzullo, M. et al. (2023). The phygital transformation: A systematic review and a research agenda. *Italian Journal of Marketing*, 323-349.

Moore, G. A. (2014). *Crossing the chasm: Marketing and selling disruptive products to mainstream customers*. HarperCollins.

Odoardi, P. (2020). Search Engine Optimization (SEO) e semiotica: Come lavorare efficacemente sulle keyword. *Lexia*, *33-34*, 73–88.

Odoardi, P. (2024). Critica (semiotica) della ragion (algoritmica) d'Instagram. *Versus*, *2*, 355–376.

Rane, N., Choudhary, S., & Rane, J. (2023). Metaverse for enhancing customer loyalty: Effective strategies to improve customer relationship, service, engagement, satisfaction and experience. SSRN *Electronic Journal*. DOI: 10.2139/ssrn.4624197

Rolle, L. (2014). *Semiotica in pratica. Strumenti per governare le strategie di brand*. Franco Angeli.

Rossolatos, G. (2012). Applications, implications and limitations of the semiotic square for analyzing advertising discourse and discerning alternative brand futures. *Signs - International Journal of Semiotics, 6*, 1-47.

Rossolatos, G. (2015). *Handbook of brand semiotics*. Kassel University Press.

Schmitt, B. H. (1999). *Experiential marketing: How to get customers to sense, feel, think, act, relate to your company and brands*. The Free Press.

Semprini, A. (1993). *Marche e mondi possibili. Un approccio semiotico al marketing della marca*. Franco Angeli.

Stigliano, G., & Kotler, P. (2018). *Retail 4.0. 10 regole per l'era digitale*. Mondadori.

Turban, E., Strauss, J., & Lai, L. (2012). *Social commerce*. Prentice Hall.

Varma, A., Varde, Y., & Ray, S. (2024). Reinventing the retail experience: The case of Amazon GO. *World Journal of Advanced Research and Reviews*, *21*(03), 1123–1133. DOI: 10.30574/wjarr.2024.21.3.0779

Zingale, S. (2009). *Gioco, dialogo, design. Una ricerca semiotica.* ATì.

Zingale, S. (2012). *Interpretazione e progetto. Semiotica dell'inventiva.* Franco Angeli.

Zingale, S. (2020). Design o progettualità? Il progetto come trasformazione inventiva. *Ocula, 24*, 51-72.

Zinna, A. (2004). *Le interfacce degli oggetti di scrittura: teoria del linguaggio e ipertesti*. Meltemi.

ENDNOTES

1 Statista. (n.d.). Global E-commerce Sales. Retrieved from https://www.statista.com/markets/413/e-commerce/ - https://www.statista.com/statistics/379046/worldwide-retail-e-commerce-sales

2 https://www.strikingly.com/blog/posts/global-ecommerce-sales-growth-factors-driving-expansion

3 Boston Consulting Group. (n.d.). The E-commerce Imperative. Retrieved from https://www.bcg.com/publications/2024/e-commerce-innovation-imperative-for-retailers

4 Paragraphs §1-4 are written by Antonio Laurino; paragraphs §5-10 are written by Paolo Odoardi.

5 Source: https://commons.wikimedia.org/wiki/File:Es515_semiotic_square.jpg

6 Source web: http://www.signosemio.com/greimas/semiotic-square.asp

7 It is worth noting that this label and the previous one (tech enthusiasts), here in contradictory relationship, recall the well-known distinction between apocalyptic and integrated proposed by Umberto Eco (1964) to describe opposing attitudes toward mass culture; a formula still in use when discussing innovations, especially digital ones.

8 English translation by the authors.

9 Statista. (2024, December 12). Click and collect retail sales in the United States from 2014 to 2025. [Online]. Retrieved January 1, 2025, from https://www.statista.com/statistics/1132001/click-and-collect-retail-sales-us

10 Source: https://www.appvizer.fr/magazine/relation-client/experience-client/click-and-collect

11 Source: https://business.trustedshops.it/blog/clicca-e-ritira-gestire-picco-ordini

12 Walmart Corporate. (2017, April 12). When convenience and technology meet, pickup customers win. [Online]. Retrieved January 1, 2025, from https://corporate.walmart.com/news/2017/04/12/when-convenience-and-technology-meet-pickup-customers-win

13 Source: https://corporate.walmart.com/news/2017/04/12/when-convenience-and-technology-meet-pickup-customers-win

14 Source: https://www.retailcustomerexperience.com/articles/boot-barn-taps-kiosks-to-deliver-endless-aisle

15 Source: https://www.vinculumgroup.com/leveraging-the-endless-aisle-strategy-for-omnichannel-retail-success

16 Source: https://www.elotouch.com.ar/news/endless-aisle-empowers-retailers-to-optimize-inventory-management-and-increase-sell-through-rates

17 https://about.nike.com/en/newsroom/releases/nike-nyc-house-of-innovation-000

18 https://hmgroup.com/news/hm-group-explores-tech-enabled-shopping-experiences-in-us-stores/

19 Source: https://www.red-dot.org/de/project/nike-bootroom-nike-digital-retail-experience-15054-15054

20 Source: https://hmgroup.com/news/hm-group-explores-tech-enabled-shopping-experiences-in-us-stores/

21 https://www.mckinsey.com/capabilities/growth-marketing-and-sales/our-insights/unlocking-commerce-in-the-metaverse

22 https://www.gucci.com/ch/en_gb/st/stories/article/gucci-town-on-roblox

23 https://www.journee.ai/en/insights/newsroom/journee-celebrates-prestigious-win-at-the-28th-annual-webby-awards/

24 https://www.thedrum.com/news/2022/03/22/nearly-7-million-people-have-visited-nike-s-metaverse-store

25 Source: https://www.gucci.com/ch/en_gb/st/stories/article/gucci-town-on-roblox

26 Source: https://www.journee.ai/en/use-cases/macys-mstylelab

27 Source: https://www.journee.ai/en/use-cases/macys-mstylelab

[28] https://www.amazon.com/b?ie=UTF8&node=16008589011

[29] Source: https://www.foodweb.it/2019/01/amazon-go-la-strategia-dei-negozi-senza-casse

[30] Source: https://eu.usatoday.com/story/tech/news/2016/12/05/amazon-go-supermarket-no-checkout-no-cashiers-artificial-intelligence-sensors/94991612

[31] Source: https://tryon.kivisense.com/blog/gucci-sneaker-ar-try-on/

[32] Source: https://www.cbinsights.com/research/report/sephora-teardown/

[33] Source: https://www.ikea.com/global/en/newsroom/innovation/ikea-launches-ikea-place-a-new-app-that-allows-people-to-virtually-place-furniture-in-their-home-170912/

Chapter 2
Digital–Physical Harmony:
The Impact of Symbols on Phygital Consumers

Esma Ebru Şentürk
https://orcid.org/0000-0002-4528-1518
Hitit University, Turkey

ABSTRACT

Digital marketing has become a necessity in today's business landscape, merging traditional and digital realms in the "phygital" era. This convergence has created the phygital consumer, who seamlessly navigates physical and digital channels, enriching their shopping experiences through both. In this hybrid landscape, semiotics is vital for brands to craft meaningful symbols that foster emotional and cognitive connections. By uniting physical and digital symbols, semiotics enhances brand recognition and builds consumer loyalty through symbolic cohesion. Phygital strategies, supported by semiotics, enable brands to address the complexities of hybrid consumer behaviors, delivering unified messages that resonate across environments. This positions phygital marketing as a transformative approach that leverages the strategic power of semiotics.

INTRODUCTION

Digital marketing is a marketing strategy critical to businesses' success today. Businesses must use digital channels effectively to promote and sell their products and services and build customer loyalty. Digital marketing allows businesses to reach a wide audience, interact with the target audience, receive real-time feedback, and

DOI: 10.4018/979-8-3693-8024-6.ch002

continuously optimize their marketing strategies. In this way, it is possible for businesses to increase brand awareness, boost sales, and gain a competitive advantage.

Marketing semiotics, which deals with the meaning-making processes of consumers in the digital world, helps us understand how consumers relate to products and services through symbols, signs, and cultural codes. Consumers' habits have been profoundly transformed by the rapid development of the internet and technology. This transformation presents significant opportunities for marketing semiotics to analyze how consumers search for meaning in the digital world and interpret the symbols they encounter in this process. Phygital consumers, especially those who prefer experiences where the digital and physical worlds merge, are pushing the traditional boundaries of marketing. The wide access and interaction opportunities offered by digital marketing make hybrid models, where consumers can experience digital and physical elements together, attractive. How consumers perceive products during the purchasing process, how they attribute meaning to these products through symbols, and how digital signs resonate in the physical world can be more easily understood through semiotics.

In addition to its contributions to businesses, digital marketing has also provided many advantages to consumers. However, with the increasing momentum of digital marketing in the last decade and the impact of the pandemic, digital marketing has gained a different dimension for consumers in terms of health, hygiene, price, and accessibility. In sectors such as furniture, optics, and textiles, it is important for many consumers to try products before buying them. However, the pandemic has made this need problematic for consumers in terms of hygiene and health. For this reason, while consumers still want to see how the product they will buy will look on them, businesses have started to look for ways to meet this need of the consumer. In this process, advanced technology such as augmented reality (AR) and virtual reality (VR) applications (Pantano et al., 2017) have paved the way for consumers to try before they buy. These technologies are being symbolized by various symbols and signs in both the digital and physical worlds, while at the same time changing the way consumers make sense of products through signs and symbols in the digital world.

Another consumer behavior that has gained momentum in this process is webrooming, which can be defined as online research and offline shopping. In order to have more information and make comparisons on topics such as electronics, automobiles, education, etc., consumers first research and compare online, and then purchase offline by actually experiencing the product they will buy. Such phygital experiences offer an important area of investigation for marketing semiotics because consumers make meaningful decisions by combining symbols from both the digital and physical worlds.

Although all the facts and situations, conscious or unconscious, that have caused even consumers who never used digital marketing applications before the pandemic to turn to digital marketing have made digital marketing more important than ever, according to Kotler et al. (2024), no matter what, the digital environment cannot replace the traditional environment. However, this has led consumers to understand the advantages and conveniences of using digital and physical media together. As a result of this understanding, it can be said that consumers tend to act by considering the two environments as one. In other words, phygital consumers tend to think of these two environments as a whole by combining the meanings of digital and physical signs.

Millennials, who hold the majority of the power to earn and spend money today, use technology well and choose the most appropriate channel for their shopping. Generation Z, which has recently gained spending power, and Generation Alpha, which drives the purchases of Generation Y, were born directly into technology. For these two young generations, the world is a combination of physical and digital environments. For this reason, only multichannel applications are not enough for brands to retain Millennials, especially Generation Z and Alpha. As Kotler et al. (2024) emphasize, brands now have to effectively use omnichannel and metaverse applications, symbolically combine these two worlds, and appeal to consumers' signification processes. This calls for new approaches to how marketing semiotics can be used to understand the interaction of digital and physical signs. In this context, marketing semiotics research offers a powerful tool for exploring phygital consumers' meaning-making processes through symbols and signs and understanding how these processes resonate in both the digital and physical worlds.

THE RISE OF DIGITAL MARKETING AND THE PANDEMIC EFFECT

Digital marketing is a set of promotion strategies and tactics in which businesses use technology and the internet to promote and sell their products and services and build customer loyalty. Through various online platforms and technologies, businesses can reach a wide audience, interact with target audiences, and optimize their marketing strategies. Websites, mobile apps, social media platforms, email marketing, search engine optimization (SEO), search engine advertising (SEM), content marketing, and other digital channels are tools that are often used to support businesses' digital marketing strategies. These tools play an important role in increasing brand awareness, boosting sales, and strengthening customer loyalty. However, digital marketing is not only about tools and techniques; it also contains symbols and codes that have meaning and value in terms of marketing semiotics. Marketing semiotics is a research discipline that deciphers the meanings underlying consumers' relationships with brands, examining how messages and images are perceived and how they influence consumer behavior (Mick et al., 2004, p. 8).

The importance of digital marketing is increasing today. Especially with the rapid development of technology and the widespread use of the internet, consumers' shopping habits have changed significantly. Consumers now research online platforms, read product reviews, and access comments about products and brands on social media before purchasing products (Chaffey & Smith, 2023). Therefore, it is important for businesses to develop digital marketing strategies and reach their target audiences by using digital channels effectively. At this point, marketing semiotics has become an important tool for understanding consumer interactions and meaning production processes in the digital world. Consumers infer certain meanings through visual symbols, colors, logos, and language used by brands (Özbölük & Kurtoğlu, 2019), and these signs influence consumer decisions. Online reviews and social media comments create shared symbolic meanings among consumers, creating an interaction environment that reinforces the layers of meaning of marketing strategies in the digital environment.

Digital interactions between consumers and brands, especially on social media, have accelerated the shift towards a more transparent approach to marketing. Today, customers who prefer digital shopping want to be able to customize not only the product or service they want to buy but even the price they are willing to pay (Wind & Mahajan, 2000, p. 20). Moreover, they have access to enough information and alternatives independent of spatial boundaries to do so. It is very important to understand how consumers understand and interpret this information and, more importantly, to manage this perception. At this point, brands not only offer products and services through social media and digital platforms but also convey various meanings to consumers through colors (Ahmed, 2020), symbols, slogans, and other signs (Gandla et al., 2023). These signs create codes and layers of meaning that influence how consumers perceive the brand and what they value in their purchasing decisions. This shift has not only left brands with anywhere to hide but given the very clear challenges facing the world and its people, many businesses have been pushed to look for ways to take a more purpose-driven, ethical approach to market. The role of semiotics in this process is to enable brands to communicate their values and ethical approach to consumers more clearly and understandably.

In addition to all these, with the effect of the COVID-19 pandemic, which started in Wuhan, People's Republic of China at the end of 2019 and spread around the world, using digital marketing strategies has ceased to be a choice for businesses and has become a necessity. Towards the end of 2020, individuals were asked to stay away from crowded environments within the scope of protection practices from COVID-19. Curfews were imposed in many countries in this context. These restrictions brought the business of physical stores to a halt. However, the existence of needs has not disappeared. For this reason, consumers have turned to meet even their most basic needs from digital stores (Tran et al., 2023, p. 7). The fear caused by the pandemic forced even consumers who had never shopped digitally before to turn to digital markets (Rahman, 2023, p. 86). In this process, the importance of symbols, language, and visual signs used on digital platforms has increased even more. Businesses tried to reassure consumers through signs and symbols specific to this period in their digital stores; symbols of health, hygiene, and social distancing played a central role in the marketing communication of brands. The main function of semiotics in this crisis period can be considered as decoding the codes that shape consumers' purchasing behavior under pandemic conditions and analyzing the emotional reactions these symbols create in consumers.

COVID-19 created a serious stress factor for consumers. At first, consumers gathered everything in physical stores and made stocks. However, as the process dragged on, it became clear that stockpiling was an insurmountable situation and consumers gradually began to return to their daily lives. However, since the fear of being exposed to the disease by mixing with the crowd persisted, they directed their shopping to digital markets as much as possible in this process, which can be perceived as a psychological crisis. In the most difficult period of this psychological crisis, digital markets gained the trust of consumers by managing the process well (Li, 2023, p. 1899). Thus, the long duration of the process both encouraged businesses to develop digital marketing strategies and permanently changed the purchasing behavior of consumers to a great extent. Digital signs and symbols are important elements that affect consumer behavior during the pandemic period. Under pandemic conditions, the visuals (Pengnate & Sarathy, 2017), icons, colors (Lee & Rao, 2010), and messages (Karimov & Brengman, 2011) used in digital stores reassured consumers. For example, "safe shopping" icons, visuals emphasizing health protection measures, and social distancing symbols during delivery were semiotic elements that reinforced consumers' trust in digital platforms. These signs, used in moments of psychological crisis, made consumers feel safe while shopping in the digital environment, which accelerated their orientation toward digital markets.

Despite all these, various studies examining consumers' views on digital channels after the pandemic have revealed that they do not want to use digital channels as much as they did during the pandemic period, especially for basic needs and shopping related to health, education, and the public sector. However, compared to the pre-pandemic period, they will not avoid using them when needed. In addition, it is another fact that consumers who used a single channel before the pandemic have diversified the number of channels they use after the pandemic (Szwajca, 2022). This change is important for understanding how consumers create meanings between digital and physical environments and how these meanings affect their purchasing behavior. During the pandemic, digital channels have led to the adoption of new shopping symbols (e.g., "contactless payment"). Consumers' attitudes toward digital channels are directly related to how these new symbols and signs are interpreted (Hegy, 2023). The fact that consumers have adopted a more selective and conscious approach to digital channels after the pandemic shows how effective these signs are in semiotic terms and in which emotional and cultural contexts they are perceived. It should also be taken into account that the messages and symbols they see on digital channels allow for a comparison of their experiences both in providing a safe shopping experience and in physical stores. In conclusion, the increasing diversity of channels in the post-pandemic era is a reflection of how consumers interact with different symbolic meanings and experiences, and this is leading to a reshaping of marketing strategies.

Digital marketing is essentially a channel marketing strategy and as such should be integrated with other channels as part of multichannel marketing. Therefore, the interaction and integration between traditional and digital channels should support the customer journey (Chaffey & Ellis-Chadwick, 2019). This integration enables consumers to make meaning between the signs and symbols they experience through different channels. Consumers' experiences through traditional and digital channels influence how marketing messages are interpreted and perceived. For example, the variation between a product's presentation in a physical store and its presentation on digital platforms (Liao et al., 2016, Cheng et al., 2022) also shapes the symbolic meanings and emotional responses consumers have to the product. However, digital marketing has complicated and intensified the competition created by traditional marketing (Chaffey & Smith, 2023). This requires brands to create more complex and multi-layered symbolic systems in their communications with consumers. In this context, the integration of digital marketing with traditional channels should enrich the customer experience while at the same time ensuring the consistency of messages delivered across channels. As consumers analyze the meanings behind these messages, brands' presentation and content strategies are of great importance. In other words, digital marketing strategies include not only the promotion of products or services but also the creation of a symbolic language that appeals to consumers' worlds of meaning. In this way, the effectiveness of marketing communication can be increased and brands can establish a deeper connection with their consumers.

PHYGITAL MARKETING: COMBINING OF TRADITIONAL AND DIGITAL

Rigby (2014), who describes the rapid developments in digital marketing as a digital-physical mashup, predicts that businesses that fail to read the impact of digitalization correctly will be hit hard. According to the author, digital change will have a wide range of effects in the media, technology, and communication sectors. The most striking impact of this major transformation has not yet been experienced (until 2014). In some sectors, such as healthcare, the change will be slower. Five years after the author's prediction, the pandemic has accelerated the digital revolution and made many of his predictions come true. Digital marketing has gained great momentum in the last five years, and the use of digital channels has become inevitable. However, traditional marketing is still influential. This means a combination of traditional shopping and digital shopping. This combination creates a significant transformation in consumer habits. This transformation affects the shopping behavior of both traditional and digital consumers. The fact that consumers experience signs, symbols, and meanings in both physical and digital environments together creates a semiotically rich interaction area.

With the popularity of digital shopping, businesses are looking to combine the traditional shopping experience with digital platforms. This aims to provide customers with the same quality and consistent experience in both physical stores and online platforms. This combination has led to the emergence of a new concept called phygital marketing. Phygital marketing is a marketing strategy that is coordinated with the marketing strategies of businesses, designed in accordance with the purpose and content, includes tactics within the main theme, is visible in both digital and physical touchpoints, and strengthens communication with consumers. This strategy causes businesses to design all marketing components in a coordinated manner across different channels (Kartal & Şentürk, 2020, p. 276). Phygital marketing utilizes modern technologies such as smartphones, tablets, and various digital platforms to interact with consumers in innovative ways by combining traditional marketing concepts with in-vogue communication technologies. The perspective of semiotics, which examines the link between signs and meanings, is reflected in the way consumers interpret physical and digital symbols in phyigital marketing. This strategy creates a coherent and engaging customer journey by presenting the best of both the physical and digital space (Ortiz, 2013). In other words, it increases the interaction of the business with consumers in both physical and digital channels. This interaction enriches the shopping experience of consumers and increases the brand awareness of businesses. Combining physical and digital shopping experiences offers consumers a wider range of choices and makes the shopping process more enjoyable. This approach aims to create a multi-channel shopping environment that better responds to consumers' needs and preferences. The layers of meaning offered by semiotics are especially important for consumers to make a meaningful connection between the signs and symbols they see across different channels in this multi-channel environment. In order to influence consumers, who prefer multi-channel shopping, integrity, consistency, continuity, and complementarity between the relevant channels are required (Chaffey & Smith, 2023; Mohammad Alzub, 2023).

With the impact of the digital revolution, consumers' shopping habits have also changed, and channel preferences have diversified. Traditional consumers differ from digital consumers in purchasing behavior due to the impact of the digital age on consumer habits (Tirpude, 2022; Jaiwant, 2023). Traditional consumers are generally guided and make decisions as a result of internal stimuli, product positioning, advertising, and other marketing activities. During the pandemic period, these stimuli have been overshadowed by environmental stimuli. Especially the millennials, who have the spending power, have turned to survival-based purchasing behavior (Niranjini & Sridevi, 2023). Among the motivations of consumers who prefer digital shopping, time-saving, price comparison, and affordable prices are at the forefront. However, perceived security concerns may slow down the digital shopping process (Tirpude, 2022). Considering the structure of semiotics in making sense of consumers' product and shopping experiences (Østergaard et al., 2015), these diverging preferences and motivations of digital and traditional consumers express the transformation of meaning across spaces.

Consumers' attitudes towards digital markets are also influenced by personal tastes, ease of use of the platform, and perceived usefulness. In addition, factors such as consumers' personal characteristics, environmental factors, economic situation, and preferred product characteristics are also important (Tran et al., 2023). Digital consumers are generally more tech-savvy and expect convenience, quick access to information, and product comparison (Bartosik-Purgat & Filimon, 2022). Therefore, they tend to shop online for price comparison and product research (Mehmeti-Bajrami et al., 2022). Traditional consumers, on the other hand, trust traditional marketing channels more and may have different shopping experience expectations (Engelbrecht, 2022). However, while it was easier to distinguish between traditional and digital customers before the pandemic, the pandemic has changed this situation. Many consumers, especially those who lack experience and knowledge about the use of technology, perceive digital shopping as risky or hesitate to use it for various reasons, have had to experience digital shopping during the pandemic. Traditional consumers who have experienced this experience are increasingly switching to digital shopping channels driven by factors such as perceived convenience, experienced use of technology, variety, and the pleasure of accessing alternatives (Tang et al., 2023; Tran et al., 2023). This transition can be taken as evidence that digital shopping channels create a new layer of meaning and value in the minds of consumers. In addition, the information, offers, and personalized experiences and communication offered by the business in digital channels, tailored to their preferences and needs, attract traditional consumers more to the digital market (Bolos et al., 2016). This accelerated shift in traditional consumers has also accelerated businesses to integrate traditional and digital shopping experiences (Alzub, 2023).

As a result, the combination of traditional and digital shopping is transforming businesses' marketing strategies and consumers' shopping experiences. This combination represents an innovative approach to the advantage of both businesses and consumers by creating a multi-layered structure of meaning through the combination of physical and digital signs.

EXPERIENCE PRIORITIZED CONSUMER BEHAVIOR

Social media has become a platform for word-of-mouth marketing, where customers share their satisfaction and frustrations. The positive or negative experience of a customer has started to be internalized by other potential customers. The Patisswiss incident in early 2024 is a good example of this (Şenses, 2024). A customer shared her disappointment with the chocolate she bought from a chain of grocery stores on social media and received a negative response that she did not expect. Other consumers who saw this disappointment and the response internalized the situation as if they had experienced it themselves and took a negative attitude toward the brand. As can be understood, the fact that consumers have more options when choosing a supplier and can make their voices heard more easily through the Internet and social media has led to a major change in the way brands communicate with consumers. In each of these interactions on social media, the symbols, images, and responses of brands to consumers create new meanings and images. Thus, communication between brands and consumers is shaped not only by text or visuals but also by creating a layer of meaning in the perception of consumers.

The fact that digital marketing has become a necessity in the last decade has directly or indirectly turned all consumers who are familiar with technology into digital customers. However, the likelihood of these consumers making digital purchases varies according to their trust in the Internet, whether they feel comfortable shopping digitally, the sector in which they shop, and their personal characteristics (Wind & Mahajan, 2000, p. 21). While it is more common among consumers to use digital in sectors such as banking, it may be less preferred to use digital in the textile sector, which has a lower risk compared to banking. The main reason for this is how the semiotic elements used by the businesses in the sector are perceived, as well as factors such as security measures taken, perceived convenience, and how the businesses in the sector direct the consumer. In addition, the importance that consumers attach to experience is also effective in this difference. Experience can occur in different dimensions as product experience, customer experience, and brand experience, and each of them creates new perspectives (Yin & Xu, 2021) with symbols and meanings in the minds of consumers. This leads to the reinterpretation of concepts such as trust and convenience offered by brands in the digital environment in the minds of consumers, creating a series of signs that reinforce or weaken brand and industry images.

In experience-first marketing, personalization and consumer experience play a critical role in increasing customer satisfaction and loyalty. This role can be both cognitive and emotional (Tyrväinen et al., 2020, Martínez-González & Álvarez-Albelo, 2021). Personalized experiences strengthen the symbolic and meaningful relationships consumers have with brands. While the effectiveness of personalized services increases with consumer trust in the seller (Pappas, 2018), privacy concerns can negatively affect the adoption of personalized services. Signs and symbols are also among the factors that affect the consumer's perception of trust. A high level of experience can compensate for low trust or negative emotions (Chellappa & Sin, 2005). For example, in digital marketing, personalized website design is very important to create consumer trust. A quality website strengthens the brand's image in the eyes of the consumer and increases online purchase intentions (Martínez-González & Álvarez-Albelo, 2021). However, not every consumer's demand for personalization is similar. Brands that understand these differences can use the advantages of digital marketing to attract traditional consumers to the online store through personalized offers. Understanding these differences allows brands to better understand consumers' needs and expectations so that their communication strategies become more effective.

In this context, augmented reality (AR) applications that can provide consumers with a product experience during online shopping allow consumers to experience the interaction of their own face and the product. Thus, the customer experience becomes enjoyable and informative, which increases the online purchasing tendencies of consumers with experience-first purchasing behavior (Smink et al., 2019, p. 8). While AR applications are perceived as useful for consumers in terms of accessing more information more easily and making sure that they get exactly the desired product, on the other hand, they contribute to experience-based online shopping (Dacko, 2017, p. 254) by causing them to perceive online shopping as fun. In this process, AR applications shape consumers' perceptions with their visual and functional elements, thus helping brands to increase the value of their products and positively influence consumers' purchasing decisions.

One of the processes that lead consumers to a brand is the brand's success in crisis management and its ability to resolve consumer complaints. Consumers want to find an interlocutor in case of a negative experience. In such a situation in online media, they are hesitant to find an interlocutor. At this point, applications such as live customer support service, chatbots, and conversational human voice (personalized and human-like tone of voice, CHV) strengthen the perception of trust by making the consumer feel heard. Such elements also reinforce the symbolic bonds that the brand establishes with the consumer, and it can be argued that the length of the response (Zhang & Wang, 2023, p. 695) influences customer satisfaction. With the power of social media, customers can immediately share negative experiences with their followers, so it is important to resolve the customer's complaint process as quickly and appropriately as possible. In the process of handling customers' complaints, a successful resolution process can reduce negative word of mouth and encourage positive word of mouth.

Brands use multichannel marketing strategies to improve the consumer experience. However, multichannel marketing strategies should be consistent and integrated. Customer experiences are positively affected when consumers can reach the same goal using the channel they want. Understanding consumer behavior in multichannel strategies is challenging (Barwitz & Maas, 2018), because different symbols and messages in each channel shape consumer perception. In addition, online and offline strategies need to be consistent with each other (Teltzrow et al., 2007). For example, the overlap between the experience in an offline store and the experience offered on digital platforms supports the consumer's holistic perception of the brand.

These developments have further increased the importance of digital customer experience and made it imperative for brands to invest in digital innovations to meet consumer expectations. As a result, consumers' experiences on digital platforms directly influence their purchasing decisions

PHYGITAL CONSUMERS AND THEIR CHARACTERISTICS

Phygital consumers are a new generation of consumers who interact in "phygital" environments where physical and digital experiences merge. These consumers benefit from the advantages of both worlds by experiencing their shopping experiences both in physical stores and on digital platforms. This new consumer group, which emerged as a result of the rapid development of digital marketing and new behaviors gained after the pandemic, tries to personalize products and services and even price. To achieve this goal, they are digitally interactive at every moment (Wind & Mahajan, 2000). The experiences, satisfaction, and criticism of other consumers' guide their purchases. Here, feedback from other consumers serves as a signifier, i.e., it creates layers of meaning about the product for phygital consumers. However, for phygital consumers, this personalization is not as easy as for digital consumers. Phygital consumers want to see, touch, and try the product/service they plan to buy first. Therefore, even if they like a product they see in the digital market, it may be difficult for them to make a purchase decision. At this point, webrooming behavior is frequently shown by phygital consumers. The desire to both research the product online and physically examine it creates a mental marker of the product; that is, the physical experience reinforces the value and meaning of the product for the consumer.

Reasons for this behavior include the desire to experience the product experience and purchase experience in the traditional way with the technology experience (Aw et al., 2021), the desire to make the smartest purchase by comparison (Kothari et al., 2021), the sense of trust arising from the traditional brand experience (Nosi et al., 2022), the category of the product they plan to buy and the risk phenomenon they perceive about the product (Hult et al., 2019), and the pleasure of getting the most useful product by getting more information (Díaz et al., 2017). At this point, experience carries a critical symbolic meaning in the purchase decision process of the phygital consumer. The phygital consumer's need to physically touch the product and interact with salespeople supports their offline purchasing tendencies as well as their online research behavior.

Phygital consumers can be highly socially interactive consumers. Therefore, they want to know whether a product they like is also liked by others. Phygital consumers' product evaluations are positively or negatively influenced by other consumers' evaluations. Social influences and learning from others play an important role in consumers' decision-making processes (Sridhar & Srinivasan, 2012). Here, the opinions of other consumers become a symbol for phygital consumers, shaping opinions about the value and reliability of the product. Interaction is therefore very important in this consumer group. In other words, even if phygital consumers like the product themselves, they may not buy it if online consumer reviews are negative. Online reviews represent symbolic meanings about the product for phygital consumers; in other words, these reviews integrate with the consumer's personal experience to form a sign system that influences the decision-making process.

Phygital consumers prefer to combine the traditional shopping experience with the digital shopping experience and engage in hybrid experiences. These experiences offer a richer and more personalized experience in consumers' shopping journey (Yao et al., 2024). On the other hand, consumers' interactions in phygital experiences often follow non-linear paths and can be characterized by complex emotional responses (Mele et al., 2024).

Phygital consumers try a product physically in the store but prefer to order from the digital store. Thus, they do not have to carry the product. Moreover, they can use digital discount coupons and gift vouchers if available. In addition, they do not have to buy the product as soon as they try it. After deciding on the product to buy in the physical store, they can order the product from the online platform of their choice at any convenient time (Garg & Kaur, 2018). The physical store offers a sense of trust and tangibility as an icon representing the product in the real world. They can also benefit from digital-specific price discounts as a result of showrooming behaviors that allow them to benefit from price competition between the physical store and the digital store (Zhang et al., 2018). After deciding on the features such as size, color, and model, they can order by choosing the most affordable one in the digital market. Digital stores function as a symbol of the opportunities that the digital world provides to the consumer by offering benefits such as price advantage and flexibility. On the contrary, when phygital consumers compare the product they have examined in the physical store with the product in the digital store, if they encounter a similar price, they may prefer to shop from the physical store without incurring time costs (Wolk & Ebling, 2010, p. 144).

One of the most important challenges for consumers in online purchases is the exchange or return process. Due to the time and cost increases that may be experienced due to shipping in this process, phygital consumers may prefer to go to the store (Akturk et al., 2018) to return or exchange a purchased product in the traditional way. This behavior can be considered as a combination of the abstract nature of the digital shopping process with the need to find a concrete response in the return process.

A study by Li et al. (2016) found that young and middle-aged female consumers are more likely to engage in phygital consumer behavior, and that they have higher levels of education and average income levels. This result may imply that education and income levels have become a symbol through which consumers reflect their identity and social status by integrating physical and digital shopping. Bae et al. (2021) states that consumers older than fifty years perceive themselves as old and therefore avoid innovative processes. Especially young adults and middle-aged consumers (Jain & Duggal, 2016, Kleinlercher et al., 2020; Eugene Cheng-Xi Aw et al., 2021) are among the prominent findings in the literature. These findings show that consumers' beliefs about technology are shaped by their emotional and cognitive perceptions. Therefore, in phygital environments, these perceptions influence consumers' approach or avoidance behaviors (Guzzetti et al., 2024).

Phygital Consumer Identity and Symbolism

Born from the combination of technology and individual characteristics, "phygital consumers" constitute a new group of consumers who live at the intersection of the digital and physical worlds, blending the symbols of these two worlds into their own identities. Phygital consumers combine the sense of trust that comes from physical experiences with the flexibility and innovation offered by digital symbols. This integration creates a unique "phygital consumer identity" where virtual symbols, avatars, and digital representations meet the symbolic experiences of the physical world.

The combination of the symbols consumers experience in physical stores and the visual and linguistic symbols they encounter on digital platforms plays an important role in the formation of a phygital consumer identity. The sustainability of a brand image for phygital consumers can be realized by ensuring consistency between physical and digital symbols (Mishra et al., 2023). Logos and slogans are critical in establishing brands' identities (Ward et al., 2020). These elements also make it easier for consumers to recognize and remember the brand. For example, a consumer makes the brand visible in the digital world by sharing a bag purchased from a physical store with the logo visible on their social media profile. This behavior is important for understanding how the brand creates a symbolic meaning on consumer identity in both the physical and digital worlds.

Social media enables phygital consumers to adopt the symbolic values of brands through digital representations. Brands, which can be positioned both functionally and symbolically, provide symbolic resources for consumers to express themselves and build their social identities (Elliott & Wattanasuwan, 1998). Symbolic brands help consumers express themselves through dimensions such as prestige and personality expression (Bhat & Reddy, 1998). In a sense, consumers identify with the symbolic values and meanings of brands. This allows brands to become part of consumers' lives (Tan & Ming, 2003). This process takes place through advertisements and product/service experiences. Consumer experiences in phygital environments can be categorized as ordinary or extraordinary. A consumer who perceives an experience as hostile or is disappointed by it for some reason may see it as ordinary, whereas a consumer who has an experience that fuels their passion or allows them to make new discoveries may describe it as extraordinary. What is important is that brands use flexible and agile strategies to shape these experiences (Pusceddu et al., 2023) and at the same time symbolize this experience for consumers.

Symbolic elements such as logos, slogans, and colors of brands become tools for consumers to express their digital identities (Osmanova et al., 2023). For example, a consumer who shares the logos of a brand emphasizing sustainability on their social media profile makes their environmental awareness visible through this brand. Thus, by transforming the meanings of the symbols offered by brands into indicators on social media, phygital consumer identity creates a form of personal expression and strengthens brand loyalty.

Phygital avatars allow digital consumers to establish an emotional connection with the brand, especially on platforms such as the metaverse, where the virtual and the physical are intertwined. Especially avatars with high behavioral realism (Lee & Choi, 2017) positively affect consumers' social communication (Verhagen et al., 2014), customer experience (Miao et al., 2022), and consumer decision-making behaviors (Al-Natour et al., 2011). On the other hand, a personalized avatar equipped with the virtual clothes of a fashion brand strengthens the digital presence of the consumer by combining their digital and physical identity. Avatars contribute to consumers' identification with the brand's values and bridge digital and physical symbols together to bridge the phygital consumer identity (Belghiti et al., 2018a).

Phygital consumers are also empowered by social approval mechanisms from digital and physical environments. Sharing the symbols of a brand in the digital world gives the consumer a sense of acceptance and prestige online. Sharing the symbolic value of a product experienced in a physical store in a digital environment gives these consumers a sense of acceptance and approval within the community. For example, a consumer carrying the brand's symbols at an event and sharing it on social media takes a physical experience to a digital level of approval. The social symbolism of these two worlds increases phygital consumers' loyalty to the brand.

Digital and physical symbols are key elements that shape phygital consumers' brand loyalty. Consistent symbols that the brand offers both in physical stores and on digital platforms deepen phygital consumers' bonds with the brand (Tan & Ming, 2003). Symbols experienced in a store are transferred to the digital world, further strengthening the relationship between the consumer and the brand (Batat & Hammedi, 2023). For example, a loyalty program where a product is integrated with digital rewards increases consumer loyalty to the brand and reinforces loyalty through the physical-digital connection.

In the future, with the proliferation of new digital platforms such as the metaverse, the identities of phygital consumers will become richer and more symbolized. In this world, consumers can bring the products they physically experience into the virtual world through their digital avatars. By increasing the importance of digital symbols, brands can offer consumers innovative experiences where the digital and physical worlds offer an integrated symbolism. For example, re-enacting an event in the physical world in a virtual environment through a digital avatar will create a powerful symbolic experience for phygital consumers that connects the two worlds.

However, younger consumers, born directly into the digital world, who today directly influence the decisions of consumers with the ability to spend, are learning symbols in the digital world. This brings opportunities and threats. For example, the signs, colors, and logos they see on web pages, in games, clips, and movies in the digital world mean a lot to this consumer group. As a result of the gamification technique used in marketing, the symbols and environments used in games create shared symbol systems among those exposed to them and this can create a different and common understanding of those symbols (Alcindor et al., 2022). For example, a child may use an arrow sign in a game to reach a secret passage or find a hidden item, but when they encounter a similar symbol in real life, they will still try to perceive it in its digital meaning. In this case, brands can achieve this semiotic unity not only by creating symbols in the digital environment but also by updating the way symbols are used in the physical environment. Digital symbols reshape communication styles in the physical world by influencing individuals' thoughts and behaviors through social media and other digital platforms (Tuğba & Ramazan, 2019). Moreover, it is easier and faster to create and share new symbols through social media. Moreover, the interactive nature of these symbols allows individuals to develop new patterns of behavior and language. This has an impact on many areas from brand recognition to purchasing behavior (Uğurlu, 2014). In other words, the symbols used in digital media correspond in various ways in physical life, and these symbols play an important role in individuals' daily lives and social interactions. This situation indicates that brands should use data analytics and market segmentation techniques together and effectively in order to better recognize their target audience (Sargın, 2024, p. 51).

Examples of Phygital Marketing That Attract Phygital Consumers

The phygital customer journey involves a combination of digital and physical tools and spaces. This enables consumers to have a more holistic shopping experience (Mele et al., 2024). In this context, the mixed reality applications they will be exposed to make it easier for them to interact between the physical world and the digital world, while the phygital personalized services they will receive make it easier for them to connect with brands. The challenges faced by omnichannel applications can be overcome with the use of semiotics in phygital marketing strategies. Community-oriented platforms such as social media can strengthen the experience of physical shoppers by keeping them interacting with their social environment, while storytelling and story creation can facilitate a much longer-lasting relationship between the consumer and the brand when the brand and the consumer's imagination combine. While implementing all these practices, the meanings of digital signs and physical signs should be reconsidered. It is clear that symbols that point to different meanings will create perception confusion for consumers.

Mixed Reality (XR) Experiences

Mixed reality enables users to interact between the physical and digital worlds. These applications enrich customer experiences, offering new encounters and sensory impacts. They can also create positive word-of-mouth by increasing social interactions (Holopainen et al., 2018). Augmented reality applications can influence consumers' brand perception and purchase decisions (Çakırkaya & Koçyiğit, 2024). Augmented and virtual reality applications enrich consumer experiences throughout the customer journey. These technologies are making a significant impact in consumer marketing and are gaining increasing attention in marketing research (Wedel et al., 2020). Technologies such as smart mirrors allow consumers to express themselves by integrating the physical experience with the digital world. These tools reveal not only the functional aspects of products, but also their visual and personal meaning. For example, smart mirrors launched by MemoMI Labs Inc. integrate the physical experience of consumers with the digital experience and make it meaningful in a sector with a large market share such as textiles. These mirrors, which can memorize the real-time view of the person from various angles, can show how the person will stand on the product in the store and different color alternatives. They also allow combinations with various accessories, further personalizing the experience (Vimeo, n.d.). In the cosmetics industry, a mirror called HiMirror can recommend products suitable for skin problems by analyzing the real-time image of the person through the camera (Slater, 2018). The virtual mirror developed by Ffface.Me offers an experience in the style of makeup artist Mario Dedivanovic, bringing together the person's snapshot with the makeup application (Marin-Lopez, 2024).

Personalized Services

Phygital marketing has the potential to increase sales by offering consumers the best of both physical and digital environments. This approach enriches the consumer experience by combining elements such as ease of payment and product engagement (Johnson & Barlow, 2021; Sağtaş, 2022). Phygital marketing increases brand loyalty by providing consumers with personalized experiences. This enables consumers to engage more and build a deeper connection with the brand (Johnson & Barlow, 2024). For example, in 2015, Rebecca Minkoff created a boutique equipped with technology that redefined the physical store shopping experience. The store features interactive mirrors that allow customers to order drinks, request different sizes, and adjust the lighting to see how clothes look in different environments. This technology, developed in collaboration with E-Bay, makes customers feel special and provides designers with data on customer expectations (Fast Company, 2015). H&M, on the other hand, offers consumers a combination of physical and digital experience with its digital applications. Consumers can find similar alternatives of the products they scan with the application and see these alternatives on their own images. In physical stores, they can check stock through the app (H&M TR, n.d.). Similarly, The H. Store in Korea uses smart mirror and camera technology to digitally visualize the results such as color, size, length before the transaction and offers personalized experience to customers (Lovethehstory, 2024).

Omnichannel Marketing

Omnichannel marketing aims to provide customers with a consistent service experience by ensuring seamless integration across different channels. Research shows that integration quality (INQ) positively influences customer value and cross-purchase behavior (Hossain et al., 2020). In this context, semiotics (Zotova, 2021), which plays an important role in the global world as a means of information, knowledge transfer, positioning, and attention-getting, has become an important tool in omnichannel marketing. In the use of different channel elements, semiotic elements should be used to create message unity in the minds of consumers. Because the correct use of signs and symbols helps brands to convey their messages in a powerful way (Zotova, 2021).

While omnichannel marketing has significant advantages, it also faces challenges such as data access and integration, marketing attribution, and consumer privacy. These challenges are particularly pronounced in the digital environment. However, technologies such as machine learning and artificial intelligence can provide solutions to these challenges and make omnichannel marketing strategies more effective (Cui et al., 2021).

At this point, phygital marketing adds a different dimension to the omnichannel experience by combining physical and digital components at the same time and in the same place. The phygital experience blends physical store elements (products, point of sale) with digital tools (touch screens, NFC cards) and presents them to consumers. This experience draws attention with its social, hedonic, sensory, and participatory dimensions (Belghiti et al., 2018b). On the other hand, findings from consumer psychology and neuroscience suggest that digital purchasing technologies can increase sales by reducing the “pain of payment” and encouraging product engagement (Johnson & Barlow, 2024).

Slatter (2018) defines consumers as “individuals who live in the digital world while breathing in real life”. In this context, Amazon Go's cashierless store service offers an ideal environment for phygital consumers. Thanks to artificial intelligence and infrared sensor technology, consumers can experience digital shopping in the physical store (Amazon, n.d.). With digital twin technology, Media Markt moves to the metaverse and offers consumers the physical store experience in digital media. Access to this store becomes possible by using VR glasses, mobile devices, or computers (Edtech Turkey, 2024).

Community Driven Platforms

Community-driven platforms, together with phygital marketing, which is a combination of digital and physical marketing strategies, deepen consumer communication and interaction through the use of semiotic tools. In addition to being channels where users and brands interact, these platforms enable the creation of meanings between users and between users and brands (Moschini, 2018). Semiotics extends the practical possibilities of sign systems in the digital age, using them as an important tool for communicating information and influence, while enabling brands to offer consumers more meaningful and contextually rich experiences (Zotova, 2021). For example, Snapchat Dress Up app allows consumers to try on outfits with AR lenses and share these images. Through this sharing, users can receive feedback from their community and make their shopping experience more interactive (Technology, 2022). Similarly, McDonald's brought phygital applications into the advertising space through outdoor billboards loaded with digital games. With the "Pick & Play" concept, it enabled consumers to connect to the game, and those who successfully completed the game received a coupon for a free product from McDonald's (Kalamut, 2011). Similarly, C&A enriched the consumer shopping experience through social communities by showing customers the number of likes the products received on social media with smart hangers (Kartal & Şentürk, 2020, p. 276).

Storytelling and Meaning Making

Storytelling allows brands to create an emotional connection with consumers. By using emotional and narrative elements, brands can effectively communicate important messages and increase consumer engagement (Menon et al., 2024). Storytelling aims to provide consumers with meaning and context rather than simply selling them a product. The combination of digital marketing, storytelling, and semiotics—the signs, symbols, media, and shared emotions used together to create meaning and context—allows brands to engage more deeply with consumers (Sandra & Noina, 2024). For example, Nike, Adidas, and Flo have offered experiences supported by AR and VR technologies, enabling consumers to create an emotional connection with the product. Smart mirrors in the sports industry aim to fill the gap between digital and face-to-face fitness experiences for consumers who want to do fitness but have limited time (Walk-Morris, 2023). These mirrors can create motivation by providing a narrative of users overcoming the challenges they face in achieving their goals. Therefore, brands that take storytelling one step further position their products on platforms that create meaning, knowing that consumers are not only buying a physical product, but also an experience and meaning. These approaches can help phygital consumers identify with the brand and build a long-term bond.

CONCLUSION

Digital marketing, which was once a new strategy, has become a mandatory strategy to keep up with the global competitive environment. However, the developments in information technologies in the last decade and challenging changes such as the pandemic have rendered digital marketing inadequate. In this process, consumers have become accustomed to experiencing physical stores and digital shopping together, and a new consumer group has emerged that has become accustomed to the convenience, entertainment, and alternatives that this experience brings. It is possible to call these consumers phygital consumers. Phygital consumers try to match the colors, symbols, signs, and logos in the physical world with the symbols in the digital world. They use both worlds together and at this point perceive semantic relationships between the two worlds. Therefore, the characteristics of this consumer group differ from those who prefer physical stores or digital stores.

This consumer group prefers mixed experiences. In this context, behaviors such as webrooming and showrooming come to the fore. Semiotic elements and their semantic integrity are important in the formation of phygital consumers' experiences and accordingly their identities. The combination of the symbols these consumers experience in physical stores and the visual and linguistic symbols they encounter on digital platforms helps them determine how they perceive the important experience and which platform (traditional, digital, or phygital) they will use. Therefore, for phygital consumers, the cognitive and emotional responses created by symbols, colors, shapes, and emotions guide their purchasing behavior.

Phygital marketing has started to gain a place in today's markets with applications such as big data, machine learning, artificial intelligence, augmented reality, and mixed reality. In particular, the metaverse and social media marketing provide brands with the means to implement phygital strategies. However, phygital consumers are highly influenced by intrinsic motivations like traditional consumers, environmental factors like digital consumers, and their own unique cyclical perceptions and expectations. Therefore, winning over this consumer group requires a high level of imagination. In addition, the expectations of this group require counter-intuitive thinking (Slater, 2018). Brands that want to appeal to this consumer group need to think about traditional consumers and digital consumers together, but also understand what the common behaviors of both groups are. They should utilize the growth hacking strategy, follow technology well, and use it without hesitation. In addition, combining two different concepts means the necessity to create a unity of meaning. At this point, they should use the science of semiotics at the maximum level.

This study is the result of a systematic literature review. However, understanding and shaping consumer behavior is a difficult process. For this reason, it is necessary to include studies in which consumers' opinions can be taken in future studies in order to understand the subject more deeply.

REFERENCES

Ahmed, K. M. (2020). Effect of design elements for social media ads on consumer's purchasing decision. *Global Media Journal, 18*(34), 1–12.

Al-Natour, S., Benbasat, I., & Cenfetelli, R. (2011). The adoption of online shopping assistants: Perceived similarity as an antecedent to evaluative beliefs. *Journal of the Association for Information Systems, 12*(5), 347–374. DOI: 10.17705/1jais.00267

Alcindor, M., Jackson, D., & Alcindor-Huelva, P. (2022). Heritage places as the settings for virtual playgrounds: Perceived realism in video games, as a tool for the re-localisation of physical places. *International Journal of Heritage Studies, 28*(7), 865–883. DOI: 10.1080/13527258.2022.2091638

Amazon. (n.d.). Amazon Go is a new kind of corner store. *Amazon.* Retrieved December 20, 2024, from https://www.amazon.com/b?node=16008589011

Amos, O. (2020, August 26). Covid-19'un uğramadığı 10 ülke. *BBC News Türkçe.* https://www.bbc.com/turkce/haberler-dunya-53909497

Aw, E. C.-X., Basha, N. K., Ng, S.-I., & Ho, J.-A. (2021). Unraveling determinants of webrooming behavior: A qualitative inquiry. *International Journal of Business and Society, 22*(3), 1550–1568. DOI: 10.33736/ijbs.4321.2021

Aw, E. C.-X., Kamal Basha, N., Ng, S. I., & Ho, J. A. (2021). Searching online and buying offline: Understanding the role of channel-, consumer-, and product-related factors in determining webrooming intention. *Journal of Retailing and Consumer Services, 58*, 102328. DOI: 10.1016/j.jretconser.2020.102328

Bae, H., Jo, S. H., & Lee, E. (2021). Why do older consumers avoid innovative products and services? *Journal of Services Marketing, 35*(1), 41–53. DOI: 10.1108/JSM-10-2019-0408

Bartosik-Purgat, M., & Filimon, N. (2022). *European consumers in the digital era: Implications of technology, media and culture on consumer behavior* (1st ed.). Routledge., DOI: 10.4324/9781003263685

Barwitz, N., & Maas, P. (2018). Understanding the omnichannel customer journey: Determinants of interaction choice. *Journal of Interactive Marketing, 43*(1), 116–133. DOI: 10.1016/j.intmar.2018.02.001

Batat, W., & Hammedi, W. (2023). The extended reality technology (ERT) framework for designing customer and service experiences in phygital settings: A service research agenda. *Journal of Service Management*, *34*(1), 10–33. DOI: 10.1108/JOSM-08-2022-0289

Belghiti, S., Ochs, A., Lemoine, J.-F., & Badot, O. (2018). The phygital shopping experience: An attempt at conceptualization and empirical investigation. In Rossi, P., & Krey, N. (Eds.), *Marketing transformation: Marketing practice in an ever-changing world* (pp. 61–74). Springer International Publishing., DOI: 10.1007/978-3-319-68750-6_18

Bhat, S., & Reddy, S. K. (1998). Symbolic and functional positioning of brands. *Journal of Consumer Marketing*, *15*(1), 32–43. DOI: 10.1108/07363769810202664

Bolos, C., Idemudia, E. C., Mai, P., Rasinghani, M., & Smith, S. (2016). Conceptual models on the effectiveness of e-marketing strategies in engaging consumers. *Journal of International Technology and Information Management*, *25*(4). Advance online publication. DOI: 10.58729/1941-6679.1293

Çakırkaya, M., & Koçyiğit, M. (2024). Consumer involvement in augmented reality applications in the context of phygital marketing communications. *ASR: Chiang Mai University Journal of Social Sciences and Humanities*, *11*(1). Advance online publication. DOI: 10.12982/CMUJASR.2024.008

Chaffey, D., & Ellis-Chadwick, F. (2019). *Digital marketing* (7th ed.)., https://books.google.com.tr/books?hl=tr&lr=&id=-1yGDwAAQBAJ&oi=fnd&pg=PT17&dq=Chaffey,+D.,+%26+Ellis-Chadwick,+F.+(2019).+Digital+Marketing.+Pearson+UK.&ots=XjQnbVnJ40&sig=pvGNpt2Btzgl9aRMbYndzvhrifk&redir_esc=y#v=onepage&q=Chaffey%2C%20D.%2C%20%26%20Ellis-Chadwick%2C%20F.%20(2019).%20Digital%20Marketing.%20Pearson%20UK.&f=false

Chaffey, D., & Smith, P. (2023). *Digital marketing excellence* (6th ed.). Routledge., DOI: 10.4324/9781003009498

Chellappa, R. K., & Sin, R. G. (2005). Personalization versus privacy: An empirical examination of the online consumer's dilemma. *Information Technology and Management*, *6*(2–3), 181–202. DOI: 10.1007/s10799-005-5879-y

Cheng, Z., Shao, B., & Zhang, Y. (2022). Effect of product presentation videos on consumers' purchase intention: The role of perceived diagnosticity, mental imagery, and product rating. *Frontiers in Psychology*, *13*, 812579. DOI: 10.3389/fpsyg.2022.812579

Chibás Ortiz, F. (2013). Ciclo do marketing digital: Tática e estratégia blended. *Revista ENIAC Pesquisa*, *2*(1), 64. DOI: 10.22567/rep.v2i1.111

Cui, T. H., Ghose, A., Halaburda, H., Iyengar, R., Pauwels, K., Sriram, S., Tucker, C., & Venkataraman, S. (2021). Informational challenges in omnichannel marketing: Remedies and future research. *Journal of Marketing*, *85*(1), 103–120. DOI: 10.1177/0022242920968810

Dacko, S. G. (2017). Enabling smart retail settings via mobile augmented reality shopping apps. *Technological Forecasting and Social Change*, *124*, 243–256. DOI: 10.1016/j.techfore.2016.09.032

Díaz, A., Gómez, M., & Molina, A. (2017). A comparison of online and offline consumer behaviour: An empirical study on a cinema shopping context. *Journal of Retailing and Consumer Services*, *38*, 44–50. DOI: 10.1016/j.jretconser.2017.05.003

Elliott, R., & Wattanasuwan, K. (1998). Brands as symbolic resources for the construction of identity. *International Journal of Advertising*, *17*(2), 131–144. DOI: 10.1080/02650487.1998.11104712

Engelbrecht, N. (2022). Responsible consumer behavior in the digital age: Empirical evidence on the impact of (micro-)environmental factors on consumers' socially responsible behavior [Dissertation, Georg-August-University Göttingen]. DOI: 10.53846/goediss-9428

Gandla, R., Vemali, L. K., Choudhary, S., Pallavi, M. S., Saurav, A., Sahoo, P., & Golla, V. (2023). Semiotics and brand perception: How symbols and signs influence consumer behavior. *Journal of Informatics Education and Research*, *3*(2), 2275–2288. DOI: 10.52783/jier.v3i2.378

Garg, V., & Kaur, A. (2018). Has physical retail lost its relevance in e-commerce world? *Journal of Business Management and Information Systems*, *5*(2), 1–8. DOI: 10.48001/jbmis.2018.0502001

Guzzetti, A., Crespi, R., & Belvedere, V. (2024). Phygital luxury experiences: A correspondence analysis on retail technologies. *International Journal of Consumer Studies*, *48*(2), e13008. DOI: 10.1111/ijcs.13008

Hegy, P. M. (2023). Symbol preaching in the digital age: From symbol recognition to symbol interpretation in Facebook ads. *Religions*, *14*(2), 229. DOI: 10.3390/rel14020229

Holopainen, J., Mattila, O., Parvinen, P., Pöyry, E., & Seppälä, K. (2018). Employing mixed reality applications: Customer experience perspective. *Proceedings of the 51st Hawaii International Conference on System Sciences,* 1168–1176. DOI: 10.24251/HICSS.2018.145

Hossain, T. M. T., Akter, S., Kattiyapornpong, U., & Dwivedi, Y. (2020). Reconceptualizing integration quality dynamics for omnichannel marketing. *Industrial Marketing Management*, *87*, 225–241. DOI: 10.1016/j.indmarman.2019.12.006

Hult, G. T. M., Sharma, P. N., Morgeson, F. V.III, & Zhang, Y. (2019). Antecedents and consequences of customer satisfaction: Do they differ across online and offline purchases? *Journal of Retailing*, *95*(1), 10–23. DOI: 10.1016/j.jretai.2018.10.003

Jain, P., & Duggal, T. (2016). The influence of transformational leadership and emotional intelligence on organizational commitment. *Journal of Commerce and Management Thought*, *7*(3), 586. DOI: 10.5958/0976-478X.2016.00033.1

Johnson, M., & Barlow, R. (2021). Defining the phygital marketing advantage. *Journal of Theoretical and Applied Electronic Commerce Research*, *16*(6), 2365–2385. DOI: 10.3390/jtaer16060130

Johnson, M., & Barlow, R. (2024). Phygital marketing through the lens of neuroscience and phenomenology: An interpretivist account. *Qualitative Market Research*, *27*(3), 471–494. DOI: 10.1108/QMR-07-2023-0098

Kalamut, A. (Southside Adguy). (2011, June 02). McDonalds "Pick N' Play" interactive - Experiential outdoor ad. Retrieved December 23, 2024, from https://www.youtube.com/watch?v=D2UkIo-0prw

Karimov, F. P., & Brengman, M. (2011). The effect of website design dimensions on initial trust: A synthesis of the empirical literature. *Journal of Electronic Commerce Research*, *12*(4), 272–301.

Kartal, C., & Şentürk, E. E. (2020). Endüstri 4.0 ve pazarlamada yeni gelişmeler. In Çetinkaya, F. F., & Şener, E. (Eds.), *Endüstri 4.0 paradigması* (1st ed., pp. 259–286). Efe Akademi Yayınevi.

Kleinlercher, K., Linzmajer, M., Verhoef, P. C., & Rudolph, T. (2020). Antecedents of webrooming in omnichannel retailing. *Frontiers in Psychology*, *11*, 606798. DOI: 10.3389/fpsyg.2020.606798

Kothari, H., Lodha, S., Joshi, N., & Khan, S. (2021). A study of the impact of online consumer buying behaviour on offline market while purchasing white goods. *MET Management Review*, *8*(2), 78–82. DOI: 10.34047/MMR.2020.8210

Kotler, P., Kartajaya, H., & Setiawan, I. (2024). *Marketing 6.0: The future is immersive* (1st ed.). John Wiley & Sons.

Lee, S., & Choi, J. (2017). Enhancing user experience with conversational agent for movie recommendation: Effects of self-disclosure and reciprocity. *International Journal of Human-Computer Studies, 103*, 95–105. DOI: 10.1016/j.ijhcs.2017.02.005

Lee, S., & Rao, V. S. (Chino). (2010). Color and store choice in electronic commerce: The explanatory role of trust. *Journal of Electronic Commerce Research, 11*(2), 110–127.

Li, H. (2023). How digital retail markets recovered China's economy and changed consumer behaviors during COVID-19. *BCP Business & Management, 38*, 1893–1901. DOI: 10.54691/bcpbm.v38i.3999

Li, Y., Zhang, Z., & Zhao, Y. (2016). Analysis on influencing factors of consumers' purchasing behavior online for furniture: A case study on furniture malls and business centers in Harbin. *Proceedings of the 18th Annual International Conference on Electronic Commerce E-Commerce in Smart Connected World - ICEC '16,* 1–8. DOI: 10.1145/2971603.2971606

Liao, C., To, P.-L., Wong, Y.-C., Palvia, P., & Kakhki, M. D. (2016). The impact of presentation mode and product type on online impulse buying decisions. *Journal of Electronic Commerce Research, 17*(2), 153–168.

Lovethehstory. (2024, December 23). AI virtual hair experience. Retrieved February 1, 2025, from https://www.instagram.com/reel/DD6l6aySjkP/?igsh=dm1qMDRkcTRqbWNp

Martínez-González, J. A., & Álvarez-Albelo, C. D. (2021). Influence of site personalization and first impression on young consumers' loyalty to tourism websites. *Sustainability (Basel), 13*(3), 1425. DOI: 10.3390/su13031425

Mehmeti-Bajrami, S., Qerimi, F., & Qerimi, A. (2022). The impact of digital marketing vs. traditional marketing on consumer buying behavior. *HighTech and Innovation Journal, 3*(3), 326–340. DOI: 10.28991/HIJ-2022-03-03-08

Mele, C., Di Bernardo, I., Ranieri, A., & Russo Spena, T. (2024). Phygital customer journey: A practice-based approach. *Qualitative Market Research, 27*(3), 388–412. DOI: 10.1108/QMR-08-2023-0102

Menon, A. S., Pillai, R., & Pai, Y. P. (2024). Customer engagement through transformational campaigns: A netnographic exploration on the storytelling power of 'Jaago Re.'. *Journal of Creative Communications, 09732586241276345*, 09732586241276345. Advance online publication. DOI: 10.1177/09732586241276345

Miao, F., Kozlenkova, I. V., Wang, H., Xie, T., & Palmatier, R. W. (2022). An emerging theory of avatar marketing. *Journal of Marketing*, *86*(1), 67–90. DOI: 10.1177/0022242921996646

Mick, D. G., Burroughs, J. E., Hetzel, P., & Brannen, M. Y. (2004). Pursuing the meaning of meaning in the commercial world: An international review of marketing and consumer research founded on semiotics. *Semiotica, 2004*(152-1/4), 1–74. DOI: 10.1515/semi.2004.2004.152-1-4.1

Mishra, S., Malhotra, G., Chatterjee, R., & Shukla, Y. (2023). Consumer retention through phygital experience in omnichannel retailing: Role of consumer empowerment and satisfaction. *Journal of Strategic Marketing*, *31*(4), 749–766. DOI: 10.1080/0965254X.2021.1985594

Mohammad Alzub, A. (2023). Navigating the disruption of digital and conventional media in changing media consumption landscape in the digital era. [JETAS]. *Journal of Engineering, Technology, and Applied Science*, *5*(1), 38–48. DOI: 10.36079/lamintang.jetas-0501.517

Moschini, I. (2018). Social semiotics and platform studies: An integrated perspective for the study of social media platforms. *Social Semiotics*, *28*(5), 623–640. DOI: 10.1080/10350330.2018.1504714

Niranjini, N., & Sridevi, J. (2023). Covid-19—Pushes marketers to sell differently to global millennials in emerging markets. *Journal of Pharmaceutical Negative Results, 13*(Special issue 7), 6993–7003. DOI: 10.47750/pnr.2022.13.S07.847

Nosi, C., Pucci, T., Melanthiou, Y., & Zanni, L. (2022). The influence of online and offline brand trust on consumer buying intention. *EuroMed Journal of Business*, *17*(4), 550–567. DOI: 10.1108/EMJB-01-2021-0002

Osmanova, I., Ozerden, S., Dalal, B., & Ibrahim, B. (2023). Examining the relationship between brand symbolism and brand evangelism through consumer brand identification: Evidence from Starbucks coffee brand. *Sustainability (Basel)*, *15*(2), 1684. DOI: 10.3390/su15021684

Østergaard, P., Hermansen, J., & Fitchett, J. (2015). Structures of brand and anti-brand meaning: A semiotic square analysis of reflexive consumption. *Journal of Brand Management*, *22*(1), 60–77. DOI: 10.1057/bm.2015.4

Özbölük, T., & Kurtoğlu, R. (2019). *The role of language and symbols in promotional strategies and marketing schemes* (Epure, M., & Mihăeş, L. C., Eds.). IGI Global., DOI: 10.4018/978-1-5225-5778-4

Pantano, E., Rese, A., & Baier, D. (2017). Enhancing the online decision-making process by using augmented reality: A two-country comparison of youth markets. *Journal of Retailing and Consumer Services*, *38*, 81–95. DOI: 10.1016/j.jretconser.2017.05.011

Pappas, I. O. (2018). User experience in personalized online shopping: A fuzzy-set analysis. *European Journal of Marketing*, *52*(7/8), 1679–1703. DOI: 10.1108/EJM-10-2017-0707

Pengnate, S., & Sarathy, R. (2017). An experimental investigation of the influence of website emotional design features on trust in unfamiliar online vendors. *Computers in Human Behavior*, *67*, 49–60. DOI: 10.1016/j.chb.2016.10.018

Pusceddu, G., Moi, L., & Cabiddu, F. (2023). Do they see eye to eye? Managing customer experience in phygital high-tech retail. *Management Decision*. Advance online publication. DOI: 10.1108/MD-05-2022-0673

Rahman, M. (2023). The impact of Covid-19 (coronavirus) on consumers' behavior towards e-commerce. *Canadian Journal of Business and Information Studies*, *5*(4), 81–91. DOI: 10.34104/cjbis.023.081091

Rigby, D. (2014, September 1). Digital-physical mashups. *Harvard Business Review*. https://hbr.org/2014/09/digital-physical-mashups

Sağtaş, S. (2022). Dijital pazarlamanın değişen yüzü: Fijital pazarlama ve uygulamaları üzerine bir araştırma. *Social Sciences Studies Journal*, *8*(95), 629–637. DOI: 10.26449/sssj.3866

Sandra, N. P. A. A., & Noina, N. M. K. (2024). Semiotic analysis of tourism soft-selling: Decoding short films as persuasive narratives. *Ultimart: Jurnal Komunikasi Visual,* 49–63. DOI: 10.31937/ultimart.v17i1.3547

Sargın, S. (2024). Dijital reklamcılığın tüketiciler üzerindeki izleri. In Kartal, C., Şentürk, E. E., & Durukan, T. (Eds.), *Teknolojik tüketiciler çağı* (pp. 39–58). Nobel Akademik Yayıncılık.

Şenses, S. (2024, April 23). Patiswiss krizinden neler öğrendik? *MediaCat*. https://mediacat.com/patiswiss-krizinden-neler-ogrendik/

Serkan Akturk, M., Ketzenberg, M., & Heim, G. R. (2018). Assessing impacts of introducing ship-to-store service on sales and returns in omnichannel retailing: A data analytics study. *Journal of Operations Management*, *61*(1), 15–45. DOI: 10.1016/j.jom.2018.06.004

Slater, J. (2018, August 28). Let's get phigital. *The Marketing Sage.* https://www.themarketingsage.com/lets-get-phigital/

Smink, A. R., Frowijn, S., Van Reijmersdal, E. A., Van Noort, G., & Neijens, P. C. (2019). Try online before you buy: How does shopping with augmented reality affect brand responses and personal data disclosure. *Electronic Commerce Research and Applications*, *35*, 100854. DOI: 10.1016/j.elerap.2019.100854

Sridhar, S., & Srinivasan, R. (2012). Social influence effects in online product ratings. *Journal of Marketing*, *76*(5), 70–88. DOI: 10.1509/jm.10.0377

Szwajca, D. (2022). The use of digital communication channels by Polish consumers – Changes caused by the pandemic. *Foundations of Management*, *14*(1), 37–50. DOI: 10.2478/fman-2022-0003

Tan, T., & Ming, M. (2003). Leveraging on symbolic values and meanings in branding. *Journal of Brand Management*, *10*(3), 208–218. DOI: 10.1057/palgrave.bm.2540117

Tang, P., Chen, J., & Raghunathan, S. (2023). Physical stores as warehouses for online channels: Implications for channel choices under competition. *Information Systems Research*, *34*(4), 1554–1581. DOI: 10.1287/isre.2023.1198

Teltzrow, M., Meyer, B., & Lenz, H.-J. (2007). Multi-channel consumer perceptions. DOI: 10.5167/UZH-65987

Tirpude, R. (2022). Study of impact of digital marketing on consumer buying behaviour for electronic goods. *International Journal for Research in Applied Science and Engineering Technology*, *10*(2), 905–909. DOI: 10.22214/ijraset.2022.40348

Tran, A. T. N., Nguyen, U. H. D., Ngo, V. M., & Nguyen, H. H. (2023). Explaining consumers' channel-switching behavior in the post-COVID-19 pandemic era. *Cogent Business & Management*, *10*(1), 2198068. DOI: 10.1080/23311975.2023.2198068

Tuğba, Ö., & Ramazan, K. (2019). *The role of language and symbols in promotional strategies and marketing schemes* (Epure, M., & Mihăeş, L. C., Eds.). IGI Global., DOI: 10.4018/978-1-5225-5778-4.ch003

Tyrväinen, O., Karjaluoto, H., & Saarijärvi, H. (2020). Personalization and hedonic motivation in creating customer experiences and loyalty in omnichannel retail. *Journal of Retailing and Consumer Services*, *57*, 102233. DOI: 10.1016/j.jretconser.2020.102233

Uğurlu, Ö. (2014). Encoding the daily life through social networks "Binboa – A social night" analysis of advertising in accordance with the new media symbols. *Journal of Media Critiques*, *1*(1), 177–194. DOI: 10.17349/jmc114111

Verhagen, T., Van Nes, J., Feldberg, F., & Van Dolen, W. (2014). Virtual customer service agents: Using social presence and personalization to shape online service encounters. *Journal of Computer-Mediated Communication, 19*(3), 529–545. DOI: 10.1111/jcc4.12066

Vimeo. (n.d.). The World's First Digital Mirror on Vimeo. Retrieved December 23, 2024, from https://vimeo.com/116120605

Vincent Jaiwant, S. (2023). Changing structure of consumer buying behaviour and expectation in the digital era. In Singh, G., Goel, R., & Garg, V. (Eds.), *Industry 4.0 and the digital transformation of international business* (pp. 207–215). Springer Nature Singapore., DOI: 10.1007/978-981-19-7880-7_12

Ward, E., Yang, S., Romaniuk, J., & Beal, V. (2020). Building a unique brand identity: Measuring the relative ownership potential of brand identity element types. *Journal of Brand Management, 27*(4), 393–407. DOI: 10.1057/s41262-020-00187-6

Wedel, M., Bigné, E., & Zhang, J. (2020). Virtual and augmented reality: Advancing research in consumer marketing. *International Journal of Research in Marketing, 37*(3), 443–465. DOI: 10.1016/j.ijresmar.2020.04.004

Wind, J., & Mahajan, V. (2000). Digital marketing. *European Business Forum.* https://faculty.wharton.upenn.edu/wp-content/uploads/2012/04/0004_The_Challenge_of_Digital_Marketing.pdf

Wolk, A., & Ebling, C. (2010). Multi-channel price differentiation: An empirical investigation of existence and causes. *International Journal of Research in Marketing, 27*(2), 142–150. DOI: 10.1016/j.ijresmar.2010.01.004

Yao, A., Chan, N., & Yao, N. (2024). Understanding consumer behavior in phygital environments: An interpretivist methodological framework. *Qualitative Market Research, 27*(3), 449–470. DOI: 10.1108/QMR-08-2023-0100

Yin, W., & Xu, B. (2021). Effect of online shopping experience on customer loyalty in apparel business-to-consumer ecommerce. *Textile Research Journal, 91*(23–24), 2882–2895. DOI: 10.1177/00405175211016559

Zhang, T., Ge, L., Gou, Q., & Chen, L. (2018). Consumer showrooming, the sunk cost effect and online-offline competition. *Journal of Electronic Commerce Research, 19*(1), 55–74.

Zhang, W., & Wang, Y. (2023). Not just apologizing: The impact of complaint handling on sustained participation behavior in live-streaming shopping. *Journal of Consumer Behaviour, 22*(3), 688–700. DOI: 10.1002/cb.2154

Zotova, A. S. (2021). Semiotics of advertising communication in WEB 2.0 network social services. *RUDN Journal of Language Studies. Semiotics and Semantics, 12*(4), 1285–1298. DOI: 10.22363/2313-2299-2021-12-4-1285-1298

ADDITIONAL READING

Belghiti, S., Ochs, A., Lemoine, J.-F., & Badot, O. (2018). The phygital shopping experience: An attempt at conceptualization and empirical investigation. In Rossi, P., & Krey, N. (Eds.), *Marketing transformation: Marketing practice in an ever changing world* (pp. 61–74). Springer International Publishing., DOI: 10.1007/978-3-319-68750-6_18

Kartajaya, H., Kotler, P., & Setiawan, I. (2024). *Marketing 6.0: The future is immersive* (1st ed.). John Wiley & Sons, Inc.

Mele, C., Di Bernardo, I., Ranieri, A., & Russo Spena, T. (2024). Phygital customer journey: A practice-based approach. *Qualitative Market Research, 27*(3), 388–412. DOI: 10.1108/QMR-08-2023-0102

Mishra, S., Malhotra, G., Chatterjee, R., & Shukla, Y. (2023). Consumer retention through phygital experience in omnichannel retailing: Role of consumer empowerment and satisfaction. *Journal of Strategic Marketing, 31*(4), 749–766. DOI: 10.1080/0965254X.2021.1985594

Pusceddu, G., Moi, L., & Cabiddu, F. (2023). Do they see eye to eye? Managing customer experience in phygital high-tech retail. *Management Decision*. Advance online publication. DOI: 10.1108/MD-05-2022-0673

Rahman, M. (2023). The impact of Covid-19 (Coronavirus) on consumers' behavior towards e-commerce. *Canadian Journal of Business and Information Studies, 5*(4), 81–91. DOI: 10.34104/cjbis.023.081091

Rigby, D. (2014, September 1). Digital-physical mashups. *Harvard Business Review*. https://hbr.org/2014/09/digital-physical-mashups

Sağtaş, S. (2022). Dijital pazarlamanın değişen yüzü: Fijital pazarlama ve uygulamaları üzerine bir araştırma. *Social Sciences Studies Journal, 8*(95), 629–637. DOI: 10.26449/sssj.3866

Smink, A. R., Frowijn, S., Van Reijmersdal, E. A., Van Noort, G., & Neijens, P. C. (2019). Try online before you buy: How does shopping with augmented reality affect brand responses and personal data disclosure. *Electronic Commerce Research and Applications, 35*, 100854. DOI: 10.1016/j.elerap.2019.100854

Tuğba, Ö., & Ramazan, K. (2019). The role of language and symbols in promotional strategies and marketing schemes. In Epure, M., & Mihăeş, L. C. (Eds.), *IGI Global.*, DOI: 10.4018/978-1-5225-5778-4.ch003

Yao, A., Chan, N., & Yao, N. (2024). Understanding consumer behavior in phygital environments: An interpretivist methodological framework. *Qualitative Market Research, 27*(3), 449–470. DOI: 10.1108/QMR-08-2023-0100

KEY TERMS AND DEFINITIONS

Augmented Reality (AR): Augmented reality enriches physical product experiences with a digital layer. It allows consumers to virtually try products, making shopping processes more enjoyable and informative while bridging the gap between the physical and digital realms.

Experiential Marketing: Experiential marketing focuses on creating emotional and meaningful consumer experiences rather than merely offering products or services. Integrating physical and digital elements, this approach aims to strengthen brand loyalty and engage consumers through personalized and enjoyable interactions.

Omnichannel Marketing: Omnichannel marketing is a strategy that integrates different marketing channels (physical stores, websites, mobile apps, etc.) to provide a seamless and consistent consumer experience. It helps enhance brand loyalty by delivering unified messaging across all touchpoints.

Phygital Consumer: Phygital consumers are a new type of consumer that combines the advantages of physical and digital worlds, preferring both online and offline experiences. These consumers connect with symbols and meanings throughout their shopping journey, benefiting from the strengths of both environments.

Phygital Marketing: Phygital marketing is a holistic approach that combines physical and digital marketing strategies to provide consumers with both the tangible experiences of physical stores and the convenience of digital platforms. This strategy enhances consumer experiences and helps brands adapt to hybrid consumer behaviors.

Semiotics: Semiotics studies how consumers interpret and make sense of symbols and signs in physical and digital environments. Marketing is crucial in helping brands convey consistent messages and build emotional connections with their audiences.

Showrooming: Showrooming occurs when consumers examine products in physical stores and then purchase them online. This behavior combines the tangible experience of physical stores with the cost advantages offered by online shopping.

Webrooming: Webrooming refers to the behavior where consumers research products online and then purchase them in physical stores. This process allows consumers to benefit from both digital convenience and the tactile experience of physical shopping.

Chapter 3
The Role of Semiotics in Digital Marketing:
Study on Consumer Interpretation and Brand Communication

Sarvesh Khaitan
https://orcid.org/0009-0002-3230-6269
Christ University, Bengaluru, India

Kartikeya Singh
https://orcid.org/0000-0002-3060-6359
Christ University, Bengaluru, India

ABSTRACT

This paper aims to examine the concept of semiotics with an emphasis on the manner in which consumers analyse brand messages through signifying practices. Being the science of meaning, semiotics in central to the formation of perception towards brand image and communication. Given the proliferation of digital communications in many different channels, it is vital for modern marketing to engage with semiotic features. Hence, the present research uses semi structured interviews as its data collection method to explore how consumers assign meaning to visuals and the symbols used to depict them as a means of gaining their attention and securing their attention and loyalty. Research results indicates semiotic assets including picture, iconography, and storyline boost brand familiarity/identity and consumer bond. Culture-sensitive signs enhances perception and ensure that messages passed do not create confusion. These observations present marketers with valuable information useful when developing cultural and interpretational strategies in the market.

DOI: 10.4018/979-8-3693-8024-6.ch003

1. INTRODUCTION

Semiotics refers to the study of properties of signs and symbols. It examines the different types of sign systems. Semiotic analysis can provide a deep understanding of consumer interpretation of a brand's advertising message and may analyze all elements of brand communication as perceived by the consumer. In digital marketing, it is known that selling is not easy, inexpensive, or straightforward. All of this needs to be understood, as there are real difficulties in achieving effective communication. The language of signs, used as a tool for analysis and interpretation of the explored world, including in the business area, can help to understand one of the main communication difficulties existing in the universe of brands. This is mainly due to the increase in the amount of goods and services offered in a context of almost daily decreases in generalized income, which translates into a permanent shortage in the search for consumption (Sitanggang, 2020; Lawes, 2023).

For business managers, semiotic analysis tools provide the possibility of producing more coherent communication with the brand, enhancing the desired brand equity. Ignoring these tools can lead to unexpected interpretations by consumers. It is important for managers to avoid hidden meanings and errors in judgment. In view of the above, this study was conducted with the objective of understanding the appreciation of brand digital marketing messages by an emerging consumer segment, discovering the importance of sequential images with semaphore messages in the reading of audiovisual sequences, and thus the roles of semiotics in the visualization of brands. Business managers may find this important from a search perspective to manage, study, consult, or work in the brand's visual communication area. Satisfying and communicating well with brand stakeholder management is a current need. This is also the case for government, academia, or any other institution that works with communication. The main research phase involves a qualitative study consisting of semi-structured interviews designed to gather the opinions of a particular consumer segment (Haghbin et al., 2022; Guibourgé, 2020; Dressler & Paunovic, 2021).

1.1. Background and Rationale

Customer behavior and marketplace demands have changed. Internet access has revolutionized countless points – whether in an emotional, operational, or even social way. Most of these changes can be attributed to the digital transformation of the company, bringing forth an opportunity to enhance internet sales. Numerous players are attempting to figure out how a company or an individual can increase virtual representation. In this context, an innovative and fluid digital marketing strategy is required, allowing companies to reach their target audience in a rapid, effective, and loyal way. Market laws applied to virtual places provoke rapid changes. This is possible due to an environment characterized by two-way dialogue between the seller and the potential consumer. In such a scenario, new communication strategies have emerged, with particular attention to the use of the two channels most used by consumers: email marketing and content marketing, which serve to send promotional messages directly or indirectly, respectively (Terho et al., 2022; Shankar et al.2022).

Market laws in cyberspace have altered the nature of advertisement in virtual environments: consumer sovereignty and rationality. Today to do effective email marketing it means to build meaningful relationships by selecting signals in a noisy digital world. Using tools which make them researchers and decision makers, consumers enjoy an impact on their preferences and consumption. They cherish informal, practical information searches improved by visuals and interaction that provide satisfaction and expectation. This shift demonstrates the consumer's new found power to select, assess, contribute and demand information that has transformed traditional advertising into a more sharing process. (Dwivedi et al.2021; Kang et al., 2020; Xi & Hamari, 2021)

1.2. Research Objectives

The main aim of this research is to understand the role of semiotics in the interpretation of brand expression on digital channels from a consumer perspective. During recent research, semiotics has often been used to assess the perception of advertising content such as campaign messages, images, and narratives. In the present study, instead, the attention is focused on the brand identity model, which translates brand expression into a set of distinctive elements, and how consumers recognize and interpret these elements during their digital experience. It is of interest to explore consumers' interpretation processes, the hermeneutic code-informed encounters, identifying the triggers that can improve memorability and usefulness of each use of brand expression. The combination of simplicity and cognitive ability to store an amount of information in a single source pushed researchers to analyze the Instagram platform. Instagram is one of the top social media platforms on which users follow, like, and save the highest number of posts each day and each moment, passing by the social media activities of brands that are designed to be revisited (Lourenção et al., 2020; Dalamu, 2021; Paraskevaidis and Weidenfeld 2021).

1.3. Scope and Limitations

This research seeks to refine the examination of digital commercial communication to brand messages. Many of the conventional forms of marketing communication dominate the market are no longer effective tools given the intense competition. Simply embedding ads, sales promotions or PR messages in the market does not work unless these messages are systematically integrated. Picking up competition, brand messages become all the more difficult to decipher and make out. As communication through and around goods to consumers, especially in digital contexts—, the paper conceptualizes consumption as a communicative process and analyzes non-Other-directed, business-related communication in digital media. A theoretical consideration is given to consumer relationship management especially within a multiple channel environment, which is relatively uncovered. The marketing paradigm change from autocratic one-way broadcasts of thousands of identical products to communicated 'experiences' with companies, consumers, and shared interests. The communications technology notably internet is the core in embracing dialogue marketing tactics and creative communication channels. Regarding this idea, this research aims at exploring how consumption-oriented organizations can engage consumers in this emergent environment dominated by digital developments. (Fraccastoro et al., 2021; Shankar et al.2022).

2. THEORETICAL FRAMEWORK

The sign is the basic unit of meaning for semiotics, and it is associated with a form of expressiveness. In other words, the sign is also made up of something that produces understanding. To this purpose, the sign is a connection formed by understanding, made up of a signifier, which is the material existence of the sign, and the signified, which is its conceptual existence, represented by the understanding of the signifier. Semiotics is interested in the informative aspect associated with the practice, identifying three layers associated with the sign: the representational production, the addressee reception, and the communicational restitution. The representational production was designed by the brand concept store, doing a semiotic analysis from the qualitative speeches addressed by consumers to this point of sale. Information and measuring aspects were also emphasized in the approach to local and multinational brands (Aiello, 2020; Ibrahim and Sulaiman2020).

Through a qualitative interviews study, we collected consumer views of the three main connotational supports present in the semiotic practice, namely object-consumer relationship, temporal, and behavioral connotational support. The results show the impact of the referred support in the conceptual construction of users, thus helping in the understanding of other meanings that determine real behaviors, in this case influenced by the brand. This is advantageous for a strategic formulation of the brand; the communicational restitution and the association of certain added values in the functional areas of the store allow for significant brand communication and for an effective purchase process experience (Ibrahim and Sulaiman2020; Aiello, 2020).

2.1. Semiotics: Definition and Principles

Semiotics is a combination of the terms sema (sign), and comes from the Greek word semiotike, meaning the study of or belief in signs. It involves four key elements: There are four elements; the signifier, referent, signified, and code. The concept of signifier and signified constitutes a complete sign. Semiotics is the study of signs in society that is linked with semantics and treats semiotics as an approach to connotation. It deals with the analysis of people's actions in the framework of semiotic formations and their functions within a society. In advertising, there is nothing as crucial as semiotics in the process of communicating brand image. There is confidence that it keeps the message being passed on through advertisements as ones that will be accepted by consumers. Of the two types of semiotics – the linguistic and visual, the former plays major roles in constructing brand images and labels given that ad visuals contain innumerable pieces of information. Promotion signals and icons' meaning in advertisements help extend and diversify the interactions of the company–product–consumer message system by noting connotation and symbol. Ads succeed because they force consumers to read between the lines, to put feelings and creativity into it. By the end of watching the ad, the creator wants the consumer to see the ad in a different way and the consumer starts to decipher the meaning behind the advertisement, which makes the process cognitive. In conclusion, the use of advertisement as a semiotic resource incites thinking, elicits feelings and creates or helps in delivering memorable brand messages. (Lawes, 2023; Lytvynenko et al., 2022; Hussain and Panggabean2024; Oswald, 2020)

2.2. Semiotics in Marketing

Semiotics is part of the wide communication models that work to express, establish, and translate the understanding or message from a subject to its recipients. In marketing, and especially in brand communication, brand communication is a widely extended marketing technique that uses symbols with meanings deep-rooted in a society to convey and communicate a message. Despite the common use of semiotics in marketing, little empirical research has been undertaken concerning its interpretation compared to the deep theoretical background of advertising semiotic theory. This research aims to clarify these inconsistencies and also develop a typical target audience: a high-use digital content group with the aim to advertise that digital content. For this typography, great entertainment value, race, gender, age, or educational level are not important to the target audience, nor is the literal message content on the Internet (Chandler, 2022; Hasyim & Arafah, 2023; Oswald, 2020).

Creating an icon that gets at least nine out of ten Internet users to click on and continue watching the digital content. The research has been conducted through a survey to determine how a sample of Internet users perceived the semiotics of digital content and the communication between the symbols and signs used in a digital marketing strategy; the icon and the content itself, and the brand shown in the marketing icon. The nature of the content found an economical relation between content brands. The brand was an expression of the content. Entertainment was what the content was mostly offering, and excitement and energy were key concepts to catch the attention of the audience. Statistics were used to analyze the consumer's perception: brand-oriented vs. content-oriented advertising (Liu et al., 2021; Beaird et al., 2020).

2.3. Digital Marketing and Semiotics

E-business, e-commerce, and e-marketing are the new marketing trends in the era of information and communication technology. All traditional marketing processes are becoming digital. This change in the habits of marketing occurs because of the change in the way in which consumers interact with service and product content. Consumers are connecting themselves to digital platforms using mobile devices. New marketing paradigms are establishing with these new digital characteristics. Traditional marketing uses a linear approach to convey messages, but new marketing uses a network approach to market and introduces a new approach and a new advertising strategy to deliver a message to the consumer. Semiotics, as a branch of linguistics, which is also used in the study of signs, is an area commonly used in advertising to create meaning beyond its own meaning in communication with individuals in advertising (Dalamu, 2021; Ibrahim and Sulaiman2020).

Over time, following developments in digital technology, traditional advertising and communication methods have evolved. The transformation of traditional media to digital has changed advertising means and reached a wider audience. Digital advertising, which has become an important communication tool in a short time, has developed in direct proportion to the increase in social media usage and internet penetration rates. Social media have become marketing tools used by advertising companies to reach large audiences with cheaper costs. Since the number of consumers using social media has increased, the profitability of customer communication has increased, and digital marketing has made it easier for companies to use advertising. The development of society and the current internet structure together enabled the spread of digital advertising. With the social media applications that emerged as a result of the development of the internet and the participation of individuals in advertising activities, interactive communication took place. With the spread of internet use, the combination of digital technology and advertising also made it possible to develop more effective advertising practices (Dwivedi et al.2021; Habes et al.2020; Makrides et al.2020).

3. LITERATURE REVIEW

Fashion industry is intensively competitive and therefore finding an appropriate marketing mix model is essential. It is required of fashion companies to pass strong marketing messages to the consumers in the best tools. New media has become inevitable platforms for brand communication in the digital age for sophistication and creativity to appeal for consumers. Incentive messages that are attention-provoking, inventive, and different looking from most ads are said to work.

This paper aims to understand how consumers make sense of digital design communication in digital marketing using semiotic theory as an analytical lens. Semiotics is not well employed in marketing studies, but it is useful when trying to understand consumer differences in the interpretation of digital communications and develop the concept of communication interpreters. Through an application of ethnographic methods, the research shows how semiotic assessment can highlight consumers' perceptions of the intentions of brand communications.

The ultimate objective is to improve the communication of digital design, offering a theoretical framework that corresponds to the consumer's understanding of it: a theoretical perspective that supports digital brand marketing approaches in consumer-centric environments (Grewal et al., 2022; Llorente-Barroso et al.2021; Chen & Cheung, 2022; Lawes, 2023).

Interest in the role of semiotics in the field of marketing clearly exists. Although the area is not new, only a few scholars have recognized consumer interpretation in marketing communication activities. This was particularly noted when initiated in social media activities. This paucity implied that there has not been any standardized understanding in the study of consumer interpretation derived from digital design communication. Marketers needing consumer interpretations are considerably limited, while the study revealed that in the steady development over the number of methodological consumer-based studies over recent years, prior semiotic studies have argued which implications may be derived from the analysis of marketing interpretation. As a result, studies attempting to understand consumer interpretation – and the semiotic elements used – are only now emerging (Schultz, 2020; John & De'Villiers, 2020; Cambier & Poncin, 2020).

3.1. Key Concepts in Semiotics

Our research operates at the intersection of three areas of analysis, arguing that the analysis of consumer interpretation of brand communication in the digital environment calls for a dialectical approach convening knowledge from the domains of semiotics, marketing, and consumer behavior. This section is devoted to presenting the key concepts of semiotics theory. The theoretical approach defines semiotics as a discipline that studies meaning creation and acquisition processes through the complex structure provided by the sign, the codes, and the messages (Wang et al.2020; Tsiotsou, 2021; Tsiotsou & Diehl, 2022).

The model of signverting, decoding the message, appearing as the sign equivalent, serves as a link between the sign and the final element, the interpretant. This becoming of the possible interpretant can be abstract, implicit, explicit, or reflexive when it becomes a sign that needs its own interpretant. In the relationship between a group of agents, a system can be outlined, where communication is the process through which codes and messages are exchanged. The interpretant in this case takes the key role as its main properties are a personal context, having an observer with an aim, and it may take one of the enunciated positions by the theory. This investigation is within the limits outlined by naming the sign as the micro-unit of communication, stressing the necessity of the interpretant and the transmitter, and also presenting two agents with their actions, the third conceptual base (West, 2021; Els, 2021; Sultan, 2021).

3.2. Semiotics in Traditional Marketing

In spite of being identified as a robust marketing school, the dominant model has its limitations, given the exponential changes caused by the digital transformation of society. The concept of a unique universal code, which orders the signs, is no longer valid. With the collapses, paradoxes, and ambiguities of the contemporary world, to understand and decode meanings, it is necessary to integrate a complex process of articulation between the different fields of social sciences to explain how individuals construct meanings and, therefore, how signs acquire value. Therefore, the marketing school that emerges from the comprehensive paradigm of integrating the so-called mixed cultural studies falls within the interpretive paradigm (Kraus et al.2021; Kraus et al.2022).

The semiotics of consumer culture is a conceptual framework that fits with certain paradigms of marketing that seek to interpret consumer activities. Briefly, semiotics refers to the study of signs, and the semiotics of consumer culture analyzes the interactions between consumers, brands, and cultural elements. The objective is to investigate the factors that motivate consumer actions and behaviors and that are related to the consumption of goods and services as a search for meanings. Consumer goods and services represent situations of concrete cultural negotiation between producers and consumers. Therefore, consumer culture is a cultural negotiation (Welch, 2020; Michaelidou et al.2021).

3.3. Semiotics in Digital Marketing

Semiotics is a relational discipline covering a system of communication based on signs and meaning. It is the study of signs, symbols, and the interpretation of communication. Semiotics creates the science of signs and systems of signs, and it uses symbols to establish any kind of meaning. In addition to being of value in studying computer icons, semiotics has functions as informers of decision-making, identifies the emotional attitude of brands, creates appropriate consumer insights, and helps marketing researchers. It is not only the relationship of consumer interpretation that uses semiotics, but also in brand communication. Indeed, the language of a brand is one of the brand communication tools using signs to establish any kind of meaning. Furthermore, it always uses an advertising language consisting of signs, and this is the key (Vanninen et al., 2023; Killen et al., 2020; Sang, 2021).

Every brand has its own story; this story is feasible to establish through signs because it is in the context of culture and society used by consumers. In order to translate it, semiotics is required to analyze for the realization of a brand that fully takes into consideration consumers' actions. A brand's communication is by sign if it is able to connect with the real and emotional aspects of the consumer, with consumers' needs and attitudes. This aspect of a brand is made possible by brand signs. Their function is to stand in for the product, although they do not have any relationship with it. This sign is fundamental, and the only way of having control over brands is to understand the consumer who is the potential buyer because the sign commentator is the potential buyer. Brands are a consumer's tool that helps the consumer to externalize the identity that they have constructed or would like to construct. They externalize this identity through signs. The brand, the consumer that defines themselves by that brand, merchandising of the brand, and will generate a million messages, whether commercial or monetized (Sherry Jr, 2020; Beverland et al.2021; Lalaounis, 2020).

4. METHODOLOGY

This study followed the positivist paradigm, which believes that reality is objective and independent of human perception. The main research method was a survey, implying that consumer opinions were shaped by binary questions (with the exception of the perceived similarity question) and multiple objective responses. The study utilized Economic Exchange Theory, according to which consumer perceptions (the key units of the analysis) are subordinated to existing traditions and conventions in the Latvian communications market. The theory indicates that the conventional product should be cheaper than the product linked with tradition. The signals from the traditional and conventional products must contain a credible guarantee (Sechi et al.2023; Ferm & Thaichon, 2021).

The survey design was influenced by the depletion model, and therefore the questionnaire was developed following good advice, applying the self-determination theory of motivation. The survey was hosted on an online survey service, which allowed for email data gathering from internal databases. The survey was performed as part of a national omnibus survey. The sample design was determined by the objectives and demographic attributes of the sample. The survey was pilot tested with a sample of 50 consumers initially and 30 random respondents who were selected during the compilation of the questionnaires. The pretest and pilot survey results gave preliminary insights into any potential flaws in the questionnaire design and therefore confirmed that the questions posed were suitable (Kumar et al.2021; Fanelli, 2021).

4.1. Research Design

Given the complexity of the study, the research design required a division into different stages of data collection and analysis. The first stage of the investigation had a qualitative nature and intended to identify cultural characteristics, values, and norms of the brand's consumption audience. In this stage, semi-structured individual interviews were conducted to obtain consumer opinions and feelings about different advertising messages, asking them to interpret possible hidden meanings and strategies used by the company in its communication process. It is pertinent to note that during these initial contacts, none of the interviewees identified it as a form of marketing research, nor was any communication related to the brand disclosed. The respondents' unconsciousness was crucial in obtaining individual interviews and reliable data, which allowed a deep understanding of their motivations and ways of thinking. Upon completion of this stage, 35 interviews were recorded and made available by the interviewees for later content analysis. The number of interviews was sufficient to achieve data saturation and meet the qualitative nature of the first stage, as it concerned the study of individual opinions (Priya, 2021; Crabtree & Miller, 2023; Levitt, 2021).

The study based on semi-structured interviews followed procedures already established in previous literature. The script was pre-tested with three potential consumers. This test aimed to verify comprehension and eliminate possible administrative problems in the data collection process. Consequently, some adjustments were made to the interview questions. This stage was concluded when there was an impossibility of new categories and/or construct validation, signaling saturation and the initiation of the second stage: data preparation. The interviews were recorded and then transcribed. Before starting the coding process developed by qualitative data analysis software, the verbatim text was subjected to a model of semantic content, aiming to facilitate the systematization of the responses. Each written discourse was organized in line with the operational and theoretical stages of qualitative content analysis. Next, the set of data was encoded by two trained graduate students in the research area, where the number of interviews with the coders was 25 tapes. Data preparation was also concluded at this stage, making the data available for testing the hypotheses and proceeding with the research objectives (Paul et al.2021; Paul & Criado, 2020).

4.2. Data Collection Methods

For this research data was collected through purposive, informal unstructured interviews to get insights of consumers' perception of signature elements. intercourse was required with consumers before completion of the intensive care studies so a pilot study was carried out to assess the consumer interpretation dimension, reference theories, credibility of the researchers carrying out the study, and context of the study. The use of questionnaire in the verified profile ensured that secondary research done was more reliable. Of the total number of questions identified above, a set of questions that formed a fully structured interview questionnaire was arrived at, given the number of questions to be asked, memory effects and quality of questions. On the basis of coherence, the interview protocol was pretested on a small scale before implementing it. (Azodo et al.2020; Moisander et al., 2020; Matyas, 2020).

All the data gathered from the interviews were in note form, so as to be able to ensure the interviewer got an accurate portrayal of results and also the gestures made during the interviews such as hand movements and facial expressions. Failure to rely on notes only could cause misunderstanding of some vital data, which is important in conducting the evaluation. That is, the researchers got the full records after completing the interviews and transcribing the data for analysis. Another set of two researchers from different background cross-checked the findings to ensure internal validity of the study and checked them against secondary themes and context factors. Knowledge coming from diverse prior experiences, including customer's view, enhanced the analysis of the study findings. (Adeoye-Olatunde and Olenik2021; Lareau, 2021).

4.3. Data Analysis Techniques

Most of the data analysis techniques are also known as multivariate analysis, due to the purpose of describing, interpreting, and testing the relationship between the variables. The variables explain the differences and measure this relationship. These data analysis techniques are appropriate when a large amount of data stemming from many informants is analyzed, with the purpose of identifying patterns and regularities across them. Structural Equation Modeling represents a general causal modeling framework and a combination of factor analysis and regression techniques that are used to study relationships among variables. SEM analysis was performed using Partial Least Squares-SEM to avoid multicollinearity issues present in estimations (Sauerbrei et al.2020; Mertler et al., 2021).

In order to link the study with Semiotics and to be sure that the scale items embraces the concept of brand elements, Exploratory Factor Analysis (EFA) was conducted. In this context, the study adapted Principal Component Analysis with varimax rotation to choose factors having a variance of at least 70 percent. The final scale included six items across two factors: Brand elements – 'Type of brand elements' and 'Brand element fit' had high reliability and validity. The Bartlett's test and Kaiser–Meyer–Olkin measure justified data applicability on the factor analysis. The validity of the scale was also established out of compound variables and factor scores thus confirming the construct for the study. (Schreiber, 2021; Widaman & Helm, 2023).

5. CONSUMER INTERPRETATION OF SEMIOTICS IN DIGITAL MARKETING

This research assesses consumer understanding of visual semiotics in digital marketing by promotional posts with athletes or individuals of prominence. Participants included twenty internet users and six brand promotional posts through focus group discussion and semi-structured interviews. The study shows that participants appreciated content appreciation when the link between a post and a brand cultural moment is comprehensible. There was a difference though when the values associated with the product and brand were similar, where the visual components were not as critical. However, the Interpretant relations formed interpreters by blending the different interpretants, which only created confused impressions and obscure meaning. As such this study postulates that the integration of sign markers can be effective in helping the users and from a communication perspective issues targets can be achieved. (Dhaoui & Webster, 2021; Hamzah et al.2021; Swani & Labrecque, 2020).

In digital marketing, brands mostly have the goal of creating visual indications and a new picture with relatively high complexity. Semiotics has a social function because it engages the consumer and produces a continuous rewriting of a meaningful image, handling and playing identity. Text and images in digital marketing explain a social phenomenon, expressing communication and dialogue which are the brand's obligation and the consumer's needs. The inclusion and transfer to the digital environment have remodified the concept of web experience and participation, where the use of a grammar of meanings becomes a natural and refined process of idiom construction. Therefore, using the semiotic terms of metaphor, metonymy, and simile is essential to describe how the consumer reproduces a "virtual" copy of the product in their imagination, as well as to perceive generic similarities that generate relational codes (Plakoyiannaki et al.2022;Dalamu, 2021).

5.1. The Influence of Semiotics on Consumer Perception

This research benefits digital marketing by providing information about the symbolism in the brand consumer relationship. This paper looks at the act of consuming brands with the spotlight laid on how consumers make sense of the brand messages that are constituted by sources of meaning. More than that, the study focuses on the cultural aspect of branded communication and thus calls for a more elaborate and expansive view to consumer behavior. Introducing the role of semiotics in a converging media environment, the study provides a basis for claiming the medium is both relevant in today's marketing communications landscape. Contrary to a common practice, this study shows how semiotic theory work for consumer construction and engages in meaning making relevant to marketing communication. (Zhang, 2020; Mandler et al., 2020; Maria-Teresa et al.2023).

6. BRAND COMMUNICATION THROUGH SEMIOTICS

Some criticism can be as follows that using control as the framework to analyze the brand-consumer relationship skews how brands are constructed via consumers. Traditionally, brands have been defined by consumers' culture, personal and social imaging techniques. The assertive work of feeling ads and linking characterizations of brand personalities to products is central. What a brand really needs is the consumer's endorsement which in this case is highlighted by the semiotics of daily existence. Brands, as important to the consumer, are expected to communicate stories about themselves. Lastly, the effectiveness of brands as forms of semiotic modulation that is being done externally is influenced by the capacity that brands have to be strategic with their semiotics, coherent and innovative. (Rindell & Santos, 2021; Lawes, 2023).

Building on modes of address and modes of reception research, this paper examines how consumers create brand meaning and the cultural position of brands in return. In the mode of address tradition, we explore how advertisers provide a context to address specific consumer outlooks. In the mode of reception we interested texts reception strategies for interpretation of brand identity. We will organize certain seminal semiotic inputs in Consumer Culture and Marketing, with an eye on how consumers create brand associations of product attributes/stones that form parts of personal myths/narratives, and interactions between peers. (Keller, 2020; Roggeveen et al.2021).

6.1. Semiotics and Brand Identity

Brand identity is developed in the semiosphere: The mass of signs that are tightly connected with culture. It's important to know which of the global values affect consumers and help brands stand out. On balance, semiotics is a defensive planning language that becomes a competitive weapon in the hands of corporations; it influences products, their designs, packaging and advertising, company's website and social media. A powerful and emotionally provocative selling proposition is something that every contemporary company needs. This research aims at establishing the semiotic significance of material and non-material signs in the development of brand image for luxury fashion brands and evaluating howushman signs create thoughts and meanings in the consumer across the digital and physical domains. Classification and system design are the two remaining phases or areas of interest for further study. (Rindell & Santos, 2021; Lawes, 2023; Oswald, 2020).

This paper includes suggestions for three levels of meaning interpretation. The 'self-centered' dimension is "logical, linguistic and factual," which is based on material brand descriptions and functional attributes. This dimension focuses on the utility of care products and the role the brand plays in culture as signalling one's status. It applies where qualifying sign refers to physically perceptible items which prompt consumer reflection and response, such as utilitarian goods or services. On the other hand, perceptual4 content that is involved in the emotional and aesthetic experience of a product entails elements eliciting emotions. Advertising of luxury brands is more of an endeavor to sell the image and not the product to the consumers. (Akkaya, 2021; Chae et al., 2020).

Second, 'attention rumors' and life theories synchronize meanings to their chronotopic worth. A model was employed to examine the modern chronotopic context approached by the brand content; the concepts as seen in advertisement were encompassed in dramatic and literary vantage points. This model focuses on contexts, content and product communication. The findings shown in the paper indicate rather homogeneity of artistic communication within market/brand segments. Chronotopes are most acute in fashion communication which creates links between consumers' cognition and the world of fashion as well as its values, past, and stars. These elements can also be successfully used by marketers to choreograph the world of luxury fashion brands. (De Fina, 2023; Perrino & Kohler, 2020).

6.2. Semiotics and Brand Messaging

A brand is a set of signs offered to the consumer, and advertising research focuses on understanding the meaning attributed to these signs. Advertising uses specific techniques to ensure that positioning and strategy are aligned with the target audience and media, considering impact, recall, recognition, and interpretation. In today's attention-based economy, brand frame and label are crucial. Successful communication triggers emotional responses, reminding consumers of the brand promise. Psychological research helps understand how emotional processing correlates with semiotic feelings, suggesting that evocative experiences enhance encoding, recall, and consumer significance. (Shanmugavel & Micheal, 2022; Shukla et al.2023; Masuda et al., 2022).

Advertising requires creative mediation to convey meaning and purpose, especially when linking product identity and consumer experience. Creative success occurs when copywriters effectively bridge manufacturers and consumers, aligning beliefs, values, and desires. Advertising's success relies on the semiotic skills of its creators. Semiotics adds sophistication to brand messaging by uncovering hidden truths, explaining why a creative solution works rather than just being preferred. It enables deeper emotional connection, tapping into consumer vulnerabilities and compelling them to purchase. (Ventalon et al., 2020; Lawes, 2023; Sitanggang, 2020).

7. IMPLICATIONS FOR DIGITAL MARKETING STRATEGY

Knowledge of how consumers semiotically perceive their brands' identity and values is beneficial to brand managers. To understand brand characteristics, consumer opinions and ideas posted on the Internet should be examined. Because brand perception is deeply rooted in strategic objectives and culture, the consumer-brand relationship can be analyzed by firms. Overall, for businesses that want to determine whether all the used digital marketing strategies reflect the established digital brand personality, semiotic research enables identification of consumers' behaviours, preferences and wants. It shows the associations connected with the brand and defines what should be promoted, what misleading or requires changes in the process of marketing. (Lawes, 2023; Senivongse and Bennet2022; Oswald, 2020).

This research focus on brand meaning from cultural angle and conveyed through digital marketing instrument; it evaluates brand strategy using semiology. It looks at how brand opinions are shared between the brand and the user in social media platforms. In this context, monitoring of semantic values and of a visual identity which is somehow acknowledged by users in Web 2.0 is the focus of the study, bringing into perspective the explicit involvement of crowdsourcing in building topics and opinions. The more the Web 2.0 languages develop, the decisive role of company ethics and values increases to affect the opinion of users. It means that both linguistic and visual semiotic resources bear consequences for the communicative effectiveness of the brand. (Alwan and Alshurideh2022; Nam & Kannan, 2020; Shankar et al.2022).

7.1. Incorporating Semiotics into Marketing Campaigns

Specifically, the application of semiotics in marketing is now one of the most important models for interpreting consumer behavior. Thereby, it will be useful to understand the extent to which the essentially embodied process of communication is in fact material. Semiotics increases the application of value by emphasizing the name of products and other related factors illustrating how consumers interact with culture and gain meanings. Although 'engagement' is nebulous, it shows that people are interested in messages they did not anticipate. In this case commercial communication acts an important milestone in marketing while at the same time placing advertising into art context. (Travere, 2023; Solano-Flores, 2021).

7.2. Measuring the Effectiveness of Semiotic Strategies

The analysis confirmed that through semiotics it was possible to make brands more expressive, establish symbols of fashion and choose characteristic elements of charitable brands. But it lacks pattern building, it have issues with negativ brand communication, and there are creativity boundaries. It helps now to get a critical perspective on strategies and offers applicable recommendations for researchers, digital marketing practitioners, and brand managers. This research is also innovative for examining the meanings of marketing communication semiotically and imaginatively assessing the effectiveness of messages with an integrated approach. (Wang and Qiao2020; Shahzadi & Maqbool, 2024; Suhaimi & Fauzi, 2021).

Semiotics application in digital marketing is relatively small, and doing research with consumers about it is even more difficult. There is empirical literature on how firms in marketing use signs and symbols to enhance consumer understanding, but its critiques are silent on consumer behavior and value co-creation. These analyses can be conducted through advertising since it makes up a two way communication channel between producers and consumers with a touch on interpretation. The purpose of this research was to analyze semiotics as the brand communication approach with regard to various public segments. (Yu et al.2024; Worakittikul et al., 2024; Wang & Li, 2024).

8. CONCLUSION AND FUTURE DIRECTIONS

Brand conversations and the processing of such messages by the user are presented in this paper as crucial on SN sites which are primary platforms for brand interaction. The study seeks to understand how consumers decode brand communication and offer brands information on engaging users in such areas. This is same agenda the study puts forward a conceptual framework on brand interpretation using social media generated images and videos. It includes roles known as connectors, influentials, and brand opposers, all of which it categorizes by means of multilevel content analysis. This research also applies to theoretical and practical aspects of user interpretations in digital marketing and stresses the importance of textual and visual analysis of textual data in consumer-generated media.

8.1. Summary of Findings

This opens the horizon for companies to position and single them out using the most diverse signs and symbols, and it opens up threats and opportunities for digital marketing. Notwithstanding the four hypotheses not having been supported, other findings are extremely relevant and innovative. First, the study makes advances in the use of social semiotics in marketing, contributes to the theory of signs, the theory of multimodal discourse, and adds to academic knowledge. Clarification of how different visual, audio, olfactory, gustatory, and tactile signs symbolize the functions, values, and experiences of the most diverse brands in such a diverse consumer culture is a substantial advance in the marketing of signification. Much marketing has confined itself to the symbolic and pragmatic functions of signs, their colors, shapes, and placement, mainly in posters and secondarily in packaging. However, increasingly, brands need sensorial signs that appeal to all the senses to transmute the company's DNA and convey the more diverse brand values and messages.

8.2. Contributions to Theory and Practice

Given the Secondary goal and objectives of this research, in this section we propose and summarize the theoretical contributions and discuss the practical implications of the research. We conclude by identifying research limitations and providing several venues for future researchers to approach.

We contribute to the body of knowledge on digital marketing, focusing on a few aspects. Convergence of Media. The theoretically explorative tendency of our work is that it contributes to the marketing scholars working on the topic of media convergence as we couple two quite different areas of knowledge to inform a new perspective. Prior research on media convergence already provides much insight into the implications of the fusion of different media for the traditional structure of the firm and the market. Although marketing scholars have examined product placement and brand support in the media, they have done so considering just a narrow combination of media or have limited their research using traditional marketing theoretical models. Our brand contributes to the existing marketing literature by integrating the characteristics of different environments in which consumers and marketers operate. Individuals and Digital Communication. An in-depth examination of the interpretation carried out by the consumer and the role of mental simulators reveals some of the psychological mechanisms underlying individual behavior when interacting with digital media. The effective and convincing use of varying characteristics of digital marketing often depends on the user's visualization of some mental representation and possible psychological factors leading to and maintaining that mental vision. Branding Strategies and Marketing Tactics. A detailed investigation of the roles of mental simulators for two brand strategies, as well as two marketing tactics, in a digitally mediated environment is depicted in the present study. The confirmation of the pervasiveness of embodied cognition in the context of digital marketing can support further development of such an understanding in wider—and possibly in non-marketing-related—areas, such as the field of human-computer interaction, in employing semantics to improve the interplay between human and visualization technologies, the area of multimedia research on the integration and coherence of visual and auditory elements enhancing message delivery. Theorizing digital interaction empowers scholars and practitioners to improve our most intimate communication with a larger world increasingly mediated by digital technologies. (Bashirzadeh et al.2022; Luangrath et al.2022)

8.3. Recommendations for Future Research

Most aspects of the methodology used in this research were aimed at developing a deep qualitative understanding. This resulted in focused and coherent findings. However, the findings of the questionnaire suggest that the links between visual elements and their connotations may not be as clear-cut as conventional semiotic codes would suggest. Hence, one possibility for future research would be to investigate this setting using an even more qualitative approach to confirm whether these types of learning processes are indeed common among consumers. Two main groups of influences that have an impact on consumer interpretation in the digital media environment were found in the study. The research focused on one type of digital media environment, which was an online brand community. This study was conducted only on one social media platform and investigated only consumer interpretational processes under the category facilitated by brand communication and interaction. The research used the semiotic aesthetic dimension as a lens but did not investigate other dimensions. Hence, these issues provide potential opportunities for future research (Ekwall et al., 2023; Deng & Wang, 2020).

REFERENCES

Adeoye-Olatunde, O. A., & Olenik, N. L. (2021). Research and scholarly methods: Semi-structured interviews. [purdue.edu]. *Journal of the American College of Clinical Pharmacy: JAACP, 4*(10), 1358–1367. DOI: 10.1002/jac5.1441

Aiello, G. (2020). Visual semiotics: Key concepts and new directions. *The SAGE handbook of visual research methods*. academia.edu

Akkaya, M. (2021). Understanding the impacts of lifestyle segmentation & perceived value on brand purchase intention: An empirical study in different product categories. [sciencedirect.com]. *European Research on Management and Business Economics, 27*(3), 100155. DOI: 10.1016/j.iedeen.2021.100155

Alwan, M., & Alshurideh, M. (2022). The effect of digital marketing on purchase intention: Moderating effect of brand equity. [growingscience.com]. *International Journal of Data and Network Science, 6*(3), 837–848. DOI: 10.5267/j.ijdns.2022.2.012

Azodo, I., Williams, R., Sheikh, A., & Cresswell, K. (2020). Opportunities and challenges surrounding the use of data from wearable sensor devices in health care: Qualitative interview study. [jmir.org]. *Journal of Medical Internet Research, 22*(10), e19542. DOI: 10.2196/19542 PMID: 33090107

Bashirzadeh, Y., Mai, R., & Faure, C. (2022). How rich is too rich? Visual design elements in digital marketing communications. [sciencedirect.com]. *International Journal of Research in Marketing, 39*(1), 58–76. DOI: 10.1016/j.ijresmar.2021.06.008

Beaird, J., Walker, A., & George, J. (2020). *The principles of beautiful web design*. uni-osnabrueck.de

Beverland, M. B., Eckhardt, G. M., Sands, S., & Shankar, A. (2021). How brands craft national identity. [cbs.dk]. *The Journal of Consumer Research, 48*(4), 586–609. DOI: 10.1093/jcr/ucaa062

Cambier, F., & Poncin, I. (2020). Inferring brand integrity from marketing communications: The effects of brand transparency signals in a consumer empowerment context. *Journal of Business Research*. nscpolteksby.ac.id

Chae, H., Kim, S., Lee, J., & Park, K. (2020). Impact of product characteristics of limited edition shoes on perceived value, brand trust, and purchase intention; focused on the scarcity message frequency. [HTML]. *Journal of Business Research, 120*, 398–406. DOI: 10.1016/j.jbusres.2019.11.040

Chandler, D. (2022). Semiotics: the basics. [HTML]

Chen, Z. T., & Cheung, M. (2022). Consumption as extended carnival on Tmall in contemporary China: a social semiotic multimodal analysis of interactive banner ads. *Social Semiotics*. arts.ac.uk

Crabtree, B. F. & Miller, W. L. (2023). *Doing qualitative research*. [HTML]

Dalamu, T. O. (2021). Social semiotic genre: Exploring the interplay of words and images in advertising. *Anuari de filologia. Llengües i literatures modernes*. ub.edu

De Fina, A. (2023). 'I especially loved the little Nana dancing on the balcony': The emergence, formation, and circulation of chronotopes in mass-mediated communication. *Language in Society*. cambridge.org

Deng, X. & Wang, L. (2020). The impact of semantic fluency on consumers' aesthetic evaluation in graphic designs with text. *Journal of Contemporary Marketing Science*. [HTML]

Dhaoui, C., & Webster, C. M. (2021). Brand and consumer engagement behaviors on Facebook brand pages: Let's have a (positive) conversation. [HTML]. *International Journal of Research in Marketing*, *38*(1), 155–175. DOI: 10.1016/j.ijresmar.2020.06.005

Dressler, M. & Paunovic, I. (2021). The value of consistency: portfolio labeling strategies and impact on winery brand equity. *Sustainability*. mdpi.com

Dwivedi, Y. K., Ismagilova, E., Hughes, D. L., Carlson, J., Filieri, R., Jacobson, J., Jain, V., Karjaluoto, H., Kefi, H., Krishen, A. S., Kumar, V., Rahman, M. M., Raman, R., Rauschnabel, P. A., Rowley, J., Salo, J., Tran, G. A., & Wang, Y. (2021). Setting the future of digital and social media marketing research: Perspectives and research propositions. [sciencedirect.com]. *International Journal of Information Management*, *59*, 102168. DOI: 10.1016/j.ijinfomgt.2020.102168

Ekwall, P. E., Ädel, A., & Nyström Höög, C. (2023). Towards a unified affordance approach: searching for congruent meaning making in COVID-19 warning designs. *Social Semiotics*. tandfonline.com

Els, D. (2021). *The role of intersemiotic translation in multimodal communication in educational textbooks*. ufs.ac.za

Fanelli, R. M. (2021). Changes in the food-related behaviour of Italian consumers during the COVID-19 pandemic. *Foods*. mdpi.com

Ferm, L. E. C., & Thaichon, P. (2021). … pre-participatory social media drivers and their influence on attitudinal loyalty within the retail banking industry: A multi-group analysis utilizing social exchange theory. [HTML]. *Journal of Retailing and Consumer Services.*

Fraccastoro, S., Gabrielsson, M., & Pullins, E. B. (2021). The integrated use of social media, digital, and traditional communication tools in the B2B sales process of international SMEs. *International business review.* sciencedirect.com

Grewal, D., Herhausen, D., Ludwig, S., & Ordenes, F. V. (2022). The future of digital communication research: Considering dynamics and multimodality. *Journal of Retailing.* sciencedirect.com

Guibourgé, J. (2020). Semiotics: about logo, identity and brand image. *Translated from Guibourgé Jérôme, Design phase 1, améliorer sa conception, L'Harmattan, Paris, 2021.* hal.science

Habes, M., Alghizzawi, M., & Ali, S., SalihAlnaser, A., & Salloum, S. A. (2020). The Relation among Marketing ads, via Digital Media and mitigate (COVID-19) pandemic in Jordan. International [researchgate.net]. *Journal of Advanced Science and Technology, 29*(7), 12326–12348.

Haghbin, F., Nambusubramaniyan, S., & Monfared, N. (2022). The semiotics of social-distance branding during the post-coronavirus crisis. *Semiotica.* degruyter.com

Hamzah, Z. L., Abdul Wahab, H., & Waqas, M. (2021). Unveiling drivers and brand relationship implications of consumer engagement with social media brand posts. [researchgate.net]. *Journal of Research in Interactive Marketing, 15*(2), 336–358. DOI: 10.1108/JRIM-05-2020-0113

Hasyim, M. & Arafah, B. (2023). Semiotic multimodality communication in the age of new media. *Studies in Media and Communication.* academia.edu

Hussain, W., & Panggabean, H. (2024). Language and Power Dynamics in Automobile Advertising: A Multimodal Discourse Analysis of Word Choice and Semiotics. [eltaorganization.org]. *Journal of Applied Linguistics, 4*(1), 71–81. DOI: 10.52622/joal.v4i1.242

Ibrahim, I., & Sulaiman, S. (2020). Semiotic communication: An approach of understanding a meaning in communication. *International Journal of Media and Communication Research, 1*(1), 22–31. uir.ac.id. DOI: 10.25299/ijmcr.v1i1.4584

John, S. P., & De'Villiers, R. (2020). Elaboration of marketing communication through visual media: An empirical analysis. *Journal of Retailing and Consumer Services.* nscpolteksby.ac.id

Kang, H. J., Shin, J., & Ponto, K. (2020). How 3D virtual reality stores can shape consumer purchase decisions: The roles of informativeness and playfulness. [HTML]. *Journal of Interactive Marketing*, *49*(1), 70–85. DOI: 10.1016/j.intmar.2019.07.002

Keller, K. L. (2020). Consumer research insights on brands and branding: A JCR curation. [HTML]. *The Journal of Consumer Research*, *46*(5), 995–1001. DOI: 10.1093/jcr/ucz058

Killen, C. P., Geraldi, J., & Kock, A. (2020). The role of decision makers' use of visualizations in project portfolio decision making. *International Journal of Project Management*. cbs.dk

Kraus, S., Durst, S., Ferreira, J. J., Veiga, P., Kailer, N., & Weinmann, A. (2022). Digital transformation in business and management research: An overview of the current status quo. [sciencedirect.com]. *International Journal of Information Management*, *63*, 102466. DOI: 10.1016/j.ijinfomgt.2021.102466

Kraus, S., Jones, P., Kailer, N., Weinmann, A., Chaparro-Banegas, N., & Roig-Tierno, N. (2021). Digital transformation: An overview of the current state of the art of research. [sagepub.com]. *SAGE Open*, *11*(3), 21582440211047576. DOI: 10.1177/21582440211047576

Kumar, S., Murphy, M., Talwar, S., Kaur, P., & Dhir, A. (2021). What drives brand love and purchase intentions toward the local food distribution system? A study of social media-based REKO (fair consumption) groups. [sciencedirect.com]. *Journal of Retailing and Consumer Services*, *60*, 102444. DOI: 10.1016/j.jretconser.2021.102444

Lalaounis, S. T. (2020). Strategic brand management and development: *Creating and marketing successful brands*. [HTML]

Lareau, A. (2021). Listening to people: *A practical guide to interviewing, participant observation, data analysis, and writing it all up*. [HTML]

Lawes, R. (2023). Using semiotics in marketing: *How to achieve consumer insight for brand growth and profits*. [HTML]

Lawes, R. (2023). *Using semiotics in marketing: How to achieve consumer insight for brand growth and profits*. [HTML]

Lawes, R. (2023). *Using semiotics in marketing*: How to achieve consumer insight for brand growth and profits. [HTML]

Lawes, R. (2023). Using semiotics in marketing: *How to achieve consumer insight for brand growth and profits*. [HTML]

Lawes, R. (2023). Using semiotics in marketing: *How to achieve consumer insight for brand growth and profits*. [HTML]

Lawes, R. (2023). Using semiotics in marketing: *How to achieve consumer insight for brand growth and profits*. [HTML]

Lawes, R. (2023). *Using semiotics in marketing*: How to achieve consumer insight for brand growth and profits. [HTML]

Levitt, H. M. (2021). Qualitative generalization, not to the population but to the phenomenon: Reconceptualizing variation in qualitative research. [HTML]. *Qualitative Psychology*, *8*(1), 95–110. DOI: 10.1037/qup0000184

Liu, W., Cao, Y., & Proctor, R. W. (2021). How do app icon color and border shape influence visual search efficiency and user experience? Evidence from an eye-tracking study. [HTML]. *International Journal of Industrial Ergonomics*, *84*, 103160. DOI: 10.1016/j.ergon.2021.103160

Llorente-Barroso, C., Kolotouchkina, O., & García-García, F. (2021). The meaning of the logo from its semiotic construction and its reliance on new formats of digital communication: The case of Apple. *Revista Latina de Comunicacion Social*, (79), 333-356. researchgate.net

Lourenção, M., Giraldi, J. M. E., & de Oliveira, J. H. C. (2020). Destination advertisement semiotic signs: Analysing tourists' visual attention and perceived ad effectiveness. [HTML]. *Annals of Tourism Research*, *84*, 103001. DOI: 10.1016/j.annals.2020.103001

Luangrath, A. W., Peck, J., Hedgcock, W., & Xu, Y. (2022). Observing product touch: The vicarious haptic effect in digital marketing and virtual reality. [HTML]. *JMR, Journal of Marketing Research*, *59*(2), 306–326. DOI: 10.1177/00222437211059540

Lytvynenko, A., Zavialova, O., Kalashnyk, M., Varadi, N., & Enska, O. (2022). Semiotics of advertisment. hnpu.edu.ua

Makrides, A., Vrontis, D., & Christofi, M. (2020). The gold rush of digital marketing: Assessing prospects of building brand awareness overseas. [sagepub.com]. *Business Perspectives and Research*, *8*(1), 4–20. DOI: 10.1177/2278533719860016

Mandler, T., Johnen, M., & Gräve, J. F. (2020). Can't help falling in love? How brand luxury generates positive consumer affect in social media. [HTML]. *Journal of Business Research*, *120*, 330–342. DOI: 10.1016/j.jbusres.2019.10.010

Maria-Teresa, M. T. G. R., Pineda, A. P. A., David, J. D. F. G. J., & Gómez, F. (2023). Brand Community and Symbolic Interactionism: A Literature Review. *Review of Communication Research*, 11, 01-32. rcommunicationr.org

Masuda, H., Han, S. H., & Lee, J. (2022). Impacts of influencer attributes on purchase intentions in social media influencer marketing: Mediating roles of characterizations. *Technological Forecasting and Social Change*. kyoto-u.ac.jp

Matyas, M. (2020). Opportunities and barriers to multimodal cities: Lessons learned from in-depth interviews about attitudes towards mobility as a service. *European Transport Research Review*. springer.com

Mertler, C. A., Vannatta, R. A., & LaVenia, K. N. (2021). Advanced and multivariate statistical methods: *Practical application and interpretation*. unt.edu

Michaelidou, N., Micevski, M., & Halkias, G. (2021). How do international advertisers use consumer culture positioning strategies? A cross-national, cross-category approach. *International Marketing Review*, *38*(2), 367–386. lboro.ac.uk. DOI: 10.1108/IMR-05-2020-0101

Moisander, J., Närvänen, E., & Valtonen, A. (2020). Interpretive marketing research: Using ethnography in strategic market development. *Marketing management*. tuni.fi

Nam, H. & Kannan, P. K. (2020). Digital environment in global markets: Cross-cultural implications for evolving customer journeys. *Journal of International Marketing*. sagepub.com

Oswald, L. R. (2020). What do affluent Chinese consumers want?: A semiotic approach to building brand literacy in developing markets. *Marketing Management*. researchgate.net

Oswald, L. R. (2020). Doing semiotics: *A research guide for marketers at the edge of culture*. [HTML]

Oswald, L. R. (2020). Doing semiotics: *A research guide for marketers at the edge of culture*. [HTML]

Oswald, L. R. (2020). *Doing semiotics: A research guide for marketers at the edge of culture*. [HTML]

Paraskevaidis, P., & Weidenfeld, A. (2021). Perceived and projected authenticity of visitor attractions as signs: A Peircean semiotic analysis. [HTML]. *Journal of Destination Marketing & Management*, *19*, 100515. DOI: 10.1016/j.jdmm.2020.100515

Paul, J. & Criado, A. R. (2020). The art of writing literature review: What do we know and what do we need to know?. *International business review*. drjustinpaul.com

Paul, J., Lim, W. M., O'Cass, A., Hao, A. W., & Bresciani, S. (2021). Scientific procedures and rationales for systematic literature reviews (SPAR-4-SLR). [researchgate.net]. *International Journal of Consumer Studies*, *45*(4), O1–O16. DOI: 10.1111/ijcs.12695

Perrino, S. & Kohler, G. (2020). Chronotopic identities: Narrating Made in Italy across spatiotemporal scales. *Language & Communication*. sciencedirect.com

Plakoyiannaki, E., Stavraki, G., & Tsapi, V. (2022). The artist and the photograph: A semiotic analysis of consumers' experiences with photographs. *Qualitative Market Research*, *25*(2), 256–271. surrey.ac.uk. DOI: 10.1108/QMR-09-2021-0119

Priya, A. (2021). Case study methodology of qualitative research: Key attributes and navigating the conundrums in its application. *Sociological Bulletin*. sagepub.com

Rindell, A. & Santos, F. P. (2021). What makes a corporate heritage brand authentic for consumers? A semiotic approach. *Journal of Brand Management*. springer.com

Roggeveen, A. L., Grewal, D., Karsberg, J., Noble, S. M., Nordfält, J., Patrick, V. M., Schweiger, E., Soysal, G., Dillard, A., Cooper, N., & Olson, R. (2021). Forging meaningful consumer-brand relationships through creative merchandise offerings and innovative merchandising strategies. [sciencedirect.com]. *Journal of Retailing*, *97*(1), 81–98. DOI: 10.1016/j.jretai.2020.11.006

Sang, S. (2021). Reconstructing the place branding model from the perspective of Peircean semiotics. [HTML]. *Annals of Tourism Research*, *89*, 103209. DOI: 10.1016/j.annals.2021.103209

Sauerbrei, W., Perperoglou, A., Schmid, M., Abrahamowicz, M., Becher, H., Binder, H., Dunkler, D., Harrell, F. E.Jr, Royston, P., & Heinze, G. (2020). State of the art in selection of variables and functional forms in multivariable analysis—Outstanding issues. [springer.com]. *Diagnostic and Prognostic Research*, *4*(1), 1–18. DOI: 10.1186/s41512-020-00074-3 PMID: 32266321

Schreiber, J. B. (2021). Issues and recommendations for exploratory factor analysis and principal component analysis. *Research in Social and Administrative Pharmacy*. academia.edu

Schultz, D. E. (2020). From advertising to integrated marketing communications. *A reader in marketing communications*. [HTML]

Sechi, G., Šķilters, J., Selecka, M., Kalnača, L., & Leškēviča, K. (2023). Knowledge exchange and growth in a hybrid community–a social-capital-based approach: Evidence from Latvia. [sagepub.com]. *IFLA Journal*, *49*(1), 87–98. DOI: 10.1177/03400352221089673

Senivongse, C., & Bennet, A. (2022, September). Semiotic inception, attitude altering, and behavioral expression: Understanding the foundation of organizational knowledge construction. *In 23rd European Conference on Knowledge Management Vol* 2. Academic Conferences and publishing limited. academic-conferences.org DOI: 10.34190/eckm.23.2.465

Shahzadi, M. & Maqbool, A. (2024). Semiotic Analysis of Pakistani Clothing Brands Advertisements using Barthes' Theory. *Competitive Linguistic Research Journal*. clrjournal.com

Shankar, V., Grewal, D., Sunder, S., Fossen, B., Peters, K., & Agarwal, A. (2022). Digital marketing communication in global marketplaces: A review of extant research, future directions, and potential approaches. [google.com]. *International Journal of Research in Marketing*, *39*(2), 541–565. DOI: 10.1016/j.ijresmar.2021.09.005

Shanmugavel, N. & Micheal, M. (2022). Exploring the marketing related stimuli and personal innovativeness on the purchase intention of electric vehicles through Technology Acceptance Model. *Cleaner Logistics and Supply Chain*. sciencedirect.com

Sherry, J. F.Jr. (2020). *The soul of the company store: Nike Town Chicago and the emplaced brandscape*. The Retailing Reader. [HTML]

Shukla, M., Misra, R., & Singh, D. (2023). Exploring relationship among semiotic product packaging, brand experience dimensions, brand trust and purchase intentions in an Asian emerging market. [HTML]. *Asia Pacific Journal of Marketing and Logistics*, *35*(2), 249–265. DOI: 10.1108/APJML-10-2021-0718

Sitanggang, A. O. (2020). The meaning of advertising'Aqua life'in the semiotic perspective of roland barthes. *International journal of multi science*. multisciencejournal.com

Solano-Flores, G. (2021). The semiotics of test design: Conceptual framework on optimal item features in educational assessment across cultural groups, countries, and languages. *Frontiers in Education*. frontiersin.org

Suhaimi, S. N., & Fauzi, T. A. (2021). Visual semiotics: identity reflection in personal symbol creation. *KUPAS SENI*. upsi.edu.my

Sultan, J. K. (2021). The War-Zone Consequences of the Deformed Linguistic Image: Iraqi Simultaneous Interpreters during the US-led Invasion.. *Journal of College of Education/Wasit*. iasj.net

Swani, K., & Labrecque, L. I. (2020). Like, Comment, or Share? Self-presentation vs. brand relationships as drivers of social media engagement choices. [HTML]. *Marketing Letters*, *31*(2-3), 279–298. DOI: 10.1007/s11002-020-09518-8

Terho, H., Mero, J., Siutla, L., & Jaakkola, E. (2022). Digital content marketing in business markets: Activities, consequences, and contingencies along the customer journey. *Industrial Marketing Management*. sciencedirect.com

Travere, A. (2023). The Interplay of Signs and Visuals: Unveiling the Symbiotic Relationship Between Semiotics and Visual Communication. [pioneerpublisher.com]. *Journal of Linguistics and Communication Studies*, *2*(3), 28–40.

Tsiotsou, R. H. (2021). Introducing relational dialectics on actor engagement in the social media ecosystem. *Journal of Services Marketing*. uom.gr

Tsiotsou, R. H. & Diehl, S. (2022). Delineating transformative value creation through service communications: an integrative framework. *Journal of Service Management*. uom.gr

Vanninen, H., Mero, J., & Kantamaa, E. (2023). Social media influencers as mediators of commercial messages. *Journal of Internet Commerce*. lut.fi

Ventalon, G., Erjavec, G., & Tijus, C. (2020). Processing visual metaphors in advertising: An exploratory study of cognitive abilities. [HTML]. *Journal of Cognitive Psychology*, *32*(8), 816–826. DOI: 10.1080/20445911.2020.1817038

Wang, J., & Li, M. (2024). *Brand transcreation as multimodal configuration: The (re) making of text, context, and meaning in brand semiotics*. Babel. [HTML] DOI: 10.1075/babel.00370.wan

Wang, W., Chen, C. H. S., Nguyen, B., & Shukla, P. (2020). Collaboration between East and West: Influence of consumer dialectical self on attitude towards co-brand personality traits. [HTML]. *International Marketing Review*, *37*(6), 1155–1180. DOI: 10.1108/IMR-01-2019-0012

Wang, Y., & Qiao, F. (2020). The symbolic meaning of luxury-lite fashion brands among younger Chinese consumers. [HTML]. *Journal of Fashion Marketing and Management*, *24*(1), 83–98. DOI: 10.1108/JFMM-09-2019-0204

Welch, D. (2020). Consumption and teleoaffective formations: Consumer culture and commercial communications. *Journal of Consumer Culture*. sagepub.com

West, D. E. (2021). *Between two minds: The work of Peirce's energetic interpretant*. Contemporary Pragmatism. [HTML]

Widaman, K. F. & Helm, J. L. (2023). Exploratory factor analysis and confirmatory factor analysis.. [HTML]

Worakittikul, W., Saenwerm, C., & Naruetharadhol, P. (2024). Unlocking the secrets of green semiotics: The revolutionary power of eco-symbols in transforming consumer perceptions and catalyzing behavioral shifts in emerging .... *PloS one*. plos.org

Xi, N. & Hamari, J. (2021). Shopping in virtual reality: A literature review and future agenda. *Journal of Business Research*. sciencedirect.com

Yu, J., Dickinger, A., & Egger, R. (2024). Leveraging emojis as visual semiotics for enhanced engagement in destination marketing. [researchgate.net]. *Journal of Destination Marketing & Management, 33*, 100925. DOI: 10.1016/j.jdmm.2024.100925

Zhang, K. (2020). The effect of para-social interaction in endorsement advertising: SEM studies based on consumers' exposure to celebrity symbols. *Language and Semiotic Studies*. degruyter.com

Chapter 4
AI, Semiotics, and Marketing:
Navigating the New Frontier of Consumer Engagement

Naga Ramesh Palakurti
https://orcid.org/0009-0009-9500-1869
Tata Consultancy Services, USA

ABSTRACT

This chapter explores the dynamic intersection of artificial intelligence (AI), semiotics, and marketing, emphasizing how AI technologies are transforming consumer engagement through the lens of symbolic interpretation. In an increasingly digitalized world, the use of semiotics in marketing is essential for understanding the deeper cultural and emotional connections that consumers form with brands. By integrating AI, brands can decode consumer behavior, personalize interactions, and predict trends in real-time, elevating the symbolic meanings that resonate with diverse audiences. The chapter discusses how AI-driven tools, such as natural language processing, machine learning, and data analytics, are revolutionizing the way marketers craft and deploy semiotic elements like logos, colors, and narratives to foster deeper consumer connections. Furthermore, it analyzes how semiotic theory supports the development of AI-enabled marketing strategies that go beyond functional benefits to engage consumers on a symbolic, emotional level.

1. INTRODUCTION

In today's digital age, consumer engagement has become more complex and nuanced than ever before. Brands are not only competing for attention, but they are

DOI: 10.4018/979-8-3693-8024-6.ch004

also vying for emotional and symbolic connections with consumers. The fusion of artificial intelligence (AI) and semiotics offers a powerful toolkit for navigating this evolving landscape. AI, with its ability to process and analyze vast amounts of data, has revolutionized how marketers understand consumer behavior. At the same time, semiotics provides deep insights into the cultural, emotional, and symbolic meanings that shape consumer decisions.

This chapter explores how AI and semiotics together create new possibilities for consumer engagement. While AI enables brands to engage with consumers on a personalized and data-driven level, semiotics enriches this engagement by ensuring that the communication resonates with consumers' cultural and symbolic expectations. By combining the strengths of AI's technical capabilities with semiotics' focus on meaning and representation, marketers can craft more compelling and meaningful consumer experiences.

2. AI IN MARKETING: THE DATA-DRIVEN REVOLUTION

AI has transformed marketing by providing unprecedented capabilities in data processing, predictive analytics, and personalization. AI-driven tools such as machine learning algorithms, natural language processing (NLP), and computer vision allow marketers to engage consumers in new, more precise ways. In recent years, artificial intelligence (AI) has revolutionized the way businesses approach marketing, ushering in what is often referred to as the data-driven revolution. This transformation is powered by the unprecedented availability of data, the rapid development of AI technologies, and the increasing need for personalized, real-time consumer engagement (Shankar, 2018).

Some key AI applications in marketing include:

- Personalization at Scale: The data-driven revolution in marketing, powered by artificial intelligence (AI), has given rise to the concept of personalization at scale. This approach moves beyond the traditional one-size-fits-all strategy and allows brands to create highly tailored and relevant experiences for individual consumers—across vast and diverse audiences—through the intelligent use of data and automation. Personalization is the key to driving deeper engagement, improving customer satisfaction, and ultimately increasing brand loyalty. In the modern marketplace, where consumers expect personalized interactions, AI is helping brands deliver these experiences at scale by analyzing data, predicting behaviors, and adjusting content in real-time.

Example: AI-powered recommendation engines, like those used by Amazon or Netflix, analyze user behavior to suggest products or content that align with individual interests. This results in a more engaging user experience and, ultimately, higher conversion rates.

- Predictive Analytics: Machine learning models can predict consumer behavior, allowing marketers to anticipate needs, preferences, and trends. Predictive analytics help brands make data-driven decisions about product development, advertising strategies, and customer retention. Predictive analytics refers to the process of using data mining, statistics, machine learning, and AI to make predictions about future consumer behaviors and outcomes. By analyzing historical data, AI can identify patterns that are likely to recur and use these insights to anticipate what actions consumers will take next.

In the context of marketing, predictive analytics can help brands understand consumer needs before they even arise, enabling them to deliver the right message at the right time. This capability is central to creating personalized marketing experiences that resonate with individual consumers (Rust & Huang, 2021).

2.1. The Role of AI in Predictive Analytics for Marketing

AI plays a critical role in enabling predictive analytics by processing vast amounts of data far more efficiently than traditional methods. AI algorithms, particularly machine learning models, can continuously improve their predictions by learning from new data and adjusting their forecasts over time. This allows brands to maintain a high degree of accuracy in anticipating consumer behavior.

2.1.1 Data Integration and Analysis

AI-powered predictive analytics systems can integrate data from multiple sources—such as consumer purchase history, website interactions, social media activity, and demographic information. By analyzing these diverse datasets, AI identifies patterns and trends that marketers can use to anticipate future actions.

2.1.2 Machine Learning and Continuous Improvement

The machine learning models used in predictive analytics become more accurate over time as they process more data. As consumer behavior evolves, AI systems can adapt to these changes, ensuring that predictions remain relevant. This continuous improvement is a key advantage of using AI for predictive analytics.

Predictive analytics represents a powerful tool in the data-driven marketing revolution, allowing brands to anticipate consumer behaviors, craft personalized experiences, and stay ahead of cultural trends.

Chatbots and Virtual Assistants: AI-powered chatbots enhance consumer engagement by offering 24/7 customer service, answering inquiries, and guiding users through purchasing decisions. These virtual assistants use NLP to understand and respond to consumer questions, creating a seamless experience.

Content Creation and Curation: AI tools are now capable of generating content such as text, images, and videos. Marketers can leverage AI-generated content to engage consumers in real-time, adapting creative assets based on user feedback and preferences.

Example: Tools like GPT-3 can generate marketing copy that is tailored to specific audiences, while platforms like HubSpot use AI to automate content curation, recommending articles or social media posts that resonate with target demographics.

AI also helps optimize content for SEO (Search Engine Optimization) by analyzing search trends and adjusting keywords in real-time. This ensures that marketing content stays relevant and visible to consumers.

2.1.3 Data Privacy and Ethical Concerns

As AI in marketing becomes more data-driven, it also raises significant concerns about data privacy and ethics. AI relies on collecting and analyzing consumer data, which poses risks related to user consent, data security, and transparency. Marketers must navigate the ethical landscape of using personal data responsibly while ensuring compliance with regulations such as GDPR and CCPA.

Transparency is key in building consumer trust. Brands must be open about how they use AI and data to avoid alienating customers who may feel uncomfortable with the extensive tracking and analysis of their behavior.

As AI-driven marketing becomes more sophisticated and personalized, concerns around data privacy and ethics are becoming increasingly prominent. In the digital marketing landscape, where predictive analytics and personalization are central to enhancing consumer engagement, the massive collection and use of consumer data presents challenges in maintaining ethical standards and protecting individual privacy.

This section explores the ethical considerations in the use of AI in marketing, focusing on issues related to data privacy, consumer consent, algorithmic transparency, and responsible data usage, and provides strategies for ensuring ethical AI practices in marketing.

2.2. The Role of Data in AI-Driven Marketing

AI marketing technologies rely heavily on data—collected from consumer interactions, purchasing behavior, social media activity, and website analytics—to deliver personalized experiences and targeted advertising. This data allows AI systems to analyze trends, predict consumer behavior, and tailor marketing messages to individual preferences.

However, the sheer volume of data being collected, often without explicit consumer awareness or consent, raises serious concerns about the potential for misuse. The line between personalization and privacy invasion becomes increasingly blurred as AI-driven systems gain deeper insights into consumers' behaviors, preferences, and even emotional states.

2.3. Ethical Concerns in AI-Driven Data Collection

2.3.1. Consumer Consent and Data Transparency

One of the core ethical concerns in AI-driven marketing is the lack of transparency regarding how consumer data is collected, stored, and used. Many consumers are unaware of the data being gathered about them or how that data is being used to influence their buying decisions. Often, data collection is embedded in terms of service agreements that consumers rarely read or fully understand.

2.3.2 Over-Personalization and Consumer Autonomy

While personalization enhances the consumer experience, there is a risk of over-personalization, where consumers feel that brands know too much about them. This can create discomfort or lead to a sense of manipulation, where consumers feel their actions and choices are being unduly influenced by AI-driven marketing strategies.

Challenge: Avoiding the creepiness factor—where consumers perceive that their personal data is being used in ways that make them feel monitored or manipulated, such as receiving hyper-targeted ads immediately after searching for a product online.

Solution: Brands should implement ethical personalization strategies that balance relevance with respect for consumer privacy. Providing transparent options for users to control the extent of personalization in their experiences can help alleviate concerns.

2.3.3. Data Security and Breach Risks

With the vast amounts of personal data being collected by AI-driven marketing systems, ensuring the security of this data is paramount. Data breaches can result in significant harm to consumers, including identity theft, fraud, and loss of trust in the brand. Moreover, poorly secured AI systems may be vulnerable to cyberattacks, putting sensitive consumer information at risk.

Challenge: Protecting consumer data from unauthorized access or breaches, especially as the volume of data being processed by AI systems continues to grow.

Solution: Implement robust data encryption and security protocols to protect sensitive consumer information. Brands should also be proactive in addressing security vulnerabilities within AI systems and ensuring compliance with data protection regulations such as GDPR and CCPA.

2.3.4 The Future of AI in Marketing

The data-driven revolution is far from over. As AI technologies evolve, we can expect further advancements in areas such as emotion recognition, voice search, and augmented reality (AR) marketing. AI will continue to redefine the boundaries of what is possible in marketing, enabling brands to offer immersive, personalized, and seamless experiences.

The future of AI in marketing will be characterized by:

Real-Time Optimization: AI will enable brands to adjust campaigns instantaneously based on consumer responses.

Deep Personalization: Hyper-personalization will allow brands to deliver unique experiences tailored to individual consumer journeys.

AI and Creativity: AI will complement human creativity by providing data-driven insights that inspire new forms of content and storytelling.

While AI provides marketers with tools for deeper engagement and personalization, it does not address the symbolic and cultural dimensions of communication. This is where semiotics comes into play.

According to Kannan and Li (2017), digital marketing involves a dynamic integration of data analytics, technology, and consumer insights, forming the foundation of modern AI-driven marketing strategies.

The data-driven revolution is transforming marketing in ways that were unimaginable just a few years ago. AI enables brands to deliver personalized experiences at scale, predict future trends, and engage with consumers in real-time. While challenges such as data privacy and ethical concerns remain, the potential for AI to revolutionize marketing is vast. As businesses continue to adopt AI-driven tools, they will unlock new opportunities for customer engagement, operational efficiency, and market growth, positioning themselves at the forefront of the next generation of consumer marketing.

3. SEMIOTICS: UNDERSTANDING THE SYMBOLIC NATURE OF CONSUMER ENGAGEMENT

Semiotics is the study of signs and symbols, and how they create meaning in communication. In marketing, semiotics helps brands decode the cultural codes and symbols that influence consumer perceptions, choices, and loyalty. Semiotic analysis focuses on the narratives, values, and emotions that underpin consumer behavior, allowing marketers to craft messages that resonate on a deeper, more symbolic level (Cosenza, 2020).

Semiotics is the study of signs and symbols, and how they create meaning in communication. In marketing, semiotics helps brands decode the cultural codes and symbols that influence consumer perceptions, choices, and loyalty (Arnould & Thompson 2005; Mick et al., 2004).

- What is Semiotics in Marketing: At its core, semiotics in marketing explores how signs—whether they be logos, colors, slogans, or product designs—represent meanings beyond their literal form. Every brand communication, from an advertisement to packaging, consists of signs that convey messages to the consumer. Semiotics helps marketers understand the cultural context and emotional responses these signs elicit, offering a more nuanced approach to consumer engagement.

Sign in semiotic terms can be divided into:

- Signifier: The form the sign takes (e.g., a logo or an image).
- Signified: The concept or meaning the sign represents (e.g., luxury, trust, or innovation).

By decoding the relationship between the signifier and the signified, marketers can gain insights into how consumers perceive and emotionally engage with brands. Semiotics helps marketers understand how consumers interpret brand messages and develop "brand literacy," or the ability to decode symbolic meaning in marketing communication (Oswald, 2015).

- Cultural Codes and Symbols: Every consumer operates within a cultural context shaped by symbols, values, and social norms. Semiotics helps marketers understand these codes and incorporate them into their branding and messaging (Greco & Boero, 2023).

For example, certain colors, imagery, or metaphors may carry specific meanings in different cultures, influencing how consumers interpret a brand's message.

Some more examples:

- Red may symbolize luck and prosperity in China but can represent danger or passion in Western cultures.
- The use of minimalist design might evoke simplicity and elegance in one market but be perceived as lacking substance in another, depending on cultural expectations.

Semiotics allows brands to align their marketing strategies with the cultural codes of their target audiences. It ensures that the meanings communicated are congruent with the cultural values and beliefs of the consumers, leading to more effective engagement.

- Brand Narratives: Brands are not just products; they are stories. Semiotics helps marketers construct brand narratives that resonate with consumers' identities and values. By understanding the symbolic meaning behind a product, brands can craft stories that evoke emotions, aspirations, and desires.

For instance:

Nike's "Swoosh" is a simple design, but through repeated association with ideas of victory, endurance, and athleticism, it has become a powerful symbol of achievement. The "Swoosh" is no longer just a visual logo—it's a cultural symbol representing sportsmanship and empowerment.

Through semiotic analysis, brands can examine whether their symbolic elements align with their desired identity and how consumers perceive those symbols in the context of broader cultural narratives. This process is essential for brands that aim to evolve their identity while maintaining symbolic consistency with their core values.

- Consumer Identity and Aspiration: Consumption is a symbolic act, often tied to identity and social status. Semiotic analysis enables marketers to understand how consumers use products and brands to express their identity, and how they aspire to certain lifestyles or social groups (Mick et al., 2004).
- Emotional Resonance: Semiotics helps marketers tap into the emotional dimensions of consumer engagement. Whether through advertising, packaging, or social media content, semiotic analysis reveals the emotional triggers that drive consumer behavior, allowing brands to build stronger, more meaningful connections.

For example:

- Disney invokes feelings of magic, nostalgia, and childhood joy through its symbols (such as the castle, Mickey Mouse, and the iconic music). Consumers develop a strong emotional connection with Disney, resulting in loyalty that spans generations.
- Starbucks uses its green mermaid logo as a symbol of quality and comfort. The symbol itself represents more than just coffee—it has become synonymous with the experience of enjoying a moment of personal indulgence. It's about offering a complete sensory experience, from the café atmosphere to the personalized drink options, creating an emotional connection with customers (Borghini et al, 2009).

Through semiotics, brands can design symbols that trigger these emotional responses, ensuring that consumers continue to engage and remain loyal over time.

- Visual and Verbal Semiotics in Advertising: Advertising is one of the most visible forms of semiotic communication in marketing. The use of visual and verbal signs in ads is a delicate process, where every element is designed to communicate a specific meaning. Semiotics helps marketers ensure that the visual symbols (such as imagery and color) and verbal symbols (such as slogans and taglines) work in tandem to deliver a cohesive and effective message.

Example: In an ad for a luxury watch brand, the visual elements (such as sleek design, gold, and elegant backgrounds) symbolize opulence and exclusivity. Meanwhile, the verbal tagline might emphasize timeless elegance, reinforcing the product's position as a symbol of both style and status.

The interaction of visual and verbal semiotics in advertising shapes consumer perceptions and plays a key role in defining how engaged they feel with a brand's identity.

The combination of AI's data-driven insights and semiotics' focus on meaning creates a powerful strategy for engaging consumers in a way that is both personalized and culturally resonant. Semiotics in marketing is essential for understanding how consumers engage with brands on a symbolic level. As consumers increasingly seek brands that align with their values and aspirations, the symbolic meaning of products becomes as important—if not more so—than the products themselves. By leveraging semiotic analysis, marketers can decode consumer behavior, craft compelling brand narratives, and create meaningful connections that lead to long-term engagement and loyalty. In an era of data-driven marketing and AI-enhanced strategies, semiotics remains an invaluable tool for understanding the deeper layers of consumer engagement. As Mick and Buhl (1992) explain, consumers derive meaning from advertising not only through information but through the emotional and symbolic experiences it evokes.

4. AI AND SEMIOTICS: A SYMBIOTIC RELATIONSHIP FOR MARKETING SUCCESS

The convergence of Artificial Intelligence (AI) and Semiotics is creating new opportunities for brands to engage consumers more effectively. While AI enhances marketers' ability to analyze vast amounts of data and predict consumer behavior, semiotics provides a framework to decode the symbolic meanings embedded in consumer culture and communication (Van den Broeck & Pauwels, 2021). Together, they form a symbiotic relationship that amplifies the power of marketing, enabling brands to build deeper, more meaningful connections with their audiences.

4.1. The Basics of Semiotics in Marketing

Semiotics, in the context of marketing, is the study of how signs and symbols—such as logos, slogans, colors, and imagery—convey messages that resonate with consumers. Every marketing communication is rich with semiotic elements that convey meanings beyond the literal product or service being offered. These meanings tap into cultural codes and individual aspirations, enabling consumers to identify with a brand on a deeper, emotional level.

4.1.1. Signifier and Signified

- Signifier: The tangible form of a symbol (e.g., a brand logo, a color, a product design).
- Signified: The concept or meaning the symbol evokes in the consumer's mind (e.g., luxury, innovation, sustainability).

Brands often employ specific symbols to convey their core values. For example, Tesla's electric vehicles signify environmental sustainability and technological advancement through the sleek design of the cars and the minimalistic nature of their marketing.

4.2. The Role of AI in Enhancing Semiotics

Artificial Intelligence provides marketers with the ability to gather and process large volumes of consumer data in real time. This allows brands to better understand how different symbols and signs are perceived by their target audience. AI tools like machine learning, natural language processing, and predictive analytics can identify patterns in consumer behavior, allowing marketers to optimize their semiotic strategies based on these insights.

4.2.1. AI's Role in Symbol Analysis

AI can be used to analyze how consumers interact with a brand's semiotic elements across various touchpoints, such as social media, online reviews, and e-commerce platforms. By tracking which symbols resonate most with different consumer segments, AI can help brands adjust their messaging to maximize relevance and emotional engagement.

- Example: AI tools can analyze social media conversations to detect whether a brand's new logo is generating positive or negative sentiment. If the AI detects that the new design is not resonating with consumers, marketers can quickly pivot their strategy to address these concerns.

4.3. AI and Semiotic Adaptability

AI's capacity for real-time analysis allows for dynamic adaptation of marketing strategies. Brands can adjust their semiotic messaging on the fly, based on consumer feedback and behavioral data. This adaptability is crucial in today's fast-paced, ever-changing consumer landscape, where trends emerge and fade quickly.

4.3.1. AI and Cultural Sensitivity

One of the most critical applications of AI in semiotic marketing is in navigating the complexities of cultural codes. Semiotic elements can carry different meanings in different cultural contexts, and a message that resonates well in one market may be misinterpreted or even offensive in another. AI helps marketers adapt their semiotic elements to ensure cultural relevance and avoid missteps.

- Example: A color like red, which signifies luck and prosperity in China, may symbolize danger or aggression in Western markets. AI can help brands analyze how certain semiotic elements are perceived in different regions, ensuring that campaigns are culturally appropriate.

4.3.2. Personalized Semiotic Messaging

AI allows for personalization at an individual level, which is crucial for creating semiotic messages that resonate with specific consumer identities. By analyzing consumer data, AI can help marketers craft tailored messages that align with individual values, beliefs, and cultural contexts.

- Example: Spotify uses AI to analyze a user's listening habits and curate personalized playlists that align with their preferences, embedding symbolic elements of identity and taste into the user experience. The branding experience becomes personal, fostering deeper emotional connections.

4.4. AI and Semiotic Storytelling

At the heart of successful marketing is the ability to tell a compelling story, and semiotics plays a vital role in constructing the narratives that consumers identify with. AI enhances this by providing data-driven insights that inform the creation of personalized brand stories. This symbiosis between AI and semiotics enables brands to craft narratives that resonate deeply with their audience on both cognitive and emotional levels.

4.4.1. Narrative Creation through Data-Driven Insights

AI tools such as predictive analytics can provide insights into what kinds of narratives are likely to engage consumers based on historical data, current trends, and individual preferences. Brands can use this data to create stories that align with consumers' cultural backgrounds, aspirations, and values.

- Example: A fashion brand using AI can track current trends in consumer conversations and social media activity, identifying symbolic elements that reflect consumer preferences. These insights can be used to develop marketing campaigns that align with consumers' evolving tastes and cultural trends.

4.4.2. Adapting Stories in Real-Time

AI allows marketers to adapt their semiotic storytelling in real-time, adjusting messaging based on how consumers are responding to a campaign. If a certain narrative is resonating particularly well with a specific audience segment, AI can help amplify that message through targeted ads, personalized emails, or social media content.

- Example: During the COVID-19 pandemic, AI helped many brands, such as Nike, adapt their semiotic storytelling to focus on themes of resilience, community, and personal health. These stories resonated deeply with consumers who were seeking comfort and solidarity during uncertain times.

4.5. The Role of AI in Semiotic Brand Identity

A brand's identity is built upon a complex network of symbols, narratives, and values. AI plays a crucial role in shaping this identity by providing insights into how consumers perceive a brand's semiotic elements. With the help of AI, brands can continuously refine their identity to stay relevant and engaging to their target audience.

4.5.1. Brand Consistency and Semiotic Evolution

AI ensures that as brands evolve, they maintain a consistent semiotic identity across all channels and touchpoints. This consistency is key to building a strong, recognizable brand that resonates with consumers.

- Example: Apple maintains a consistent semiotic identity centered around innovation and minimalism. AI helps the brand track how this identity is perceived across different markets, enabling them to adjust their messaging without losing the core elements that define their brand.

4.5.2. Brand Perception and Consumer Data

AI provides marketers with real-time data on how their brand is being perceived in the marketplace. By analyzing consumer sentiment and engagement patterns, AI can help brands adjust their semiotic elements to ensure that their identity is aligned with the values and aspirations of their target audience.

4.6. AI, Semiotics, and the Future of Consumer Engagement

The future of consumer engagement will be defined by the symbiotic relationship between AI and semiotics. As AI technologies continue to evolve, they will provide marketers with even deeper insights into how symbols, signs, and narratives resonate with consumers. These insights will be crucial in crafting the personalized, culturally relevant messages that drive consumer engagement and brand loyalty.

4.6.1. Hyper-Personalization

As AI becomes more advanced, brands will be able to deliver hyper-personalized experiences that are tailored to individual consumer identities. This will involve not only targeting consumers based on their demographic information but also understanding their emotional and cultural needs.

- Example: Hyper-personalized ads that take into account not only a consumer's purchase history but also their cultural background, emotional triggers, and aspirational goals. These ads will use semiotic elements that resonate with the consumer on a deeply personal level.

4.6.2. Predicting Cultural Shifts

AI will play an increasingly important role in helping brands predict cultural shifts and adapt their semiotic strategies accordingly. By analyzing large datasets of social media interactions, consumer behavior, and global trends, AI can provide insights into emerging cultural movements and help brands stay ahead of the curve.

- Example: AI can track conversations related to sustainability and ethical consumption, providing brands with the information they need to align their messaging with the growing demand for eco-friendly products.

The symbiotic relationship between AI and semiotics is revolutionizing the way brands engage with consumers. While semiotics provides a framework for understanding the symbolic meanings that drive consumer behavior, AI offers the tools to analyze, predict, and adapt these meanings in real-time. Together, they empower brands to create personalized, culturally relevant marketing strategies that resonate deeply with their target audience.

As the capabilities of AI continue to expand, brands will be able to harness the full potential of semiotics to craft marketing messages that not only meet the needs of their consumers but also reflect their values, aspirations, and cultural identities. This symbiosis between AI and semiotics is the future of marketing success, enabling brands to navigate the complexities of consumer engagement in an increasingly interconnected and data-driven world.

5. CHALLENGES AND ETHICAL CONSIDERATIONS IN AI-SEMIOTICS MARKETING

The intersection of Artificial Intelligence (AI) and semiotics is transforming marketing strategies, allowing brands to create more meaningful, data-driven, and personalized consumer engagements. However, this convergence also introduces a range of challenges and ethical considerations (Ransbotham et al., 2017). As AI technologies enable brands to harness the symbolic power of semiotics on a massive scale, questions about data privacy, cultural sensitivity, algorithmic bias, and consumer autonomy become increasingly important.

This section will explore the critical challenges and ethical dilemmas that arise when integrating AI and semiotics into marketing, and how brands can navigate these issues while fostering responsible and ethical marketing practices.

5.1. Data Privacy and Consumer Consent

One of the most pressing concerns in AI-driven marketing is the collection and use of consumer data. AI relies heavily on vast datasets to analyze consumer behavior, predict trends, and personalize marketing messages (Kaplan & Haenlein, 2019). However, the extensive use of personal data can raise concerns about privacy and the ethical boundaries of how data is gathered and utilized.

5.1.1. Challenge: Transparency in Data Collection

AI requires access to consumer data—such as browsing history, purchase patterns, and social media activity—to generate personalized marketing experiences. Many consumers are not fully aware of how much data is being collected, leading to concerns about informed consent.

- Ethical Concern: Consumers may not fully understand how their data is being used in AI-driven semiotic analysis. Without transparent communication, they may feel that their privacy is being invaded or that their personal information is being exploited without proper consent.

5.1.2. Solution: Transparent Data Practices

Brands must ensure that their data collection practices are transparent and comply with privacy regulations like GDPR (General Data Protection Regulation) and CCPA (California Consumer Privacy Act). Providing consumers with clear, accessible information about how their data is collected and offering them the choice to opt out of data collection is essential.

- Best Practice: Implement a clear opt-in mechanism for consumers, allowing them to control what personal information is used and how it is processed for personalized marketing.

5.2. Algorithmic Bias and Fairness

AI systems are only as unbiased as the data they are trained on. When used in marketing, algorithmic bias can lead to unintended discrimination or stereotyping, especially when applied to semiotic analysis. Since AI models are trained on historical data, they may replicate and amplify existing societal biases.

5.2.1. Challenge: Bias in AI Algorithms

AI systems can unintentionally perpetuate racial, gender, and cultural biases. When analyzing semiotic symbols—such as the use of color, imagery, or language—AI might over-represent or under-represent certain groups, reinforcing harmful stereotypes.

- Example: An AI-driven marketing campaign may favor certain demographics based on historical purchasing data, leading to unequal targeting or exclusion of minority groups.

5.2.2. Solution: Bias Detection and Mitigation

Brands must take proactive steps to ensure that their AI algorithms are trained on diverse datasets that reflect a wide range of consumer identities and experiences. Regular audits of AI models are necessary to identify and mitigate biases that could harm consumer engagement or perpetuate inequality.

- Best Practice: Develop algorithmic fairness tools to monitor AI performance, ensuring that all demographic groups are equally represented in marketing campaigns.

5.3. Cultural Sensitivity and Semiotic Misinterpretation

Semiotics plays a key role in shaping consumer perceptions by using symbols, narratives, and imagery to create meaning. However, cultural sensitivity is crucial when applying semiotic analysis across global markets. Symbols carry different meanings across cultures, and the risk of misinterpretation or cultural appropriation is high when AI is used to scale these efforts.

5.3.1. Challenge: Cultural Missteps in Semiotic Messaging

A symbol or color that resonates positively in one culture might carry negative or inappropriate connotations in another. When using AI to analyze and deploy semiotic elements, brands must be cautious not to overlook these cultural differences.

- Example: The color white, which symbolizes purity in Western cultures, may symbolize mourning or death in other parts of the world, such as certain Asian cultures. An AI-driven marketing campaign that fails to account for this difference could lead to cultural insensitivity.

5.3.2. Solution: Cross-Cultural Semiotic Analysis

To avoid cultural missteps, AI systems should be trained to understand the cultural nuances of different markets. Collaborating with local cultural experts and implementing region-specific semiotic strategies can help brands ensure that their messaging is appropriate and respectful across diverse audiences.

- Best Practice: Use geo-targeted marketing campaigns that adapt semiotic symbols to the specific cultural context of each target market, ensuring relevance and sensitivity.

5.4. Hyper-Personalization and Consumer Autonomy

Hyper-personalization, enabled by AI, allows brands to tailor marketing messages to an individual's preferences, behaviors, and even emotional states. While this can enhance the consumer experience, it also raises concerns about consumer autonomy and the potential for manipulation.

5.4.1. Challenge: Manipulation Through Personalization

With hyper-personalized marketing, brands can create experiences that are so tailored to the individual that it feels as though their decisions are being influenced or manipulated. When semiotic symbols are used to tap into deep emotional or cultural triggers, consumers may feel they are being pushed toward certain actions without fully realizing it.

- Ethical Concern: Over-personalization can lead to feelings of discomfort or loss of autonomy, as consumers may perceive that brands are using personal data to steer their behavior too aggressively.

5.4.2. Solution: Balance Between Personalization and Consumer Choice

While personalization can improve consumer engagement, brands must ensure that their strategies respect consumer autonomy. Instead of using AI to push consumers toward predetermined decisions, marketers should use personalization to offer options and empower consumers to make informed choices.

- Best Practice: Implement ethical AI frameworks that prioritize consumer welfare, ensuring that personalization is used to enhance the user experience rather than manipulate it.

5.5. Automation vs. Human Oversight

AI enables the automation of many marketing processes, from ad targeting to content creation. However, relying too heavily on AI systems without adequate human oversight can result in ethical lapses, particularly when dealing with semiotic messaging that requires nuanced interpretation.

5.5.1. Challenge: Lack of Human Sensitivity

While AI is highly efficient in processing large datasets and deploying marketing campaigns at scale, it lacks the empathy and contextual awareness that human marketers possess. This can be especially problematic when addressing sensitive topics, such as cultural values, identity, or social justice issues.

- Example: An AI system might generate semiotic messaging that aligns with data-driven insights but misses the deeper emotional context or cultural significance of certain symbols, leading to tone-deaf campaigns.

5.5.2. Solution: Combining AI Automation with Human Oversight

Brands should not rely solely on AI to develop and deploy semiotic marketing strategies. Human marketers must be involved in reviewing and interpreting AI-generated insights, ensuring that marketing messages are culturally appropriate and emotionally resonant.

- Best Practice: Use AI for data analysis and insight generation, but involve human experts in the final decision-making process to ensure that the messaging is in line with ethical and cultural standards.

5.6. Ethical Dilemmas in Semiotic Storytelling

Semiotics plays a critical role in crafting brand stories that resonate with consumers. However, when AI is used to create semiotic narratives, ethical dilemmas can arise regarding the manipulation of emotional and cultural symbols for commercial purposes.

5.6.1. Challenge: Exploitation of Emotional Symbols

Semiotic elements—such as language, imagery, and symbols—can evoke powerful emotional responses. When AI-driven systems deploy these elements at scale, there is a risk that emotional symbols will be over-exploited for commercial gain, leading to consumer alienation or distrust. Kaplan and Haenlein (2019) highlight that marketers must not only adopt AI tools but also interpret their societal implications responsibly.

- Ethical Concern: Consumers may feel that their emotions and cultural identities are being commodified, especially if semiotic symbols that hold deep personal or cultural meaning are used in a manipulative way.

5.6.2. Solution: Ethical Storytelling in AI-Driven Marketing

Brands must ensure that their semiotic storytelling is genuine and respectful. AI-driven marketing strategies should aim to enhance the consumer-brand relationship by telling stories that align with consumers' values and cultural identities, rather than exploiting them for profit.

- Best Practice: Use authentic storytelling that reflects the brand's core values and resonates with consumers on a meaningful level, while ensuring that semiotic symbols are used ethically and respectfully.

The integration of AI and semiotics in marketing offers powerful tools for creating personalized, culturally relevant, and emotionally resonant campaigns. However, it also introduces a range of challenges and ethical considerations that brands must address to maintain trust and integrity in their consumer relationships. By adopting transparent data practices, mitigating algorithmic bias, respecting cultural nuances, and ensuring human oversight in AI-driven campaigns, brands can harness the full potential of AI-semiotics marketing while upholding ethical standards and fostering meaningful consumer engagement.

6. THE FUTURE OF CONSUMER ENGAGEMENT: AI, SEMIOTICS, AND MARKETING SYNERGY

As technological advancements in Artificial Intelligence (AI) continue to transform the marketing landscape, the convergence of AI and semiotics is poised to redefine the future of consumer engagement. The synergy between AI's data-driven capabilities and semiotics' deep understanding of cultural symbols, signs, and meanings offers brands a powerful toolkit to craft more meaningful, personalized, and contextually relevant experiences for consumers.

This section explores how AI and semiotics will work together in the future to create a new paradigm for consumer engagement, characterized by hyper-personalization, real-time interaction, cultural sensitivity, and a deeper emotional connection between brands and consumers.

6.1. Hyper-Personalization: AI and Semiotics for Individualized Experiences

In the future, hyper-personalization will be at the forefront of consumer engagement. While personalization has already become a major trend in marketing, AI and semiotics will enable brands to create even more tailored experiences that align with individual consumer identities, emotions, and cultural contexts.

6.1.1. AI's Role in Analyzing Consumer Data

AI will continue to evolve, with enhanced capabilities for analyzing vast datasets that include consumer behaviors, preferences, demographics, and social interactions. By processing this data in real time, AI can predict what consumers want and need, enabling brands to anticipate preferences and deliver personalized content, offers, and experiences.

Example: A streaming platform like Netflix can use AI to analyze a user's viewing history, but with semiotics, it can delve deeper into the symbolic meanings of preferred genres, themes, and character archetypes to curate content that resonates on a personal and emotional level.

6.1.2. Semiotics and Personalization at Scale

Semiotics enables brands to understand the symbolic language that resonates with different audiences. As AI systems become more sophisticated, they will be able to adapt these semiotic cues—such as colors, images, and narratives—based on individual consumer preferences and cultural contexts, delivering personalized messages that go beyond product recommendations to engage consumers on a symbolic and emotional level.

Example: An AI-driven fashion retailer could use semiotics to recognize that certain colors or clothing styles carry specific cultural significance for different consumer groups. The retailer could then tailor its advertising to reflect these cultural codes, enhancing relevance and engagement.

6.2. Real-Time Consumer Interaction: AI-Driven Semiotic Engagement

In the future, real-time interaction between brands and consumers will be essential for maintaining engagement in a world where consumer expectations are constantly evolving. AI's ability to process data in real-time, combined with semiotic analysis, will allow brands to continuously adapt their messaging to reflect consumers' shifting needs, preferences, and emotional states.

6.2.1. AI for Dynamic Marketing Adjustments

AI enables brands to respond immediately to real-time consumer feedback, adjusting marketing messages, offers, and content on the fly. As AI becomes more integrated into marketing systems, brands will be able to adjust their semiotic strategies in response to changes in consumer sentiment or behavior.

Example: A brand might launch a campaign featuring a specific symbol, such as a celebrity endorsement. AI systems can monitor real-time responses on social media and other platforms. If consumers respond negatively, the brand can adjust the campaign's semiotic elements in real time, replacing the symbol with something more aligned with the audience's preferences.

6.2.2. AI-Powered Conversations and Engagement

The future of consumer engagement will also involve AI-powered conversational agents, such as chatbots, that understand and engage with consumers in real time. These AI systems will use natural language processing (NLP) to decode the semiotic meaning embedded in consumer interactions, allowing brands to communicate more effectively and meaningfully with their audiences.

Example: A retail brand could use AI-driven chatbots that understand the symbolic value of certain words, images, and narratives used by consumers during their shopping journey. By interpreting the emotional and cultural significance of these symbols, the chatbot can engage consumers in more personalized and contextually relevant conversations.

6.3. Cultural Sensitivity and Global Marketing: AI-Semiotics for Cross-Cultural Engagement

As brands expand into global markets, the ability to understand and respect cultural differences will be crucial for successful consumer engagement. The synergy between AI and semiotics will allow brands to navigate these cultural nuances, ensuring that their marketing messages resonate with diverse audiences without falling into cultural missteps.

6.3.1. AI for Cultural Analysis and Adaptation

AI will play a significant role in helping brands analyze cultural contexts and adapt their semiotic messaging accordingly. By leveraging machine learning algorithms trained on vast datasets of global consumer behavior and cultural trends, AI can identify how different symbols, colors, and narratives are perceived in various regions.

Example: A brand launching a new product globally might use AI to analyze how certain product symbols are interpreted in different markets. In one region, the color red might symbolize excitement and passion, while in another, it might be associated with danger or caution. AI will help the brand adjust its semiotic elements to ensure that the product is marketed appropriately in each cultural context.

6.3.2. Balancing Global Consistency with Local Relevance

AI and semiotics will enable brands to strike a balance between maintaining a consistent global brand identity and tailoring their messaging to be culturally relevant in local markets. AI systems can analyze cultural symbols and values in real-time, ensuring that a brand’s messaging aligns with local expectations while staying true to the brand's overarching identity.

Example: A luxury brand like Gucci can use AI to maintain its global identity of exclusivity and craftsmanship while adapting its advertising and product presentation to align with local cultural aesthetics and preferences.

6.4. Emotional Engagement: AI and Semiotic Storytelling

The future of marketing will be defined by the ability to create emotional connections with consumers. AI, combined with semiotics, will empower brands to craft personalized narratives that evoke strong emotional responses and deepen consumer loyalty.

6.4.1. AI in Semiotic Storytelling

AI will be instrumental in analyzing consumer data to identify the emotional triggers and symbolic narratives that resonate with different audience segments. By combining this data with semiotic analysis, brands will be able to tell stories that connect with consumers on both a cognitive and emotional level.

Example: A car manufacturer like Tesla could use AI to analyze how consumers engage with the symbolic elements of its brand—such as innovation, sustainability, and status—and craft personalized advertisements that highlight the specific emotional values that resonate most with each consumer.

6.4.2. Personalized, Contextual Narratives

As AI becomes more sophisticated, it will enable brands to deliver contextualized semiotic narratives that are tailored to the specific needs, emotions, and desires of individual consumers. These personalized stories will enhance consumer engagement by making consumers feel understood and valued.

Example: A wellness brand could use AI to create personalized content for consumers based on their health goals and lifestyle preferences. Semiotic analysis would ensure that the brand's messaging—such as imagery related to wellness, mindfulness, or vitality—aligns with the consumer's aspirations, creating a deeper emotional connection.

6.5. Ethical Consumer Engagement: AI and Semiotic Responsibility

As AI-driven semiotic marketing becomes more advanced, ethical considerations will play a critical role in shaping the future of consumer engagement. Brands will need to ensure that their use of AI and semiotics respects consumer privacy, autonomy, and cultural integrity.

6.5.1. Data Privacy and Consumer Autonomy

With the increasing use of personal data to deliver hyper-personalized experiences, brands must prioritize data privacy and ensure that consumers maintain control over how their data is used. The future of AI-semiotic marketing will require brands to be transparent about data collection and to respect consumer autonomy in the decision-making process.

Best Practice: Implement ethical AI frameworks that prioritize transparency and give consumers the option to opt-in or out of personalized marketing campaigns, ensuring that consumer trust is maintained.

6.5.2. Cultural Sensitivity and Inclusivity

AI-driven marketing strategies must be designed with cultural sensitivity and inclusivity in mind. As brands leverage semiotics to engage with global audiences, they must ensure that their messaging is culturally respectful and inclusive of diverse perspectives.

Best Practice: Use AI to conduct cultural audits and ensure that all semiotic elements are culturally appropriate and do not reinforce harmful stereotypes or exclude minority groups.

The future of consumer engagement lies in the synergy between AI and semiotics. Together, these technologies will enable brands to create more personalized, culturally relevant, and emotionally resonant marketing experiences that drive deeper consumer connections. By leveraging AI's data-driven capabilities and semiotics' understanding of symbolic meaning, brands will be able to anticipate consumer needs, adapt to real-time feedback, and craft powerful narratives that engage consumers on a personal and emotional level.

As this synergy evolves, the most successful brands will be those that not only harness the power of AI and semiotics to enhance consumer engagement but also do so ethically, ensuring that their marketing strategies are transparent, inclusive, and respectful of cultural diversity. The future of consumer engagement is one where AI, semiotics, and marketing work hand in hand to create experiences that resonate deeply with consumers, fostering lasting loyalty and brand success.

7. THE ECONOMICS OF EXPERIENCE: AI AND SEMIOTICS IN THE EXPERIENCE ECONOMY

In today's marketplace, consumers are no longer simply buying products or services—they are seeking immersive experiences that resonate emotionally, culturally, and symbolically with their identities. This shift toward the experience economy places new demands on brands to craft compelling, meaningful, and personalized experiences that go beyond traditional marketing. The intersection of Artificial Intelligence (AI) and semiotics offers an unprecedented opportunity for brands to deliver these tailored experiences at scale, leveraging both data-driven insights and symbolic communication to create deeper, more impactful consumer relationships.

This topic explores how AI and semiotics together drive the economics of experience (Borghini et al., 2009), providing brands with tools to deliver personalized, immersive experiences that reflect cultural and emotional symbols, increasing consumer engagement and loyalty.

7.1. Understanding the Experience Economy

The experience economy, a term coined by B. Joseph Pine II and James H. Gilmore in 1998, represents a shift from goods and services to experiences as the primary drivers of consumer value. In the experience economy, consumers seek meaningful, emotionally resonant experiences that engage multiple senses, fulfill personal or social needs, and allow them to connect with brands in deeper, more immersive ways.

- Example: Starbucks isn't just about selling coffee—it's about offering a complete sensory experience, from the café atmosphere to the personalized drink options, creating an emotional connection with customers.

In this context, AI and semiotics play crucial roles in delivering experiences that are symbolically meaningful and personalized to the consumer, allowing brands to differentiate themselves in a crowded marketplace.

7.2. AI's Role in Shaping the Experience Economy

AI enables brands to collect and analyze vast amounts of data related to consumer behavior, preferences, emotions, and interactions, allowing them to predict what experiences will resonate with everyone. By understanding consumer patterns, AI helps brands tailor their offerings to create more personalized experiences, fostering deeper engagement and loyalty.

7.2.1. Personalization and Predictive Analytics

AI-powered predictive analytics allows brands to anticipate what experiences will resonate with consumers by analyzing past behavior, preferences, and emotional responses. AI can create tailored experiences based on individual preferences, whether in retail, entertainment, or hospitality.

- Example: Netflix uses AI to recommend movies and shows based on individual viewing history, tailoring the user experience to match emotional and symbolic preferences for certain genres or narratives (e.g., adventure, drama, or comedy).

7.2.2. Real-Time Adaptation of Experiences

With AI, brands can adjust experiences in real-time based on consumer engagement and feedback. AI allows brands to collect data continuously from consumer interactions and adjust the experience to maintain relevance and engagement.

- Example: In e-commerce, AI can track how a consumer navigates a website in real-time and adjust the content, product recommendations, or offers to create a more engaging, personalized experience. Visual attention is critical in semiotic communication; as Pieters and Wedel (2007) noted, eye movement and goal-directed attention determine how consumers interpret advertising symbols.

7.2.3. Multi-Sensory Engagement

AI can also help brands optimize multi-sensory experiences, understanding how consumers react to different sensory stimuli (visual, auditory, tactile) and personalizing these elements to enhance the overall experience.

- Example: AI-powered virtual or augmented reality (AR/VR) applications in retail allow consumers to experience products in a virtual setting, creating an immersive, sensory-rich experience before making a purchase.

7.3. The Role of Semiotics in the Experience Economy

Semiotics provides the framework for understanding how consumers interpret the symbols, signs, and cultural codes embedded in a brand's experiences. By decoding these elements, brands can craft experiences that align with consumers' symbolic worlds—whether related to identity, values, or aspirations.

7.3.1. Symbolic Meaning and Brand Engagement

Brands use semiotics to communicate symbolic meanings through everything from logos and colors to store designs and narratives. In the experience economy, semiotics helps ensure that the experiences brands create carry the right symbolic connotations to evoke emotional engagement.

- Example: A luxury brand like Chanel uses semiotic elements such as the color black, elegant store designs, and minimalist packaging to signify exclusivity, sophistication, and timelessness in every customer interaction, reinforcing its brand image.

7.3.2. Crafting Narrative-Driven Experiences

Semiotics allows brands to build narratives around their experiences that resonate with cultural symbols or values. Consumers don't just buy products; they buy into the stories those products represent. AI enhances this process by delivering narratives that are personalized to the consumer.

- Example: Outdoor brands like Patagonia create narratives around environmental sustainability and adventure, using semiotic elements like rugged landscapes in their marketing and AI to tailor these narratives to individual consumer preferences for outdoor activities.

7.3.3. Cultural Sensitivity in Global Markets

As brands expand globally, semiotics helps ensure that their experiences are culturally relevant in different markets. Cultural symbols carry different meanings in different regions, and brands need to adapt their messaging accordingly. AI can assist in analyzing these cultural differences and providing real-time adjustments.

- Example: A global brand like McDonald's uses different semiotic elements in its restaurants around the world to reflect local cultures—whether through menu options or visual branding elements—while maintaining a consistent global identity.

7.4. AI and Semiotics: Creating Immersive Brand Experiences

The synergy between AI and semiotics allows brands to craft immersive experiences that not only engage consumers but also resonate with their personal and cultural identities. Through real-time data analysis and symbolic messaging, AI and semiotics together create emotional, sensory-rich, and meaningful interactions that align with the experience economy's core principles.

7.4.1. Hyper-Personalization of Experiences

AI, combined with semiotics, allows brands to deliver hyper-personalized experiences by understanding the symbolic significance of specific narratives or visuals to individual consumers. AI can continuously adapt these experiences, making them more engaging and meaningful.

- Example: A theme park like Disney can use AI and semiotics to deliver personalized experiences based on the symbolic meaning of different characters, stories, and settings that resonate with each visitor's cultural background and preferences.

7.4.2. Emotional Engagement Through Symbolic Resonance

AI-driven semiotic analysis allows brands to identify the emotional triggers that resonate with consumers. By leveraging the right symbols, colors, or narratives, brands can create experiences that evoke positive emotional responses—whether excitement, nostalgia, or comfort.

- Example: In hospitality, a hotel chain might use AI to deliver personalized in-room experiences based on the emotional meaning of comfort or luxury to different types of guests, from vacationers to business travelers.

7.4.3. AI-Powered Storytelling

AI can enhance storytelling by using semiotic analysis to adapt narratives in real time, ensuring that the brand's story aligns with the consumer's current context and emotions. This creates dynamic, evolving experiences that stay relevant and engaging over time.

- Example: In interactive entertainment platforms, AI-driven storytelling engines can use semiotics to adjust the plot and character development based on the user's symbolic interpretation of the story, creating a tailored narrative experience.

7.5. AI and Semiotics in the Retail Experience

In the experience economy, retail spaces are becoming less about selling products and more about creating immersive brand environments. AI and semiotics together allow retailers to create store experiences that engage consumers through symbolism and personalized interaction.

7.5.1. Personalized Retail Experiences

AI-powered systems can analyze consumers' preferences and behaviors to deliver personalized shopping experiences that align with their personal tastes and cultural symbols. These experiences can be extended through augmented reality (AR) or virtual reality (VR) to provide deeper engagement.

- Example: A fashion brand like Gucci might use AI to provide in-store personalized experiences, offering product suggestions based on the symbolic significance of colors, styles, or designs that resonate with the consumer's identity.

7.5.2. Semiotic Symbols in Retail Design

The design of retail spaces can be optimized using semiotics to reflect symbolic elements that align with the brand's values and create meaningful experiences. AI can analyze how consumers interact with different design elements and adjust them to improve the experience.

- Example: Apple stores use minimalistic, clean designs that symbolize innovation and simplicity, enhanced by AI systems that adjust in-store experiences based on consumer behavior and interaction patterns.

7.6. The Future of AI and Semiotics in the Experience Economy

As AI technologies continue to evolve, the potential for creating even more immersive and meaningful experiences through semiotic analysis will only grow. Brands will be able to use AI to predict emotional responses, adjust symbolic messaging, and create multi-sensory, personalized experiences in real-time.

7.6.1. Predictive Experience Design

In the future, AI will be able to predict consumer emotions and design experiences in advance that align with their symbolic and emotional needs, ensuring a frictionless and engaging experience across both digital and physical spaces.

7.6.2. AI-Driven Cultural Adaptation

AI will enable brands to continuously adapt their symbolic messages and experiences to reflect the cultural shifts happening in real-time, ensuring that they remain relevant and engaging in an increasingly diverse global marketplace.

8. CONCLUSION

The future of consumer engagement is being shaped by the integration of AI and semiotics. AI's ability to analyze data and predict behavior offers marketers a powerful tool for personalization and precision. However, without semiotic insight, these efforts risk becoming purely technical and devoid of the cultural, symbolic, and emotional depth that makes marketing truly effective.

By combining AI's capabilities with semiotics' understanding of meaning and representation, brands can navigate the complexities of consumer engagement in the digital age. Together, AI and semiotics offer a new frontier for marketers—one where data-driven precision meets cultural relevance, and technology works in harmony with human-centered meaning.

8.1. The Harmonization of AI Precision and Semiotic Depth in Modern Marketing

The integration of artificial intelligence (AI) and semiotics presents a groundbreaking approach to consumer engagement that leverages the strengths of both technologies. While AI excels at processing vast amounts of data and delivering personalized marketing experiences at an unprecedented scale, semiotics provides the essential cultural and emotional depth needed to make those interactions meaningful. Together, they form a powerful symbiosis that can help brands connect with consumers in ways that transcend mere functionality, engaging them at a deeper, more symbolic level.

The modern consumer landscape is shaped by rapid technological advances, shifting cultural values, and an ever-evolving marketplace where brand loyalty is driven by experiences, identity, and emotional connections. In this context, AI's ability to predict, personalize, and optimize consumer interactions is invaluable. However, AI alone cannot fully account for the intricate and symbolic nature of human behavior. This is where semiotics fills a crucial gap, ensuring that the data-driven insights provided by AI are aligned with the cultural and emotional narratives that resonate with consumers.

As consumer behavior becomes increasingly symbolic and identity-driven, the need for marketing strategies that are both technologically advanced and deeply meaningful grows stronger. The future of marketing lies in this dual approach:

8.2. From Personalization to Cultural Resonance

AI has the capacity to deliver hyper-personalized marketing messages tailored to individual preferences, browsing behaviors, and purchase history. However, personalization is only the beginning. To create lasting consumer engagement, brands must also ensure that these messages resonate within the broader cultural and symbolic framework of the consumer's world.

Semiotics plays a pivotal role in bridging this gap by analyzing the underlying symbols, metaphors, and narratives that shape consumer perceptions and choices. By integrating semiotic analysis into AI-driven marketing strategies, brands can move beyond personalization and tap into the deep emotional and cultural currents that drive consumer behavior. The result is not just a more personalized experience, but a more meaningful one—an experience that connects with consumers' identities, values, and aspirations.

For instance, an AI-driven campaign for a luxury brand might identify a consumer's preference for high-end products, but semiotics ensures that the brand's message communicates not just exclusivity, but also status, aspiration, and identity in a way that aligns with the consumer's cultural context. This dual-layered approach turns a functional message into an emotionally compelling one, fostering deeper brand loyalty.

8.3. Navigating Global Markets with Cultural Sensitivity

As brands increasingly operate on a global scale, the challenges of engaging culturally diverse audiences become more pronounced. AI offers valuable insights into local consumer behavior, preferences, and trends by analyzing data from various regions. However, this data must be contextualized through a semiotic lens to ensure that marketing messages are culturally appropriate, respectful, and effective.

The risk of cultural missteps is high when brands attempt to expand globally without a nuanced understanding of local values, symbols, and social norms. Semiotics provides a roadmap for navigating these cultural complexities, helping brands avoid pitfalls such as cultural appropriation or tone-deaf messaging. By combining AI's data-driven insights with semiotic analysis, marketers can craft campaigns that resonate across different cultural landscapes while maintaining authenticity and respect.

For example, a global fast-food brand might use AI to understand dietary preferences in different regions, but semiotics ensures that their advertising reflects local cultural practices, values, and identities—whether that means respecting religious dietary restrictions or incorporating culturally significant symbols in a respectful manner.

8.4. The Emotional Connection: AI and Semiotics in Storytelling

One of the most powerful ways that brands engage consumers is through storytelling. Stories are a universal human experience, and they are particularly effective in marketing because they evoke emotions, foster connections, and build loyalty. While AI can provide valuable insights into which types of stories resonate with specific audiences, it is semiotics that reveals why those stories are effective.

Semiotics helps brands craft narratives that are not only emotionally engaging but also symbolically rich, drawing on cultural myths, archetypes, and values that consumers identify with. AI can optimize the delivery of these narratives—determining the best platforms, timing, and formats—but it is semiotics that ensures the message has emotional and cultural relevance.

For example, a brand might use AI to identify that younger audiences prefer video content over written content. Semiotics can then be applied to design video narratives that tap into cultural references, emotions, and identity markers that resonate with this demographic—whether it's the symbolism of freedom, creativity, or social justice.

8.5. The Ethical Imperative: Balancing Automation with Human Sensitivity

As AI continues to automate various aspects of marketing, there is a growing concern that marketing strategies may lose their human touch. Automated systems can sometimes produce impersonal, mechanical, or culturally insensitive content when not carefully guided by human oversight. The combination of AI and semiotics offers a solution to this dilemma by maintaining the balance between technological efficiency and human-centered communication.

AI-driven marketing strategies must be ethically grounded, especially when dealing with sensitive cultural, social, or personal issues. Semiotics provides the necessary human sensitivity to ensure that marketing messages are not only effective but also respectful, inclusive, and aligned with ethical standards. As marketers increasingly rely on AI, the semiotic framework will become even more critical in guiding the ethical use of AI technologies, ensuring that consumer engagement remains not only effective but also empathetic and humane.

8.6. The Road Ahead: AI and Semiotics as a Unified Strategy for Consumer Engagement

Looking toward the future, the relationship between AI and semiotics will continue to shape the evolution of consumer engagement. Brands that succeed in this new era will be those that harness the power of AI to understand and predict consumer behavior while using semiotics to craft messages that are culturally resonant, emotionally engaging, and ethically sound.

As AI technology advances, its potential to deliver more personalized and predictive marketing experiences will grow exponentially. However, the true impact of these advancements will depend on how well they are integrated with semiotic principles. This integration will allow marketers to create not just personalized experiences, but meaningful ones—experiences that engage consumers on a deeper level, resonate with their identities, and foster lasting relationships with brands.

8.7. A Holistic Approach to the Future of Marketing

In conclusion, the future of consumer engagement lies at the intersection of AI's technological capabilities and semiotics' cultural insights. By combining data-driven precision with symbolic meaning, brands can navigate the complexities of modern consumer behavior, building relationships that are not only based on convenience and personalization but also on cultural relevance and emotional connection. The challenge for marketers in the coming years will be to strike the right balance between AI-driven efficiency and the human-centered understanding that semiotics offers.

As we move further into the digital age, this holistic approach will become the new standard for successful marketing strategies. AI and semiotics, working in harmony, will redefine how brands engage with consumers, ensuring that marketing remains both technologically advanced and deeply human at its core.

REFERENCES

Arnould, E. J., & Thompson, C. J. (2005). Consumer Culture Theory (CCT): Twenty Years of Research. *The Journal of Consumer Research*, *31*(4), 868–882. DOI: 10.1086/426626

Borghini, S., Diamond, N., Kozinets, R. V., McGrath, M. A., Muniz, A. M.Jr, & Sherry, J. F.Jr. (2009). Why Are Themed Brandstores So Powerful? Retail Brand Ideology at American Girl Place. *Journal of Retailing*, *85*(3), 363–375. DOI: 10.1016/j.jretai.2009.05.003

Cosenza, G. (2020). Semiotic Perspectives on Digital Marketing: Tools for AI Integration in Branding. *Journal of Cultural Marketing*, *8*(3), 101–115.

Greco, G., & Boero, R. (2023). Semiotics and Digital Marketing: Synergies in AI and Consumer Engagement. *Journal of Semiotics and Marketing Research*, *12*(2), 123–139.

Kannan, P. K., & Li, H. A. (2017). Digital Marketing: A Framework, Review, and Research Agenda. *International Journal of Research in Marketing*, *34*(1), 22–45. DOI: 10.1016/j.ijresmar.2016.11.006

Kaplan, A., & Haenlein, M. (2019). Siri, Siri, in My Hand: Who's the Fairest in the Land? On the Interpretations, Illustrations, and Implications of Artificial Intelligence. *Business Horizons*, *62*(1), 15–25. DOI: 10.1016/j.bushor.2018.08.004

Mick, D. G., & Buhl, C. (1992). A Meaning-Based Model of Advertising Experiences. *The Journal of Consumer Research*, *19*(3), 317–338. DOI: 10.1086/209305

Mick, D. G., Burroughs, J. E., Hetzel, P., & Brannen, M. Y. (2004). Pursuing the Meaning of Meaning in the Commercial World: An International Review of Marketing and Consumer Research Founded on Semiotics. *Journal of Business Research*, *57*(6), 760–768.

Oswald, L. R. (2015). Developing Brand Literacy among Consumers. *Journal of Business Research*, *68*(8), 1634–1642.

Pieters, R., & Wedel, M. (2007). Goal Control of Attention to Advertising: The Yarbus Implication. *The Journal of Consumer Research*, *34*(2), 224–233. DOI: 10.1086/519150

Ransbotham, S., Kiron, D., Gerbert, P., & Reeves, M. (2017). Reshaping Business with Artificial Intelligence. *MIT Sloan Management Review*, *59*(1), 1–17.

Rust, R. T., & Huang, M.-H. (2021). The AI Revolution in Marketing. *Journal of the Academy of Marketing Science*, *49*(1), 24–42.

Shankar, V. (2018). How Artificial Intelligence (AI) is Reshaping Retailing. *Journal of Retailing*, *94*(4), 6–11. DOI: 10.1016/S0022-4359(18)30076-9

Van den Broeck, E., & Pauwels, K. (2021). Visual Storytelling and AI in Marketing: Enhancing the Consumer-Brand Relationship. *Journal of Interactive Marketing*, *55*(2), 134–149.

Chapter 5
Semiotics, Advertising, and Classification: Developments of Floch's Models in the Italian Context

Antonio Laurino
https://orcid.org/0009-0006-8544-4525
Università di Bologna - Alma Mater Studiorum, Italy & Università della Repubblica di San Marino, San Marino

ABSTRACT

The square of the axiology of consumption and the square of the advertising philosophies are two milestones within the semiotics of advertising. Developed around the mid-1980s by the French semiotician and consultant Jean-Marie Floch, they crossed the boundaries of applied semiotics and became part of the tools available to marketing researchers. The chapter aims to propose some developments of these two models, illustrating them and conducting both a theoretical review and an empirical investigation, focused on the Italian context. In this way, it will be possible to advance some integrative proposals – the mapping of narrative configurations and the square of declensions of the discursive genres – able to increase the heuristic power of the original typologies.

INTRODUCTION

The work of French semiotician and consultant Jean-Marie Floch is deeply tied to the development of two models that have been particularly successful: the square of the axiology of consumption and the square of advertising philosophies, both proposed in his *Sémiotique, marketing et communication* (1990/1992). These are

DOI: 10.4018/979-8-3693-8024-6.ch005

two semiotic squares[1] that transcended the boundaries of applied semiotics and became tools for marketing researchers. While their use by scholars and practitioners is still widespread, it is legitimate to ask whether and how they need to be (and can be) updated in light of the changes that have occurred in the advertising landscape from the time they were developed to the present.

Around the mid-1980s – the period when Floch fine-tuned his proposal – the advertising industry was enjoying a particularly dynamic moment, which was also the result of a phase of expansion in the world economic system. In the West, there was a steady growth in advertising investment, driven by the medium of television, and also on the rise were the affluence and enjoyment of consumption by ever larger segments of the population. One was, in short, in France as in Italy, in what is generally considered the golden age of advertising. An era, in which, among other things, it was accorded considerable importance from both an economic and a social point of view. Many things have changed since then, not only in terms of new general sociocultural arrangements and coordinates, but also, and perhaps above all, in terms of the relationship between the individual, communication and consumption. The elements of discontinuity are numerous, and among them should be mentioned:

- the radical innovations introduced by the rise of digital technologies and networks that have profoundly transformed the models of content consumption and the forms of interaction among the various actors involved in the flow of communication and production itself: a relationship that is increasingly egalitarian and focused on co-creation;
- the proliferation of approaches and theories that have emphasized the consumers and some of their previously under-explored traits: their emotional and passionate dimension; the relational implications of their behaviors; the centrality of the esthetic dimension in their consumption practices; their experiences of purchasing and consuming products/services (Pine & Gilmore, 2000; Ferraresi & Schmitt, 2006);
- the cyclical waves of protest against big brands and advertising itself (Klein, 2001), which have contributed to creating a new, widespread sensibility towards the world of consumption, its dynamics and its implications.

All of this occurs within the context of a progressive decline in advertising investments since the beginning of the new millennium. These factors have contributed to the shaping of the so-called postmodern consumer:

a disenchanted and secular individual, autonomous and responsible, aware that consumption is now also a form of language through which they communicate, to themselves and others, pieces of their identity, their moods, or the trends of the moment. This consumer has a often playful and non-submissive relationship with commodities, yet is capable of new enchantments that have nothing to do with commodity fetishism. They engage with interest – albeit for uses quite different from those intended by the producers and user manuals – in the market's offerings. (Fabris, 2009, p. 143)

As a target audience, this consumer has challenged all traditional systems of categorization, posing ever-new challenges to creatives and advertising agencies. Given this, one wonders how and to what extent all these socio-economic-cultural aspects can influence advertising production. In this regard, it is important to note that

advertising messages are created on the basis of the languages, values, narrative forms, musical competencies, etc., of their intended recipients. From this perspective, [...] far from being a truly creative activity, the work of the advertising agency appears rather as a skillful job of packaging, reworking and adapting elements and configurations that are already established on the cultural scene. (Ferraro, 1999, pp. 56-57)

In other words, while the power of advertising to propose (and influence) not only consumer choices but also lifestyles and value systems has often been highlighted, what is of interest here is what lies upstream, namely the process of selecting specific features of social reality that the advertiser carries out when designing a campaign: values, tastes and aesthetics are carefully chosen to be as aligned as possible with those of a specific target audience. At this point, the creative's job is to anchor the product, service or brand to the selected characteristics in the most effective way; whether this occurs through systematic research or intuition, what matters is that advertising, in its production and reproduction, crystallizes certain features of a society, an era and a culture, proposing them to those subjects who, more or less consciously, have previously staged them.

Therefore, it is reasonable to hypothesize that the emergence and affirmation of new trends, sensibilities and aesthetics in the social fabric have influenced advertising production. This chapter will explore this hypothesis, focusing on the Italian landscape and referring to previous research conducted in this context (Laurino, 2020a, 2020b).

We will, therefore, start by introducing the two models, focusing on the characteristics that underlie their success; we will then continue by reviewing the main readings and applications proposed by scholars and practitioners; finally, we will proceed to illustrate and analyze a large textual corpus through which some proposals aimed at supplementing and deepening the original categories will be elaborated.

1. THE ORIGINS OF THE CATEGORIES

1.1. The Axiology of Consumption: Genesis and Fortune of a Model

Starting from the analysis of a large number of print ads and TV commercials in the automotive sector, Floch (1990/1992) develops a typology of the possible ways in which the automobile object can be valorized. To do so, he uses and tests some theoretical tools of narrative grammar. In particular, he takes up the distinction between basic values and use values: the former "correspond to the level of fundamental concerns of being and of which the search underlies life and gives meaning to the realization of multiple secondary, more superficial, 'more practical' action programs" (Floch, 1990/1992, p. 172), expression, precisely, of use values.

Floch observes how in advertising texts the relationship linking basic values and use values is not one of implication, but of opposition: in other words, while in a narrative one is accustomed to reasoning in terms of presupposition between actions aimed at achieving a final goal and actions linked to the acquisition of objects or instrumental capacities, in advertising one often witnesses a parallel opposition between ends and means: "it is as if one had to – a priori – choose between the use of a car that meets your needs and the possession, indeed the joy, of a car that corresponds to your tastes or your desires" (Floch, 1990/1992, p. 172).

Having ascertained this, Floch refers to use values a type of valorization that he defines as practical, and to basic values a type that he defines as utopian. Subsequently, by articulating this fundamental semantic opposition on the semiotic square, he identifies two further forms of valorization that he calls critical and ludic, corresponding respectively to the negation of basic values and to the negation of use values. The resulting scheme is the following (Figure 1):

Figure 1. Square of the axiology of consumption drawn up by Floch (1990).

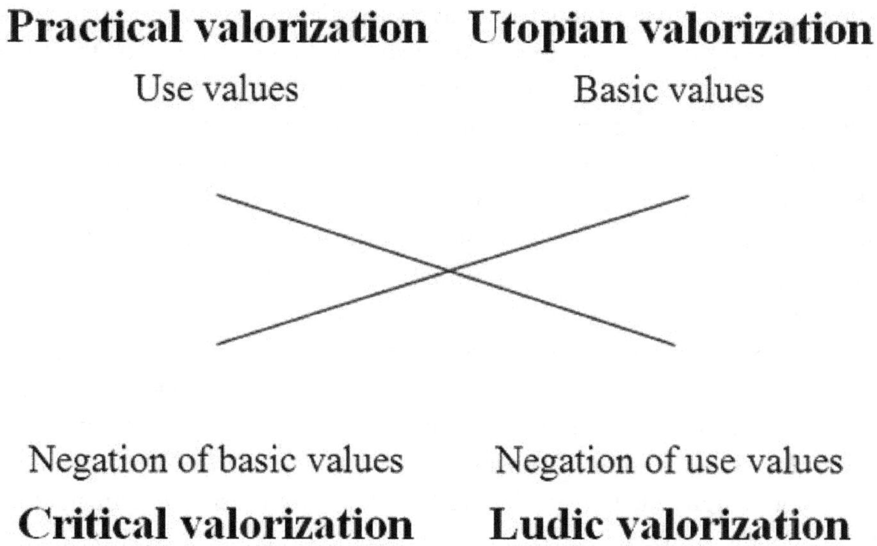

The four forms of valorization that he thus delineates are:

- practical valorization (corresponding to use values), which is based on the magnification of the object's functional characteristics and to which, in the product sector considered, the characteristics of handling, comfort or robustness of the car can be attributed;
- utopian valorization (corresponding to basic values), which invokes existential values, that is, those linked to a real life project, such as the spirit of adventure or the search for freedom;
- ludic valorization (corresponding to the negation of use values), which exalts the product as a source of pleasure, leisure and fun, and which is embodied in the characteristics of luxury or refinement of the object;
- critical valorization (corresponding to the negation of basic values), which involves a kind of cognitive distance in the valorization of the object and translates into the creation of quality/price or cost/benefit ratios.

Taken together, these four ways of valorizing the advertising object form a "system of consumer values" (Floch, 1990/1992, p. 163), or an axiology.

Although it was developed starting from a specific sector, the square of the axiology of consumption has proven to be a useful tool for accounting for the positioning of both products belonging to product categories very far from the automotive segment, and of brands (Floch, 2013; Marrone, 1999, 2007; Ceriani, 2001). The four terms of the square, in fact, must be understood as "semantic reservoirs" (Zannin, 2009, p. 104), empty forms that can be filled with specific values depending on the product, the conjuncture and, ultimately, the individual advertising text.

It is not difficult to imagine, for example, a commercial for a detergent in which the product is magnified for its cleaning power (practical valorization); of a liqueur that becomes an expression of an adventurous lifestyle (utopian valorization); of a laptop whose unparalleled ratio between performance and occupied volume is underlined (critical valorization); of a smartphone for which the pleasure/fun that its use procures is highlighted (ludic valorization).

This is therefore a model that, from its introduction, has presented significant potential for generalization, so much so that, already in the concluding pages of his essay, Floch foresaw the possibility that it could be the basis of "an axiology of everyday life and not just of consumption" (Floch, 1990/1992, p. 190). And, in fact, one could argue the universal validity of these four terms: practical, utopian, critical and ludic would represent four necessary and sufficient ways of looking at the advertised object (and at the world). At the same time, however, this hypothesis has often led to mechanical and trivializing applications of Floch's model, which risk leading to a substantial, yet useless, undifferentiation. It is therefore necessary to look at the literature in the field and search for readings and applications capable of further increasing the operational power of this tool.

1.2. The Advertising Philosophies: At The Roots of a Typology of Discursive Genres

Starting from the analysis of a considerable number of publications dedicated to some well-known advertisers – Jacques Séguéla, David Ogilvy, Philippe Michel and Jean Feldman – Floch identifies and defines four different "conceptions of advertising" (Floch, 1990/1992, p. 232).

The variety of concrete occurrences is ordered starting from a fundamental semantic category that sees a representational function and a constructive function of language opposed. For Floch, this opposition appears particularly relevant since advertisers ask themselves whether the value of the product, for the consumer, pre-exists advertising or whether it is advertising that creates it; semioticians, whether language is the representation of a meaning that is already there or whether it is its construction. Coming from practice on the one hand and theory on the other, advertising and semiotics in fact arrive at the same double issue: the function of language and the "origin" of meaning (Floch, 1990/1992, p. 236).

More specifically, on the one hand, there would be advertising understood as an action aimed at highlighting the properties of an object that is already there and that simply needs to be represented for what it is and what it does. On the other hand, there are those who, ultimately, consider the concrete nature of the product to be irrelevant and emphasize its discursive doing that constructs its meaning and value. Projecting this opposition onto the semiotic square, Floch enriches his typology with two other ways of understanding advertising: an extreme of representativeness, corresponding to the negation of the constructive function, which focuses on the intrinsic, often material characteristics of the product, and an extreme of constructivism, linked to the negation of the representative function, which seems to even set aside the product, seeking first of all to establish a sort of intellectual complicity with its interlocutor.

At this point, the French semiotician adopts labels for each style identified and associates a specific ideologue with it, that is, the most representative exponent of that particular way of understanding and doing advertising. Schematically (Figure 2):

Figure 2. Square of advertising philosophies drawn up by Floch (1990).

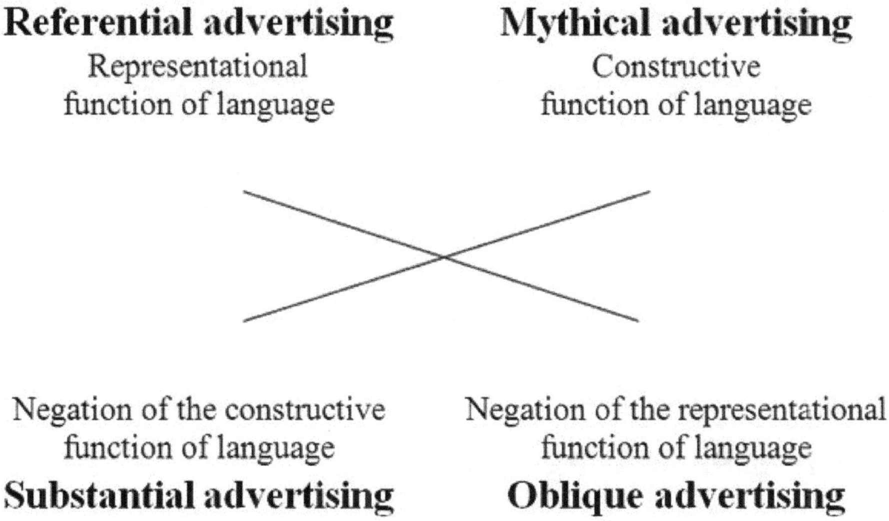

The four advertising philosophies identified by Floch are:

- referential advertising (linked to the representational function of language) which invokes realistic and plausible situations that the reader/viewer can easily recognize as their own. Although the term 'referential' is used, it should not be understood as referring to a presumed actual reality, but rather as a communicative strategy aimed at making it seem real. Its ideologue is Ogilvy;

- oblique advertising (linked to the negation of the representational function of language) which aims to stimulate the viewer's intelligence. It is an advertising that exploits and stimulates lateral thinking, that stages the unexpected and that often makes use of paradox and irony. In it, meaning is not given immediately as in the case of referential advertising, but is to be constructed through a more or less massive intervention of interpretative cooperation (Eco, 1979). Its ideologue is Michel;
- mythical advertising (linked to the constructive function of language) which aims to endow the product with a meaning deeply detached from its function and its context of use. It is a spectacular advertising, full of magical, sometimes mysterious, often fantastic elements, whose objective is to endow the product with a personality, a soul. Its ideologue is Séguéla;
- substantial advertising (linked to the negation of the constructive function of language) which focuses on the details, the most intimate, often material aspects of the product. Its objective is to bring out the essence of things starting from their sensory qualities. Its ideologue is Feldman.

Beyond the reference to the thought and work of individual professionals, when you look closely, with this model Floch classifies advertising genres based on the contract between the enunciator and the enunciatee that each text proposes. In fact, "each conception of the relationship between discourse and reality – each ideology – implies a certain intersubjectivity, a particular relationship between the enunciator and the enunciatee" (Floch, 1990/1992, p. 247). In these terms, this classification could have had, and in fact has had, numerous applications and its operational relevance also in other communicative contexts.

2. THE THEORETICAL REVIEW

2.1. The Axiology of Consumption: Readings and Applications

The heuristic potential of Floch's model has been understood and discussed by numerous authors, not only semioticians, who have proposed re-readings and applications of it, since

> *it is universally recognized that it is among the primary tasks of advertising to valorize a product, a service or a brand. Neither products (or services, or brands) on the one hand, nor values on the other hand, are constructed in the*

context of advertising; what is done in this context is only an act of connection between entities belonging to two different "universes": the universe of products on the one hand and that of meanings, values, culturally relevant ideas on the other. (Ferraro, 1999, p. 26)

Floch himself (1995/1997), a few years after its elaboration, intervened again on the model by renaming the ludic valorization as ludic-aesthetic, thus anticipating the eventual magnification of the object for its aesthetic characteristics and/or its design. While such an operation remedied a rather evident gap in the original model, on the other hand, it undermined its formal purity, since the positions articulated on the square became five. As Maria Pia Pozzato notes (2001), in fact, the ludic and the aesthetic are united by being both expressions of the negation of use values (and therefore of practical valorization) but still maintain significant differences that not only make their juxtaposition rather problematic, but do not exclude that in the same text they may even be opposed.

Gianfranco Marrone (2001) highlights a further problematic aspect of Floch's square. The latter, in fact, "overlaps and ends up flattening two different levels of relevance of the narrative structure: that of deep values [...] and that of narrative programs" (Marrone, 2001, p. 187). Thus, within the ludic pole, we find commercials in which we see the subject having fun using the object, but also advertisements in which the focus of the narrative is on the object valued for its aesthetic qualities. Within each category, therefore, it would be possible to find three different narrative perspectives: one linked to the subject, one to the object and one focused on the relationship between the two. Schematically (Figure 3):

Figure 3. Restatement of the axiology of consumption by Marrone (2001).

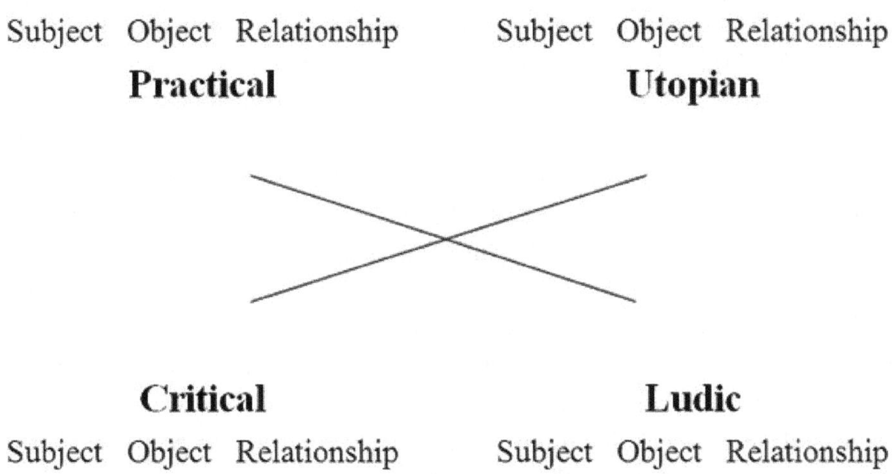

On an operational level, this integration has the merit of accounting more fully for the narrative richness of advertising texts, further refining the analytical potential of the model.

Of a completely different nature are the observations of Ugo Volli (2003), according to whom the upper vertices of the square (practical and utopian) would concern values that can be considered inherent to the object itself, while the lower ones (critical and ludic) would involve dimensions attributed to the object by advertising communication. Furthermore, the vertices on the right would articulate immaterial, intangible qualities, while those on the left would have essentially concrete and tangible qualities. Such an interpretation, however,

> *instead of insisting on formal and narrative positions (the subject's relationship with the object) seems to return to somewhat referentialist explanations that distinguish based on the very substance of values: material vs. immaterial, functional vs. emotional on the horizontal axis; values of the object itself, intrinsic, vs. values provided by advertising communication, constructed by secondary discourses, on the vertical axis. (Zannin, 2009, p. 107)*

Furthermore, there is nothing to prevent us from considering aesthetic values (and to some extent also critical ones) as inherent to the object itself and not exclusively provided by communication.

Cinzia Bianchi (2005), for her part, emphasizes a strength of Floch's model: the semiotic square, in fact, in addition to allowing a paradigmatic, or static, organization of the various concepts, also allows for a syntagmatic reading, that is, a dynamic one, capable of accounting for the evolutions of positioning of a single product/service or brand over time. Through the logical operations of negation (passage from term a to its contradictory non-a) and affirmation (passage from non-a to its complementary b) it is possible to trace a "butterfly wings" path on the square and therefore, within certain limits, predict towards which pole a product or brand could (and should) tend that is seeking a more distinctive positioning compared to its competitors. Beyond this, however, in her re-reading of Floch, Bianchi focuses on the possibility of tracking value transformations within a single advertising text, in particular a commercial. If on the one hand this reading risks appearing too restrictive, on the other it calls into question a situation that is easily found in the analysis phase: the co-presence of multiple forms of valorization within a single advertisement or commercial. It is worth noting that in all these cases, given the exclusive nature and, from this point of view, excessively rigid nature of the semiotic square, it is customary to reason in terms of dominant valorizations, polarizing the text around a single vertex of the square.

A possible solution to this limit is provided by Andrea Semprini (1992/1993), who takes up the four terms of the Floch square (practical, utopian, critical, ludic), but arranges them in a way as to form a mapping, "a logical system that opposes, crossing them, two different categories" (Semprini, 1992/1993, p. 121): on the vertical axis the two contrary terms practical/utopian are placed, while on the horizontal one the two subcontrary terms critical/ludic which thus go to specify the semantic areas defined by the first two. In this way, the author aims to produce a conceptual representation more familiar to marketing professionals; a representation that, unlike the semiotic square, allows us to capture overlaps and nuances of meaning by mixing the original categories two by two. Furthermore, the intersection of the four dimensions gives rise to quadrants – called Mission, Information, Euphoria and Project – within which it is possible to proceed with the positioning of products and brands (Figure 4).

Figure 4. Semiotic mapping of consumption values proposed by Semprini (1992).

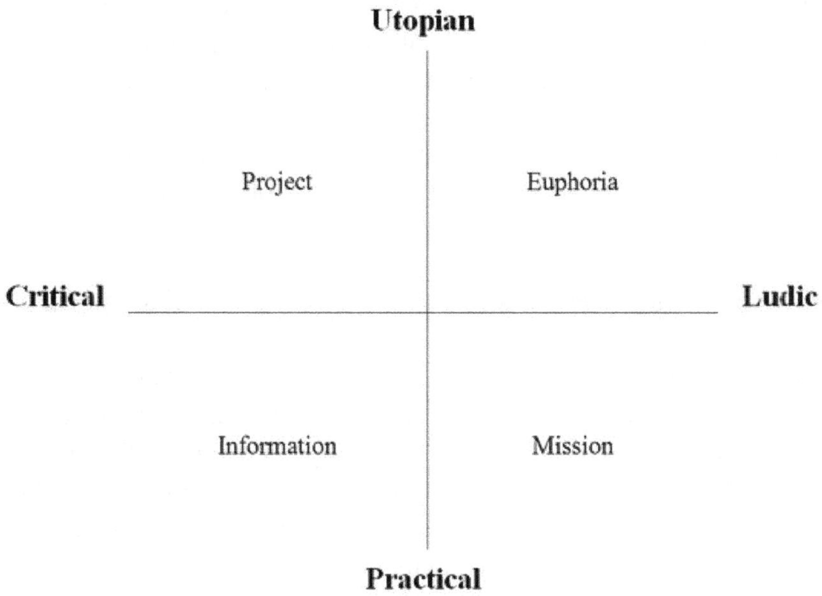

Despite possessing several operational advantages, on a theoretical level Semprini's proposal has been the subject of various criticisms, including those raised by Giulia Ceriani (2001), who contests this schematization for wanting to descend from a semiotic square and, specifically, for using terminology properly linked to a well-defined square, namely that of the axiology of consumption. In the latter, the two subcontrary poles, critical and ludic, are defined by negation with respect to the respective contraries, utopian and practical. If they are not obtained by negation – but are independent and constitute another category – these two terms take on a different meaning, for which it would be correct to use another terminology capable of clearly stating the difference between the two uses.

Secondly, it is not clear how these two subcontraries can represent the qualifications and specifications of terms of which they are precisely the negation and contradiction.

Finally, the third problem, and probably the most serious, is that of articulating an "absolute" schematization that is not dependent on a given context. One can never obtain an absolute square, since the category it opens up is always derived from an analyzed text of which the fundamental isotopy has been found. Thus, the four terms related to values – already generic in Floch's square but at least interdefined – are here so generic as to become unfortunately useless (Ceriani, 2001, pp. 115-116).

For these reasons, the mapping of consumption values, although openly inspired by Floch's axiology, seems to actually retain only the terminological labels, presenting itself as something profoundly different from it. On the other hand, Semprini's proposal brings to light the debated issue of whether or not to abandon the semiotic square model: on the one hand, being an a priori square, one wonders how well it can account for a complex and changing reality such as advertising; on the other hand, its logical coherence is questioned, since the four valorizations would represent semantic areas too broad to be in a relationship of contrariety, contradiction and implication.

2.2. The Advertising Philosophies: Readings and Applications

A first application of Floch's square is that of Ventura (2005), who uses it to outline four different product packaging strategies; Mangano (2008), on the other hand, uses it to identify four different types of design; Marrone (2007), for his part, proposes a reworking of it, further expanding its heuristic scope and making it a useful tool for classifying the different genres of brand discourse. His reformulation develops the Flochian categories by highlighting in each of them "the degree of subjectification and objectification present in the relationship between utterance and enunciation [...] and the discursive dimension – pragmatic, passionate, cognitive or aesthetic – most solicited in the communicative act" (Marrone, 2007, pp. 203-204). In this way, he arrives at identifying four genres of brand discourse (Figure 5):

Figure 5. Square of brand discourse genres proposed by Marrone (2007).

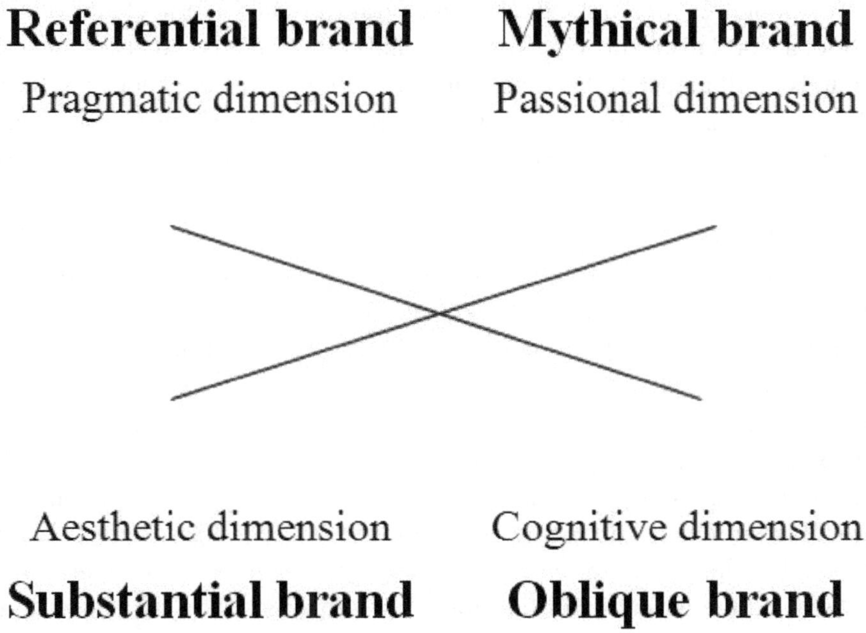

Following Marrone (2007, pp. 204-205):

The referential brand discourse tends to produce effects of objectivity, so as to bring out a universe made up of concrete things, effective practices, field tests and action plans. The values at stake in this type of brand will therefore be more pragmatic; and the way of life it summons will be directed towards concreteness, the position and solution of daily problems, the ability to deal with the situations that life presents us day by day. The discourse of a mythical brand, on the other hand, tends to produce an effect of subjectivity, so as to bring out a whole intense universe of intimate affections and proclaimed feelings, in a very broad passionate arc that ranges from family and love relationships to great collective enthusiasms for media and political myths, from the indeterminate 'I-don't-know-what' minimalist to the obsessive adherence to strong and totalizing ideologies. Hence a passionate and exciting way of life, programmatically detached from the prosaic logic of everyday life and directed instead towards dreams and daydreams, 'the whim', the poetic journey towards the exotic, the other, the unknown. The substantial brand negates all this, whose experiences are not at all dreamlike or imaginary but, conversely, physical, sensory, corporeal. This type of brand contradicts any form of individual or collective subjectivity to take refuge in the world of the prepersonal, fragmentary, partial body, where eroticism and sexuality are generally understood as the most banal form of somatic experience. What dominates is then the vast, entire range of sensory experiences, which stands as an ancestral and auroral form of knowledge of the world; a world made up of consistencies and colors, smells and tastes, materials and sounds of all kinds. To bring into play the mind and its ingenious intellectual capacities is instead the oblique brand, which proposes a world that is the absolute negation of all practicality and concreteness, pure thought that delights in its own intelligence, that enjoys logical and mathematizing wit, the enigma to be solved, the mystery to be unraveled, the investigation to be carried out. It is the realm of engineers and technicians, of those who enjoy bending practical life to their cerebral needs, stubbornly trying to improve it in a sense that is logically a priori, thus coming close to the very thin ridge that connects pure logic to imaginative delirium, the mathematician to the poet and the dreamer.

Another model that, in a way, draws inspiration from the square of advertising philosophies is the typology of discursive regimes proposed by Ferraro (1999). Often placed in continuity with Floch's square of the axiology of consumption and, in particular, with its reworking by Semprini (1992/1993), this scheme is halfway between a description of the values at stake in a communication (commercial and otherwise) and the definition of the strategies with which they are staged. In this case, the chosen modeling is that of mapping: through the intersection of the objective/subjective and relative/absolute categories, the author defines four quadrants characterized by certain values and discursive forms, to which it is possible to refer to four types of advertising (Figure 6).

Figure 6. Typology of discursive regimes proposed by Ferraro (1999).

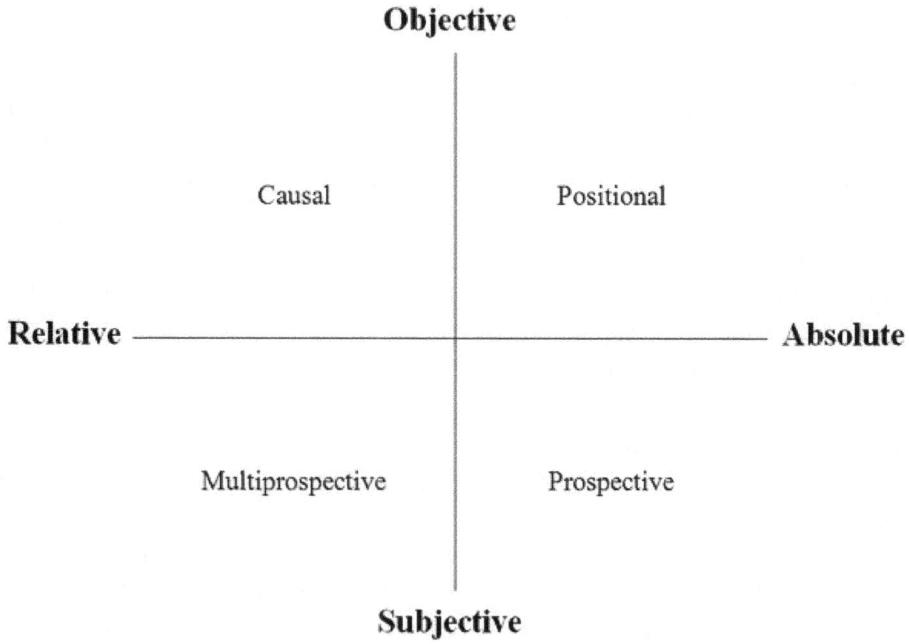

- In the positional regime, values are based on characteristics that are actually possessed and on stable and evident identities. Consequently, the narrative coincides with a discovery and an approach to the essence of things. In this case, "advertising often takes on the modes of definition, of affirming a precise correspondence between an object and an idea" (Ferraro, 1999, p. 66).
- In the causal regime, "the value of things derives from their interaction, and therefore represents a variable, continuously questioned. It is therefore, quite evidently, not absolute but relative values" (Ferraro, 1999, p. 67). Advertisements that are situated in this area often stage solutions and brilliant ways of addressing complex problems.
- The prospective regime "corresponds in some way to the declaration of a certain specific worldview" (Ferraro, 1999, p. 69). And, on the other hand, in advertising, the absolute subjectivity of such a worldview is often associated with the absolute value of the product.
- The multiprospective regime "introduces a complex vision of the relativity of values and the centrality of the component of interaction in all human affairs" (Ferraro, 1999, p. 71). Often, in advertising, this regime is concretized in the

staging of seduction processes, considered as the emblem of human intersubjective modalities.

Despite the internal coherence of this model, Zannin (2009) has pointed out that it ends up overlapping the level of values and that of discursive regimes: an operation that appears risky and that can be misleading. It is necessary to clear the field of possible misunderstandings regarding the relationship between the square of the axiology of consumption and that of advertising philosophies. The proximity of the exposition, the terminological closeness and, last but not least, the diffusion of the models among non-semioticians have meant that the terms of the two squares have often been considered as interchangeable one by one. In other words, it has been erroneously hypothesized that a practical valorization could be conveyed mainly, if not exclusively, through a referential communicative style, a utopian valorization through a mythical advertisement and so on. On closer inspection, however, this reading does not hold: the two models, in fact, must be considered completely independent of each other since, referring to the generative path of meaning (Greimas & Courtés, 1979/2007), they articulate dimensions belonging to two different levels.

> *The model of the axiology of consumption concerns the semio-narrative level, the level of values within the utterance. It is about the construction of the relationship between subject and object: what has value for whom. Conversely, the square of advertising philosophies concerns the level of enunciation and manifestation of the narrative within the discourse and is independent of the type of values: theoretically it is possible to express the same value (and the same type of values) both in a referential, mythical, oblique or substantial way, that is according to any of the four advertising ideologies. (Zannin, 2009, p. 103)*

We are therefore dealing with two distinct tools, which account for profoundly different aspects of an advertising text: "the first concerns the narrative utterance while the second concerns the enunciative strategies" (Marrone, 2007, p. 195). In other words, with the model of the axiology of consumption we refer to what can be communicated, while with the square of advertising philosophies to how it is possible to do so. Certainly, there may be a correlation between some forms of valorization and certain discursive genres, insofar as, for example, in a particular sector, a practical valorization may be conveyed more frequently by a referential advertising. However, in principle, these are independent tools that have, among other things, the advantage of being able to be used synergistically, thus accounting in a more complete way for a communication strategy or a positioning.

Finally, a further elaboration that follows in the footsteps of Floch's square of advertising philosophies is the mapping of discursive regimes proposed by Zannin (2009): taking up Ferraro's (1999) category of Objective vs. Subjective and intersecting it with the opposition Emotional vs. Cognitive, widely and sensibly adopted in advertising, the author outlines a scheme capable of accounting for and translating different contributions elaborated by scholars who have variously dealt with advertising. According to Zannin, in fact, Floch's proposal needs to be integrated and further systematized because

> *it seems to us that referential, mythical, oblique and substantial are necessary operational terms, not coincidentally derived from a logical opening of a category, which therefore safeguards a single semantic criterion for defining the typology. And yet, they do not seem to us to be totally sufficient, insofar as [...] a review of the literature shows that within what can be defined as referential it is necessary to distinguish [...] on the one hand a properly referential with a dominant narrative and on the other a regime by no means residual based on a dominant argumentative, which not coincidentally seems to adhere perfectly to what Ferraro defines as causal. (Zannin, 2009, p. 265)*

Therefore, the model he arrives at, in which Floch's categories (also) find a place, is the following (Figure 7):

Figure 7. Mapping of discursive regimes elaborated by Zannin (2009).

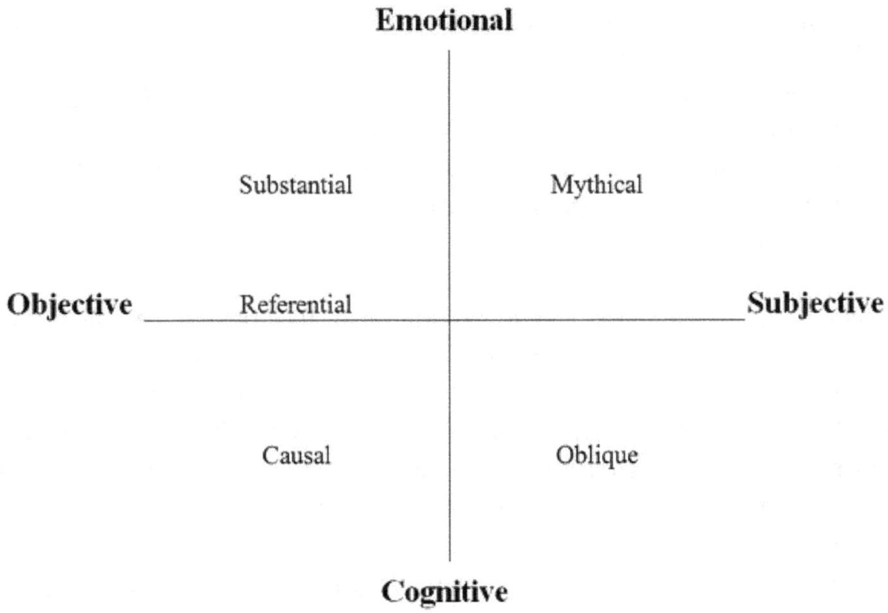

3. THE EMPIRICAL INVESTIGATION

3.1. The Definition of the Corpus

How can we put to the test what has had a strong ambition of generality from the very beginning? Which and how many texts should be taken into consideration, from which product category and within what time interval? In short, the delicate but crucial question of corpus construction emerges strongly. If semiotic tools have often proven to work excellently on "concrete" and well-defined objects (spots, posters, print ads, etc.) and if the observations that derive from them can aspire to a certain degree of generalization, this is due, even before the researcher's abilities, to the skill with which he or she identifies his or her horizon of action. Not just any collection of texts can be considered a corpus, and its definition is an operation that hides numerous pitfalls, capable of conditioning the outcome of the analysis. The main risks are poor representativeness, poor observability and constructivism. To avoid them, or at least reduce their incidence, it is necessary

- to consider a quantity of objects that is manageable and adequate to the scarce resources of the analyst, but at the same time is representative of the universe that one wants to account for;
- that the texts selected on paper are then in concrete terms actually retrievable to be collected and observed by the analyst;
- to ensure that the researcher's initial hypotheses do not influence him or her to the point of putting together a corpus aimed essentially at finding what he or she is looking for.

A good corpus, therefore, should be significant in terms of the quantity and quality of the texts, even if it will not be (and can never be) complete. At the same time, it is essential – but not trivial – that it is well-defined and not open-ended. Last but not least, it must be adequate to the object of analysis. Given the centrality of this operation, and bearing these principles in mind, we will now dwell on the construction of the corpus and will expose in detail the choices that led to its definition.

The universe of commercial communication is one of the most prolific and changing discursive domains in our society. The very high density of messages goes hand in hand with their rapid obsolescence, to which corresponds a considerable speed of the production process. Isolating, in this incessant flow, a defined, coherent and somehow cohesive set is not simple. It is necessary to make choices that are, to a certain extent, arbitrary but as well-argued and consistent as possible with the research objective. The first step, if one wants it to be immediate – but by no means obvious, given the transversality of the model's application – was to choose a single product category to focus on. For a number of reasons, the automotive sector was chosen.

Firstly, there are philological reasons. As mentioned, Floch's typology of forms of valorization was born precisely from the analysis of print and TV campaigns in the automotive sector, carried out in France between the early and mid-1980s. It seemed particularly relevant to return to observing the same sector to possibly identify differences, evolutions and trends.

Secondly, there are strategic reasons: the major automotive groups, in fact, are consistently among the largest advertising investors and it is reasonable to assume that a substantial and relatively constant advertising investment by companies corresponds to a significant search for distinctive concepts and innovative campaigns by agencies and creatives.

On the other hand, even by restricting the field of investigation to the automotive sector, numerous questions remain open. The first: on which type/s of text to focus attention? Spots, print ads, posters, banners, viral? Or a combination of these? Needs for economy and observability have made it necessary to make a further selection towards a specific form: the spot; by virtue of considerations of both a theoretical and practical nature.

Firstly, the advertising audiovisual format allows, by its very nature, greater semantic richness and narrative expansion compared to the still image; which could affect the forms of valorization that advertisers resort to.

Secondly, some empirical observations on the dynamics of creating and planning advertising campaigns indicate that where the creation and dissemination of a commercial is planned, there will probably also be a print or poster campaign. While, for obvious budget reasons, the same degree of correlation does not hold true in reverse. This calls into question both the principle of coherence and that of representativeness of the corpus: the choice of considering a single type of text, in fact, guarantees greater uniformity during the analysis phase, but can also raise objections regarding the relevance, within the advertising landscape, of the chosen form. One might ask, for example, whether it is correct and appropriate to omit the innovative and more engaging forms linked to the Internet. In this regard, Marco Lombardi (2007) observes that, although we are in the midst of the post-spot era, in which the dynamics and interaction models of the network are now indispensable for marketing, there is still a need for

> *a big, powerful communication idea [...] and the simplest way to produce it is to have a TV commercial at the center of the off and online multimedia plan. [...] Its role [of the commercial] will be less important, some of the media modalities alternative to generalist TV will be the most relevant to engage the person, but the big idea must be synthesized at the center to ensure a cohesive whole. And the best synthesis, the clearest and the strongest, remains the one that arises*

from the iron discipline of the very short time on video: the thirty-second TV commercial. (Lombardi, 2007, pp. 29-30)

At the same time, if we understand the commercial as an audiovisual advertising form, we immediately realize how reductive it is to reduce it to the television medium alone and its specific type of consumption: we regularly come across video advertisements, both on the web – think of campaigns (which aspire to become) viral, focused precisely on the creation of audiovisual products, or the practice, widespread on information portals and platforms with a high number of accesses, of inserting advertisements before their content – as well as in outdoor spaces, such as airports, train stations and subway stops.

For these reasons, it seemed possible and profitable to focus on audiovisual advertising texts.

On the other hand, aware of the need to guarantee a certain degree of variety within the corpus, no discrimination was made between commercials aired on national generalist or thematic, terrestrial or satellite, free-to-air or pay-per-view channels. Furthermore, no selections were made based on industry classifications, target or positioning. All this because it can be hypothesized that certain forms of valorization are more frequently adopted in specific segments. Therefore, it would have been risky to make a priori differentiations of this kind, at the risk of drastically reducing the representativeness of the corpus.

Finally, it was necessary to define a sufficiently large time interval to allow for the collection of a significant but manageable number of elements. A two-year period was therefore considered, from July 1, 2011 to June 30, 2013.

Once the principles through which the elements of the corpus were identified were chosen and duly argued, the knot of their actual retrievability and observability remained to be untied. This is a crucial point in any extensive investigation and is also the one that most often conditions its success. In this case, it was possible to use a tool that guaranteed a high level of systematicity in the collection of spots: the Creative Dynamix platform[2]. This was a web service offered by the Nielsen Media Research institute that allowed you to track the commercial disseminated on the main media and to view them online after their launch.

By setting the different parameters based on the reflections made so far and further refining the initial search results, we finally arrived at the definition of a well-defined and easily observable corpus. Initially, we worked on the search variables that concerned:

- the product category (automotive);
- the different product category classifications identified by the AdEx System (institutional campaigns, off-road, luxury, upper-medium, lower-medium, minivan, multi-segment, sports, premium, supermini, mini, microcars);

- the type of content (spot);
- the distribution channels (TV);
- the time frame (2 years).

In this way, the items returned by the system amounted to 1915. Despite the high degree of customization, however, it was realized that further filtering was necessary. For the purposes of the research, in fact, the following appeared to be of little relevance and therefore negligible:

- calls to listen and quotes;
- diaries;
- different versions of the same spot that differed only in the closing frames (e.g., invitations to test drive the car at dealerships in a certain period or to take advantage of promotions valid for a certain period);
- the same spots aired on multiple television networks and therefore considered by the system as different elements;
- the same spots broadcast at different times of the year and therefore classified by the system as different commercials;
- tele-promotions inserted within television programs;
- spots that differed due to small differences in dubbing;
- non-Italian language versions of the same spot.

Finally, where multiple versions of different lengths of the same spot were present (15, 20, 30, 45 or 60 seconds), it was decided to consider the most widespread format, both within the corpus and in the media system: that of 30 seconds. This was also a somewhat arbitrary choice, but one aimed at increasing the degree of uniformity of the analysis. In light of this further selection, the corpus was reduced to 490 spots from 36 different car brands: Alfa Romeo, Audi, Bmw, Chevrolet, Citroen, Dacia, Dr, Fiat, Ford, Honda, Hyundai, Infiniti, Jaguar, Jeep, Kia, Lancia, Land Rover, Lexus, Mahindra, Mazda, Mercedes, Mini, Mitsubishi, Nissan, Opel, Peugeot, Porsche, Renault, Seat, Skoda, Smart, Subaru, Suzuki, Toyota, Volkswagen, Volvo. At this point, bearing in mind the findings of the theoretical excursus and with an adequate, defined and observable corpus, it was possible to move on to the analysis.

3.2. The Axiology of Consumption: Confirmations and Developments

Delving into the analysis of the commercials, it soon became evident that the values invested in the car object can all be traced back to one of the forms originally identified and illustrated by Floch. In other words, the characteristics and attributes that make the product desirable are varied and numerous, but the rationalities underlying them and the semantic areas they call into play are those described by the French semiotician. As proof of this, for each form of valorization, concrete occurrences emerged during the analysis and it was chosen to describe in detail a particularly significant spot. The selected text is a prototype (Rosch & Lloyd, 1978), namely the best representative and the clearest case of belonging to the category. It was chosen based on the possession of the greatest number of salient features with respect to the definitions of each form of valorization given previously and served as a model on the basis of which to establish, by gradual similarity, the belonging or not of other texts to the category.

3.2.1. Practical Valorization

Concrete attributes present in the corpus: technical features, optional extras, functional solutions, performance.

Most representative text: Citroen C3 commercial.

Description: the commercial focuses on a quirky individual driving an old utility car, but he simulates with gestures and voice a whole series of latest-generation features and accessories that make the use of the car more efficient and comfortable (from the anti-theft device to electric windows, from the seatbelt warning to the navigator, from air conditioning to parking sensors). In conclusion, the advertised car appears, naturally fully equipped.

3.2.2. Utopian Valorization

Concrete attributes present in the corpus: spirit of adventure, freedom, elitism, nonconformism, environmental sensitivity.

Most representative text: Alfa Romeo Mito commercial.

Description: the commercial features numerous invitations that adults, presumably parents and grandparents, address to a young girl. These are advice to do things that can be considered transgressive and nonconformist (getting a tattoo, changing hair color, wearing a shorter skirt, leaving everything and leaving, buying a "bad" car). At the end of the video, the car appears, and the voice-over invites you to "live rock".

3.2.3. Critical Valorization

Concrete attributes present in the corpus: convenience and value for money, performance/consumption, comfort/size.

Most representative text: Hyundai i20 commercial.

Description: the commercial opens by listing the increasing costs associated with buying, managing and maintaining a car: fuel, insurance, tolls. The car is then presented, highlighting its many advantages in terms of cost/benefit: starting with standard options (climate control, ESP, multimedia equipment) at a particularly advantageous price, to the excellent ratio between performance and consumption, passing through the possibility of taking advantage of a subsidized loan.

3.2.4. Ludic Valorization

Concrete attributes present in the corpus: fun, leisure, driving pleasure.

Most representative text: Renault Scenic X-Mod commercial.

Description: a young couple takes their nephew for a drive in their car. They announce to the boy that they will go to some places of amusement (the amusement park, the park, the sea), but once they reach the vicinity of each of these, they do not stop: they continue to speed with their car, preferring the pleasure of driving to any other source of amusement. The whole thing ignoring the desires and requests of the boy.

While the overall validity of Floch's categories has been confirmed, some problematic aspects have emerged during the analysis. A first discontinuity is linked to the importance of aesthetic valorization: in a considerable number of cases, the automobile is valued exclusively for its aesthetic qualities or, conversely, for the refined taste of the subjects who own and use it. This data, in itself, may seem of little relevance and essentially linked to the specific product category under examination: the car market, where look and line have considerable importance and where it is common practice to resort to prestigious design firms, not only for high-end cars. Moreover, this aspect can be significant insofar as in the original formulation the aesthetic dimension did not have such relevance as to deserve a place within the Flochian scheme. Only to be subsequently incorporated in a rather problematic way into the ludic one.

This is why, in addition to the previous focuses, dedicated to the four original forms of valorization, another must be added, reserved for the aesthetic one, which has now acquired full relevance.

3.2.5. Aesthetic Valorization

Concrete attributes present in the corpus: beauty, charm, exterior appearance, interior design.

Most representative text: BMW Series 6 Coupé commercial.

Description: the commercial, without a voice-over, shows a succession of details of various external parts of the car (the front, the side, the rear lights), interspersed with rapid shots of a nearly complete solar eclipse. As the soundtrack builds, the commercial culminates in a scene where the car speeds down a deserted road in the light of the eclipse, and the words "A spectacle of rare beauty" appear superimposed.

After acknowledging the relevance acquired by aesthetic valorization, an overall look at the corpus was taken, highlighting how the presence of texts in which there is a coexistence of multiple forms of valorization is significant. In most cases, values are used that can be traced back to two distinct dimensions, but it happens to come across spots in which the semantic areas solicited are even three. An exemplary case is the Kia Carens commercial, which opens with an adult man accompanying his mother to her new car, where his wife and children are also present. Once on board, the elderly woman begins to underline some technical characteristics such as the spaciousness of the interior and the size of the sunroof, referring at the same time to what these characteristics can allow from a strictly practical point of view. However, after each of her statements, a playful use of the car is shown, such as celebrating with the whole team after a five-a-side football victory, playing with spraying water from the open sunroof or making love in the moonlight. Finally, the mother is pleased that her son has finally settled down and the commercial ends with the phrase "Growing up can be fun", thus alluding to an existential maturity – apparently – reached and thus giving the commercial a strong utopian nuance.

Generally, we almost always encounter texts where various valorization strategies coexist in a form that, following Lévi-Strauss (1958/1990), can be defined as mythical: the product is presented as a solution that manages to reconcile multiple dimensions that are normally perceived as opposites in common sense. This can concern both dimensions belonging to distinct forms of valorization – as in the case of a Lancia Musa commercial where we witness one of the typical reconciliations of advertising communication, that between comfort/economy (practical-critical values) and luxury/refinement (aesthetic values) – and values that are located within a single one of them – in the case of the Kia Carens commercial, examined previously, we move within the utopian pole, where we find the taking on of responsibilities of starting a family and at the same time maintaining a lifestyle marked by lightheartedness and fun.

In other cases, however, the opposition is not so clear and we are rather in the presence of a dominant valorization to which values are added that call into question another or two other forms of valorization. If the possible recourse to more than one form of valorization within a single text was a possibility foreseen by Floch himself, in the analyzed texts this occurrence appears qualitatively relevant, insofar as part of the distinctiveness of a brand's proposal seems to be entrusted precisely to these nuances of meaning, to a certain continuum of significations.

While the pertinence and relevance of what has been said so far remain unchanged, it is evident that many aspects of the protean textual reality, equally crucial for a greater systematization of the individual semantic areas, remain elusive. Many of these aspects can be attributed to narrative configurations. Indeed, there is no doubt that ads often characterized by the same form of valorization differ radically in the scripts they stage. The latter, however, are difficult to grasp, given their enormous variety, unless a detailed analysis of individual texts is carried out. It would therefore be necessary to develop tools capable of focusing on some of these dimensions and allowing this to be done in an effective and efficient manner, that is, with a high degree of differentiation and flexibility. To this end, we believe it is appropriate to start again from some interesting observations by Marrone (2001), partly already highlighted previously, but on which it is worth reflecting more extensively. According to the semiotician:

> *Floch's model of the axiology of consumption overlays and ends up flattening two different levels of relevance in the narrative structure: that of deep values (articulated, precisely, by the semiotic square) and that of narrative programs (which involve the presence of actants such as the Subject and the Object). (Marrone, 2001, p. 187)*

As mentioned, the author starts from these observations to highlight how it is possible to find, within texts that use a specific form of valorization, different narrative perspectives: one that focuses on the Subject, one on the Object and one on their relationship. Putting aside the last case for a moment, the suggestion seems interesting and useful for analytical purposes. Of course, it must be emphasized that, as a rule, the dimensions of the Object and the Subject, that are those of the product and the consumer, are co-present within a text. Therefore, it is very difficult to insert a text discreetly into one of the two classes. It seems much more sensible to reason in terms of a tendency. In other words, in a commercial – for example – the same valorization can be dynamized through a narrative program focused more on the Subject or on the Object, which in fact allows us to account for further and strategic nuances of meaning, but also confronts us with the problem of how to arrive at an effective and non-arbitrary categorization.

A second, equally interesting point is provided a few pages later: focusing on the utopian pole, the author highlights how the identity dynamics that characterize this semantic field can be traced not only to a doing of the Subject, as highlighted by Floch (1995/1997, pp. 32-59) in his analysis of a print advertisement for the Waterman fountain pen, but also to a being, as emerged during an analysis conducted by Marrone himself (2001, pp. 196-214) on another advertisement of the same campaign.

If the author uses this opposition to highlight the importance of the passionate dimension within advertising texts (a dimension that accompanies and often surpasses the more pragmatic one), this opposition could also be useful in a broader sense: during the analysis process, in fact, we have found it within all the other semantic areas and moreover not only in relation to the Subject. Let's focus on practical valorization and refer to two commercials: in one the car is presented as spacious and comfortable and in the other it is valued as powerful and suitable for tackling different terrains in the most diverse weather conditions. Although in both cases within the same valorization, it is evident that there is a subtle difference between the two texts: in the first, the focus is on characteristics that concern the being of the Object, while in the second its doing is called into question. Let's try to expand our reasoning by completely changing the product category and looking for a moment at the mineral water market: reflecting on it, it is very likely that we will think of commercials for low-sodium water and one that instead stimulates diuresis, finding once again the aforementioned opposition. But – one might say – it is not always easy (and perhaps even possible) to separate the being of the Object from its doing. On the other hand in an advertising text one can choose to present and enhance one or the other dimension of the product. Ultimately, these are precise textual strategies that can give rise to specific effects of meaning. Effects that it can be useful to keep track of.

These two interesting observations, as originally presented, seem disconnected and, above all, difficult to use in the analysis phase. We have therefore tried to make them more operational, and the most useful and heuristically interesting way to make them interact seemed to be to make them semantic axes within a mapping. In other words, a diagram was created composed of the intersection of two axes: that of Object vs. Subject and that of Being vs. Doing (Figure 8). In this way, we arrived at the definition of four quadrants capable of accounting with the right flexibility for the perspectives and narrative dimensions that one can choose to magnify within each semantic area.

Figure 8. Mapping of narrative configurations.

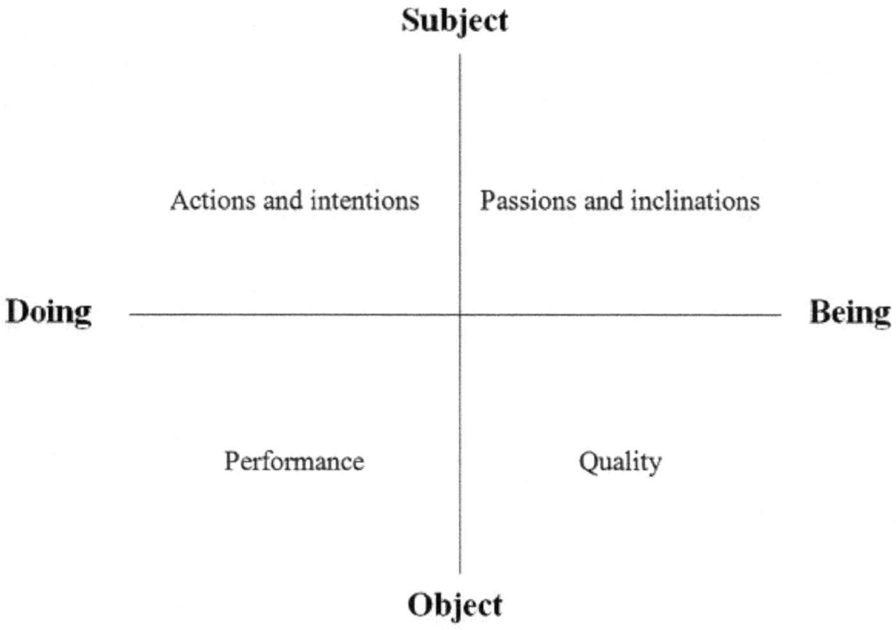

Regarding this schema, it should be said that:

- The ultimate goal of this operation is to introduce a certain degree of differentiation where there is an almost indistinct whole. In this sense, the choice of mapping as a model seemed to us the most suitable: it takes into account the substantial continuum existing between the dimensions of being and doing, on the one hand, and the frequent narrative co-presence of the Subject and the Object, on the other. It goes without saying that the nuances of meaning present within the texts become graspable only and exclusively in relative terms, through an almost infinite series of intermediate positions.
- Even where one would expect certain specific dimensions to be stimulated more (as in the case of the being and doing of the Subject within commercials that resort to a utopian valorization), in fact, the use of this tool has allowed us to capture some "deviant" and therefore particularly interesting texts: commercials that focus on dimensions alternative to those more frequently staged.
- The labels chosen for each quadrant suggest very general aspects. To avoid them being excessively generic, we will try to define them in more detail. First of all, the term "Passions" does not refer to hobbies, but to all those

elements that refer to the emotional dimension and the state of mind of the subject, to which are added “Inclinations”, understood as their character attributes. Similarly, “Actions” are associated with “Intentions”, to be understood as an expression of a wanting-to-do and of a being-able-to-do not put into action by the subject within the text, but simply stated. As for the terms “Performance” and “Quality”, it should be emphasized that they can take on slightly different shades of meaning depending on the semantic area in which they are found.

To further clarify all these aspects, we propose an application, focusing on the critical area. In the current economic situation, characterized by deep uncertainty and limited purchasing power, there is a widespread and transversal recourse to rational consumption values linked to a logic of calculation. And the automotive sector does not seem to be exempt from this trend. In the corpus under analysis, in fact, the critical area, closely linked to the value of convenience, is very crowded. The phenomenon appears even more interesting because it does not only concern commercials for city cars or low-end cars, but also involves brands and models traditionally foreign to such rationality, as in the case of Mercedes C-Class commercials. Given this, there is a need for additional categories that can help us capture the differences between the individual commercials that resort to this form of valorization. For these reasons, it can be particularly useful – and interesting – to test our mapping. Among the commercials that present this form of valorization, four have been selected, each of which can be considered the most representative example of a specific quadrant.

In the area of the subject’s doing, we place an Opel Corsa commercial focused on a young subject who, chatting in the office with a colleague, exposes everything he can do thanks to his new car, both in terms of performance/consumption and savings.

In the quadrant of the subject’s being, we find a series of Suzuki Swift commercials set in a dealership, in which different individuals with particular attitudes and needs alternate, but united by the desire to find the perfect compromise for their needs. The dealer always proposes the same car to each of them.

In the area of the object’s doing, a Fiat 500 L commercial is located. In this case, images and voice-over focus on how our life would be if there were a car able to satisfy our daily mobility needs more and better, balancing consumption and performance, comfort and size.

Finally, in the area of the object’s being, we find a Renault Clio commercial where the only and sole protagonist is the car, with its convenience and comfort, listed in detail as detailed images of its technical and functional characteristics.

Figure 9. Application of mapping of narrative configurations to the critical pole.

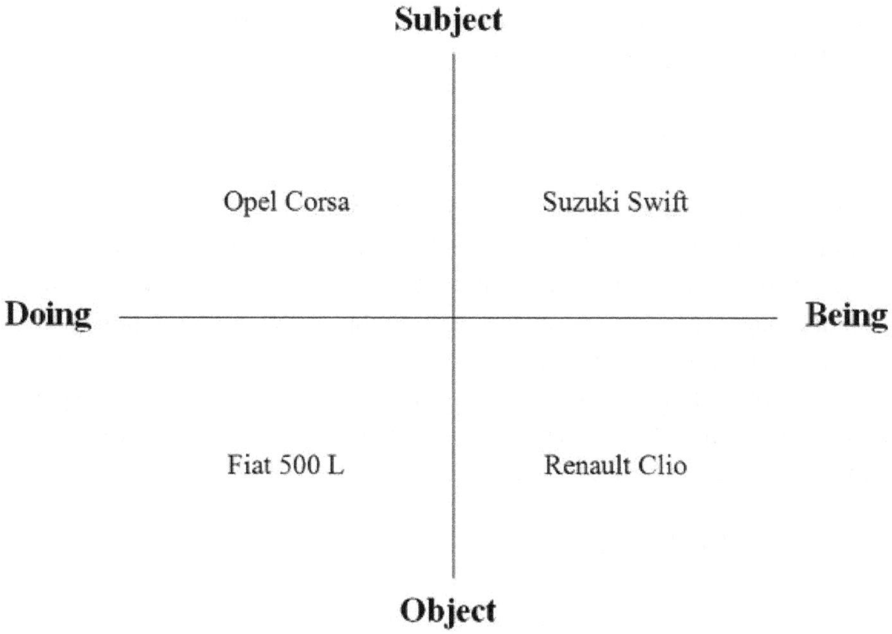

Naturally, around these four "exemplary" texts, many others are located that occupy a long series of intermediate positions, depending on whether the text fades from the subject to the object, from being to doing and so on.

Finally, it is worth noting that with the development of this tool we have actually moved from the values level, attributable to deep semio-narrative level, of the spots, to that of their narrative structures, attributable to surface semio-narrative level.

3.3. The Advertising Philosophies: Confirmations and Developments

We started by the classification of the commercials according to the correspondence with one of the four categories originally outlined by Floch; then, for each of them, the most representative text was identified, which can be briefly illustrated.

3.3.1. Referential Strategy

Most representative text: dr5 commercial.

Description: in this commercial, the only protagonist is the car, which travels on city roads, mountain paths and a sunny seaside promenade; real places, or rather, shown in a way as to generate a high effect of reality. Overall, in fact, the commercial is extremely linear, with an almost documentary approach. All this is also thanks to a composed and natural editing, the total absence of superimposed visual effects and the choice not to resort to any voice-over.

3.3.2. Mythical Strategy

Most representative text: Nissan Juke commercial.

Description: the commercial is articulated in a series of unreal and spectacular scenes; it opens in fact with a man who jumps out of a plane and, while falling in free fall, a group of parachutists begins to assemble the various components of the car around him. Shortly after, the car and the driver land on a racetrack and the workers, this time on motocross bikes, continue their work completing and painting the bodywork. Finally, before arriving on a quiet city street, the car dives into the water, where some divers put the finishing touches.

3.3.3. Substantial Strategy

Most representative text: Hyundai i30 commercial.

Description: in this case too, the car is at the center of the commercial, but this time it is shown in its materiality, through a series of details filmed so closely that the grain of the surfaces can be appreciated and a tactile sensation can be generated in the viewer. Not by chance, various gestures are shown, such as grasping, pressing or caressing parts of the car. To each of these actions, characteristics of refinement, comfort, beauty and quality are then associated, both of the interiors and the exteriors of the car.

3.3.4. Oblique Strategy

Most representative text: Fiat Punto commercial.

Description: the commercial refers to some models of cars of competing brands; in particular, the Mini, the Polo and the Fiesta. The cars, however, are not shown, but recourse is made to scenes that are in a certain sense evocative: in fact, we see girls in miniskirts, men playing polo and young people partying on the edge of a swimming pool. At the end of each sequence, there are superimposed writings (in order, "this is the mini we love", "this is the polo we love", "this is the fiesta we love"), then there is a reference to the advertised car, emphasizing that it is this "that we like". There is therefore a gap that the viewer must fill, leaving the text and drawing on their automotive competence.

This first division of the commercials has allowed us to note that in the vast majority of texts either a referential or a mythical strategy was used. Oblique commercials, in fact, were significantly fewer in number and the substantial ones were only about ten. In turn, this data has led to the advancement of hypotheses and to make some choices.

Firstly, it can be stated that the massive use of the same enunciative strategies contributes to creating that effect of indistinguishability that is frequently noticed in automotive advertising communication. In fact, it often happens to have a sort of déjà vu watching car commercials of different brands. If this effect arises primarily from some discursive characteristics of the texts, in particular with regard to themes and figures, on the other hand, it is the use of the same enunciative strategies that, presupposing the same contract with the user, stimulates practically identical discursive dimensions. In most cases, these texts leverage the emotional dimension, but, due to the inflated use of such strategies, they paradoxically end up generating a certain habituation and, therefore, indifference.

Secondly, the significant crowding of the referential and mythical poles has led us to focus on these two areas and to give a precise cut to the analysis, questioning the opportunity and the possibility of identifying different ways of declining the same advertising genre. Although there are numerous advertising taxonomies – among them, those of Giaccardi (1996) and Saba (2006) should be mentioned –, in fact, none can be considered sufficiently exhaustive, and often distinct tools are difficult to integrate and use coherently with each other. From this point of view, Floch's categories are only one of the possible classifications, but they have proven to be particularly effective and less ambiguous than others in accounting for the complexity of the textual reality. For this reason, it was considered useful to try to increase their heuristic power by deepening them internally while balancing empirical research and theoretical reflection.

The theoretical contributions that seemed useful to take into consideration were, on the one hand, the elaboration of the causal regime carried out by Ferraro (1999), on the other, the reading that Zannin (2009) gave of it. Ferraro, in introducing his category, makes explicit the numerous points of contact with Floch's referential genre. Yet, it is not a simple overlap. As Zannin notes, in fact, the argumentative component represents a peculiar feature compared to the original Flochian formulation. In this way, he suggests that the causal regime can be considered in all respects a specific declination of the referential genre. It was decided to proceed in this way. Therefore, both for coherence and for relevance, we focused precisely on the referential genre, focusing on the discursive configurations of the commercials and searching for further textual dimensions that could serve as distinctive features.

Firstly, the presence of an argumentative dimension was traced and verified in a significant number of elements of the corpus belonging to the referential genre. To this, then, it was chosen to contrast a properly narrative dimension, distinguishing a "superficial level of storytelling, [...] from a universal level of narrativity as a mode of generation (perception and reconstruction) of meaning" (Zannin, 2009, p. 261). In other words, we are referring to all those commercials in which the discourse takes the form of a story: it is not a matter of supporting one's thesis but, more simply, of staging a chain of events, a more or less linear and complex story that substantiates the semantic nucleus that one wants to communicate.

At this point, starting from the category /Argumentative Dimension Vs Narrative Dimension/ the semiotic square was used to expand it and try to account for further empirical cases. In this way, two new positions were obtained, corresponding respectively to the negation of the argumentative dimension and to the negation of the narrative one. To each of the four terms of the square, a label was then assigned that suggested in the most immediate and unambiguous way possible the different types of referential that emerged during the analysis of the commercials (Figure 10).

Figure 10. Semiotic square of the declensions of the referential genre.

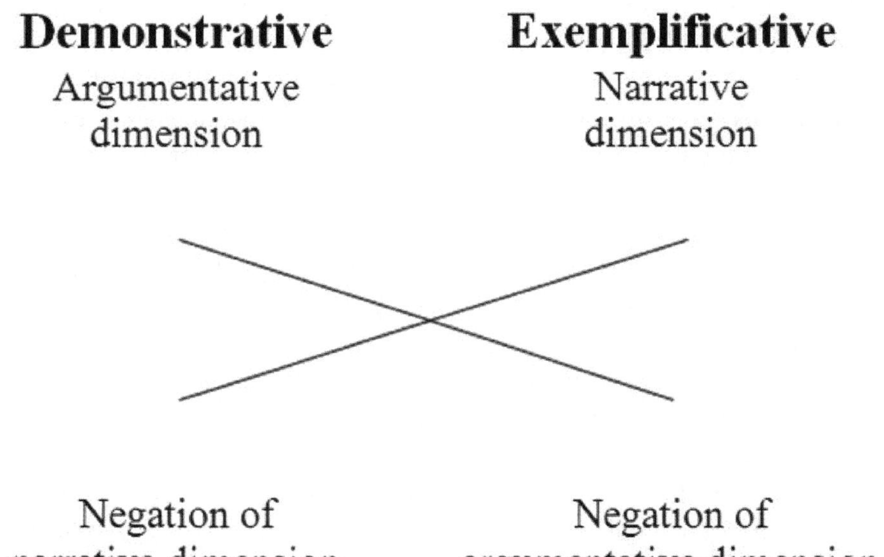

In commercials attributable to the demonstrative type of referential genre, a discursive strategy is used that revolves around the presentation of arguments in support of one's own proposal of meaning, of field tests, of (presented as) objective tests, of expert opinions or testimonies from users. In all these cases, the text presents a certain argumentative dimension, which makes this type of referential attributable to Ferraro's causal regime (1999). In the corpus, some examples of this declension are the Ford Focus commercials in which footage of tests carried out on and by the cars is shown, as in the case of the stopping technology or the automatic parking system. All this through a strategy aimed at obtaining a very marked effect of reality, with images taken from cameras placed in the cockpit that show the car's performance from multiple angles.

In commercials attributable to the exemplificative type of referential genre, a choice is made to place the product in the lives of people, in stereotypical use occasions and characterized by dynamics of behavior that are considered particularly significant. Being within the referential, this choice is not surprising and reflects the representational function of advertising language that characterizes it. What is interesting, however, is the absence of any argumentative implication and the simultaneous relevance assumed by the narrative one: we are in the presence of a narrative that is explicitly figurativized and of logically ordered concatenations of events. Within the corpus this way of declining the referential is among the most widespread. To give an example, we can cite the Dacia Lodgy commercial, in which the hectic morning moments are told in which two families, both very large, have to accompany their respective children to school. The first has a sports car, not suitable for family needs, and is therefore forced to leave two unlucky children on foot. All the members of the second, on the other hand, can enjoy the spaciousness and comfort of the advertised car.

In commercials attributable to the illustrative type of referential genre, nothing happens, in the sense that what is shown is not linked by cause-effect relationships. In other words, the explicit narrative dimension is decidedly marginal, if not entirely absent. Rather, we witness the parallel juxtaposition of elements aimed at presenting and depicting what is enunciated. This strategy invests each of the languages that characterize a syncretic text such as a commercial. Thus, we have highly iconic images of the product and/or its context of use, which often translate visually what is heard on the verbal level. All this is generally accompanied by a massive use of verbo-visual elements such as superimposed writings and graphic texts that further reinforce the effect of objective presentation of the product. A brilliant example is the Hyundai ix20 commercial where, for its entire duration, voice-over, short filmed sequences and textual elements present and describe the car, in terms of consumption, comfort and convenience, moreover referring to and reinforcing each other.

Finally, the entertaining type of referential genre can be found in a limited number of elements of the corpus, but it has considerable importance in the Italian advertising landscape. This type of referential explicitly denies any argumentative dimension and leaves room for the playful one: in other words, with this discursive strategy, the aim is to entertain the user or to try to make commercials an opportunity for the viewer to relax. In some cases, there may be a certain narrative dimension, but the distinctive feature is precisely the playful component, without which the textual mechanism would not be adequately explained. Moreover, although there is usually a comic effect, we are not within the oblique genre: these are gags that aim to elicit a smile, but that do not require a particular interpretative leap, on the contrary, the sketch often turn out to be banal or cloying, and therefore the degree of cooperation required of the viewer is generally low. This declension of the referential genre calls into question that particular way of advertising, all Italian, which was Carosello (Ballio & Zanacchi, 1987) and not by chance it is characterized both by the presence of short stories with a humorous tone or that borrow from other mass media genres some features capable of amusing and entertaining the viewer – as in the case of musical jingles – as well as by the almost constant use of testimonials from the world of entertainment and sports. Concrete examples in the corpus are the numerous Fiat commercials interpreted by the comedians Luca and Paolo or those of the Volkswagen Polo in which several Roma footballers give life to some sketches.

At this point, a clarification is necessary: although we have tried to emphasize the different types and to present some exemplary texts, it could be objected that on this occasion the model of the semiotic square is excessively rigid. In the end, in fact, we are talking about dominants: dimensions that often coexist in texts and that can be more or less marked; articulating them according to relations of contrariety, contradiction and implication, therefore, could be theoretically problematic. On the other hand, it was decided to use this tool to account for the logical and analytical path that allowed this classification to be developed: a strongly comparative path, whose categories make sense to the extent that they are mutually defined in relation to each other.

Once this categorization of referential commercials was completed, we moved on to the mythical one, and we asked ourselves if it was possible to trace the same dimensions in the texts attributable to this second genre. In principle, in fact, the work of abstraction and isolation of the discursive dimensions could have allowed us to identify different textual declensions in a transversal but coherent way within the different enunciative strategies. Thus, returning to observe the commercials, it was possible to ascertain that each dimension was also present in the mythical genre and allowed for a classification. At this point, it was decided to invert the perspective, that is, to start from the individual common declensions (demonstrative, exemplificative, illustrative, entertaining) and then to compare referential and mythical commercials belonging to each of them. This operation allowed us to grasp further differences and thus to identify some particularly exemplary commercials.

In the case of the demonstrative with a dominant argumentative dimension, on the one hand (the referential one) we have the Toyota Rav4 commercial, in which, to demonstrate the road holding on icy ground, footage of a real test drive is shown; on the other hand (the mythical one) the BMW xDrive commercial, in which, to demonstrate once again the road holding on icy ground, the fictitious xDrive Village is used, a location created ad hoc, characterized by such unpredictable weather conditions that there are "365 seasons a year".

In the case of the exemplificative with a dominant narrative dimension, on the one hand (the referential one) we have a Volvo V40 commercial, in which we see a man, visibly down, dealing with a series of daily chores, such as queuing at the pharmacy or the supermarket. Shortly after, however, he returns to his car, gets behind the wheel and, speeding through the city streets, finds his full existential dimension; on the other hand (the mythical one) we have several Toyota Auris Hybrid commercials where a future is outlined, as dystopian as it is bizarre, in which it will be allowed to own only one pet or one phone for the rest of your life: all perspectives that a subject imagines concretely and whose consequences push him to speak up and distinguish himself from the mass.

In the case of the illustrative with a dominant non-narrative dimension, on the one hand (the referential one) we have the Kia Ceed commercial, in which the voice-over and the images expose and show in detail some of the car's features, filmed as it travels along a normal city street; on the other hand (the mythical one) the Ford C Max commercial, in which the voice-over informs us that "there is a car designed for our desires" and lists the features of the car, while a series of subjects assembles it in real time by arranging the various components mentioned in the air.

In the case of the entertaining with a dominant non-argumentative dimension, on the one hand (the referential one) we have some commercials in which the comedians Luca and Paolo play two unlikely Fiat dealers, giving life to misunderstandings and gags; on the other hand (the mythical one) a Skoda Yeti commercial, shot like a music video: in fact, we see a Tyrolean folk group that, to the notes of a South Tyrolean ballad, reprimands the owners of many SUVs, represented as real clouds of smog, which pollute the pristine landscapes.

That said, it is worth making two final clarifications: first of all, the most disparate forms of valorization are used in the selected and described commercials, proving the independence of what one decides to communicate from the way in which it is possible to do so, not only in relation to the enunciative strategies, but also with respect to their different discursive declinations. Secondly, in relation to the oblique and substantial genres, the subcategories identified seem to be of little relevance: indeed, the small number of commercials within the corpus that resorted to the latter two strategies did not allow us to advance hypotheses that could be generalized to some extent.

CONCLUSIONS

Both the theoretical review and the empirical investigation have made it possible to propose some developments of Floch's models. But after such a taxonomic effort, it is legitimate to ask what the operational impact of these models and their related integrations could be. In this regard, we adopt the words of Zannin, according to whom semiotics can contribute

> *to the conception, development, launch and verification of brands, advertising packaging, new products, product/brand names, claims-pay-off and everything that makes up the brand's communication. [...] Semiotic analysis, in fact, provides a set of operational tools that allow the monitoring, management and optimization of the image effects connected to brand and product communication. In this way, marketing is able to:*

- speak the language and use the codes most appropriate to its targets;
- monitor and limit as much as possible the unintended or unelected meanings as "primary meanings" of one's communication;
- make the specificities of one's own proposal (of product and communication) more evident;
- read and interpret the results of consumer surveys, being able to trace opinions, sensations, impressions and motivations to specific communicative sign elements; this happens because only the semiotic method can place the various effects of meaning (and collaterally the consumers' decoding) at specific levels of signification;
- and, therefore, react in a timely and precise manner to unwanted communicative effects. (Zannin, 2008, p. 131)

Therefore, semiotics can, first of all, intervene in the preparatory phase of the conception of a communicative artifact, bringing benefits in terms of intelligibility, relevance and differentiation (Floch, 1990/1992). But, at the same time, it can intervene in the choice of the paths of meaning to be undertaken and the expressive solutions to be adopted to achieve a specific objective or a certain target (Deni & Proni, 2008; Bianchi et al., 2010).

Returning then to the strictly advertising field, we can say that semiotics can help us take stock and offer us ideas on what to communicate and how to do it. In the conception of a new campaign for a product, for example, we could:

- start from the analysis of the competitive context, observing which semantic areas are most solicited in that particular product category, and based on these choose an alternative proposal that is different and relevant for the target;

- choose from which perspectives and narrative dimensions to decline our proposal, so that even these aspects contribute to generating precise effects of meaning and increase the distinctiveness of the texts;
- finally, identify the most suitable way to communicate the chosen value nucleus, in terms of enunciative strategy and discursive declension, according to competitors, target, medium, etc.

Of course, in the creation of a commercial, a print ad or an entire campaign, many other aspects would remain to be defined. The point, in fact, is not to create a combination of elements based on which to produce texts in a mechanical way, thus confining the creative process in paths established a priori. Rather, we believe that semiotics can orient it and in some ways enhance it, even deciding, at the design stage, to hybridize or subvert those categories that one has tried to outline, deepen and integrate.

REFERENCES

Ballio, L., & Zanacchi, A. (1987). *Carosello story. La via italiana alla pubblicità televisiva*. Eri.

Bianchi, C. (2005). *Spot. Analisi semiotica dell'audiovisivo pubblicitario*. Carocci.

Bianchi, C., Montanari, F., & Zingale, S. (Eds.). (2010). *La semiotica e il progetto 2. Spazi, oggetti, interfacce*. FrancoAngeli.

Ceriani, G. (2001). *Marketing moving: L'approccio semiotico. Analizzare il mix di comunicazione, gestirne gli effetti di senso*. FrancoAngeli.

Deni, M., & Proni, G. (Eds.). (2008). *La semiotica e il progetto. Design, comunicazione, marketing*. FrancoAngeli.

Eco, U. (1979). *Lector in fabula. La cooperazione interpretativa nei testi narrativi*. Bompiani.

Fabris, G. (2009). *Societing. Il marketing nella società postmoderna*. Egea.

Ferraresi, M., & Schmitt, B. H. (2006). *Marketing esperienziale. Come sviluppare l'esperienza di consumo*. FrancoAngeli.

Ferraro, G. (1999). *La pubblicità nell'era di internet*. Meltemi.

Floch, J.-M. (1992). *Semiotica, marketing e comunicazione* (Semprini, A., & Franceschetti, M., Trans.). FrancoAngeli. (Original work published 1990)

Floch, J.-M. (1997). *Identità visive* (Ranelletti, L., Trans.). FrancoAngeli. (Original work published 1995)

Floch, J.-M. (2013). *Bricolage. Analizzare pubblicità, immagini e spazi*. FrancoAngeli.

Giaccardi, C. (1996). *I luoghi del quotidiano. Pubblicità e costruzione della realtà sociale*. FrancoAngeli.

Greimas, A. J., & Courtés, J. (2007). *Semiotica. Dizionario ragionato della teoria del linguaggio* (Fabbri, P., Trans.). Mondadori. (Original work published 1979)

Klein, N. (2001). *No Logo* (Borgo, S., Trans.). Baldini & Castoldi. (Original work published 2000)

Laurino, A. (2020a). Per una nuova assiologia del consumo. Una proposta di ampliamento, approfondimento e aggiornamento del modello flochiano, *Ocula*, 1-29.

Laurino, A. (2020b). Intorno al quadrato delle filosofie pubblicitarie. Per una sottoarticolazione di alcune delle categorie flochiane originarie, *Filosofi(e) Semiotiche, 7*(1), 116-129.

Lévy-Strauss, C. (1990). *Antropologia strutturale* (Caruso, P., Trans.). Il Saggiatore. (Original work published 1958)

Lombardi, M. (Ed.). (2007). *La marca, una come noi. La personalità di marca nell'era post spot*. FrancoAngeli.

Mangano, D. (2008). *Semiotica e design*. Carocci.

Marrone, G. (1999). *C'era una volta il telefonino. Un'indagine sociosemiotica*. Meltemi.

Marrone, G. (2001). *Corpi sociali*. Einaudi.

Marrone, G. (2007). *Il discorso di marca. Modelli semiotici per il branding*. Laterza.

Pine, J. B., & Gilmore, J. H. (2000). *L'economia delle esperienze. Oltre il servizio* (Monkhouse, A. S., Trans.). Etas. (Original work published 1999)

Pozzato, M. P. (2001). *Semiotica del testo. Metodi, autori, esempi*. Carocci.

Rosch, E., & Lloyd, B. B. (Eds.). (1978). *Cognition and Categorization*. Erlbaum Associates.

Saba, C. (2006). *Lo sguardo che insegue. Strumenti per l'analisi delle forme audiovisive pubblicitarie (spot, trailer, videoclip e rich media)*. Lupetti.

Semprini, A. (1993). *Marche e mondi possibili. Un approccio semiotico al marketing della marca* (Semprini, A., Trans.). FrancoAngeli. (Original work published 1992)

Ventura, I. (2005). Di che packaging sei? Generi discorsivi e confezioni dei prodotti, sulla scia di J.-M. Floch. *E|C*, 1-23.

Volli, U. (2003). *Semiotica della pubblicità*. Laterza.

Zannin, A. (2008). Per una semiotica al lavoro. Approcci e toolkit semiotici nei progetti di marketing e comunicazione. In Deni, M., & Proni, G. (Eds.), *La semiotica e il progetto. Design, comunicazione, marketing* (pp. 130-157). FrancoAngeli.

Zannin, A. (2009). *Analisi, progettazione e valutazione dell'efficacia dello spot pubblicitario. Una semiotica per la ricerca di mercato*. [Unpublished doctoral dissertation]. Università di Bologna - Alma Mater Studiorum, Bologna, Italia.

ENDNOTES

1 The semiotic square is the model developed by Algirdas Julien Greimas (Greimas & Courtés, 1979/2007) through which it is possible to visualize the logical relations governing a micro-universe of meaning, such as a text or a set of advertising texts may be. The process of constructing a square starts with the identification of a semantic category formed by two terms in a contrariety relation (a Vs b). This category is expanded through the identification of the respective contradictors (not-b and not-a), obtained by negating the starting terms. They, in turn, are in contrariety relation. Moreover, in a well-placed square, each of these two terms must have an entailment relation with the opposite term than the one from which it was generated by negation.

2 The platform offered companies the opportunity to monitor their competitors' activities. Nielsen guaranteed very high media coverage and almost constant updates, providing its customers with a series of information (such as ads, when, where and how often) that could represent a competitive advantage.

Chapter 6
Challenging Beauty Norms in the Digital Age:
An Analysis of Dove's "The Code" Campaign

Alice Venturini
https://orcid.org/0000-0002-0022-5790
University of Modena and Reggio Emilia, Italy

ABSTRACT

Nowadays brands are increasingly expected to adopt activist stances on political, social, and environmental issues. Popular examples include Patagonia's commitment toward the conservation and restoration of the natural environment and Nike's longstanding support for the Black community in the US, to name a few. These corporate efforts have come to be known as 'brand activism' and concern publicly stated positions on sensitive issues by means of advertising, public relations, and other media. Despite the increasing dissemination of activist marketing campaigns, however, brand activism remains underexplored from a semiotic standpoint. This chapter aims to fill this gap by proposing a new methodological tool merging semiotics and netnography to analyze both the narrative strategies used within activist commercials and consumers' reactions to these messages. Dove's 2024 'The Code' campaign will serve as a case study to illustrate this approach. Results will furnish interesting insights into the relationship between consumers, brands, and social issues.

INTRODUCTION

In May 2020, four days after the death of the 46-year-old George Floyd, who was held down by a Minnesota police officer's knee, Nike released a text-only video on

DOI: 10.4018/979-8-3693-8024-6.ch006

its social media platforms entitled "For once, Don't Do It," creatively subverting its iconic claim "Just Do It." The post encouraged viewers to not turn their backs on racism and not remain silent about injustice and inequality.

Nike has a long history of standing against hatred and racism, emphasizing the role the firm wants to play in these racially fractured times (Cohen, 2020). In 2018 the brand released another ad featuring former San Francisco 49ers quarterback Colin Kaepernick, who was rejected by the National Football League for kneeling during the national anthem at the start of a game to protest police brutality. The campaign ensured that the protest movement against racism and social injustice started by Kaepernick expand beyond the US most powerful sports league.

Over the past two decades, pressing political, social, and environmental challenges have compelled many brands to adopt an 'activist' role by taking deliberate stands on sensitive issues (Koch, 2020; Sibai, Mimoun, & Boukis, 2021). This shift in companies' conduct has given rise to the emergence of 'brand activism' (Sarkar & Kotler, 2018), a values-driven approach where a brand takes a public stance on sensitive issues to drive social change and achieve marketing success (Vredenburg, Kapitan, Spry, & Kemper, 2020).

Stakeholders – especially consumers – play a crucial role in shaping the success of brand activism messages and practices. Empowered by digital technologies, consumers now actively scrutinize and challenge companies' activist stances, often leading to 'buycotts' (Pimentel, Bassi-Suter, & Didonet, 2024) – e.g., financially supporting brands that align with their values – or 'boycotts' – e.g., publicly opposing brands for their moral positions (Hydock, Paharia, & Blair, 2020; Klostermann, Hydock, & Decker, 2022). For instance, Adidas faced a severe backlash on social media and public forums after Kanye West's repeated antisemitic remarks, which led the company to terminate its partnership with the celebrity (The New York Times, 2023). Within a similar vein, consumers on X (formerly Twitter) heavily criticized Balenciaga for the 2022 holiday campaign featuring children holding teddy bears adorned in BDSM-style attire. Online protests prompted the brand to issue multiple apologies and remove the campaign, demonstrating how public outcry can now force brands to backtrack on their marketing strategies (Paton, Friedman, & Testa, 2022).

Although studies on brand activism have recently gained momentum (see Cammarota, D'Arco, Marino, & Resciniti, 2023; Pimentel, Bassi-Suter, & Didonet, 2024) and marketing academics have shown growing interest in brand activism as an emerging business strategy (Shoenberger, Kim, & Sun, 2021), semiotic research in this area remains limited (Boero, 2022). Moreover, since traditional semiotics of advertising has primarily focused on understanding the intended ad message from the brand's perspective, contemporary approaches must acknowledge the crucial role of consumer interpretation, exploring both how meaning is constructed within the advertisement and how that meaning is received and understood by the audience. To address this gap, this chapter proposes a methodological framework that combines semiotic analysis with netnography – a particular form of online ethnography that examines the social interaction on digital platforms through a cultural lens (Kozinets & Nocker, 2018) – in order to better understand the effectiveness of brand activism campaigns.

To demonstrate the effectiveness of this integrated methodological approach in understanding the contemporary advertising landscape, an analysis of Dove's "The Code" 2023 campaign will be provided. Two decades after the release of the "Real Beauty" ads, the Unilever-owned personal care brand takes a stand against the use of generative AI to create idealized and often unrealistic female images, condemning the practice as it poses significant risks to women's self-esteem and self-perception worldwide. The campaign will first be analyzed using Greimas and Courtés' structural semiotics framework (1979). Subsequently, considering the crucial role of consumers' interpretations of the ad, a netnographic analysis of social media user commentaries will be conducted to gain deeper insights into audience reception and the actual success of the campaign.

The current investigation underscores the urgent need for semiotics to dialogue with other methodologies, such as netnography, to effectively analyze contemporary cultural phenomena through direct observation of everyday online practices. This interdisciplinary dialogue answers Bianchi's (2020) call for expanding the scope of ethnosemiotics to encompass the study of cultural communities' texts and practices within online environments.

The chapter will be structured as follows: the first section will examine the emergence of brand activism, exploring its significance from a semiotic standpoint and establishing it as the contextual framework of the study. Then, the suitability of netnography as a complementary tool for conducting semiotic analysis within digital realms will be discussed. In the third paragraph, the methodological relevance of this integrated approach will be demonstrated through a case study analysis of Dove's 'The Code' campaign. Finally, the results section will demonstrate how this integrated approach provides a comprehensive understanding of contemporary branding. By combining the brand's intended meaning (as revealed through semiotic analysis) with audience interpretation (as captured through netnography), valuable insights can be gained into the success or failure of brand activism campaigns in the digital age.

1. BRAND ACTIVISM IN MARKETING

The concept of brand activism was first introduced by Sarkar and Kotler (2018), and is defined as the 'business efforts to promote, impede, or direct social, political, economic, and/or environmental reform with the desire to promote or impede improvements in society' (p. 468). Growing societal expectations demand that companies take public positions on contemporary issues (Maks-Solomon & Drewry, 2020), fuelled by a belief that firms are better equipped than governments to effectively address social, political, and environmental challenges (Edelman, 2018).

Driven by a genuine commitment to creating a better world (Chandy, Johar, & Roberts, 2021), brands may advocate for or against a wide range of topics, including racism, immigration, child rights, gender discrimination, abortion, public health, gun control, and environmental issues (Hydock, Paharia, & Blair, 2020; Varghese & Kumar, 2020; Vredenburg, Kapitan, Spry, & Kemper, 2020). Recognizing that such positioning can enhance market value, companies strategically leverage brand activism as a marketing tool (de Oca, Mason, & Ahn, 2022; Pimentel, Bassi-Suter, & Didonet, 2024) to foster deeper connections with their target audience.

The foundation of modern brand activism has its roots in the 'cultural branding' paradigm (Holt, 2002; 2004). This paradigm challenges the traditional view of brands as mere corporate entities, instead positioning them as powerful cultural symbols that both shape and are shaped within particular socio-cultural contexts (Schroeder, 2017). More than twenty years ago, Douglas Holt (2002) suggested that since corporate civic responsibilities were becoming increasingly important to individuals, consumers increasingly sought brands that aligned with their own values and demonstrated a commitment to civic duties. Drawing on the cultural branding premises, brand activism positions brands as 'moral subjects' (Sibai, Mimoun, & Boukis, 2021, p. 2) driven by purpose and values (Vredenburg, Kapitan, Spry, & Kemper, 2020). By leveraging their cultural authority, activist companies can challenge existing power dynamics and contribute to significant cultural and socio-political change (Moorman, 2020). In other words, brands were expected to function as responsible corporate citizens, actively contributing to their communities driven by inherent values rather than solely by profit motives. This groundbreaking framework has significantly shaped how businesses approach brand management and communication in the 21st century.

Within this context, Patagonia represents a prominent case study in successful brand activism. Widely recognized for its authentic and genuine commitment to sustainability, the brand consistently takes impactful actions to reduce its environmental footprint. These include for instance using a high proportion of recycled fabrics, discouraging customers from purchasing too many of its products by offering a repair and reuse program; and founding an organization that encourages businesses to donate at least 1% of their annual sales to environmental nonprofits. In this way, the outdoor and adventure-wear brand is paving the way in mitigating the negative impact of the textile and fast fashion industry, fostering a real and actual transformation both globally and within the sector (Boström & Micheletti, 2016; Simões & Sebastiani, 2017).

Hence, in order to be successful, brand activism hinges on its perceived authenticity (Hydock, Paharia, & Blair, 2020; Vredenburg, Kapitan, Spry, & Kemper, 2020), requiring a strong alignment between the advocated issues and the firm's core mission and values (Schmidt, Ind, Guzmán, & Kennedy, 2021). Additionally, consumers evaluate activism efforts based on consistency, with the historical congruency between a firm's core values and the supported cause heavily influencing their judgments and feelings (Pasirayi, Fennell, & Follmer, 2023). Thus, consistency between a company's stated commitments and its actual business practices (Vredenburg, Kapitan, Spry, & Kemper, 2020) is also essential for activist firms.

1.1. Brand Activism in Semiotics

As previously mentioned, despite the growing interest shown by marketing scholars toward brand activism (e.g., Cammarota, D'Arco, Marino, & Resciniti, 2023; Pimentel, Bassi-Suter, & Didonet, 2024), semiotic research on activist campaigns is still in its early stages.

A first attempt has been undertaken by Marianna Boero (2022), who examined the intersection of ethics and semiotics by analyzing some advertisements concerning environmental protection and sustainability released within a ten-year timeframe, concluding in the first half of 2022. Instead of directly talking about brand activism, Boero focuses on social advertising, namely a form of non-profit advertising that seeks to encourage the adoption of specific behaviours or to address critical social issues to promote social change, rather than directly selling products or services (Boero, 2022).

Within this research, she argues that the lines between social and commercial advertising are increasingly blurred, as both public and private entities can effectively convey ethical messages as powerful instruments for social change. Furthermore, she acknowledges that consumers have become increasingly aware of both the non-profit and profit purposes of social communication and commercial advertising, respectively. The long-held notion of a passive and easily manipulated audience is now obsolete, thanks to the numerous tools available to consumers for evaluating and verifying information, such as online reviews and readily accessible information (see, for instance, Filieri, Alguezaui, & McLeay, 2015; Kozinets, de Valck, Wojnicki, & Wilner, 2010; Swaminathan, Sorescu, O'Guinn, & Schmitt, 2020).

For what concerns the register used, ethical advertising, whether promoted by non-profit organizations or private business, was found to predominantly employ emotional appeals to foster a deeper and more direct connection with the audience (Boero, 2022). This approach aims to establish an emotional pact built upon shared values that the organization or the company seeks to convey. By blending rhetorical strategies based on irony or fear with images, payoffs, and sounds, these campaigns engage with increasingly informed and responsible consumers, sensitive both to the emotional content and tone of the ad message. This emotional impact is achieved through a careful selection of soundtracks, as well as the use of evocative imagery such as pregnancy, family, and suffering animals. Hence, from a consumption values standpoint, mythical and oblique advertising predominate (Floch, 1990) as well as utopian values, emphasizing a sense of belonging and the aspiration for a better world (Boero, 2022). Furthermore, an aspect worth noting is that, within these advertisements, nature is often portrayed as an actant to be protected and safeguarded from the harmful actions of humans (that is, in generative semiotic terms, the Opponent). Put simply, nature is depicted as a victim of human activity, highlighting an unbalanced relationship that can only be rectified through commitment and responsible actions on behalf of humans (Traini, 2020).

Finally, Boero (2022) acknowledges that the relationship between advertising and ethics from a marketing standpoint has been historically complex, as corporate initiatives have long been criticized for engaging in the logic of 'greenwashing', that is, presenting an environmentally friendly image without reflecting a genuine commitment toward the exposed issues and values. This discrepancy is particularly evident in cases where brands utilize ethical advertising while failing to implement the values they claim to embody in their actual business practices. Consequently, conflicts have arisen between firms and activist organizations, as exemplified by the Greenpeace campaign against the Lego-Shell partnership (Vaughan, 2014). This victory, achieved by means of viral videos and appealing to childhood themes, led the Danish brand to terminate its over 50-year marketing relationship with the fossil-fuel group due to their plans to drill for oil in the Arctic.

Recognizing the limited exploration of brand activism – or ethical advertising, as defined by Boero (2022) – within the semiotic realm, the following section will introduce a methodological framework that integrates semiotics with netnography to address this gap, thus providing deeper insights into the impact of these advertising strategies within the contemporary communication landscape.

2. THE INCREASED EMPOWERMENT OF THE CONSUMER IN THE DIGITAL AGE

Companies can purposefully publicize their activist stances on sensitive issues through various channels, including marketing campaigns, press releases, social media, and celebrity endorsements (Campbell, Freeman, & Gannon, 2021; Hydock, Paharia, & Blair, 2020; Klostermann, Hydock, & Decker, 2022; Koch, 2020; Sterbenk,

Ward, Luttrell, & Summer Shelton, 2022). The communication of brand activism can yield positive outcomes, such as economic support from those who align with the issues the company supports (Pimentel, Bassi-Suter, & Didonet, 2024). On the other hand, negative consequences can arise when brand activism is perceived as opportunistic or when the company's activist conduct does not align with stakeholders' expectations (Johnson, Bauer, & Carlson, 2022; Pöyry & Laaksonen, 2022), potentially leading to significant backlashes such as online protests and boycotts.

Consumers' reactions to brand activism are strictly influenced by their political ideology (Flight & Coker, 2021; Hydock, Paharia, & Blair, 2020; Klostermann, Hydock, & Decker, 2022; Neureiter & Bhattacharya, 2021). Political ideology encompasses the values and beliefs that shape one's attitudes, opinions, and behaviours, serving as a framework for interpreting the world, affirming their self-concept, and fostering a sense of belonging within a shared community of like-minded individuals (Flight & Coker, 2021). By taking a stance on sensitive issues, companies implicitly align themselves with a particular political ideology (Vredenburg, Kapitan, Spry, & Kemper, 2020). The perceived alignment between a brand's political stance and the consumer's own ideology significantly influences the success or failure of brand activism campaigns, since consumer decisions to support or boycott a brand are often driven by the extent to which the brand's political stance aligns with their political beliefs (Hydock, Paharia, & Blair, 2020; Klostermann, Hydock, & Decker, 2022). For instance, companies that advocate for the rights of LGBTQIA+ communities may anticipate increased engagement and empowerment among their target audience, while simultaneously experiencing financial losses from consumers holding conservative or right-wing viewpoints.

Predicting stakeholders' reactions to brand activism can be extremely challenging (Warren, 2021) and the consequences of a failure can be severe (Weinzimmer & Esken, 2016). A poorly executed brand activism strategy can indeed significantly damage both intangible corporate assets, such as brand image and reputation (Dodd & Supa, 2014), and tangible assets, including economic and financial performance (Vredenburg, Kapitan, Spry, & Kemper, 2020). When brand actions fail to demonstrate a genuine commitment to addressing sensitive issues, they can be perceived as 'woke washing' (de Oca, Mason, & Ahn, 2022; Mirzaei, Wilkie, & Siuki, 2022; Vredenburg, Kapitan, Spry, & Kemper, 2020). While genuine 'woke activism' involves a sincere commitment to addressing social and political issues, particularly those related to inequality and social justice (Sobande, 2019), woke washing has been defined as the act of publicly expressing support for a sociopolitical issue, either through statements or by presenting a concrete action plan, without genuinely implementing meaningful changes to address those issues (Ahmad, Guzmán, & Al-Emran, 2024). For instance, brands can be accused of woke washing when they publicly advocate for topics like racial equality or minority rights but fail to translate those promises into concrete actions within their own organization. Popular examples include the beauty brand Glossier, which, despite pledging a $1 million donation to support black-owned beauty businesses and organizations addressing racial injustice, faced criticism when former brand employees wrote a public letter denouncing a racist and inequitable work environment (O'Brien, 2020). Within a similar vein, the contested Audi's 2017 Super Bowl commercial, 'Daughter', whose emotional storytelling underlined the need to resolve gender inequalities in the workplace, faced strong backlash for the company's limited number of female workers in executive leadership roles (Kauflin, 2017).

The widespread adoption of social media has empowered brands to amplify their commitment toward brand activism, offering a powerful megaphone to turn the spotlight on their commitment toward certain socio-political issues. However, on the other hand, the increased visibility allowed by online environments has also put companies under an intense scrutiny (Karunakaran, 2024) from social media users. Social media platforms have indeed transformed into a public forum where users closely observe, examine, and judge firms' statements and actions, looking for subtle evidence of mismatch and inconsistency between declared brand purpose and brand actions. This heightened scrutiny compels brands to consistently demonstrate alignment between their advocated stances and their actual conduct, as any inconsistencies can quickly be exposed and disseminated across the digital landscape.

Of course, the rapid dissemination of dissent on social media can significantly amplify negative reactions to companies' failures in addressing sensitive issues (Hesse, Niederle, Schön, & Stautz, 2021; Pöyry & Laaksonen, 2022). For instance, in 2017 the beverage corporation Pepsi released a commercial featuring Kendall Jenner joining a protest and offering a police officer a can of the famous fizzy soda. The campaign faced widespread backlash for trivializing the Black Lives Matter movement and appropriating the theme of social justice. The hashtag #BoycottPepsi quickly went viral and gained traction on platforms like Twitter and Instagram, leading to a public outcry and prompting Pepsi to withdraw the controversial ad (Smith, 2017).

Brand activism initiatives indeed generate a wide range of discourse and conversations among consumers that are uncovered, amplified, and discussed, particularly on social media platforms. This intense consumer scrutiny stems from the rise of the 'participatory culture' of the Internet (Jenkins, 2006), where users actively engage in content creation and sharing, fuelled by the perceived 'empowerment' and 'democratization' allowed by the web (Beer, 2009, p. 986). Furthermore, the accessibility of 'clicktivism' – users easily and rapidly expressing their ideas and standpoints by means of a 'click' of their mouse (Halupka, 2014) – on social media platforms has greatly expanded the opportunities for individuals to readily express their opinions and engage in collective actions, facilitating the rapid dissemination of both support and criticism for brand activism efforts, depending on consumers' ideological alignments.

These dynamics have been found to create a fertile ground for the outbreak of controversies against brands by means of online protests such as boycotts and 'online firestorms' – the digital manifestation of brand crises (Hansen, Kupfer, & Hennig-Thurau, 2018; Pfeffer, Zorbach, & Carley, 2014). These counter-power movements aim not only to unveil brand opportunistic behaviours by impacting corporate reputation and financial performance (Neureiter & Bhattacharya, 2021), but also to create active resistance in order to challenge existing power hegemonies and social order within economic and societal contexts (Kozinets & Seraj-Aksit, 2024).

Social media has thus revolutionized consumer empowerment, enabling the rapid mobilization of collective action and transforming bottom-up movements into standard elements of the modern marketing environment. Before the advent of social media, consumers' dissatisfaction with a brand was largely confined to individual expressions, such as contacting the firm directly or sharing complaints within a very limited social circle (Rauschnabel, Kammerlander, & Ivens, 2016). Subsequently, the rise of digital platforms has empowered consumers by facilitating real-time information sharing among peers, co-creating and spreading brand-related content through their digital networks (Hennig-Thurau, Wiertz, & Feldhaus, 2015; Labrecque, Vor Dem Esche, Mathwick, Novak, & Hofacker, 2013). This shift has notably amplified the voice of the consumer and empowered them to exert greater influence on brand behaviour and conduct.

As these consumer movements against brands' stances and actions mainly unfold on social media, netnography emerges as a particularly suitable research methodology for unveiling how brand activism is received and interpreted by users. Netnography, rooted in ethnography, is a branch of digital anthropology that examines the dynamics of meaning-making within online communities (Kozinets, 2019). As a qualitative research method focused on analyzing online traces – e.g., social media posts, comments, online forums, and user-generated content – it can provide valuable insights into the social interactions, cultural meanings, and consumer behaviours that emerge within digital spaces (Kozinets & Nocker, 2018).

The capabilities of netnography in accounting for the complex dynamics and interactions that occur online will be further explored in the analysis section.

3. CASE STUDY ANALYSIS: 'THE CODE' (2024) BY DOVE

Dove, a Unilever-owned personal care brand, has a long history of commitment to promoting authentic beauty. For two decades, the brand has been at the forefront of transformative campaigns, challenging societal norms and contributing to the redefinition of beauty standards within and outside the cosmetic industry.

With its 'Campaign for Real Beauty', launched in September 2004, Dove became the first company to challenge traditional beauty standards and promote self-acceptance among women. The campaign was composed by a photography exhibit, a series of billboard advertisements, and several viral videos, including 'Evolution' (2006)[1], 'Oneslaught' (2007), 'Dove Real Beauty Sketches' (2013), and 'Free Being Me' (2013). The campaign featured images of real women of different ages, shapes, sizes and ethnicities to showcase that women's unique differences should be celebrated, rather than ignored, and that physical appearance should be transformed from a source of anxiety to a source of confidence (Bissell & Rask, 2010).

By showcasing real women, Dove has reframed its previous advertising approach, shifting from a beauty and toiletries product-centric focus emphasizing practical or critical values – what Floch (1990) would have called *referential* or *substantial* advertising – to a more *oblique* one that aims to subvert societal norms and beauty standards. By purchasing Dove's products, consumers and especially women can show that they too believe society's values regarding beauty need to change, thus actively participating in the brand's mission to challenge societal beauty standards. This innovative consumer-centric approach which prioritizes values over product features, significantly diverged from the advertising tactics of those years. Dove's innovative strategy was rooted in the insight that only 2% of women globally considered themselves to be beautiful, primarily due to the pervasive influence of the idealized and often unattainable images of women presented in advertising, media and popular culture (Dove, n.d.).

The company employed a multi-channel approach, utilizing TV commercials, magazine spreads, talk shows, and a worldwide online conversation to disseminate its sensitive and groundbreaking message. However, despite its popularity and commercial success, the Real Beauty campaign has also been subject to much criticism, as consumers argued that Dove was exploiting feminist values for commercial purposes, namely to increase sales of its beauty products. Although Dove was among the first brands to build its identity around 'femvertisements', a growing marketing trend that leverages feminist values and female empowerment to drive consumer engagement (Akestam, Rosengren, & Dahlen, 2017), Dove was accused of appropriating feminist ideals and reconstructing feminism as an ideal that could, arguably, be gained through the consumption of their products (Taylor, Johnston, & Whitehead, 2016).

Notwithstanding the criticism it faced, one of the greatest achievements of the Dove campaign was that it initiated a global conversation about a broader definition of beauty. By selecting real women whose appearances are outside the stereotypical norms of beauty (e.g., older women with wrinkles, overweight women), Dove has challenged conventional beauty standards and made positive beauty experiences more accessible to a wide range of women.

Furthermore, Dove continues to develop new initiatives that promote positive body image, with its latest being 'The Code'. Marking the 20th anniversary of Real Beauty campaign, with this new ad the brand recognizes the new challenges posed by the evolving digital landscape and adapts its approach to address the impact of the new technologies on the representation of authentic beauty. Among these technologies, artificial intelligence (AI) has emerged as one of the most discussed topics, due to its profound influence on how individuals – young people, but also adults – perceive reality.

First released in the US in April 2024, The Code shed lights on the potential negative impact of AI-generated imagery on women's self-esteem. Drawing upon its latest research, the beauty care brand found that one in three women feels the need to change their physical appearance after being exposed to AI-generated images depicting unattainable aesthetic standards (Dove, 2024). In a world where beauty ideals are constantly evolving, and technology rapidly shapes how individuals perceive reality, Dove recognizes the urgent need to address the influence of digitally altered images that blur the line between reality and fantasy, undermining women's self-perception. In this way, Dove reaffirms its commitment to fostering a more inclusive and realistic portrayal of beauty in the digital age as well.

The following paragraph will delve deeper into The Code commercial, using semiotics to deconstruct the narrative strategies employed by the brand to convey its activist message. Then, netnography will be applied to analyze consumer reactions to the campaign, exploring the online discourse surrounding The Code through Youtube comments. By combining these two methodologies, this study aims to gain a comprehensive understanding of the multifaceted dimensions of Dove's social message, including its intended meaning, its reception by consumers, and its broader implications within the context of contemporary brand activism.

3.1. Semiotic Analysis of 'The Code' (Dove, 2024)

Dove's advertising campaign 'The Code' was created by the Brazilian agency Soko and has been transmitted on television networks as well as published on several social media throughout 2024. The spot is available in 115-, 60-, 30- and 15-second lengths. For the sake of completeness, this analysis focuses on the 115-second version published on Dove UK's Youtube channel[2].

The spot begins with two text-only frames, stating that Artificial Intelligence is predicted to generate 90% of online content by 2025 and that all images featured in the ad are created using AI. From a denotative standpoint, the commercial unfolds a straightforward narrative: a young girl sitting in the dark of her living room is experimenting with an AI image-generation software. As she inserts prompts such as 'imagine a gorgeous woman', 'imagine the perfect skin', 'imagine the most beautiful girl is the world', flawless images of conventionally attractive women in idyllic settings appear, emphasizing AI's inherent biases which reinforce narrow and stereotypical notions of beauty. Within this narrative, the girl assumes both the role of the *Subject* and the *Receiver* of the ad's message (Greimas & Courtés, 1979), metaphorically representing all the women struggling with AI-driven unattainable beauty standards. The *Opponent* is the societal pressure perpetuated by these representations, embodied by the tendency of AI – and, more broadly, all technologies – to create and disseminate these unrealistic norms.

The video then transitions to another text framing, showing how AI-generated images can be transformed when guided by Dove's principles. The prompts 'imagine the most beautiful woman in the world', 'imagine perfect skin' and 'imagine a gorgeous woman', when modified to include 'according to Real Beauty Ad', notably alters the AI-generated output, triggering a series of images depicting women of different ethnicities, skin tones, hair textures, and facial features, including a woman with thick, curly hair in a wheelchair, as well as other ones with visible skin imperfections. By contrasting with the previously AI-generated images of stereotypical and idealized beauty, these more inclusive and diverse representations serve both as an homage to the 2004 iconic 'Campaign for Real Beauty' and a reaffirmation of the brand's enduring commitment to authentic beauty, even in increasingly digital and technologically driven environments. In Greimasian terms (1979) Dove acts as both as the *Sender* and the *Helper*, respectively identifying the problem of AI bias in generating idealized and homogeneous images of beauty, and offering a solution by promoting more inclusive beauty standards through the creation of a real 'code' that can be applied in AI prompts. Through these actions, Dove builds *Competence* by equipping the audience with the knowledge to discern genuine beauty from unattainable beauty, as well as with the necessary toolkit (i.e., the prompt code 'according to Real Beauty Ad') to actively reshape the portrayal of beauty in digital spaces.

Subsequently, the commercial cuts to another text-only frame, posing the provoking question 'what kind of beauty do we want AI to learn?' as a sort of *enunciational debrayage* (disengagement) addressed to the audience. By encouraging viewers to reflect on the desired outcomes of AI-generated imagery, the ad positions them as active participants in shaping the cultural narrative surrounding beauty. The video then shifts to a close-up of a television screen displaying behind-the-scenes footage from the 2004 Real Beauty campaign shot by renowned photographer Ian Rankin. The intertextual reference reinforces the historical relevance of the brand's core message even in the face of new challenges posed by AI technology. Next, the commercial shows a montage of videos and photos showcasing women of different sizes and ethnicities, celebrating the multifaced nature of beauty as envisioned by

Dove. Within this *Performance* phase, women embrace and promote authentic and unaltered beauty standards, redefining beauty in a way that respects individual diversity and rejects the homogenizing effects of AI-created images.

The montage concludes with a close-up of a black woman with braids, followed by a shot of a large billboard displaying a video of her as a child, and then a grown-up version of herself hugging her mother. Another woman, holding her daughter, notices the billboard and smiles, positively sanctioning the positive impact of Dove's message across generations. The commercial concludes with Dove's pledge to never use AI to create or distort women's images, calling on viewers to change the hegemonic representation of beauty.

On a connotative level, the campaign can be interpreted as a critique of the growing influence of technology in dictating beauty standards. By juxtaposing AI-generated images representing both artificial and authentic beauty ideals[3], the spot encourages viewers to reflect on how to responsibly manage AI to expand, rather than restrict, the representation of beauty. From a plastic semiotics perspective, the AI-generated images adhering to traditional beauty standards depict women with an unrealistic perfection, exaggerated smooth skin, and unnaturally symmetry. These uncanny visual features connote a sense of deception and distance from real human portrayals, serving as allegories of the detrimental effects of idealized beauty tropes perpetuated by technology. In contrast, those aligned with Dove's principles – though still exhibiting a subtle artificiality due to their synthetic origins (e.g., consistently blurred backgrounds, excessively glossy lighting) – seek to appear more inclusive, presenting women of different ethnicities, body types, and ages, depicted in relaxed poses and showcasing natural imperfections, such as freckles or wrinkles. Despite their inevitable traces of artificiality, Dove's synthetic images aim to celebrate authenticity and diversity, depicting imperfections and natural beauty as virtues that challenge traditional idealized norms and foster a sense of representation among the target of the brand.

A few notes need to be made regarding the cultural relevance of the campaign. The commercial inserts itself into the debate on the role of technology in shaping the perception of reality, aligning with global body positivity movements that advocate for diversity, inclusion, and representation in media. In line with the cultural branding paradigm (Holt, 2002; 2004), Dove's campaign can be seen as an articulation of the brand's cultural mission to challenge conventional beauty norms. Whilst acknowledging the potential of AI to create visual representations, the campaign also critiques the way AI algorithms, trained on existing datasets, often reinforce existing biases and stereotypes, particularly those related to beauty standards. The commercial thus directly addresses contemporary anxieties (Holt, 2004) surrounding AI, urging the need for a collective effort to educate AI ethically and responsibly to ensure that it does not perpetuate or amplify harmful biases and social inequalities.

In doing so, Dove's commitment to promote authentic beauty extends beyond the commercial itself. To tangibly contribute to the ongoing conversation about ethical AI use, the brand has introduced the 'Real Beauty Prompt Playbook'. As a free guide available on the Dove website, the playbook is designed for creators, brands, and anyone using AI to create visual content, providing practical guidance on how to use AI responsibly to widen the representation of beauty through the most popular Artificial Intelligence programs (Unilever, 2024).

Hence, the positive Sanction to Dove's initiative can be also fulfilled outside the spot, through viewers' alignment with the brand's message serving as a key element of success. By equipping users with the knowledge and tools to generate more inclusive and diverse AI-powered images, Dove invites viewers to become active participants in shaping the future of AI and its influence on the perception of reality. When using Dove's prompt in AI tools, consumers are not merely interacting with a software, but they are actively contributing to a collective shift toward a more inclusive representation of beauty.

3.2. Netnographic Analysis of 'The Code' (Dove, 2024)

Dove's 'The Code' commercial was released on Dove UK's official Youtube page on April 9, 2024, and has gained 118.870 views and 327 comments as of this writing. This volume of engagement provides a suitable dataset for netnographic analysis, as this methodological approach works with smaller and more focused collections of online traces compared to large-scale trends typically explored through big data analytic approaches (Kozinets, 2019, p. 224).

The comments section on YouTube proved to be a significant and rich data source, hence meeting the selection criteria for a netnographic study. The analysis furnished valuable insights into viewers' perceptions of the commercial's message, their reactions to the brand's usage of AI, as well as their opinions on the evolving definition of beauty. The gathered data have been divided into two primary groups, highlighting both alignment with and resistance to the campaign's message: (1) positive and supportive reactions to Dove's activism and (2) criticism toward Dove's failure in adopting an activist stance. The findings will be explained in depth in the following subparagraphs.

3.2.1. Positive and Supportive Reactions to Dove's Activism

In the Youtube comments section under 'The Code' video, several viewers were found to express admiration for the campaign, highlighting positive outcomes such as viewers being impressed or captivated by the ad. These responses ranged from simple remarks such as 'A beautiful ad' and 'Stunning and brave' to more detailed and reflective statements. Consider for instance these two traces[4]:

@Smile333: What a beautiful commercial. I had to look it up to watch again.

@Japanlover: This is a beautiful advert. I usually go do something else until the ads are on, but I stay to watch this one.

A recurring theme among these comments is the profound engagement with the ad, with users actively seeking it out or choosing to watch it again, thus bucking the trend of ad avoidance. This voluntary attention within a media landscape saturated with commercial messages testifies activist communication's ability to engage even those who typically ignore commercials. Furthermore, both comments use the terms 'beautiful' to express appreciation for the emotional impact and the overall quality of the commercial.

Other comments were found to delve more deeply into the emotional impact of the Dove's campaign:

@foxy2010: This commercial made me cry, because there's so much pressure for us to be beautiful.

@partofme: This just makes me feel like crying, and it makes me feel beautiful, thank you. <3

By addressing the theme of societal pressure to conform to unattainable beauty standards, Dove's commercial is perceived as fostering a sense of emotional release and catharsis among users. Many comments reflect a personal connection with the ad's message, likely tied to their own lived experiences and individual struggles with societal beauty expectations. The second user also expresses gratitude for the brand's effort to challenge established norms, indicating that the campaign help consumers to feel understood and validated. Moreover, the recurring theme of the ad making viewers 'feel beautiful' suggests that Dove is successfully achieving its goal of challenging traditional beauty norms and helping women to enhance their self-perception.

The last group of positive reactions reflects audience's admiration for the social and educational impact of the campaign:

@candycandy: I love when corporations can help their bottom line and humanity at the same time. It sets a precedent for the rest.

@maryhay: Showing this in my Advertising Issues class as we talk about stereotypes in AI (and the need to break them). Thanks Dove.

The first comment acknowledges Dove's alignment between profit and values, which can benefit both its business and society at large. This synergy sets Dove as an example for other brands to follow, since its campaign is not only beneficial for its own reputation but also has the potential to inspire broader shifts within the industry. Within a similar vein, @maryhay points to the campaign's educational dimension, expanding its relevance beyond the commercial sphere. The potential integration of the commercial into a school setting offers an opportunity for Dove's message to extend its reach and shape the next generation's understanding of purpose-driven branding.

3.2.2. Criticism towards Dove's Failure in Adopting an Activist Stance

Despite Dove's efforts to convey a sensitive and impactful social message, not all viewers found the campaign well-executed and convincing. This scepticism stems from various motives, ranging from dissatisfaction with the campaign's execution to disagreement with the advocated stance. Let's delve further into the first group of negative reactions concerning consumers' criticism toward corporate motives:

@oneglance: Sorry but this is just stupid. [...] Those are just different questions with no relevance to each other. Also, we all know that Dove will be posting ads of 1%ers again when the ad doesn't get enough traction. Same thing as all ads, including this one. The only purpose is to get people to buy their products.

@sportyboy99: When I want a lesson on morality, I always look to greedy multinational corporations who got rich by mixing chemicals together. Thanks, Dove! What would we do without your glory? You should use AI to write a new bible so we can all worship you together!

Both users express doubt about Dove's sincere commitment to social change, portraying the campaign as a marketing trap hiding the intent to exploit sensitive issues for commercial gain. More specifically, the sarcastic tone of the second comment indicates a strong disdain for what is perceived as moral posturing by a profit-driven entity. When brands address societal issues, some consumers may perceive their efforts as hypocritical or insincere, highlighting a critical aspect of purpose-driven marketing that brands must carefully navigate: the need to demonstrate genuine commitment and authenticity in their messaging and actions to build trust and avoid potential backlashes.

Another category of criticism emerged among Youtube comments, concerning the perceived 'wokeness' and 'political correctness' of the campaign:

@Eddy02: Dove as always being as cringe and DEI as possible.

@Williambros: So according to Dove: average is the most beautiful?
Dove: We're afraid to stand up for what is true beauty thanks to wokeness.
Dove: It's okay to be ugly.
What a cringy piece of shit of advertising.

@redhead: I really can't imagine someone in the marketing dept accepting to use this bs, worst ad in the world, so bigot, so unbearably politically correct.

The expression 'as cringe and DEI as possible' reflects a disparaging view toward campaigns promoting values such as diversity, equity, and inclusion. As in Dove's case, advertising revolving around inclusivity is perceived as forced or inauthentic by audiences resistant to such themes, who associate this kind of messages with political correctness and virtue signalling. The use of the term 'wokeness' represents the second commenter's cultural resistance to campaigns that align with social movements, which are perceived as prioritizing political correctness to capitalize on current trends. The tension between Dove's advocated values and conservative consumers' standpoint underscores the difficulty of shifting cultural ideologies in an audience that is attached to conventional beauty standards.

A third set of negative reactions provides critical perspectives on perceived stereotypes and unintentional implications carried on by Dove's campaign:

@kimikim: Funny how most of people who are attractive according to dove are of different races. It kind of feels like their trying to say 'only white women who have blonde hair are attractive by average standards, but if you have perfect skin other than a few wrinkles then don't worry! Dove loves you'. And if you don't fit into either box, then, well... I guess you aren't attractive in their opinion (which is wrong: their a billion dollar company they don't care about what you think as long as you buy their products [...])

@instapro: I find it amusing that Dove actually think that people do not perceive Black and Asian women as beautiful. It looks like they are so racist in their thoughts and projecting that opinion on others. It is like when you are riding in a car with a black dude and turn on rap music, then looking at him and smiling, thinking: "Oh my god, I am so not racist that I even turned on his favourite music". Or saying to an Asian that you like Chinese culture, not knowing where they actually from. Yeah. Totally not racist.

Whilst @kimikim raises concerns about the risk for such campaigns to inadvertently reinforce existing stereotypes about racial diversity – for instance, implicitly creating new beauty ideals and suggesting that true beauty only exists within these specific categories – @instapro points to a more insidious concern: the potential for these campaigns to reinforce racist assumptions by overcompensating in the representation of non-white beauty. By using the analogy of 'turning on rap music for a black dude', the commenter depicts Dove's efforts as superficial and performative. Hence, activist brands should consider that inclusivity campaigns, if not handled with nuance, can sometimes be interpreted as reinforcing what they are trying to overcome, i.e., stereotypes.

The fourth group of comments focuses on the perceived inconsistency and hypocrisy of the commercial:

@mcr55: All this did was make me want MidJourney soap. And also, you said you'll never use AI to create or distort images of women. But you literally did that very thing to make this ad. So, you are lying to women as well.

@claudette: For Dove the most beautiful girl in the world is a computer girl. It doesn't exist. Absurd.

@MotherOfDragons: So to fight beauty standards in generative AI pics, you... Keep using generative AI...? Am I missing something??

Several posters were found to critique the personal care brand for contradicting its own promise to avoid using AI in its advertisement, paradoxically employing the same tool that the campaign condemns for its biases in generating images of women. Despite the positive intentions behind the social message, inconsistency in the execution of the campaign can undermine and weaken the credibility of activist advertisements.

Finally, some comments reflect disappointment and frustration from viewers who attempted to engage with the campaign by using the prompts promoted by Dove but found the experience to be unsuccessful:

@oatmilk999: I just searched "/imagine a gorgeous woman", and nothing but AI showed up.

@thomas: I tried and it doesn't work.

As previously mentioned, Dove's commitment toward authentic beauty was not limited to a positive social message inside the spot, but was also concretized in a guidebook for responsibly using AI in order to broaden the representation of beauty. However, several users reported the malfunctioning of the prompts promoted by the ad. More specifically, the first commenter expected the prompt to generate images aligned with the diverse and inclusive standards advocated by Dove in the campaign, but the AI-generated images did not meet the expectations. The user experience @ thomas is negative as well, although he only states that the inserted code does not work. Dove's idealistic message of promoting wider beauty standards through AI tools was found to clash with the reality of tangible experiences, revealing that even well-intentioned campaigns can struggle when trying to implement complex ideas in real-life. When launching tangible brand activism initiatives, brands should ensure of the actual effectiveness of the instruments they are promoting, since negative outcomes can be seen as a failure of the campaign's conveyed message.

4. CONCLUSION

From urging society to widen the representation of women's beauty to advocating for transparency in digital manipulation, Dove has long sought to act as a catalyst for change, with 'The Code' campaign standing as its latest attempt.

On a semiotic level, the commercial presents a clear narrative: a young girl experiments with AI image generation software, observing how the AI initially produces idealized, often unrealistic images of women, but then, when prompted with 'Real Beauty' criteria, evolves to generate more diverse and inclusive representations. By acting both as a Sender and Helper within the Greimasian framework, Dove seeks to position itself as a leader in promoting positive body image also in an increasingly digital world. Through this campaign, Dove inspires the audience (Subject) to challenge AI-influenced beauty ideals (Opponent) and achieve the goal of redefining beauty in broader and more inclusive terms. Without demonizing AI, the commercial, along with the brand's tangible effort in creating a real prompt guide for users, emphasizes the importance of responsible AI usage, encouraging viewers to take concrete actions to educate AI in generating more authentic and inclusive representations. Hence, consistently with Boero's (2022) analysis of social advertising, the audience represents an active agent of change, with the possibility to frame a better future through collective commitment and action. However, the ultimate sanction – metaphorically represented within the commercial by the smile of the mother and the daughter – lies in real-world societal and cultural shifts. Thus, a first attempt to search for this sanction through netnography has been made.

Notwithstanding the noble intention behind Dove's campaign message, in line with the literature on brand activism and woke branding (Buyukozturk, Gaulden, & Dowd-Arrow, 2018; Flecha-Ortiz, Rivera-Guevarrez, Santos-Corrada, & Fonseca, 2024) the commercial was found to strongly polarize audiences. Whilst many viewers expressed positive and emotional reactions, praising Dove's commitment and feeling understood through the campaign's alignment with their lived experiences, a subset of the audience perceived the campaign as opportunistic and full of contradictions. First, a plethora of criticisms targeted the brand's corporate motives, seeing the campaign as a mere profit-driven marketing strategy rather than a purpose-driven effort. Additionally, some commenters questioned the campaign execution by pointing out inherent contradictions, such as the unintentional reinforcement of existing stereotypes as well as the decision of critiquing AI-generated beauty standards while in turn relying on AI-generated imagery for the campaign. Furthermore, others testify that the provided prompts for responsible AI use did not function as expected, implying that the practical application of the campaign failed to convey the intended message. For brands like Dove, success requires not only promoting sensitive and impactful messages through advertising but also ensuring that the tools and resources provided to support such messages must be accessible and effective in fostering real-world change.

Given its straightforward language and widespread reach, advertising possesses significant potential to raise awareness on current issues and promote ethical values (Boero, 2022). As the dissemination of AI continues to grow, activist communication can play a pivotal role in making the audience aware of its ethical and responsible development, thereby igniting necessary transformations. Within this context, the Code campaign offers a nuanced case study in contemporary advertising. While it effectively sparks meaningful conversations about beauty standards perpetuated by AI, it also highlights the challenges that brands face under increasing consumer scrutiny in a rapidly evolving cultural landscape. Nonetheless, the campaign's actual success will depend on its ability to inspire a lasting change in how beauty is portrayed and perceived in the digital age. Whether the campaign will be beneficial, harmful, or something in-between, will ultimately depend on the audience's interpretation and reception.

REFERENCES

Ahmad, F., Guzmán, F., & Al-Emran, M. (2024). Brand activism and the consequence of woke washing. *Journal of Business Research, 170*, 114362. DOI: 10.1016/j.jbusres.2023.114362

Akestam, N., Rosengren, S., & Dahlen, M. (2017). Advertising 'Like a Girl': Toward a Better Understanding of 'Femvertising' and Its Effects. *Psychology and Marketing*, *34*(8), 795–806. DOI: 10.1002/mar.21023

Beer, D. (2009). Power through the algorithm? Participatory web cultures and the technological unconscious. *New Media & Society*, *11*(6), 985–1002. DOI: 10.1177/1461444809336551

Bianchi, C. (2020). Nuove forme di testualità nel digital marketing. *Lexia. Rivista di semiotica, 33–34*, 13–29.

Bissell, K., & Rask, A. (2010). Real Women on Real Beauty: Self-Discrepancy, Internalization of the Thin Ideal, and Perceptions of Attractiveness and Thinness in Dove's Campaign for Real Beauty. *International Journal of Advertising*, *29*(4), 643–668. DOI: 10.2501/S0265048710201385

Boero, M. (2022). Natura, clima, sostenibilità. Il linguaggio pubblicitario tra etica e semiotica. *Filosofi(e). Semiotiche*, *9*(1), 21–31.

Boström, M., & Micheletti, M. (2016). Introducing the sustainability challenge of textiles and clothing. *Journal of Consumer Policy*, *39*(4), 367–375. DOI: 10.1007/s10603-016-9336-6

Buyukozturk, B., Gaulden, S., & Dowd-Arrow, B. (2018). Contestation on Reddit, Gamergate, and movement barriers. *Social Movement Studies*, *17*(5), 592–609. DOI: 10.1080/14742837.2018.1483227

Cammarota, A., D'Arco, M., Marino, V., & Resciniti, R. (2023). Brand activism: A literature review and future research agenda. *International Journal of Consumer Studies*, *47*(5), 1669–1691. DOI: 10.1111/ijcs.12967

Campbell, R., Freeman, O., & Gannon, V. (2021). From Overt Threat to Invisible Presence: Discursive Shifts in Representations of Gender in Menstrual Product Advertising. *Journal of Marketing Management*, *37*(3–4), 216–237. DOI: 10.1080/0267257X.2021.1876752

Chandy, R. K., Johar, G. V., & Roberts, J. H. (2021). Better Marketing for a Better World. *Journal of Marketing*, *85*(3), 1–9. DOI: 10.1177/00222429211003690

Cohen, S. (2020, May 30). *'For Once, Don't Do It': The Powerful Idea Behind Nike's New Anti-Racism Ad.* Retrieved from Forbes: https://www.forbes.com/sites/sethcohen/2020/05/30/for-once-dont-do-it---the-powerful-idea-behind-nikes-new-anti-racism-ad/

de Oca, J. M., Mason, S., & Ahn, S. (2022). Consuming for the greater good: "Woke" commercials in sports media. *Communication & Sport, 10*(6), 1165–1187. DOI: 10.1177/2167479520949283

Dodd, M. D., & Supa, D. W. (2014). Conceptualizing and measuring "corporate social advocacy" communication: Examining the impact on corporate financial performance. *The Public Relations Journal, 8*(3), 2–23.

Dove (2024). *The Real State of Beauty: A Global Report.*

Dove (n.d.). *The world's largest beauty report*. Retrieved from Dove: https://www.dove.com/us/en/campaigns/purpose/global-state-of-beauty.html

Edelman (2018, May 1). *Edelman Trust Barometer: Expectations for CEOs.* Retrieved from Edelman Trust Barometer: https://www.edelman.com/post/trust-barometer-expectations-for-ceos

Filieri, R., Alguezaui, S., & McLeay, F. (2015). Why do travelers trust TripAdvisor? Antecedents of trust towards consumer-generated media and its influence on recommendation adoption and word of mouth. *Tourism Management, 51*, 174–185. DOI: 10.1016/j.tourman.2015.05.007

Flecha-Ortiz, J. A., Rivera-Guevarrez, R., Santos-Corrada, M., & Fonseca, M. (2024). Boycott and Buycott Intent to Actions: Unpacking the Role of Political Ideology and Advertising through The Society of the Spectacle. *Journal of Political Marketing*, •••, 1–27. DOI: 10.1080/15377857.2024.2397964

Flight, R. L., & Coker, K. (2021). Birds of a feather: Brand attachment through the lens of consumer political ideologies. *Journal of Product and Brand Management, 31*(5), 731–743.

Floch, J. M. (1990). *Sémiotique, marketing et communication. Sous les signes, les stratégies*. Presses Universitaires de France.

Greimas, A. J., & Courtés, J. (1979). *Sémiotique. Dictionnaire raisonné de la théorie du langage*. Hachette.

Halupka, M. (2014). Clicktivism: A systematic heuristic. *Policy and Internet, 6*(2), 115–132. DOI: 10.1002/1944-2866.POI355

Hansen, N., Kupfer, A. K., & Hennig-Thurau, T. (2018). Brand crises in the digital age: The short-and long-term effects of social media firestorms on consumers and brands. *International Journal of Research in Marketing, 35*(4), 557–574. DOI: 10.1016/j.ijresmar.2018.08.001

Hennig-Thurau, T., Wiertz, C., & Feldhaus, F. (2015). Does twitter matter? The impact of microblogging word of mouth on consumers' adoption of new movies. *Journal of the Academy of Marketing Science, 43*(3), 375–394. DOI: 10.1007/s11747-014-0388-3

Hesse, A., Niederle, F., Schön, L., & Stautz, D. (2021). Consumer responses to brand communications involving COVID-19. *Journal of Marketing Management, 37*(17–18), 1783–1814. DOI: 10.1080/0267257X.2021.2000008

Holt, D. B. (2002). Why Do Brands Cause Trouble? A Dialectical Theory of Consumer Culture and Branding. *The Journal of Consumer Research, 29*(1), 70–90. DOI: 10.1086/339922

Holt, D. B. (2004). *How Brands Become Icons: The Principles of Cultural Branding*. Harvard Business Press.

Hydock, C., Paharia, N., & Blair, S. (2020). Should Your Brand Pick a Side? How Market Share Determines the Impact of Corporate Political Advocacy. *JMR, Journal of Marketing Research, 57*(6), 1135–1151. DOI: 10.1177/0022243720947682

Jenkins, H. (2006). *Convergence culture: Where old and new media collide*. New York University Press.

Johnson, C. D., Bauer, B. C., & Carlson, B. D. (2022). Constituency building: Determining consumers' willingness to participate in corporate political activities. *International Journal of Research in Marketing, 39*(1), 42–57. DOI: 10.1016/j.ijresmar.2021.06.004

Karunakaran, A. (2024). Frontline Professionals in the Wake of Social Media Scrutiny: Examining the Processes of Obscured Accountability. *Administrative Science Quarterly, 69*(3), 747–790. DOI: 10.1177/00018392241256303

Kauflin, J. (2017, February 6). *Why Audi's Super Bowl Ad Failed*. Retrieved from Forbes: https://www.forbes.com/sites/jeffkauflin/2017/02/06/why-audis-super-bowl-ad-failed/

Klostermann, J., Hydock, C., & Decker, R. (2022). The effect of corporate political advocacy on brand perception: An event study analysis. *Journal of Product and Brand Management, 31*(5), 780–797. DOI: 10.1108/JPBM-03-2021-3404

Koch, C. H. (2020). Brands as activists: The Oatly case. *Journal of Brand Management, 275*(5), 593–606. DOI: 10.1057/s41262-020-00199-2

Kozinets, R. V. (2019). *Netnography: The essential guide to qualitative social media research*. Sage.

Kozinets, R. V., & Nocker, M. (2018). Netnography: Online ethnography for a digital age of organization research. In Bryman, A., & Buchanan, D. A. (Eds.), *Unconventional methodology in organization and management research* (pp. 127–146). Oxford University Press.

Kozinets, R. V., & Seraj-Aksit, M. (2024). Everyday activism: An AI-assisted netnography of a digital consumer movement. *Journal of Marketing Management, 40*(3–4), 347–370. DOI: 10.1080/0267257X.2024.2307387

Labrecque, L. I., Vor Dem Esche, J., Mathwick, C., Novak, T. P., & Hofacker, C. F. (2013). Consumer power: Evolution in the digital age. *Journal of Interactive Marketing*, *27*(4), 257–269. DOI: 10.1016/j.intmar.2013.09.002

Maks-Solomon, C., & Drewry, J. M. (2020). Why do corporations engage in LGBT rights activism? LGBT employee groups as internal pressure groups. *Business and Politics*, *23*(1), 124–152. DOI: 10.1017/bap.2020.5

Mirzaei, A., Wilkie, D. C., & Siuki, H. (2022). Woke brand activism authenticity or the lack of it. *Journal of Business Research*, *139*, 1–12. DOI: 10.1016/j.jbusres.2021.09.044

Moorman, C. (2020). Commentary: Brand activism in a political world. *Journal of Public Policy & Marketing*, *39*(4), 388–392. DOI: 10.1177/0743915620945260

Neureiter, M., & Bhattacharya, C. B. (2021). Why do boycotts sometimes increase sales? Consumer activism in the age of political polarization. *Business Horizons*, *64*(5), 611–620. DOI: 10.1016/j.bushor.2021.02.025

O'Brien, S. A. (2020, August 18). *Glossier, a billion-dollar beauty brand, apologizes to former retail workers after racism allegations*. Retrieved from CNN: https://edition.cnn.com/2020/08/18/tech/glossier-apology-retail-workers/index.html

Pasirayi, S., Fennell, P. B., & Follmer, K. B. (2023). #Activism: Investor reactions to corporate sociopolitical activism. *Business & Society*, *62*(4), 704–744. DOI: 10.1177/00076503221110457

Paton, E., Friedman, V., & Testa, J. (2022, November 29). *When High Fashion and QAnon Collide*. Retrieved from The New York Times: https://www.nytimes.com/2022/11/28/style/balenciaga-campaign-controversy.html

Pfeffer, J., Zorbach, T., & Carley, K. M. (2014). Understanding online firestorms: Negative word-of-mouth dynamics in social media networks. *Journal of Marketing Communications*, *20*(2), 117–128. DOI: 10.1080/13527266.2013.797778

Pimentel, P. C., Bassi-Suter, M., & Didonet, S. R. (2024). Brand activism as a marketing strategy: An integrative framework and research agenda. *Journal of Brand Management*, *31*(2), 212–234. DOI: 10.1057/s41262-023-00335-8

Pöyry, E., & Laaksonen, S. M. (2022). Opposing brand activism: Triggers and strategies of consumers' antibrand actions. *European Journal of Marketing*, *56*(13), 261–284. DOI: 10.1108/EJM-12-2020-0901

Rauschnabel, P. A., Kammerlander, N., & Ivens, B. S. (2016). Collaborative brand attacks in social media: Exploring the antecedents, characteristics, and consequences of a new form of brand crises. *Journal of Marketing Theory and Practice*, *24*(4), 381–410. DOI: 10.1080/10696679.2016.1205452

Sarkar, C., & Kotler, P. (2018). *Brand Activism: From Purpose to Action*. Idea Bite Press.

Schmidt, H. J., Ind, N., Guzmán, F., & Kennedy, E. (2021). Sociopolitical activist brands. *Journal of Product and Brand Management*, *31*(1), 40–55. DOI: 10.1108/JPBM-03-2020-2805

Schroeder, J. E. (2017). Corporate branding in perspective: A typology. *European Journal of Marketing*, *51*(9/10), 1522–1529. DOI: 10.1108/EJM-07-2017-0450

Shoenberger, H., Kim, E. A., & Sun, Y. (2021). Advertising during COVID-19: Exploring perceived brand message authenticity and potential psychological reactance. *Journal of Advertising*, *50*(3), 253–261. DOI: 10.1080/00913367.2021.1927914

Sibai, O., Mimoun, L., & Boukis, A. (2021). Authenticating brand activism: Negotiating the boundaries of free speech to make a change. *Psychology and Marketing*, *38*(10), 1651–1669. DOI: 10.1002/mar.21477

Simões, C., & Sebastiani, R. (2017). The nature of the relationship between corporate identity and corporate sustainability: Evidence from the retail industry. *Business Ethics Quarterly*, *27*(3), 423–453. DOI: 10.1017/beq.2017.15

Smith, A. (2017, April 5). *Pepsi Pulls Controversial Kendall Jenner Ad After Outcry*. Retrieved from NBC News: https://www.nbcnews.com/news/nbcblk/pepsi-ad-kendall-jenner-echoes-black- lives-matter-sparks-anger-n742811

Sobande, F. (2019). Woke-washing: "Intersectional" femvertising and branding "woke" bravery. *European Journal of Marketing*, *54*(11), 2723–2745. DOI: 10.1108/EJM-02-2019-0134

Sterbenk, Y. M., Ward, J., Luttrell, W. R., & Summer Shelton, S. (2022). Silence has no place: A framing analysis of corporate statements about racial inequity, immigration policy and LGBTQ rights. *Corporate Communications*, *27*(2), 404–421. DOI: 10.1108/CCIJ-09-2021-0106

Swaminathan, V., Sorescu, A. S., O'Guinn, T. C., & Schmitt, B. H. (2020). Branding in a hyperconnected world: Refocusing theories and rethinking boundaries. *Journal of Marketing*, *84*(2), 24–46. DOI: 10.1177/0022242919899905

Taylor, J., Johnston, J., & Whitehead, K. (2016). A Corporation in Feminist Clothing? Young Women Discuss the Dove 'Real Beauty' Campaign. *Critical Sociology*, *42*(1), 123–144. DOI: 10.1177/0896920513501355

The New York Times. (2023, October 27). *Kanye and Adidas: Money, Misconduct and the Price of Appeasement*. Retrieved from The New York Times: https://www.nytimes.com/2023/10/27/business/kanye-west-adidas-yeezy.html

Traini, S. (2020). Comunicazioni emotive dei media nell'epoca della «post-verità»: le isole di plastica negli oceani raccontate da la Repubblica. *Rivista Italiana di Filosofia del Linguaggio*, 188–202.

Unilever (2024, April 23). *20 years on: Dove and the future of Real Beauty*. Retrieved from Unilever: https://www.unilever.com/news/news-search/2024/20-years-on-dove-and-the-future-of-real-beauty/

Varghese, N., & Kumar, N. (2020). Feminism in advertising: Irony or revolution? A critical review of femvertising. *Feminist Media Studies*, *22*(2), 441–459. DOI: 10.1080/14680777.2020.1825510

Vaughan, A. (2014, October 9). *Lego ends Shell partnership following Greenpeace campaign*. Retrieved from The Guardian: https://www.theguardian.com/environment/2014/oct/09/lego-ends-shell-partnership-following-greenpeace-campaign#:~:text=Lego%20will%20not%20renew%20its,that%20dates%20to%20the%201960s

Vredenburg, J., Kapitan, S., Spry, A., & Kemper, J. A. (2020). Brands taking a stand: Authentic brand activism or woke washing? *Journal of Public Policy & Marketing*, *39*(4), 444–460. DOI: 10.1177/0743915620947359

Warren, N. L. (2021). Boycott or Buycott: The aftermath of corporate activism. *NIM Marketing Intelligence Review*, *13*(2), 32–37. DOI: 10.2478/nimmir-2021-0014

Weinzimmer, L. G., & Esken, C. A. (2016). Risky business: Taking a stand on social issues. *Business Horizons*, *59*(3), 331–337. DOI: 10.1016/j.bushor.2016.01.007

Xu, Y., Liu, X., Cao, X., Huang, C., Liu, E., Qian, S., Liu, X., Wu, Y., Dong, F., Qiu, C.-W., Qiu, J., Hua, K., Su, W., Wu, J., Xu, H., Han, Y., Fu, C., Yin, Z., Liu, M., & Zhang, J. (2021). Artificial intelligence: A powerful paradigm for scientific research. *Innovation (Cambridge (Mass.))*, *2*(4), 1–20. DOI: 10.1016/j.xinn.2021.100179

KEY TERMS AND DEFINITIONS

Artificial Intelligence: The simulation of human intelligence processes in machines, enabling them to perform complex tasks previously exclusive to humans, such as reasoning, decision-making, and problem-solving (Xu, et al., 2021).

Brand Activism: The business efforts to promote, impede, or direct social, political, economic, and/or environmental reform with the desire to promote or impede improvements in society (Sarkar & Kotler, 2018).

Clicktivism: A low quality and less effective form of social mobilization within digital environments where users can easily and quickly express their ideas and standpoints around socio-political issues by means of a ‘click’ of their mouse (Halupka, 2014).

Cultural Branding: A branding perspective that challenges the traditional view of brands as mere corporate entities and position them as powerful cultural symbols that both shape and are shaped within particular socio-cultural contexts (Holt, 2002; Schroeder, 2017).

Femvertising: A growing marketing trend utilized by brands, such as Dove, that appropriates feminist values and female empowerment to encourage brand consumption (Akestam, Rosengren, & Dahlen, 2017).

Mythical Advertising: A type of advertising language that transcends the mundane aspects of consumerism by imbuing products with dreams and emotions (Floch, 1990).

Netnography: A particular kind of online ethnography whose use is commonplace in marketing and consumer research and whose purpose is to examine the dynamics of meaning making and its understanding, studying social interaction that occurs on interactive media by means of a cultural perspective (Kozinets & Nocker, 2018).

Oblique Advertising: An advertising language that employs rhetorical strategies like irony and paradox to subvert expectations and challenge the interpretive abilities of the consumer (Floch, 1990).

Online Firestorms: The sudden discharge of large quantities of messages containing negative word of mouth and complaint behaviour against a person, company, or group in social media environments (Pfeffer, Zorbach, & Carley, 2014).

Prompt: The information, sentences or questions that are entered by the user into a generative AI software.

Woke Washing: A marketing trick undertaken by brands by superficially aligning with public social movements to capitalize on consumer trends and build ephemeral connections based on perceived socio-political shared values (Mirzaei, Wilkie, & Siuki, 2022).

ENDNOTES

1 Evolution (https://www.youtube.com/watch?v=iYhCn0jf46U) has achieved significant recognition, leading the brand to win two Cannes Lions Grand Prix Awards in June 2007 at the Cannes Lion International Advertising Festival in France.

2 https://www.youtube.com/watch?v=13WZij3xmCA&t=3s

3 As mentioned at the beginning of the commercial, all images were generated by means of an AI software.

4 For purposes of confidentiality, Youtube users' profile names have been replaced with pseudonyms. Moreover, minor spelling corrections have been undertaken to improve readability.

Chapter 7
Digital Marketing and Semiotics

Nilesh Anute
https://orcid.org/0000-0001-6599-813X
Sri Balaji University, India

Prashant Kalshetti
https://orcid.org/0000-0003-3553-2093
Global Business School and Research Centre, Dr. D.Y. Patil Vidyapeeth, India

Jayashree Patole
https://orcid.org/0000-0001-9251-0654
Ramachandran International Institute of Management, India

Mohit Sharma
https://orcid.org/0009-0007-2280-8077
Maharshi Dayanand University, India

Priyanka Pawar
https://orcid.org/0009-0005-1043-419X
Indira College of Engineering and Management, India

P. Selvakumar
https://orcid.org/0000-0002-3650-4548
Department of Science and Humanities, Nehru Institute of Technology, Coimbatore, India

ABSTRACT

In the fast-evolving world of digital marketing, businesses, brands, and organizations are constantly searching for ways to engage consumers, shape perceptions, and create meaningful interactions in the vast expanse of the online environment. The rise of digital technologies and the increasing prominence of social media, e-commerce, and mobile applications have transformed the way people connect, shop, and interact with brands. In this digital landscape, communication extends beyond words and images to encompass a rich and complex system of signs, symbols, and cultural references. It is here that the field of semiotics— the study of signs and symbols— becomes critically important for understanding how meaning is constructed and transmitted in online spaces. Digital marketing and semiotics

DOI: 10.4018/979-8-3693-8024-6.ch007

are inextricably linked in the modern world. While digital marketing refers to the strategies and tactics used by businesses to promote products, services, or brands using digital technologies.

INTRODUCTION

While digital marketing refers to the strategies and tactics used by businesses to promote products, services, or brands using digital technologies, semiotics provides the framework for understanding how meaning is created, communicated, and interpreted through those very same technologies. Semiotics explores the intricate relationships between signs (such as logos, text, images, videos, and even sounds) and the cultural and social contexts that give them meaning. This could take the form of creating memes, writing reviews, or even modifying a brand’s message to fit its narrative. Marketers must, therefore, consider how their content will be coopted and recontextualized by consumers. Semiotics can help brands understand how their messages might be interpreted or reinterpreted when taken out of their original context. For example, a viral campaign might take on a life of its own, as consumers create alternative meanings or humorous twists on the brand's message. Marketers who understand semiotics can better anticipate these shifts in meaning and craft campaigns that are adaptable and resilient in the face of such transformations. Digital Storytelling: Crafting Meaning Through Narrative: Storytelling has become an increasingly important element in digital marketing, as brands strive to connect with consumers on an emotional level. Storytelling allows marketers to use semiotic tools like narrative structure, symbolism, and character development to create a compelling story that consumers can relate to and engage with. By weaving signs and symbols together into a cohesive narrative, brands can create powerful, emotionally charged content that resonates with consumers on a deeper level. As technology advances and the digital ecosystem continues to evolve, the role of semiotics in digital marketing will only grow in importance, helping brands navigate the complexities of an ever-changing online space and build lasting relationships with their audiences. Through the careful application of semiotic principles, marketers can ensure that their messages not only capture attention but also create a deeper connection with consumers, driving engagement and fostering brand loyalty in the process.

SEMIOTICS: THE SCIENCE OF SIGNS AND SYMBOLS IN MARKETING COMMUNICATION

In the world of marketing communication, effective messaging is the key to attracting, engaging, and retaining consumers. However, understanding how messages are constructed and interpreted is far from straightforward. In a world filled with an overwhelming amount of information, consumers must be able to decode the meanings behind marketing content to engage with it meaningfully. The importance of semiotics in marketing cannot be overstated, as it allows brands to craft more effective communication strategies by understanding not only what their messages say, but how those messages are likely to be perceived and interpreted by consumers (Lytvynenko A., et al, 2022). In marketing, these cultural codes play a pivotal role in the creation of meaning. Advertisements, for instance, often rely on a shared set of cultural codes—such as specific visual symbols, language, or narratives—to convey their message. The "code" of luxury, for example, may be represented by a sophisticated design, muted colors, and premium materials. These codes are designed to evoke feelings of exclusivity and wealth, influencing consumer perceptions of the brand. When these cultural codes are used effectively, they help to establish a connection between the brand and the consumer, as the message is immediately recognizable and understood. Signs, Symbols, and Consumer Behavior The power of semiotics in marketing lies not just in how signs are constructed, but in how they influence consumer behavior (Dunleavy D., 2020). These emotional connections are often rooted in cultural codes and semiotic associations that consumers recognize and internalize over time.

A classic example of this is Coca-Cola's use of red and white in its branding. These colors are not only eye-catching, but they also evoke feelings of joy, energy, and excitement, which the brand wants to associate with its soft drinks. The Role of Semiotics in Branding and Advertising: Branding is one of the most critical areas where semiotics plays a significant role (Bakshi & Kaur, 2023). A brand is essentially a collection of signs and symbols that communicate a unique identity, personality, and value proposition to consumers. These signs can be visual (logos, color schemes, packaging), auditory (slogans, jingles, sound logos), or linguistic (brand name, tagline), but they all contribute to the creation of meaning. Understanding how these signs interact and how they are decoded by consumers is vital for building a strong brand identity. The process of brand building is, in many ways, the process of creating and managing a semiotic system that conveys the desired meanings to the target audience. Consider how Apple's minimalist design aesthetic and sleek product packaging convey messages of innovation, simplicity, and high-end sophistication. The brand's logo, product design, and advertisements all work together to create a unified, consistent semiotic message that has helped Apple build one of the most valuable and recognizable brands in the world (Aiello G., 2020). However, marketers must be aware that consumers are also active interpreters of these messages. If a brand's message does not resonate authentically or aligns poorly with the cultural codes of the influencer's audience, it can backfire.

DIGITAL MARKETING LANDSCAPE: TRENDS, CHALLENGES, AND OPPORTUNITIES

The landscape of digital marketing is continually shifting, driven by technological advancements, evolving consumer behaviors, and emerging platforms. As businesses strive to meet the ever-changing demands of modern consumers, understanding the latest trends, navigating the challenges, and seizing the opportunities presented by the digital age are crucial for success. Digital marketing has transformed the way brands interact with their audiences, providing a myriad of ways to engage and build relationships. Machine learning algorithms help analyze large datasets, predict consumer behavior, and optimize marketing campaigns for greater effectiveness (Gupta N., 2020). AI is also transforming content creation, with tools that can generate blog posts, product descriptions, and even social media posts based on specified parameters. Automated email marketing campaigns, personalized recommendations, and predictive analytics are just a few of the ways AI is being used to improve targeting and customer engagement. Voice Search and Smart Devices: The increasing use of voice assistants, such as Amazon Alexa, Google Assistant, and Apple's Siri, has transformed the way consumers search for information and interact with brands. Marketers are increasingly leveraging influencers to build brand credibility and reach new customers (Ghorbani Z., et al, 2021). However, the influencer marketing space is also evolving, with a focus shifting towards authenticity and micro-influencers—individuals with smaller but more engaged and loyal audiences. This shift has led brands to prioritize building long-term partnerships with influencers who align with their values and message. As digital ads become more pervasive, consumers are increasingly ignoring or blocking them (Araújo S O., et al, 2021). Brands can use these platforms to engage with their audience in real time, answer questions, share behind-the-scenes content, and foster conversations. Building an online community creates a sense of belonging among consumers, who can become advocates for the brand. By focusing on engagement rather than just promotion, brands can cultivate trust, loyalty, and long-term relationships with their customers (Chaffey D., et al, 2022). The rise of social commerce, where consumers can make purchases directly through platforms like Instagram and Facebook, also presents a major opportunity for brands to drive sales and increase visibility.

SEMIOTICS OF SOCIAL MEDIA: DECODING SYMBOLS, ICONS, AND INFLUENCERS

In today's digital age, social media has become an integral part of modern life, influencing everything from communication and entertainment to commerce and culture. As a result, the semiotics of social media—understanding how signs, symbols, and meanings are created, communicated, and interpreted—have gained significant importance. Semiotics, the study of signs and symbols and how they produce meaning, is a powerful tool for decoding the complex layers of communication in social media. Every post, image, video, or comment is a complex web of semiotic elements that work together to communicate a message (Elhamy H M., 2022). These icons not only function as interactive elements but also shape the way users participate in the social media experience. Hashtags and Trending Topics: Creating Collective Meaning: Hashtags are among the most powerful semiotic tools on social media, allowing users to link content to larger conversations, movements, or trends. A hashtag is a signifier, composed of the pound symbol followed by a specific word or phrase (Januartha I W., 2024). For brands, hashtags present an opportunity to tap into cultural moments, align with social causes, and engage in real-time conversations with their audiences. However, marketers must be careful when using trending hashtags to ensure they are being used authentically and in line with their brand values to avoid backlash or accusations of "hashtag hijacking."

The symbols they use—whether it's a specific brand of clothing, a set of hashtags, or even the locations they frequent—serve as signifiers that communicate specific meanings to their followers. These meanings are often tied to values, aspirations, and identity, with followers using the influencer's content to shape their self-image (Travere A., 2023). For brands, influencers provide a direct line to their target audiences. The influence they wield comes from the perceived authenticity and relatability of their posts. Unlike traditional celebrity endorsements, influencers often build relationships with their followers by sharing personal experiences, opinions, and lifestyles. They provide an easy way for users to engage with trending topics, express opinions, and contribute to collective discourse. From a semiotic perspective, memes are unique because they are inherently collaborative. They invite users to participate in the construction of meaning by remixing and adapting the original content. This participatory nature aligns with the core principles of social media, where content is created, shared, and interpreted by users, rather than just producers or marketers (Moinuddin S., et al, 2021). These visual cues create an emotional connection, allowing followers to relate to the influencer's persona and lifestyle. When brands collaborate with influencers, they tap into these carefully constructed semiotic systems to convey messages that align with their own visual identities and brand values.

THE SEMIOTICS OF ONLINE ADVERTISING: SIGNS, SYMBOLS, AND STORYTELLING

In the digital age, online advertising has become an omnipresent force, transforming how businesses communicate with audiences and how consumers perceive products and services. At its core, online advertising is not merely about promoting products but about crafting stories and invoking emotions through signs and symbols. Semiotics, the study of signs and symbols as elements of communication, offers profound insights into how these advertisements create meaning. The semiotic approach emphasizes the interplay of denotation (literal meaning) and connotation (implied or cultural meaning), both of which advertisers manipulate to resonate with diverse audiences. By combining visual elements, linguistic cues, and narrative strategies, online advertising functions as a dynamic system of storytelling, capable of forging deep emotional connections and influencing consumer behavior (Belova A., 2021). Advertisers adeptly leverage symbols to target specific demographics, tailoring messages that resonate with localized cultural norms while maintaining global appeal. This dual approach is particularly relevant in international advertising campaigns, where universal symbols like smiles or sunsets are paired with culturally nuanced elements to ensure inclusivity and relatability. Storytelling in Online Advertising: At the heart of online advertising lies the art of storytelling. Effective ads go beyond presenting a product; they weave narratives that position the brand as part of the consumer's life story (Michael N., et al, 2022).

Unlike traditional advertising mediums, online ads often invite interactivity, adding a new layer to the semiotic process (Damayanti N P W., et al, 2021). Clickable banners, quizzes, and interactive videos allow users to engage with advertisements actively, transforming them from passive viewers into participants. This participatory aspect enables advertisers to personalize messages, enhancing the sense of relevance and connection. For instance, retargeting ads that display products previously viewed by a user create a narrative of continuity and personalized attention, fostering stronger brand affinity. Additionally, the rise of social media has transformed online advertising into a two-way dialogue. Comments, shares, and likes act as signs of user engagement, shaping how other consumers perceive the ad and, by extension, the brand. Memes, hashtags, and user-generated content amplify this dynamic, blurring the lines between advertiser and audience while reinforcing the storytelling framework. Challenges and Ethical Considerations: While semiotics enhances the effectiveness of online advertising, it also raises ethical concerns. The manipulation of signs and symbols to influence consumer behavior can verge on exploitation, particularly when targeting vulnerable populations such as children or individuals experiencing financial hardship (Zhou S., et al, 2021). The use of aspirational imagery or idealized lifestyles can perpetuate unrealistic expectations, fostering dissatisfaction or anxiety among audiences.

EMAIL MARKETING SEMIOTICS: UNPACKING MEANING IN DIGITAL MESSAGES

The signifier includes visible elements such as subject lines, headers, images, and buttons, while the signifier refers to the intended meaning or emotional response these elements evoke. For example, a subject line like "Exclusive Offer Just for You!" signals urgency and personalization, leveraging the signified meanings of exclusivity and privilege to entice recipients to open the email (Kuiler E W., 2022). Symbols in email marketing often rely on shared cultural or brand-specific meanings. Emojis, for instance, have become a ubiquitous element in subject lines and body text, serving as visual cues to elicit emotions, emphasize messages, or inject a sense of playfulness. Dynamic content further amplifies personalization by tailoring visuals and messaging to individual preferences. For example, an email promoting travel packages might display beach destinations for one recipient and mountain retreats for another, aligning the signifiers in the email with the recipient's inferred desires. This targeted approach enhances the relevance of the message, increasing the likelihood of conversion (Bonarou C., 2021).

A retail brand might use a carousel to showcase how a product fits into different lifestyles, weaving a story that aligns with the recipient's aspirations. The Role of Language: The linguistic semiotics of email marketing is equally vital, with tone, style, and vocabulary shaping the message's interpretive potential. Brands often use conversational tones to establish relatability or formal language to convey authority, depending on their audience and objectives (Shi D., 2021). Similarly, a message received in the morning might be interpreted as a proactive start to the day, while an evening email may suggest reflection or relaxation. Context also extends to the broader relationship between the brand and the recipient. Emails from trusted brands are likely to be interpreted more positively, as the signifiers within the message are viewed through the lens of established trust and familiarity. Conversely, unsolicited or poorly timed emails may evoke annoyance or distrust, undermining the intended meaning (Wiggins R J., 2022). These strategies raise questions about the ethical boundaries of persuasion in digital marketing. Conclusion: Email marketing is a powerful semiotic system that blends visual, linguistic, and contextual elements to create meaningful and engaging messages. By understanding the semiotics behind signs, symbols, and narratives, marketers can craft emails that resonate deeply with recipients, fostering loyalty and driving action. However, the power of semiotics must be wielded responsibly, ensuring that persuasive techniques are balanced with transparency and ethical considerations. As email marketing continues to evolve, its semiotic richness will remain a key factor in its effectiveness and influence.

BRAND IDENTITY IN DIGITAL ENVIRONMENTS: SEMIOTICS OF LOGOS, COLOR, AND TYPOGRAPHY

In the digital age, brand identity is more than a name or a product; it is a complex system of visual and conceptual signs that convey meaning, values, and personality to consumers. Semiotics, the study of signs and symbols, offers a powerful framework for understanding how logos, colors, and typography function as critical elements in constructing brand identity in digital environments. These visual components do more than attract attention—they shape perceptions, establish emotional connections, and build loyalty by embedding cultural, psychological, and emotional meanings into every interaction. This exploration delves into the semiotics of brand identity, examining how these elements are designed, interpreted, and leveraged in the fast-paced, highly visual landscape of digital media. The Semiotics of Logos serves as the cornerstone of brand identity, encapsulating a company's essence in a single, often simple, visual symbol. Semiotic analysis reveals that logos operate as signs with both denotative and connotative meanings. The denotative aspect refers to the literal, visual form of the logo, such as a swoosh, a golden arch, or an apple with a bite taken out of it (Guibourgé J., 2020). The connotative aspect, however, is far richer, encompassing the emotional and cultural associations the logo evokes. For example, the Nike swoosh not only signifies the brand but also connotes movement, victory, and determination, qualities that align with its "Just Do It" ethos. Logos can take various forms, including wordmarks (text-based logos), symbols, or a combination of both. Each form carries distinct semiotic implications (Yezhova O., et al, 2024). These custom typefaces not only differentiate the brand but also create a sense of ownership over the visual language, preventing the dilution of the brand identity (Singla V., et al, 2021). Typography's semiotic power extends beyond the choice of font to include size, spacing, and alignment. Challenges and Ethical Considerations: As brands increasingly rely on semiotics to shape their digital identities, ethical considerations have come to the forefront (Indrawati D., et al, 2020). The use of color and typography to manipulate emotions, for example, raises questions about transparency and authenticity. Overuse of certain colors, like red for urgency in sales or green for Eco-friendliness, can create skepticism if not backed by genuine practices.

DIGITAL STORYTELLING AND NARRATIVE SEMIOTICS: CRAFTING COMPELLING BRAND STORIES

In the digital age, storytelling has become a cornerstone of brand communication, transforming traditional marketing messages into immersive narratives that engage audiences on a deeper level. The art of digital storytelling lies in the ability to convey meaning through a seamless blend of visual, linguistic, and interactive elements. Narrative semiotics, the study of how stories create meaning through signs and symbols, provides a framework for understanding how brands craft compelling stories that resonate with diverse audiences. By leveraging archetypal structures, cultural symbols, and multimedia tools, digital storytelling elevates brands from mere product providers to relatable, aspirational entities that connect emotionally with their audiences. The Semiotics of Narrative Structures: At the heart of digital storytelling lies the use of narrative structures that audiences find familiar and emotionally engaging. Many brand stories are built on archetypal frameworks, such as the hero's journey, which follows a protagonist overcoming obstacles to achieve a transformative goal. For instance, Nike frequently uses the hero archetype in its campaigns, featuring athletes who push boundaries and redefine success, aligning with the brand's ethos of perseverance and excellence (Peho C., 2020). A vibrant color palette might evoke energy and optimism, while monochromatic tones suggest elegance or introspection. Video content, in particular, has emerged as a powerful medium for digital storytelling. Shortform videos on platforms like Instagram and TikTok leverage quick cuts, music, and relatable visuals to tell stories within seconds. Longer formats, such as branded documentaries, allow for deeper narrative development, showcasing the brand's values and mission (Sergio F., 2020).

In a globalized digital landscape, brands must consider cultural and contextual factors when crafting their narratives. Symbols, metaphors, and even story structures may carry different meanings across cultures, requiring careful localization to avoid misinterpretation (Valdivieso Benavente D J., 2023). For example, a story emphasizing individual achievement may resonate in Western cultures but might need to shift focus toward community or family values in collectivist societies. Cultural sensitivity also extends to the representation of characters and settings. Inclusive storytelling, which features diverse voices and perspectives, not only reflects contemporary social values but also broadens a brand's appeal. AI-driven personalization will enable brands to craft highly tailored narratives that adapt in real-time to user preferences, while VR will immerse audiences in three-dimensional story worlds, offering unprecedented levels of engagement (Himmelmann N., 2024). Social media platforms will remain central to digital storytelling, with features like live streaming and ephemeral content encouraging spontaneous, authentic interactions. Meanwhile, advances in analytics will provide deeper insights into audience responses, allowing brands to refine their narratives for maximum impact. Conclusion: Digital storytelling, enriched by the principles of narrative semiotics, is a powerful tool for crafting compelling brand stories that resonate across platforms and cultures. By leveraging familiar structures, evocative symbols, and immersive multimedia elements, brands can create narratives that inspire, engage, and drive action. However, the growing influence of digital storytelling demands a commitment to authenticity, inclusivity, and ethical responsibility. As brands continue to explore the potential of this medium, their ability to tell meaningful stories will remain a defining factor in their success in an increasingly connected world.

THE SEMIOTICS OF BRAND COMMUNITIES: ONLINE ENGAGEMENT AND SOCIAL INTERACTION

These identities emerge through the interplay of various semiotic elements, including logos, taglines, and brand narratives. For example, Harley-Davidson's logo and "Live to Ride" mantra are not just marketing tools but cultural symbols that embody freedom and rebellion, values embraced by its community (Rossolatos G., 2023). Online, brand identity is reinforced through digital touchpoints like social media pages, forums, and apps, where visual and textual elements consistently reflect the brand's ethos. These semiotic cues help members identify with the brand and with each other, creating a sense of belonging and exclusivity. Signs and Symbols in Online Interaction: The signs and symbols within brand communities are integral to fostering engagement and interaction. Discourse within these communities often mirrors the brand's tone and values (Ge J., 2020). Challenges in Managing Brand Communities: While brand communities offer significant benefits, they also pose challenges (Rossolatos G., 2021). This requires conscious efforts in content creation, community management, and user engagement. The Future of Brand Communities: As technology evolves, brand communities are likely to become even more immersive and interactive. Virtual reality (VR) and augmented reality (AR) experiences could enable members to interact in simulated environments, enhancing the sense of presence and engagement (Haghbin F., et al, 2022). For instance, fashion brands could create virtual runways where members can showcase their styles, while automotive brands might offer virtual test drives or design workshops. Artificial intelligence (AI) will also play a significant role in shaping brand communities, from personalized recommendations to AI-driven moderation that enhances inclusivity.

CONSUMER SEMIOTICS: UNDERSTANDING MEANING-MAKING IN DIGITAL CONSUMPTION

The Semiotics of Digital Consumption: In digital contexts, consumption extends beyond purchasing products to include experiences, information, and interactions. Each of these acts is mediated by signs and symbols that influence how consumers assign meaning to what they consume (Hasyim M., et al, 2023). For example, a luxury brand's website, with its minimalist design, high-quality visuals, and elegant typography, communicates exclusivity and sophistication, shaping the consumer's perception of its products before a purchase is made. In this environment, semiotics helps decode the implicit messages embedded in digital interfaces, advertisements, and packaging. Colors, shapes, typography, and imagery all work together to signal quality, trustworthiness, or innovation. For instance, eco-friendly brands often use green hues, earthy tones, and natural imagery to signify sustainability and ethical values, appealing to environmentally conscious consumers. Nike's campaigns often incorporate themes of empowerment and social justice, resonating with audiences who share these ideals. Such strategies use semiotics to position the brand within broader cultural conversations, enhancing its relevance and emotional appeal (Grace S C., 2021). Platforms like Instagram and Pinterest are prime examples, where high-quality visuals and aesthetic curation drive engagement and shape consumer perceptions. Brands leverage visual semiotics by crafting cohesive visual identities that align with their values and target audiences (Lawes R., 2023). While tailoring content to individual preferences enhances relevance, it can also create echo chambers that limit exposure to diverse perspectives. Brands must navigate these challenges carefully, ensuring that their semiotic practices align with ethical standards and respect consumer autonomy (Bankov K., 2022). The Future of Consumer Semiotics: As technology advances, the semiotics of digital consumption will continue to evolve. Artificial intelligence and augmented reality are creating new opportunities for meaning-making, enabling consumers to interact with brands in more immersive and personalized ways. For example, virtual try-ons and AR shopping experiences allow consumers to visualize products in their contexts, adding new layers of meaning to the consumption process.

THE SEMIOTICS OF ONLINE SEARCH: UNPACKING CONSUMER INTENT AND BEHAVIOR

Online search is a central component of the digital experience, functioning as a gateway to information, products, and services. From a semiotic perspective, search behavior represents a process of meaning-making, where consumers use keywords, phrases, and queries to express their intentions, desires, and needs. These searches are not merely technical actions; they are rich with cultural, contextual, and symbolic meaning. Understanding the semiotics of online search can illuminate how consumers interact with digital platforms, interpret search results, and make decisions based on the signs and symbols presented to them. This exploration delves into the ways consumer intent and behavior are shaped by semiotic codes, platform algorithms, and the broader cultural frameworks that underpin digital communication. (Lawes R., 2022). Each element on a SERP, from the headline to the meta description, functions as a signifier that communicates value, relevance, and credibility. Similarly, featured snippets or "position zero" results are perceived as definitive answers, leveraging their prominent placement to establish authority (Li H., et al, 2023). These semiotic cues guide user behavior, shaping perceptions of what is most relevant or trustworthy. Intent and Context in Search Semiotics: Understanding consumer intent is central to decoding the semiotics of online search. Intent can be broadly categorized into informational, navigational, and transactional, each carrying distinct semiotic implications. Informational queries, such as "How to bake a cake," signify a desire for knowledge and are often accompanied by searches for tutorials or guides.

Language plays a significant role in this process, as the same intent may be expressed differently across cultures. For example, a user in the United States might search for "cheap flights," while a user in the UK might use "low-cost flights," reflecting subtle linguistic and cultural variations. Search behavior also reflects broader cultural values. In collectivist societies, users may prioritize community-oriented queries, such as "family-friendly vacation spots," while individualistic cultures may focus on personal preferences, like "solo travel destinations." Brands and marketers must understand these cultural nuances to optimize their content and align with the semiotic expectations of diverse audiences. Visual and Voice Search: Evolving Semiotic Paradigms: The rise of visual and voice search technologies introduces new dimensions to the semiotics of online search (Polat E., et al, 2023). Visual search, which allows users to upload images or use their device's camera to find information, shifts the focus from text-based signs to visual ones. For example, a user photographing a pair of sneakers to find similar products engages with semiotic cues such as color, design, and branding. Voice search, on the other hand, relies on conversational language, emphasizing natural phrasing and spoken syntax. Queries like "What's the weather today?" reflect a shift toward more intuitive, context-aware interactions. While personalization enhances relevance, it can also feel invasive, prompting users to question how their data is being used. Ethical semiotics requires a balance between delivering meaningful, relevant content and respecting user autonomy (Hamdy A., et al, 2024). The Future of Online Search Semiotics: As technology continues to evolve, the semiotics of online search will become increasingly complex and multifaceted. Artificial intelligence and machine learning are likely to enhance the semantic understanding of queries, enabling more nuanced interpretations of intent and context. Augmented reality (AR) and virtual reality (VR) could introduce immersive search experiences, where users interact with 3D representations of products or environments.

DIGITAL CONSUMER JOURNEY MAPPING: A SEMIOTIC APPROACH

Each stage of the journey—awareness, consideration, decision-making, and post-purchase—contains its semiotic landscape, marked by distinct signs and symbols that influence consumer behavior. For instance, in the awareness stage, a brand's logo, tagline, or advertising imagery might serve as the initial signifiers that capture attention and create interest (Khan A H., et al, 2020). These elements are imbued with cultural and emotional meanings that resonate with target audiences. A tech startup, for example, may use futuristic fonts and sleek design to signify innovation, while a heritage brand might emphasize tradition through vintage typography and nostalgic imagery. Semiotics in the Awareness Stage: At the awareness stage, consumers encounter brand touchpoints that serve as entry points into the journey. These touchpoints are heavily reliant on visual and verbal semiotics to establish relevance and credibility. Advertisements, social media posts, and search engine results are crafted to function as signifiers of value, often leveraging cultural codes and emotional appeals. For example, a travel company targeting millennials might use adventurous imagery, casual language, and hashtags like Wanderlust to create a sense of excitement and relatability. These semiotic choices are designed to align with the values and aspirations of their audience, effectively drawing them into the consumer journey. The Consideration Stage: Signs of Trust and Differentiation: In the consideration stage, consumers evaluate their options by comparing products, reading reviews, and engaging with brand content. Semiotic analysis reveals how elements like website design, product descriptions, and customer testimonials function as signs that convey trust, quality, and differentiation. A minimalist website design, for instance, can signify professionalism and focus, while a cluttered interface might evoke confusion or distrust. Product descriptions that highlight sustainability or ethical sourcing tap into cultural values associated with social responsibility, appealing to eco-conscious consumers. Reviews and ratings also play a crucial semiotic role, acting as peer-generated signs of credibility and satisfaction. Decision-making and

Purchase: Closing the Semiotic Loop: The decision-making stage is where semiotic cues converge to influence the final purchase (Berners-Lee B., 2024

A seamless omnichannel experience ensures that the signs and symbols used in one channel resonate across others, creating a cohesive narrative. For example, a brand's Instagram profile might emphasize aspirational imagery and playful captions, while its website focuses on detailed product information and professional design. While the tone and style may differ, the underlying semiotic codes—such as color schemes, logos, and messaging—remain consistent to reinforce brand identity (Shukla M., et al, 2023). Emotional and Cultural Semiotics in Consumer Journeys: The digital consumer journey is not only functional but deeply emotional and cultural. This personalization extends to the semiotics of communication, as brands tailor signs and symbols to resonate with specific segments. For example, an e-commerce platform might use predictive analytics to identify a user's interest in eco-friendly products and then display green-themed visuals, nature-inspired language, and badges indicating sustainability. These semiotic cues reinforce the brand's alignment with the consumer's values, increasing the likelihood of engagement and conversion. Ethical Considerations in Semiotic Journey Mapping: A semiotic approach to consumer journey mapping raises important ethical questions, particularly regarding transparency and manipulation. Brands must ensure that the signs and symbols they use to guide consumer behavior are authentic and respectful. Overly aggressive tactics, such as using fear or false urgency, can erode trust and damage long-term relationships. Moreover, as personalization becomes more sophisticated, brands must strike a balance between relevance and privacy. Consumers should feel that their data is being used to enhance their experience, not exploit their vulnerabilities. Ethical semiotics involves creating meaningful, positive interactions that respect consumer autonomy (Girginkaya Akdağ S., 2021).

THE SEMIOTICS OF VISUAL CONTENT: IMAGES, VIDEOS, AND INFOGRAPHICS

Similarly, videos employ motion, sound, and sequencing to construct dynamic narratives, while infographics blend text and visuals to synthesize data into digestible, visually compelling formats (Simakova S., 2020). Each form of visual content carries its own semiotic rules and conventions, shaped by cultural, technological, and contextual factors. For instance, minimalist design in infographics often signifies clarity and modernity, while intricate visuals may convey complexity or depth. Understanding these semiotic frameworks allows creators to align their visual messages with audience expectations and cultural norms. The Semiotics of Images: Images are perhaps the most immediate and universally understood form of visual content. From photographs to illustrations, they communicate through a combination of denotation (literal meaning) and connotation (implied or symbolic meaning). The Semiotics of Information Design: Infographics combine text, visuals, and data to communicate complex information concisely and engagingly (Leal V C., 2021). From a semiotic perspective, every element of an infographic—charts, icons, typography, and color schemes—functions as a signifier that conveys meaning. A pie chart, for instance, visually represents proportions, while an upward arrow may symbolize growth or success.

Cultural and Psychological Codes in Visual Content: The semiotics of visual content is deeply influenced by cultural and psychological codes, which shape how audiences interpret signs and symbols. Colors, for example, carry different connotations across cultures. While blue often signifies trust and reliability in Western cultures, it may represent spirituality or mourning in others. Psychological factors also play a role in visual semiotics. Certain shapes and patterns evoke instinctive responses; circles, for example, are often associated with harmony and unity, while sharp angles may signify aggression or tension. These subconscious associations influence how audiences perceive and react to visual content. Understanding these cultural and psychological codes allows creators to craft visuals that align with their audience's values and expectations. For instance, a global brand may adapt its color palette and imagery to reflect local cultural norms in different markets, ensuring that its messages are both relevant and respectful. The Role of Technology in Visual Semiotics: Advancements in technology have expanded the possibilities for visual content creation, introducing new semiotic elements and platforms. Augmented reality (AR) and virtual reality (VR), for example, allow users to engage with immersive visual experiences, where every element—textures, spatial relationships, and interactivity—functions as a signifier. Social media platforms have also transformed the semiotics of visual content, introducing new formats and conventions (Zeghdani M B., 2023). Ethical Considerations in Visual Semiotics: The use of visual content raises important ethical questions, particularly around representation and manipulation. Images and videos are powerful tools for shaping perceptions, but they can also reinforce stereotypes or present misleading information. For example, heavily edited photos may create unrealistic beauty standards, while selective framing in videos can distort reality. Transparency and authenticity are essential in ethical visual semiotics. Brands and creators must ensure that their visual content aligns with their values and accurately represents the subjects they portray. They should also be mindful of cultural sensitivities, avoiding imagery or symbols that could be misinterpreted or offensive (Udris-Borodavko N., et al, 2023).

SEMIOTICS OF TEXT-BASED CONTENT: LANGUAGE, TONE, AND STYLE

Each word functions as a sign, with a denotative (literal) meaning and a connotative (implied) significance shaped by context and culture. For example, the word "home" denotes a place of residence but connotes warmth, security, and belonging. These dual layers of meaning enable language to communicate ideas that go beyond the surface level. Cultural codes also play a pivotal role in shaping how language is interpreted. Words and phrases that resonate in one culture may carry different connotations—or even offend—in another. For instance, the term "bold" may be celebrated as a positive trait in Western cultures, while it might be perceived as aggressive in more reserved societies (O'Halloran K L., 2023). An exclamation mark, for example, conveys enthusiasm or urgency, while ellipses might imply hesitation or suspense. Typography and formatting—such as bold text, italics, or headers—also contribute to the semiotics of style, guiding readers' attention and emphasizing key points. Stylistic choices can also evoke specific emotions or associations (Bezemer & Cowan, 2022). For instance, alliteration and rhyme can create a playful, memorable rhythm, making the text more engaging. Similarly, the use of metaphors or storytelling adds depth, allowing readers to connect with the content on a symbolic level. Text Semiotics in Digital Contexts: The semiotics of text-based content is particularly dynamic in digital environments, where interactivity, brevity, and visual integration shape how text is consumed. On social media, for example, hashtags function as semiotic tools that categorize and amplify messages while also signaling cultural relevance. A hashtag like Sustainable Living not only organizes content but also connotes environmental consciousness and ethical responsibility. In email marketing, subject lines and CTAs (calls to action) serve as critical semiotic elements, designed to grab attention and drive action. A subject line like "Don't Miss Out!" uses urgency as a semiotic cue, while a CTA such as "Learn More" signals an invitation to explore further SEO-driven content introduces another layer of semiotics, where keywords act as signifiers of relevance and search intent. Writers must balance the technical demands of SEO with the symbolic richness of language, ensuring that their content is both discoverable and meaningful.

The Role of Context in Text Semiotics: Context is essential for interpreting the semiotics of text-based content. The same word or phrase can carry different meanings depending on its cultural, situational, and temporal context. For example, the phrase "stay home" took on heightened symbolic significance during the COVID-19 pandemic, connoting safety, responsibility, and solidarity (Logi L., et al, 2023). In digital marketing, contextual cues such as platform, audience demographics, and timing influence how text is perceived. A playful tone that works on Twitter might seem out of place in a formal email campaign. The Future of Text-Based Semiotics:

As digital communication continues to evolve, the semiotics of text-based content will adapt to new platforms, technologies, and audience expectations (Hmidi Z., 2023). AI-driven tools, such as natural language processing (NLP), are already transforming how text is created and analyzed. These technologies enable personalized content that aligns with individual preferences, introducing new dimensions of semiotic complexity. Emerging formats, such as interactive text in chatbots and augmented reality (AR) applications, will further expand the possibilities for text-based semiotics. These innovations challenge traditional notions of language, tone, and style, requiring writers to explore new strategies for engaging and resonating with audiences. Conclusion: The semiotics of text-based content offer profound insights into how language, tone, and style work together to create meaning. By analyzing these elements through a semiotic lens, writers and communicators can craft messages that resonate deeply, evoke emotion, and inspire action. As the digital landscape evolves, the principles of text semiotics will remain essential for creating impactful, ethical, and culturally relevant content.

MULTIMODAL SEMIOTICS: INTEGRATING VISUAL, AUDITORY, AND TEXTUAL ELEMENTS

In today's fast-paced digital world, communication is increasingly multimodal, encompassing various forms of media that blend text, visuals and sound to create rich, engaging, and dynamic experiences. Multimodal semiotics is the study of how these different modes—visual, auditory, and textual—work together to convey meaning. Each mode brings its own set of semiotic tools and codes, influencing how a message is interpreted and experienced. For instance, colors, shapes, compositions, and spatial arrangements within an image can trigger both emotional and cognitive responses. For example, the color red often symbolizes urgency, passion, or danger, while blue may convey calmness, trust, or stability (Oja M., 2023). The positioning of objects within a visual frame also carries semiotic meaning. A figure positioned in the foreground may represent importance or dominance, while an object in the background could suggest subordination or context. Similarly, composition choices such as symmetry versus asymmetry evoke different emotional responses. In multimodal content, these visual signs are combined with other modes, often to reinforce or contrast with the message being communicated. Sound effects also play an important role in how messages are constructed and perceived (Tyrer C., 2021). In films or video advertisements, a sound effect such as a ringing phone or the sound of a heartbeat can heighten the emotional intensity of a scene, guiding the viewer's response. In digital content, sound effects might be used to underscore actions or transitions, reinforcing the flow and pacing of the message. The Semiotics of Textual Elements: Text, whether written or spoken, serves as one of the primary means through which meaning is explicitly conveyed in multimodal communication. As a semiotic system, text functions through both denotation (literal meaning) and connotation (implied or symbolic meaning). In multimodal communication, the text is often carefully crafted to align with the visual and auditory elements, creating a cohesive experience for the audience. Typography itself carries semiotic weight. The font choice can convey various emotional or thematic cues. For instance, a bold, sans-serif font might signify strength and modernity, while a serif font might evoke tradition or authority. Italics can suggest emphasis, while capital letters may indicate urgency or importance. These typographic choices, when combined with the content of the text, guide how the audience interprets the message.

The auditory elements may include a sophisticated soundtrack with orchestral music, enhancing the feeling of prestige and luxury. The textual content—whether it's a voiceover or onscreen text—might describe the car's cutting-edge technology or timeless design. Together, these elements work synergistically to convey a message of exclusivity, innovation, and luxury (Kravchenko N., et al, 2023). The visuals tell the story of the car's beauty and performance, the music enhances its emotional appeal, and the text provides key details that validate the car's value This shift has significant implications for how communicators craft messages. On social media platforms, for instance, posts often combine text with visuals (photos, GIFs, or videos) and sound (background music or voiceovers). The brevity of many digital formats, such as Twitter or Instagram, forces creators to distill their message into a limited amount of space, making the integration of these different modes crucial for delivering an impactful message quickly. The power of combining text, sound, and visuals can be used to manipulate emotions or persuade individuals toward particular actions or beliefs. For example, advertisers may use soothing music, a beautiful visual scene, and persuasive text to create a sense of longing or desire, subtly influencing consumer behavior. As such, ethical concerns around transparency, representation, and authenticity are critical in multimodal semiotics. Communicators must ensure that the combination of modes doesn't mislead or deceive audiences, particularly when the content is meant to inform rather than entertain or sell (Sommer V., 2021). For instance, in political campaigns, the use of emotionally charged visuals, music, and text can sway public opinion, raising questions about the ethical responsibility of those creating and distributing such content.

DIGITAL MARKETING AND SEMIOTICS NEW FRONTIERS AND EMERGING TRENDS

In the digital landscape, where consumers are inundated with information, being able to craft messages that resonate deeply with them is critical (Xiao H., et al, 2023). Semiotics provides a way for marketers to decode the hidden meanings behind consumer behavior and brand perception, enabling more targeted, personalized marketing strategies. The Role of Semiotics in Digital Marketing: Semiotics in digital marketing works by analyzing how images, words, logos, colors, and other elements communicate certain values, emotions, or ideas to the consumer. A digital ad featuring a specific color scheme, for example, may evoke feelings of trust or luxury, depending on the context and the consumer's cultural background. They interpret and make meaning of brand messages based on their personal experiences, values, social influences, and even their psychological predispositions. Semiotics allow marketers to understand these factors and predict how certain messages or symbols will be received by different segments of their audience (Gamiz Sandoval J., 2024).

The cultural connotations of certain visual elements must be taken into account to avoid missteps and ensure that the message is both effective and appropriate for the intended audience. Data Driven Semiotics: The Intersection of Analytics and Meaning: One of the most significant advancements in digital marketing is the increasing reliance on data analytics to drive decision-making. By leveraging big data, machine learning, and artificial intelligence, marketers can gain a wealth of insights into consumer behavior and preferences (Huaqi Y., et al, 2023). This shift toward data-driven marketing has profound implications for semiotics, as it allows marketers to track how different symbols, colors, and messages resonate with their audience in real time. Data-driven semiotics is an emerging field where brands use consumer data to refine their use of semiotic codes and make more informed decisions about their marketing strategies. By analyzing user interactions, clicks, and engagement metrics, marketers can assess the effectiveness of different semiotic elements in their campaigns. In these contexts, semiotics will be crucial in designing virtual spaces and experiences that communicate the right messages and foster positive brand associations (Badloe & Rho, 2024). The continued evolution of AI and machine learning also promises to enhance the application of semiotics in digital marketing. As these technologies become more advanced, they will enable brands to analyze vast amounts of consumer data and identify emerging trends in real-time.

FUTURE DIRECTIONS FOR DIGITAL MARKETING AND SEMIOTICS: IMPLICATIONS FOR RESEARCH AND PRACTICE

These shifts will have profound implications for both academic research and practical application in the field of marketing. The Role of Artificial Intelligence and Data Analytics in Semiotics: One of the most transformative trends in digital marketing is the integration of artificial intelligence (AI) and machine learning (ML) to better understand consumer behavior. AI and data analytics have already revolutionized how marketers approach audience segmentation, personalized content delivery, and real-time engagement. However, the next frontier in digital marketing lies in the intersection of AI, data analytics, and semiotics. As AI tools become more sophisticated, they will be able to analyze vast quantities of consumer data to identify patterns in how people respond to different semiotic elements—such as colors, images, language, and cultural references—in marketing messages (Grewal D., et al, 2022). While certain semiotic codes may carry universal meanings, others are deeply rooted in cultural contexts (Rathi R., et al, 2022). The challenge for marketers is to navigate these cultural differences to ensure their messages are interpreted as intended and resonate with local audiences. For example, the use of color in digital marketing varies widely across cultures. In Western cultures, the color white is often associated with purity and simplicity, while in many Eastern cultures, it may be linked to mourning and funerals. Similarly, symbols such as the peace sign or certain hand gestures can have vastly different meanings depending on the region.

Marketers could use semiotics to design these virtual experiences by carefully selecting visual elements, sounds, and even movements that evoke specific emotional responses. These immersive experiences would rely heavily on semiotic codes to create a coherent and engaging narrative that resonates with consumers on a deeper level. For instance, the use of color, lighting, and spatial arrangements in a virtual environment could communicate brand values such as innovation, luxury, or sustainability. The future of semiotics in digital marketing will be shaped by the need to understand how consumers perceive and engage with these immersive environments. Research will focus on how signs and symbols function in virtual and augmented realities, and how these new spaces change how consumers assign meaning to brands and products. The design of VR and AR experiences will need to take into account the psychological and emotional impact of semiotic codes, ensuring that these immersive environments are both captivating and effective in communicating brand messages. The Rise of Video Content and Multimodal Semiotics: Video content has become the dominant form of communication in digital marketing, particularly with the rise of platforms such as YouTube, TikTok, and Instagram. Videos combine multiple semiotic modes—visual, auditory, and textual—into a single piece of content, allowing marketers to convey more complex messages in a relatively short time (Gramigna R., et al, 2023). This multimodal nature of video presents both challenges and opportunities for semiotic analysis, as marketers must consider how different signs and symbols interact across various modalities to create a unified and coherent message. Similarly, the use of personal data to create hyper-targeted ads raises concerns about privacy and consumer autonomy. As digital marketing becomes more pervasive, ethical considerations will play a crucial role in shaping the future of the field. Researchers will need to explore the ethical dimensions of semiotics in digital marketing, particularly about how signs and symbols are used to influence consumer behavior. This will involve examining the power dynamics inherent in marketing communications and considering how to balance persuasive techniques with respect for consumer autonomy and privacy. In practice, marketers will need to adopt ethical frameworks that guide the responsible use of semiotics in their campaigns, ensuring that their messages are not only effective but also transparent, fair, and respectful (Rokka J., 2021).

CONCLUSION

The intersection of digital marketing and semiotics represents a powerful convergence of creativity, technology, and cultural insight that is reshaping the way brands communicate with consumers. As the digital landscape continues to evolve, the role of semiotics in shaping consumer perceptions, behaviors, and brand identities becomes increasingly essential. Semiotics, with its ability to decode the signs, symbols, and meaning-making processes embedded in digital content, provides a deeper understanding of how consumers interact with brands in an ever more interconnected world. By incorporating semiotic analysis into their digital marketing strategies, companies can craft messages that resonate more deeply with their target audiences, fostering engagement, loyalty, and long-term success. One of the key takeaways from the integration of semiotics into digital marketing is the ability to move beyond surface-level communication and tap into the deeper, often subconscious, layers of consumer behavior. Consumers today are not just passive receivers of marketing messages; they are active participants in a dynamic, interactive process of meaning-making. Through their engagement with digital media, consumers interpret and assign meaning to a vast array of semiotic elements—ranging from visual imagery, language, and typography, to more subtle cues such as tone, humor, and cultural references. By understanding these semiotic codes, brands can tailor their messaging to speak directly to the values, emotions, and expectations of their audience, creating more personalized, impactful, and memorable experiences. In this context, the role of digital marketing has expanded from simply promoting products and services to actively shaping the cultural and emotional landscapes in which consumers live. For brands, this means taking into account not only the functional attributes of their products but also the symbolic meanings attached to those products. For instance, a luxury brand does not just sell a product; it sells an experience, a status, and an aspiration. Through the careful selection of semiotic elements—whether it's the use of specific colors, logos, or the language of scarcity—brands can position themselves within the larger cultural narrative and create associations that go beyond the functional utility of their offerings.

From social media platforms to online reviews, blogs, and websites, each point of interaction is an opportunity for brands to communicate meaning and influence consumer behavior. Semiotics will play a central role in analyzing how these different touchpoints work together to create a cohesive brand narrative. By leveraging semiotic analysis across multiple platforms and mediums, marketers can create a more holistic approach to brand communication, ensuring that every interaction contributes to a unified and compelling brand identity. In conclusion, the integration of semiotics into digital marketing represents a profound shift in how brands communicate with consumers. As the digital landscape continues to evolve, the ability to decode and understand the deeper meanings embedded in signs, symbols, and cultural codes will be a crucial skill for marketers. By embracing the power of semiotics, brands can develop more effective, meaningful, and culturally resonant marketing strategies that not only capture consumer attention but also foster deeper connections and long-term loyalty. As new technologies and platforms continue to emerge, the role of semiotics in digital marketing will only grow in importance, helping brands navigate an increasingly complex and dynamic communication environment. Ultimately, semiotics provides the key to unlocking the full potential of digital marketing, enabling brands to create experiences that truly speak to the values, emotions, and identities of their audiences.

REFERENCES

Aiello, G. (2020). *Visual Semiotics: Key Concepts and New Directions*. The SAGE Handbook of Visual Research Methods SAGE Publications.

Araújo, S. O., Peres, R. S., Barata, J., Lidon, F., & Ramalho, J. C. (2021). Characterising the Agriculture 4.0 Landscape—Emerging Trends, Challenges and Opportunities [MDPI.]. *Agronomy (Basel)*, *11*(11), 2206. DOI: 10.3390/agronomy11040667

Badloe, T., & Rho, J. (2024). Enabling New Frontiers of Nanophotonics with Metamaterials, Photonic Crystals, and Plasmonics. *Nanophotonics*, *13*(7), 965–969. DOI: 10.1515/nanoph-2024-0100 PMID: 39634002

Bakshi, A., & Kaur, S. (2023). A Conceptualization of Marketing through the Perspective of Semiotics. *Academy of Marketing Studies Journal*, *27*(2), 1–15.

Bankov, K. (2022). *The Digital Mind: Semiotic Explorations in Digital Culture*. Springer. DOI: 10.1007/978-3-030-92555-0

Belova, A. (2021). Storytelling in Advertising and Branding. *Cognition, Communication, Discourse*, *19*, 5–18.

Berners-Lee, B. (2024). The Semiotics of Digital Cartography at the Geoguessr Interface: A Practice-Oriented Case Study. *New Media & Society*, *26*(12), 6881–6899. DOI: 10.1177/14614448231160132

Bezemer, J., & Cowan, K. (2022). "Exploring Reading in Social Semiotics: Theory and Methods" Reading.

Bonarou, C, (2021). "The Poetics of Travel through Unravelling Visual Representations on Postcards: A Critical Semiotics Analysis" Journal of Tourism, Heritage & Services Marketing.

Chaffey, D., & Smith, P. R. (2022). *Digital Marketing Excellence: Planning, Optimizing and Integrating Online Marketing*. Taylor & Francis. DOI: 10.4324/9781003009498

Damayanti, N. P. W., Santika, I. D A D. M., & Eka, D. P. (2021). Semiotic Analysis of Mentos Advertisement. *Humanis*, *25*(2), 1–12.

Dunleavy, D. (2020). "Visual Semiotics Theory: Introduction to the Science of Signs" Handbook of Visual Communication Taylor & Francis.

Elhamy H M, (2022). "Social Semiotics for Social Media Visuals: A Framework for Analysis and Interpretation" … on Advanced Research Methodologies for a Digital Age IGI Global.

Gamiz Sandoval J, (2024). "Globalization of Visual Media in Marketing: The Impact of Immigration in Marketing Media in Finland".

Ge, J. (2020). The Functional Building Blocks of Emoji in Consumer Engagement: A Visual Semiotic Perspective. *International Journal of Semiotics and Visual Rhetoric*, *4*(2), 16–32. DOI: 10.4018/IJSVR.2020070102

Ghorbani, Z., Kargaran, S., & Saberi, A. (2021). Trends and Patterns in Digital Marketing Research: Bibliometric Analysis [Springer.]. *Journal of Marketing Trends*, *8*(1), 1–17.

Girginkaya Akdağ, S. (2021). *"Small Icons with Wide Borders: The Semiotics of Micro-Mobility in Urban Space" The Dialectics of Urban and Architectural.* Springer.

Grace, S. C. (2021). "The Intermingling of Meanings in Marketing: Semiology and Phenomenology in Consumer Culture Theory" AMS Review, Springer.

Gramigna R, Madisson M L, (2023). "Unravelling Semiotics in 2022: A Year in Review" Sign Systems Studies.

Grewal D, Herhausen D, Ludwig S, Ordenes F V, (2022). "The Future of Digital Communication Research: Considering Dynamics and Multimodality" Journal of Retailing, Elsevier.

Guibourgé J, (2020). "Semiotics: About Logo, Identity and Brand Image" Translated from Guibourgé Jérôme, Design phase 1, hal.science.

Gupta, N. (2020). Digital Marketing: Trends, Opportunities, and Challenges. *Asian Journal of Management*, *11*(2), 53–60.

Haghbin, F., Nambusubramaniyan, S., & Monfared, N. (2022). The Semiotics of Social-Distance Branding during the Post-Coronavirus Crisis. *Semiotica*, *2022*(249), 145–175. DOI: 10.1515/sem-2021-0157

Hamdy, A., & Eid, R. (2024). *COVID-19, Destination Image, and Destination Visit Intention: Unpacking the Impacts of Familiarity, Generation, and Gender Amidst COVID-19.* Consumer Behavior in Tourism and Hospitality, Emerald.

Hasyim, M., & Arafah, B. (2023). *Social Media Text Meaning: Cultural Information Consumption.* Wseas Transactions on Information Science.

Himmelmann N, (2024). "Creative Storytelling in IKEA Advertising: Furnishing Narratives: A Multimodal Discourse Analysis of Creative Storytelling Techniques in IKEA Advertising".

Hmidi Z, (2023). “Text and Context in Multimedia Translation” Journal of Translation and Interpretation Studies.

Huaqi Y, Meng L, (2023). “Exploring the Innovation of Calligraphy Art in Animation in the Context of Globalisation—Based on Semiotics” Frontiers in Art Research.

Indrawati, D., & Amalia, R. R. (2020). “Semiotic Analysis of Typography in Virtual Advertisements” *Proceeding Conference.*

Januartha, I. W. (2024). Semiotic Analysis: Decoding Signs and Messages on Grand Filano YouTube Ads. *RETORIKA: Jurnal Ilmu Bahasa, 11*(1), 1–15.

Khan, A. H., Snow, S., Heiner, S., & Matthews, B. (2020). “Disconnecting: Towards a Semiotic Framework for Personal Data Trails” *Proceedings of the 2020 ACM.* DOI: 10.1145/3357236.3395580

Kravchenko N, Yudenko O, (2023). “Multimodal Advertising: Semiotic and Cognitive-Pragmatic Aspects” Scientific journal «International.

Kuiler, E. W. (2022). *“Semiotics” Encyclopedia of Big Data Springer.*

Lawes R, (2022). “Using Semiotics in Retail: Leverage Consumer Insight to Engage Shoppers and Boost Sales”.

Lawes R, (2023). “Using Semiotics in Marketing: How to Achieve Consumer Insight for Brand Growth and Profits”.

Leal, V. C. (2021). *Rhetoric and Visual Argument: Proposition of Methodological Models Based on the Analysis of Infographics.* Revista da ABRALIN.

Li, H., Zhang, L., & Hsu, C. H. C. (2023). “Research on User-Generated Photos in Tourism and Hospitality: A Systematic Review and Way Forward” Tourism Management, Elsevier.

Logi, L., & Zappavigna, M. (2023). A Social Semiotic Perspective on Emoji: How Emoji and Language Interact to Make Meaning in Digital Messages. *New Media & Society, 25*(12), 3222–3246. DOI: 10.1177/14614448211032965

Lytvynenko A, Zavialova O, Kalashnyk M, Varadi N, (2022). “Semiotics of Advertisement”.

Michael, N., & Fusté-Forné, F. (2022). Marketing of Luxurious Gastronomic Experiences on Social Media: The Visual Storytelling of Luxury Hotels [Wiley Online Library.]. *International Journal of Tourism Research, 24*(3), 235–248. DOI: 10.1002/jtr.2548

Moinuddin, S., & Moinuddin, S. (2021). *Geographies of Semiotics in Social Mediasphere in India*. Digital Shutdowns and Social Media Springer. DOI: 10.1007/978-3-030-67888-3_5

O'Halloran, K. L. (2023). Matter, Meaning and Semiotics. *Visual Communication*, *22*(1), 174–201. DOI: 10.1177/14703572221128881

Oja, M. (2023). Semiotic Mode and Sensory Modality in Multimodal Semiotics: Recognizing Difference and Building Complementarity Between the Terms. *Sign Systems Studies*, *51*(3-4), 604–637. DOI: 10.12697/SSS.2023.51.3-4.05

Peho C, (2020). "Storytelling as a Means of Brand Building-Building Authenticity and Emotions through Brand Stories".

Polat E, Çelik F, Ibrahim B, (2023). "Unpacking the Power of User-Generated Videos in Hospitality and Tourism: A Systematic Literature Review and Future Direction" Journal of Travel & Tourism Marketing, Taylor & Francis.

Rathi R, Garg R, Kataria A, (2022). "Evolution of Luxury Marketing Landscape: A Bibliometric Analysis and Future Directions" Journal of Brand.

Rokka J, (2021). "Consumer Culture Theory's Future in Marketing" Journal of Marketing Theory and Practice, Taylor & Francis.

Rossolatos, G. (2021). The Depth of Brand Engagement Funnel: Dimensionalizing Interaction in Social Media Brand Communities. *Qualitative Market Research*, *24*(2), 200–220. DOI: 10.1108/QMR-03-2019-0041

Rossolatos G, (2023). "Advances in Brand Semiotics & Discourse Analysis".

Sergio, F. (2020). "Storytelling in the Luxury Industry: Narratives as a Tool for Experiential Branding-The Case of Christian Dior Couture" dspace.unive.it

Shi, D. (2021). Exploring Digital Interactivity: A Multimodal and Social Semiotic Approach to Intersemiotic Construction in COVID China Website. *Multimodal Communication*, *10*(3), 311–327. DOI: 10.1515/mc-2021-0010

Shukla, M., Misra, R., & Singh, D. (2023). *Exploring Relationship Among Semiotic Product Packaging, Brand Experience Dimensions, Brand Trust and Purchase Intentions in an Asian Emerging Market*. Asia Pacific Journal of Marketing and Logistics, Emerald. DOI: 10.1108/APJML-10-2021-0718

Simakova, S. (2020). *Media Aesthetic Component of Communication and its Manifestation in Infographic Content*. Lumina. DOI: 10.34019/1981-4070.2020.v14.30188

Singla V, Ongsakul V, Raj S, (2021). "Investigating the Relationship of Semiotics Associated with Colour and Font of Google Logo with Brand Perception" Journal for Global.

Sommer, V. (2021). Multimodal Analysis in Qualitative Research: Extending Grounded Theory Through the Lens of Social Semiotics. *Qualitative Inquiry*, *27*(8-9), 1102–1113. DOI: 10.1177/1077800420978746

Travere, A. (2023). The Interplay of Signs and Visuals: Unveiling the Symbiotic Relationship Between Semiotics and Visual Communication [Pioneer Publisher.]. *Journal of Linguistics and Communication Studies*, *5*(1), 1–12.

Tyrer, C. (2021). "The Voice, Text, and the Visual as Semiotic Companions: An Analysis of the Materiality and Meaning Potential of Multimodal Screen Feedback" Education and Information Technologies, Springer.

Udris-Borodavko, N., Oliinyk, V., & Bozhko, T. (2023). *Aesthetics and Semiotics in 21st Century Visual Communications: Pedagogical and Sociocultural Aspects*. Research Journal in Advanced Humanities.

Valdivieso Benavente, D. J. (2023). "Homogenized Branding: A Semiotic and Cultural Inquiry into Visual Identity" politesi.polimi.it

Wiggins R J, (2022). "Semiotic Analysis for More Thoughtful Marketing Mix Decision-Making in the Age of Online Consumer Discourse".

Xiao, H., & Li, L. (2023). A Bibliometric and Visual Analysis of Social Semiotics: Development, Hotspots, and Trend Directions. *Semiotica*, *2023*(251), 193–213. DOI: 10.1515/sem-2021-0089

Yezhova, O., Pashkevych, K., & Bezuhla, R. (2024). *Semiotics and Cognitive Dimensions in the Design of Corporate Visual Identity for Chemical Enterprises*. Linguistic and Philosophical Studies.

Zeghdani M B, (2023). "A Semiotic Analysis of the 'Reflect Your Respect' Infographic Poster for the World Cup Qatar 2022".

Zhou, S., Barnes, L., McCormick, H., & Cano, M. B. (2021). Social Media Influencers' Narrative Strategies to Create eWOM: A Theoretical Contribution [Elsevier.]. *International Journal of Information Management*, *56*, 102245. DOI: 10.1016/j.ijinfomgt.2020.102293

Chapter 8
A Semiotic Approach to Brand Storytelling in Social Media

Caterina Scianna
University of Messina, Italy

ABSTRACT

Since the first semiotic analyses of advertising, the discursive forms of branding have undergone a significant evolution, particularly in the context of the accelerated development of information technology and social media. These have been rapidly integrated into the field of advertising communication and have become an indispensable part of the marketing apparatus for a significant number of companies. Social media have led to the development of new marketing strategies within a visual-centric digital culture. With this evolution of marketing, the consolidated practice has become visual storytelling. This is a strategy that goes beyond traditional advertising and uses narrative to create an emotional and authentic connection between the brand and its consumers. This chapter looks specifically at how brands are using visual storytelling in their social media channels.

INTRODUCTION

Advertising is a form of persuasive communication aimed at selling products, but it is also a powerful tool for the creation of social and ideological meanings that influences perceptions, using a variety of signs ranging from words to images, sounds to colors. The semiotics of advertising is, in turn, a rich and complex field concerned with analyzing the symbols and meanings present in advertising campaigns and marketing strategies, investigating how signs, codes, and cultural conventions

DOI: 10.4018/979-8-3693-8024-6.ch008

are employed to convey messages that reach the audience through mechanisms of identification, desire, and cultural recognition (Bianchi, 2005). These mechanisms illustrate, for example, how an image of a luxury car is associated with an image of a smiling, successful person, suggesting that purchasing the product may lead to happiness and success. Similarly, advertising a food product through the image of a family gathered around a table constructs a narrative of familial unity and comfort, fostering a positive emotion around the product. One of the focal points of investigation within the semiotics of advertising concerns brands and the ways in which they present themselves to consumers, with the aim of establishing a relationship of trust that ensures stability and reliability over time. Brands possess a narrative character intrinsic to their nature, which over time has enabled them not only to stand as guarantors of products, but also to tell their own values and traditions, with the products acting as manifestation of these values (Baker & Boyle, 2009; Marrone, 2007).

The chapter specifically addresses how brands have altered their narrative strategies with the advent of social media, a channel that has revolutionized advertising in several respects (Ferraro, 1999; Laurita & Venturini, 2016). Among the various changes, two are particularly significant. The first is that content creation is no longer exclusively managed by companies, and meaning it is no longer a top-down process; rather, it is a creation in which the audience also participates. The second major change is that, on social media, communication is predominantly visual: images hold much more space and importance compared to verbal language, as opposed to other media. Nowadays, the narrative structure favored in advertising is storytelling, where the goal is to construct a story that builds an identity with which the consumer can identify. Specifically, social media storytelling is a visual form of storytelling, which relies more on images than on verbal language. We will explore what this entails and how brands organize this type of narrative.

The chapter is structured as follows. The first section, *"A Brief History of Semiotic Analyses of Advertising Images,"* will provide an introduction to the semiotic analysis of advertising. It will explore the rhetorical analysis of advertising images introduced by Roland Barthes, as well as the classification of different advertising philosophies outlined by J.M. Floch in the early 1990s. The second section, *"Semiotics, Branding, and Storytelling,"* will introduce the concept of branding and explain how storytelling has become the predominant technique in advertising today. It will highlight what brand storytelling is and outline its essential characteristics. The third section, *"How Social Media Have Transformed the Advertising Industry,"* will describe the changes introduced by social media within the advertising context and their implications for brands. Specifically, it will explain what visual storytelling is. Finally, in the fourth section '*One case study of brand storytelling on Instagram platform*', a specific case study of the company Barilla will be presented, demonstrating how it has successfully developed marketing strategies over time. The section will show how the company has adapted its narrative approach on a particular social media platform, Instagram.

1. A Brief History Of Semiotic Analyses Of Advertising Images

The semiotic analysis of advertising has undergone a significant evolutionary path, starting in the mid-twentieth century and continuing to the present day, with increasing attention to the interaction between signs, culture, and ideology (Volli, 2012). The beginnings of semiotics applied to advertising can be traced back to the 1950s and 1960s, with the contributions of scholars such as Roland Barthes, one of the leading theorists of twentieth-century semiotics. Although Barthes did not specifically focus on advertising, his work revolutionized its approach by showing how advertising creates a second level of signification, that is, a connotation that transcends the literal meaning of the signs. Barthes analyzes how visual and verbal signs in advertisements not only convey objective information about a product but also construct myths and connotations that shape public perception, creating social and ideological values through the use of symbols, images, and subliminal messages (Barthes, 1972). His distinction between denotation (literal meaning) and connotation (cultural and emotional meaning) becomes central to semiotic analyses of advertising (Barthes, 1964).

Using structuralist semiotics, Barthes examines how advertising employs images, words, and colors to associate emotional and cultural meanings with a product. A classic example of this is his study of the Panzani pasta advertisement, which, through the use of visual and symbolic signs, evokes an entire cultural and ideological narrative. The advertisement depicts a typical scene in which a bottle of tomato sauce, pasta, and a variety of vegetables are arranged on a table. This setting evokes an image of purity, naturalness, authenticity, and tradition. It represents an idealized view of Italian cuisine and conviviality, strongly linked to family values and an idyllic vision of life. Barthes' analysis shows how a simple food product is associated with a series of cultural, symbolic, and ideological meanings.

From a visual perspective, the photograph used reveals two layers of meaning. One is the literal level of the image, the level of denotation, that is, the level of recognition: we identify certain visual configurations as representations of specific objects in a certain way (a tomato, a pepper, a shopping bag). It is an image that describes the act of preparing a meal. From this level, the connotative level is distinguished, i.e., the level of meaning that is associated, according to one's cultural background, with the denoted meanings. The connotative level—i.e., the level of symbolic meaning—is precisely what enables advertisements to convey the more subtle meanings that make the message effective. In this case, the tomato and the pepper, within the context of 1960s French culture, evoke values such as genuineness, health, quality, and, above all, a connection to Italian culinary tradition. These values are suggested not only by the products themselves but also by the colours in the image - green, white, and red - which are not coincidentally the colours of the Italian flag. Furthermore, the semi-open shopping bag on the table refers to someone who has just returned from the market, thus acting as a code that evokes values of freshness and natural agriculture. The arrangement of the products on the table evokes a sense of homemade preparation, calling to mind a harmonious view of family life. One of the meanings conveyed by the photograph is, in fact, the authenticity of the products, expressed through the connection or juxtaposition created between the origin (real tomatoes and peppers) and the final result of the product (the jar) (Barthes, 1972). The image employs a metonymic mechanism to suggest that the final product is as genuine as the actual tomatoes and peppers (Polidoro, 2008). Panzani pasta, therefore, is not just a food product; it becomes a symbol of an entire culture and way of life. The mechanisms of the advertising image are far from arbitrary or accidental, and they refer to the concept of encyclopaedia (Eco 1979; 1984): it is experience and culture that create the connection, for instance, between tomatoes and Italian identity.

Thus, advertising does not merely promote a product but constructs a 'myth,' that is, a meaning that goes beyond the object itself. In this case, the 'myth' concerns the idea of Italian cuisine as synonymous with good food, family, love for cooking, and authenticity. It is not simply pasta that is being promoted, but an idea of Italian culture that is appreciated worldwide, suggesting that the purchase and consumption of this product allow one to partake in a cultural tradition that is authentic, natural, and of superior quality. The advertisement uses naturalness and authenticity as elements that legitimize the product, implying that Panzani pasta is the expression of a centuries-old tradition, connected to an image of quality and genuineness that the consumer can 'purchase' with the product (Barthes, 1972). The consumer is not merely buying food but is drawn into an ideal and shared lifestyle.

Since the initial semiotic analysis of advertising, initiated by Roland Barthes with his work on the rhetoric of the advertising image, the discursive forms of branding have undergone significant evolution. This has prompted reflections and debates on the potential, limitations, and relevance of semiotic tools. In this respect, the contribution of Floch, who adapted Greimas' semiotic theories to forms easily applicable in marketing contexts, was pivotal (Floch, 1990; 1995).

Floch develops a more systematic and practical approach, focusing on the analysis of visual and linguistic codes in advertising. He proposed a semiotics of visual communication, emphasizing the relationship between image and text, and how different visual and verbal elements combine to construct more complex meanings. In his 1990 essay *'Tués dans l'œuf'* (Killed in the Egg), starting from the question that preoccupied advertisers of the time—whether the value of a product preexists advertising or if it is something created by advertising—he describes the different ideologies and approaches to understanding advertising. Beginning with the opposition between the inherent value of the product and the value created by advertising, i.e., on one side the idea that advertising discourse aims to highlight the intrinsic properties of the advertised object, and on the other side, the idea that the product has no inherent value and that this value is exclusively determined by advertising discourse, Floch identifies four different advertising philosophies, each with its own rules and communicative contract.

The referential advertising philosophy, based on the representational function of language, advocates for a 'truthful' advertising approach. This does not mean declaring the truth about the product but rather adopting a realistic and truthful advertising style: using procedures and techniques that make the product known by presenting the facts in a credible and coherent way. In this type of advertising, the product is placed in realistic, everyday scenes, within the contexts of use that allow it to acquire its meaning. The verbal text is close to a scientific text, with no overuse of slogans or adjectives. There is a clear narrative structure, in which, for example, the difference between the situation before and after using the product is evident.

The negation of referential advertising is oblique advertising. This is a more sophisticated form of advertising, where meaning is not directly given but must be constructed by the consumer. It is a type of advertising that requires careful interpretation and is targeted at a niche audience that possesses superior interpretative skills, for example, where the reader is asked to interpret an ironic meaning. Substantial advertising, in contrast to oblique advertising, focuses exclusively on the product. Particularly suitable for substantial advertising is the so-called *pack shot*—the product photograph, i.e., the shot of a specific product against an abstract background, which has the effect of presenting the object directly to the subject. This type of image is commonly used in magazines, flyers, and billboards: still life photography that enhances the advertised object, making it desirable not only from a practical perspective but also from a sensory and aesthetic point of view. The product is almost always photographed in the same manner: the best angle is chosen (frontal, three-quarter, or lateral), with variations in height or distance of the camera, which can be placed above, below, neutral, or in line with the horizon. The background may be a solid colour, a surface upon which the object is placed, or a social situation in the background. In all these cases, the background represents a symbolic void, a non-space that the object, as a signifier, fills. The structure underlying this type of photograph is an antithesis: an opposition is created between the product and the background, with the goal of focusing attention on the object.

Among Floch's examples of substantial advertising are the photograph of a beer mug and the image of a magnified butter biscuit—images that highlight the qualities of the product through an underlying synaesthesia: the visual component is tightly interconnected with other sensory and somatic experiences. The viewer is invited not only to see but also to use other senses, such as touch or taste.

The negation of substantial advertising is mythical advertising, which opposes the principles of referential advertising and based on the constructive function of language, becomes an advertising style of imagination and fantasy: it invests the product with meaning and value through the story it tells. In this case, it is the narrative that constructs the value of the product, enriching it. Moreover, this type of advertising does not just create the product's value but also the value of the brand itself. As Floch explains, this happens "progressively and coherently over time," even over several years.

2. SEMIOTICS, BRANDING AND STORYTELLING

Already since the 1970s, with the understanding that consumption is driven not only by the need but also by a deeper, continuous search for meaning, semiotic research has focused its attention on brands, the core of the construction of meaning and symbolic value reflected in the purchased objects (Baudrillard, 2016; Eco, 1975). Semiotic analysis of brands is not merely a study of signs; it is an understanding of the identity processes and symbolic narratives that brands build to seduce and retain their consumers. These narratives naturally involve visual signs (such as logos and colours), but also the stories and experiences that the brand seeks to convey. A brand is not simply identifiable as a name or a logo, but rather as a set of distinctive elements, a complex system of signs, symbols, messages, values, and experiences that identify or differentiate a product, service, or company from others on the market. It is a cultural construct that creates a coherent and recognizable perception in the public, with which it aims to establish an emotional bond, evoke trust, and represent a specific identity in the marketplace (Oswald, 2011). Brands like Nike, Coca-Cola, and Apple are paradigmatic examples of brands built through coherent narratives that become cultural and social symbols, not just products to be bought.

The brand serves a number of functions in its relationship with consumers (Wheeler & Meyerson, 2024). Primarily, it conveys positive values and enhances the image, enabling the consumer to define their identity both for themselves and for their reference group, thereby demonstrating their belonging or aspiration to belong to a particular social group. Secondly, it mitigates the risk of erroneous purchasing decisions by ensuring greater reliability, preventing depreciation in value over time and ensuring consistent satisfaction with use. It provides reassurance regarding the expected quality and continuity of the relationship and trust between the company and the consumer. In conclusion, it enables the comprehension of essential data pertaining to the elements of provenance, orientation, interpretation and recognition, thereby facilitating informed decision-making (Brown, 2016).

A strong brand is thus one that is able to evoke emotions and create a collective identity around itself, binding the consumer not only to the product but also to a worldview or lifestyle. For example, the Nike brand does not simply sell sportswear, but promotes an ideal of performance, determination, and personal success. Likewise, Apple does not just sell electronic devices, but represents an idea of innovation, elegance, and simplicity. These are cases of brands that succeed in building a strong, recognizable, and authentic identity, which goes beyond the product itself, becoming a symbol of belonging, aspiration, and cultural experience (Aimé, 2021). The brand is therefore a semiotic entity, as the signs that constitute it (logo, name, slogan, images) are not simply distinguishing elements, but convey a set of meanings that influence the consumer's perception (Manning, 2010). This complex system of meanings is constructed through visual communication, storytelling, consumer experiences, and public image (Holt, 2004).

In the 2000s, with the advent of digital advertising and social media, advertising changed in several ways (Cosenza, 2014). Brands became cultural performances, increasingly tied to social values such as authenticity, sustainability, and social responsibility, and were transformed into multimedia and interactive entities that are built and evolve through interaction with consumers. These brands no longer rely on one-way communication but engage users in active participation (Voorverd, 2019). As a result, semiotic analysis has expanded, starting to explore new phenomena such as digital branding, the use of multimodal images and languages, and the personalization of advertising messages through algorithms and social media (Bianchi, 2020; Boero & Greco, 2023; Cosenza, 2024).

With this evolution of marketing and the expansion of digital platforms, the consolidated practice became storytelling. *Storytelling* is communicating through a narrative, creating representations—whether textual, visual, auditory, or perceptual—that aim to move and engage an audience (Fontana, 2020; Marchese, 1983; Mazzoni, 2011). Applied to the brand, it is a marketing strategy that goes beyond traditional advertising, using narration to create an emotional and authentic connection between the brand and its consumers (Quesenbery & Brools, 2010; Woodside et al., 2008). A brand inherently has a narrative character: it tells a story not so much to guarantee the products but to represent values and traditions, of which the products become the manifestation (Baker & Boyle, 2009; Marrone, 2007). In this case, storytelling primarily concerns brand management and, in this sense, is brand storytelling, a narration of the brand's identity (Lund et al., 2018).

The reason brands turn to this strategy is tied to a shift in consumer expectations and behaviours. Companies have become aware that it is no longer enough to promote the functional characteristics of a product, and that consumers, increasingly exposed to multiple advertising messages, need a deeper meaning in their purchasing choices (Escalas, 2004). The act of purchasing becomes inextricably linked with the sharing of experiences, and the utilisation of storytelling has emerged as a key strategy employed by organisations and companies to foster a sense of biographical recognition between the producer and the consumer (Kristensen et al., 2012).

In this context, the primary objective of storytelling is to present the brand. Narrative becomes a means of conveying the brand's identity, its purpose, and its worldview, so that the consumer no longer sees the brand as just a simple object of consumption, but as an entity with its own history and personality (Miller, 2017). When the market is saturated with similar products, telling a unique story allows the brand to stand out. The narrative creates emotional differentiation that goes beyond price or product features. Consumers tend to be more loyal to a brand that makes them feel part of a story, where ideals, values, and traditions are conveyed in a way that allows the consumer to reflect upon them (Martinus & Chaniago, 2017). The objective is no longer to launch a campaign that will last for a few weeks and then be replaced and forgotten. Instead, the goal is to build a profile that will represent the company, the brand, and the consumer on a daily basis. Brand storytelling can be defined as the art of creating a compelling narrative about a brand that fosters emotional connections between the brand and consumers. Such elements as actors, plots, causality and chronology of events are included. In the field of marketing, the strategic positioning of a company can be enhanced through the use of a carefully crafted narrative. This narrative serves to define the brand and to reinforce its identity, while simultaneously facilitating the communication of its key attributes and values.

There are key elements that define brand storytelling. The first is naturally the brand's story. Every brand has its own origin, an evolutionary path, a 'dream' that guides it, and a set of values that define it. Brand storytelling leverages these stories to highlight its uniqueness and create an emotional connection with the audience (Rodriguez, 2020). The narrative can include the brand's foundation, the challenges it has faced, the people who are part of it, or the ideals it stands for. Another key element is a character with whom the audience can identify. In the context of brand storytelling, the 'character' can be represented by the founder, employees, customers, or even the brand itself, understood as an entity with its own personality and distinctive values. Often, the brand presents itself as a 'hero' who solves the consumer's problems, as in the case of Nike, which encourages the user to push their limits with the famous slogan 'Just do it'. Following the canonical narrative structure, brand storytelling also includes a conflict, which represents a challenge or a problem to be overcome. This conflict can be exemplified by the problem that the product or service solves, or by the mission that the brand sets to improve the world. The resolution of this conflict is shown through the brand's benefits, its positive impact, or its ability to address the consumer's needs.

Another key element of brand storytelling is its ability to evoke emotions. By telling authentic and engaging stories, the brand creates an experience that goes beyond rationality and the product itself. Emotions foster deeper connections, helping to build brand loyalty. For example, Apple does not only sell technological products, but tells a story of innovation, creative freedom, and simplicity, making consumers feel part of an exclusive community. Finally, brand storytelling highlights the social, environmental, or cultural causes that the brand supports. By communicating the brand's values and mission, storytelling reinforces its image and the perception consumers have of it.

Brand storytelling is based on a consistent narrative that unfolds across various channels and platforms, such as social media, video content, packaging, events, and direct customer interactions. The important thing is that each touchpoint with the consumer contributes to telling the same story, authentically and engagingly. In this way, consumers no longer view advertising as just a message to receive, but as part of a larger story, one that involves their own experiences and identity. For example, Coca-Cola has built its brand storytelling around the idea of sharing, joy, and friendship. Its iconic Christmas campaign with the red trucks, the presence of Santa Claus, and the idea of shared holidays tells a story that goes beyond the simple sale of a fizzy drink, evoking family experiences, moments of collective happiness, and the sense of belonging to a community.

3. HOW SOCIAL MEDIA HAVE TRANSFORMED THE ADVERTISING INDUSTRY

Over the past two decades, the accelerated evolution of information technology and the proliferation of social media platforms have had a profound impact on consumer culture, bringing new dynamics techniques and opportunities (Poulsen & Kvale, 2018). Social media have demonstrated their capacity to transform the advertising industry in a relatively short period of time, offering brands a novel and effective marketing avenue (Cara, 2019). These have been rapidly integrated into the domain of advertising communication, becoming an indispensable component of the marketing apparatus for a considerable number of companies. The success of social media can be attributed to their capacity to expand their reach, facilitating the formation of connections with customers across the globe, fostering engagement, and offering a relatively cost-effective alternative to other media tools (Kerpen, 2011).

The changes introduced by social media are numerous (Maggio, 2024). First of all, they offer an unprecedented level of targeting: thanks to real-time data collection and sophisticated algorithms, companies can optimize and direct their advertising campaigns to highly specific audience segments. The platforms provide detailed metrics such as engagement rates, views, clicks, and more, which allow for continuous refinement of strategies. Advertising campaigns are selected based on past behaviors, interactions with similar content, and expressed preferences, creating a highly personalized experience for users. This naturally optimizes the return on investment, allowing advertising that, compared to traditional advertising channels, is low-cost. In this way, even small and medium-sized enterprises have the opportunity to reach a global audience with relatively low investments.

Secondly, social media makes advertising more visible and interactive: on Instagram, for example, with the story format, brands can create ads that integrate naturally into the content flow, making them less intrusive compared to traditional ads. Furthermore, interactive features such as polls, questions, and clickable links encourage direct and immediate engagement from users (Boero, 2019). Social media thus enables real-time communication, allowing businesses to quickly respond to events, trends, or changes in user behavior. This reactivity allows brands to join the conversation and take advantage of moments of collective attention, such as viral hashtags or global events. Another advantage is that social media offer 'shopping' features that allow companies to sell directly to consumers through the platform, an approach that facilitates the conversion process by eliminating the barrier between the ad and the purchase, thereby reducing the number of steps needed to finalize a purchase.

While it is true that social media has brought numerous advantages in terms of higher engagement at lower costs, on the other hand, they have presented a new challenge for brands: previously, companies communicated messages through television, radio, and print, with full control over how the brand and its products were represented; with social media, however, consumers are no longer passive recipients, but actively participate in the communication process. This shift has led to the so-called *shift from spot to post* (Mayer, 2015), as brands had to adapt, moving from one-way communication (from the brand to the consumer) to interactive and participatory communication. The ability to share content, interact with consumers, and allow them to contribute to the brand's narrative has led to the creation of shared storytelling. Social media have provided brands the opportunity to become part of a collective narrative, rather than being the sole protagonists of a story told exclusively by the brand. In this way, brands are no longer the only ones speaking to consumers, but people themselves – now followers – become active participants in the communication process, creating active and loyal communities around brands. Incorporating user-generated content (UGC), such as reviews, testimonials, photos, and videos that consumers share on social media, is a powerful storytelling tool. People trust content created by other consumers more, and this type of content helps create an authentic and relational narrative around the brand. For example, a clothing brand could encourage its customers to post pictures wearing its items with a specific hashtag. These images become part of the brand's visual story and reinforce the sense of community.

Storytelling on social media is not just a monologue but a conversation. Brands need to actively engage with the audience, respond to comments, ask for opinions, and encourage participation. Polls, questions, and interactive content (such as Instagram stories with polls or quizzes) are excellent ways to engage followers. Nike is a classic example of visual storytelling that combines motivation, performance, and brand identity. Its visual campaigns tell stories of courage, resilience, and change, using powerful images that evoke strong emotions. Consumer participation occurs in different ways: they generate content related to the brand, share opinions, and create collective experiences around brands, thus creating brand-related stories through their experiences, reviews, shares, and posts; they interact directly with the brands; and even become brand ambassadors – influencers – who influence the perception and thus the purchasing decisions of other users. The presence of these influencers has reduced the distance between brands and consumers, creating a more authentic and personal relationship. Influencers are often perceived as "trusted voices," and their recommendations are considered more genuine than traditional advertisements. An aspect that has made brands more democratic and participatory, but on the other hand, has made them more vulnerable, as a single mistake or a lapse in managing the online community can immediately damage a brand's reputation.

Another important change introduced by social media is the shift towards communication centered on the predominance of images over verbal language. Since the mid-twentieth century, the advent of screens, initially television and subsequently multimedia, has resulted in the creation of a continuous stream of visual content and imagery (Branzaglia, 2011; Pezzini, 2008). However, it is the advent of new media, particularly social media, that has precipitated a shift towards a visual-centric mode of communication, including advertising, that is characterised by rapidity and brevity. Consequently, there is a greater tendency to communicate through images, or more specifically, through icons, than through verbal language. Verbal language is relegated to a secondary position in comparison to the image, which assumes the role of the primary protagonist in the narrative. Images are more persuasive than words and are therefore more significant in advertising because they have a greater impact on the brain. Similarly, certain musical compositions have the capacity to induce a sense of well-being and harmony. In advertisements, music that is both captivating and dreamlike, as well as scenes of familiar harmony, serve a similar function: to convey a message without explicitly stating it. If language fully reveals the intentionality of the broadcaster, images do not reveal as clearly the relationship between the broadcaster's intention and their content (Morales, 2008).

The technique primarily used on social media has been visual storytelling, a narrative that utilizes images, videos, graphics, and other visual elements to convey emotions and engage the audience (El-Desouky, 2020). In a world where people are constantly bombarded with content and information, visual storytelling has proven to be a powerful way to capture attention, communicate brand values, and promote products or services in an engaging and memorable way (Heejin & Childs, 2020). Visual storytelling has become essential on social media for several reasons. First, for its immediate impact: images and videos capture attention much faster than text (Seifert & Chattaraman, 2020). On platforms like Instagram, TikTok, Facebook, and Pinterest, where visual content is at the center, the first impression is crucial. Videos are one of the most powerful tools for storytelling, as they combine movement, sound, and emotions. People quickly scroll through their feeds and often decide whether to stop on content based on how visually appealing or interesting it is. This could be short videos for TikTok, Instagram Reels, or YouTube Shorts, or longer, more detailed videos on YouTube or Facebook. Videos can tell brand stories, product demonstrations, tutorials, interviews, or behind-the-scenes footage.

A second key point in storytelling is the ability to tell emotional stories more effectively (Ferraro, 2020). Visual storytelling is much more than showing a product or service; it must tell stories that emotionally resonate with the audience. As mentioned earlier, people don't just buy products; they buy experiences and values that make them feel connected to a brand. Visual stories are easier to remember and more memorable compared to verbal or written stories. Images evoke emotions that stay in the audience's memory much longer, which can lead to greater brand recognition and loyalty. Images and videos can also overcome linguistic and cultural barriers, enabling the brand to connect with a global audience. In an international context, visual storytelling can convey complex or emotional messages in a universal way. Some examples of emotion-based visual storytelling include telling stories of how the brand has improved its customers' lives or solved a problem. For example, a clothing brand promoting inclusivity might show stories of people of different sizes or ethnicities wearing its products. Or a fitness brand might tell visual stories of people who have achieved their health and wellness goals using its products. Alternatively, behind-the-scenes stories, interviews with founders, or authentic employee testimonials can help show the human side of the brand and build trust.

Visual storytelling for brands on social media develops in various ways but must follow some key steps that allow the creation of a strong visual brand identity. First, the brand's message and mission must be clearly defined. It's essential for the brand to define its message, values, and what differentiates it from the competition; how it wants the public to perceive it. For example, an eco-friendly brand could tell visual stories that emphasize environmental respect, the use of sustainable materials, and eco-friendly choices. Second, the visual content created must be consistent with the brand, reflecting its visual identity—logos, typography, and visual style all contribute to creating a coherent user experience and making the brand immediately recognizable (Agnello, 2013). This means using a relevant color palette, selecting a photographic or video style that aligns with the brand's image, and maintaining consistency in the use of logos and other graphic elements. For example, a beauty brand might use soft, refined tones, while a sports brand could opt for vibrant, dynamic colors. Even the fonts used in posts should reflect the brand's personality. For instance, a luxury brand will likely have an elegant, sophisticated typeface. The type of photography (minimalistic, natural, vintage, etc.) or the use of graphics and illustrations should always align with the tone and vision of the brand.

Another crucial aspect is choosing the right format for each platform. Each social media platform has its peculiarities in terms of format and the type of visual content that works best. For example, Facebook and Twitter are more text-based compared to Instagram and TikTok, but images and videos are still essential. Here, visual storytelling can be used to create content that stimulates discussions or provides information (such as infographics). TikTok, on the other hand, relies on short and engaging videos. Here, visual storytelling can be more informal and creative, using music and viral trends. Many brands create content that goes beyond traditional advertising, trying to be more authentic and naturally participating in trends. One of the primary channels for visual storytelling is Instagram. Brands use high-quality images and videos, stories (Stories) for daily updates, and reels for short but engaging video content. The images must be meticulously curated to capture attention in a competitive visual feed.

Lastly, it is evident that the narrativity of an image does not necessarily correlate with its level of attractiveness. For an image to be considered narrative, it is not sufficient for it to be aesthetically pleasing or to evoke emotions. In order for an image to be considered narrative, it must adhere to the criteria of semiotic processes of sense production (Polidoro, 2008). Of course, the presence of at least one element from the narrative scheme is required, ensuring that the image is not open to interpretation. A narrative image is defined by its capacity to declare a position and convey an unambiguous message through the grammatical elements of the narrative (Pozzato, 2001; Orzati, 2019). This necessitates the increased utilization of mythical advertising, whereby campaigns are replete with dream and imagination, thus enabling the construction of a scenario imbued with meaning and form. This kind of narrative technique provides new economic opportunities for companies and offers businesses a means of connecting with customers. The contemporary consumer is seeking experiences that will stimulate and enhance their senses, rather than merely focusing on the product itself.

4. ONE CASE STUDY OF BRAND STORYTELLING ON INSTAGRAM PLATFORM

We have therefore understood the changes introduced by social media in the way advertising is done and the main marketing strategies. Let's now see how all of this applies to a specific social platform, Instagram, which is currently the main platform used by brands to increase their visibility and level of engagement.

Using Instagram is very simple. Instagram is a social media platform designed primarily for sharing photos and videos. It allows users to upload images or videos to their profile, which can then be shared with their followers or kept private. Users can engage with the content they see by liking, commenting, or sharing it. Additionally, Instagram offers various interactive features such as Stories (temporary photos and videos that disappear after 24 hours), Reels (short, engaging video clips), and IGTV (for longer video content).

Instagram also allows users to apply filters, edit their photos and videos, and add text or stickers before sharing. The platform uses an algorithm that suggests posts based on a user's interests, previous interactions, and other behaviors. Another significant feature is the ability for users to follow other profiles, allowing them to see the content shared by friends, influencers, celebrities, or brands. Brands also use Instagram as a marketing tool, often employing paid advertisements to reach specific audiences based on demographic data and user behavior.

Users account is automatically ordered in a chronological order, where each new post appears above the previous one. Photos have both a diachronic and synchronic dimension. Each individual photo tells something about the moment it was taken and, image after image, the profile is built, which in its entirety represents a real narrative journey, something that tells more than a single image. The profile becomes the context of the photo, which, while it might be a non-narrative image on its own, becomes a semantically relevant part of a story within this context (Bevins, 2014). Each text, each photo becomes a piece of a more complex text. An Instagram profile, as a sequence, a studied arrangement of different photos, tells more than a single image (Barthes, 1980), and is a narrative comparable to a verbal text (Mohammadreza et al., 2017; Zoe, 2023).

Instagram was launched in 2010. Over time, the platform grew in popularity, attracting millions of users globally. Brands quicky recognized Instagram's potential as a visual marketing tool. The key reasons why Instagram became attractive for marketing include its emphasis on visual content, the growing number of active users, and its innovative features. By 2014, Instagram had 300 million users, which made it an essential platform for marketers. The massive and continually growing user base made Instagram a valuable channel for reaching specific demographics. Instagram allows brands to connect with consumers on an emotional level through storytelling. By sharing photos, behind-the-scenes content, and lifestyle images, brands can give followers a more authentic and relatable experience. This type of visual storytelling helps brands communicate their values, mission, and identity in a way that resonates with their audience.

Let us analyze an effective case of brand storytelling, focusing on values such as sustainability, tradition, quality, and social commitment. A company that has successfully developed a brand storytelling strategy is Barilla, one of the most well-known food brands in Italy and worldwide. Over time, Barilla has launched several storytelling campaigns that highlight its values, tradition, and social commitment (Ganapini & Gonizzi, 1994).

Founded in 1877 with a small bakery and pasta shop, Barilla opened its first industrial plant in 1910. In 1975, it launched its own brand of baked goods, Mulino Bianco — which has become iconic — and in the 1990s, it expanded by acquiring significant brands from around the world. As a result, Barilla has evolved into an international food group that exports its products to over 100 countries (Briganti, 2024). One of the company's most impactful campaigns was titled "Dove c'è Barilla c'è casa" ("Where there is Barilla, there is home"), focused on telling stories of inclusivity, family, and food tradition. The campaign centered around the idea that Barilla pasta represents not only food, but also a symbol of unity and sharing. Through images and videos depicting Italian families gathered around the table, Barilla emphasized the emotional connection created around food. The core message was that pasta, particularly Barilla pasta, has the ability to transform any meal into a special moment, an opportunity to come together and celebrate tradition.

In Barilla's Instagram campaign, several distinguishing elements can be identified, which together make it an effective campaign. Let's examine the main visual elements. First, the choice and maintenance of a single color: Barilla's blue is emblematic of familiarity and reliability, often associated with Italian tradition. Blue is also a color that evokes warmth and security, qualities that are amplified by the concept of "home" and "family." Regarding composition, the images tend to depict laid tables, families, or groups of people sharing a meal. These images of tables are often rich and welcoming, suggesting abundance and gratification. This type of composition communicates the idea of unity and social connection through food. Cultural symbols are also employed: the pasta itself becomes a symbol of Italian tradition, while the family is a symbol of deeply rooted values in Italian culture. Barilla plays on the symbol of pasta as a vehicle for tradition, home warmth, and human connection. It is not just selling a food product but a social and familial experience.

Furthermore, Barilla's Instagram profile also highlights strong emotionality and a sense of community. The images used are highly emotional, showing families coming together around the table and people sharing meals with friends and relatives, evoking feelings of familial warmth and belonging. The people in the photos are often smiling, creating a positive atmosphere that fuels the desire to share such moments with others (Boero, 2018). The concept of "food as ritual" is very strong in these images, which tell stories related to the Italian pasta tradition and its centennial heritage, linking the brand to the country's history and deeper values. Barilla leverages shared values: the message of unity and family is universal and easily recognizable, especially in a country like Italy, where cooking and shared meals are central to the culture.

Additionally, an inclusive storytelling approach is employed: Barilla strives to make every family feel represented, not just traditional families, but also modern and diverse ones, thus expanding its target audience. Barilla naturally integrates user-generated content by inviting its followers to share their family stories using a dedicated hashtag, such as #DoveCèBarillaCèCasa, thereby fostering direct interaction with the public. In this way, the company has established a strong emotional connection with consumers over time, positioning itself as a brand that transcends the simple food product and represents a deep value and part of the everyday life of Italians. Barilla pasta becomes the bond between people, a connection made visible through images that evoke inclusivity and culture.

The main difference between Barilla's storytelling on Instagram and its television advertising campaign lies in the type of content and how the message is communicated to the audience. While both platforms use storytelling to create an emotional connection with the audience, significant differences exist in terms of expression modes, consumption, and interaction. In terms of format, Instagram features short visual content, meaning that images and videos are generally very brief and dynamic. The visual format takes precedence, with images needing to capture attention immediately. Stories, posts, and reels are designed for quick consumption, often on the go, as part of users' daily routines. The focus is on immediate visuals: Instagram is a platform that prioritizes visual content. In this context, Barilla uses engaging photos and videos that tell stories visually without necessarily requiring a complex verbal narrative. The connection with the audience is established through visual emotions, such as familial bonds or conviviality around the table.

Interactivity is also central: Instagram allows for direct interaction with the audience through likes, comments, hashtags, and interactive stories (polls, questions). Users can respond or share their own experiences, creating a direct, personal relationship with the brand. On television, however, advertisements are longer: Barilla's TV commercials have more space to tell longer, more complex stories. A television commercial can last anywhere from 30 seconds to 2 minutes, providing ample time to develop a more complete narrative, with music, voiceovers, and dialogues that allow for a deeper emotional connection, also employing verbal storytelling. The visuals are more cinematic: television allows for richer visual quality and cinematography, with professional productions that use directing techniques to tell stories in an engaging and sophisticated way. Barilla's TV campaigns often depict emotional scenes and complex narratives, with cinematic moments emphasizing the importance of family, tradition, and values tied to food.

Another difference between Instagram and television lies in the type of storytelling used. On Instagram, the company favors immediate visual storytelling, based on strong images that tell brief and concise stories, more focused on immediate emotional reaction. Visual stories are designed to be consumed quickly and to elicit an instant connection. The visual content on Instagram is simple, direct, and immediate, aiming to convey visual emotions in a matter of seconds. For example, images of a family eating together at the same table can quickly and intuitively convey the concept of "home" and "family" without the need for a complex verbal discourse. On television, however, the narrative is longer and more detailed: Barilla's TV campaigns tend to tell more complex stories and structure a plot that develops over a narrative arc. For example, scenes of food preparation, family gatherings, and moments of shared emotion are included, all accompanied by a voiceover or emotional music. In this case, the central message is clear and articulated: in television advertising, the message Barilla wants to communicate (such as family unity, Italian tradition, product quality) is supported by a narrative that leverages the power of emotional storytelling. The visuals are designed to evoke deep emotion, prompting the viewer to reflect on the value of food as a unifying element.

A fundamental difference between Instagram and television lies in audience interaction. On Instagram, the interaction is direct and bidirectional: Barilla can engage directly with consumers through comments, direct messages, and interactive content. For instance, it can ask followers to share their recipes or family moments using the campaign's official hashtag. This kind of continuous engagement creates a more personal and immediate relationship. Instagram Stories allow Barilla to continuously update the audience, making followers feel like an integral part of the narrative. They can comment in real time, participate in polls and quizzes, and even create content themselves.

In contrast, television communication is unidirectional: the brand communicates a message, and the audience passively receives it. Interaction happens later, when the consumer decides to purchase the product or feels engaged by the advertisement, but there is no immediate dialogue as there is on Instagram. Here, the emotional impact is greater: television has the power to evoke stronger emotions over a longer time period, but it does not allow the same kind of direct feedback that Instagram offers.

The two channels also target different demographics. Instagram targets a young, digitally engaged audience: Instagram is a platform more frequently used by a younger, digital-savvy audience, often more inclined to seek fast, visual, and interactive content. Barilla on Instagram caters to consumers accustomed to quick visual communication and who prefer personalized and interactive content. Brand engagement is essential in this case: Barilla seeks to build an online community where consumers feel involved in the brand's narrative. On television, however, the target is broader and more general: television has a wider reach and can connect with a more diversified and traditional audience. Barilla's TV campaigns target a more generic consumer base, including families, adults, and individuals who are not necessarily digital natives. Here, brand awareness and tradition are stronger: television is an ideal platform to reinforce Barilla's image as a brand of quality and family tradition.

Another difference concerns the time and frequency of the message. On Instagram, the frequency is higher, and content is updated more frequently: here, Barilla can post content more often, with a shorter content lifecycle. Campaigns come and go quickly, and updates are continuous. Stories, posts, and reels allow for a constant presence in users' feeds. Instagram is a platform where the audience is used to scrolling through their feed continuously, so the visual communication must be immediately engaging. On television, however, the frequency is lower, but the impact is greater: television advertising has a lower frequency but tends to have a more significant impact due to its evocative power and ability to tell complete stories over a longer time span.

In conclusion, Barilla's visual storytelling on Instagram is characterized by a more immediate, visual, and interactive approach, with a strong focus on direct engagement and the creation of an online community. In contrast, Barilla's television advertising tends to be more intricate, emotional, and cinematic, with a unidirectional message.

CONCLUSION

In this chapter, we have explored the transformations brought about by social media in the realm of advertising, particularly in the domain of brand storytelling. A brand is a multifaceted system composed of signs, symbols, messages, values, and experiences that serve to identify or differentiate a product, service, or company from its competitors in the marketplace. It is not merely a commercial entity but rather a cultural construct that seeks to create a coherent and recognizable perception in the minds of the public. The brand aims to forge an emotional connection with consumers, evoke a sense of trust, and represent a distinctive identity in a competitive and often saturated market.

In the context of social media, the primary technique adopted by brands is visual storytelling—an approach that relies on the art of communicating through images and visual elements. This method employs a wide range of media, including photographs, videos, illustrations, and graphics, to elicit emotions, communicate abstract concepts, and engage audiences in ways that transcend traditional verbal or written communication. Rather than telling a story through words alone, visual storytelling involves creating a narrative that unfolds visually, where each image, color, and composition plays a crucial role in constructing the plot, atmosphere, and deeper meaning of the message.

When applied to branding, visual storytelling becomes a powerful marketing strategy that transcends conventional advertising. It goes beyond merely showcasing a product or service, focusing instead on creating an emotional and authentic connection between the brand and its consumers. By weaving narratives that resonate with the audience, brands are able to foster a sense of belonging and loyalty. This approach allows consumers to not only recognize a brand but also identify with it on a deeper, more personal level. Through this narrative framework, brands communicate values, traditions, and aspirations—elements that serve to construct an identity that consumers feel they can align with.

Visual storytelling for brands on social media manifests in various forms, each tailored to the specific objectives of the brand and the preferences of its target audience. Through the careful use of visual elements, brands can create a compelling visual identity that stands out in an increasingly crowded digital space. The key to this process lies in understanding how to employ visuals in a way that communicates the essence of the brand in an engaging and memorable way. In this regard, we have highlighted the essential steps that lead to the development of a strong visual brand identity, from the selection of the right imagery to the creation of a cohesive visual narrative that resonates across various platforms.

Moreover, visual storytelling has the unique ability to break down language and cultural barriers. While words may be subject to interpretation and translation, images have a universal quality that allows them to connect with a diverse and global audience. In this sense, visual storytelling facilitates an emotional and intuitive connection with the public, making the brand's message accessible and relatable to a wide range of consumers across different cultural contexts.

In summary, visual storytelling represents a universal language that transforms the act of seeing into an immersive, narrative experience. It is a dynamic and multifaceted tool that enables brands to craft stories that evoke emotion, create bonds, and establish a lasting presence in the minds of consumers. One exemplary case study of a brand that has successfully utilized visual storytelling is the Italian company Barilla. By adopting storytelling as its core marketing strategy, Barilla has been able to engage its audience through powerful and evocative images and videos that convey not just the quality of its products but also the values and emotions associated with its brand. Through this visual approach, Barilla has built a brand narrative that resonates deeply with its audience, forging an emotional connection that extends beyond mere consumption to create a sense of shared experience and cultural identity.

REFERENCES

Agnello, M. (2013). *Semiotica dei colori*. Carocci.

Aimé, I. (2021). The dynamic construction of brand storytelling. *Journal of Strategic Marketing*, *31*(7), 1243–1262. DOI: 10.1080/0965254X.2021.1908404

Baker, S., & Boyle, M. (2009). The timeless power of storytelling. *Journal of Sponsorship*, *3*(1), 11–26.

Baudrillard, J. (2016). The consumer society: Myths and structures. *Sage (Atlanta, Ga.)*.

Bevins, C. (2014). *Get Schooled: A visual social semiotic analysis of Target's branding using Instagram*. Liberty University.

Bianchi, C. (2005). *Spot. Analisi semiotica dell'audiovisivo pubblicitario*. Carocci.

Bianchi, C. (2020). *Semiotica e digital marketing*. Lexia.

Boero, M. (2018). *La famiglia della pubblicità*. Franco Angeli.

Boero, M. (2019). Il metodo etnosemiotico per lo studio delle pratiche di consumo. *E (Norwalk, Conn.)*, *C*, 25, 51–60.

Boero, M., & Greco, M. (2023). Semiotics, artificial intelligence, and ChatGPT: Research lines, analytical perspectives and potential applications. *Filosofi(e) semiotiche*, 10(1).

Branzaglia, M. (2011). *Comunicare con le immagini*. Mondadori.

Briganti, A. (2024). *Barilla. Made in Italy*. Mondadori Electa.

Brown, S. (2016). *Brands and branding*. Pearson Education.

Cara, M. (2019). The semiotic layers of Instagram: Visual tropes and brand meaning. *American Journal of Semiotics*, *34*(3/4), 331–352.

Cosenza, G. (2014). *Introduzione alla semiotica dei nuovi media*. Laterza.

Cosenza, G. (2024). Semiotica per campagne di digital marketing: Alcune proposte operative. *Ocula*, 25(29).

Eco, U. (1975). *Trattato di semiotica generale*. Bompiani.

Eco, U. (1979). *Lector in fabula: La cooperazione interpretativa nei testi narrativi*. Bompiani.

Eco, U. (1994). *Sei passeggiate nei boschi narrativi*. Bompiani.

El-Desouky, D. F. (2020). Visual storytelling in advertising: A study of visual storytelling as a marketing approach for creating effective ads. *International Journal of Humanities* [IJHSSE]. *Social Sciences and Education, 7*(10), 118–127.

Escalas, J. E. (2004). Narrative processing: Building consumer connections to brands. *Journal of Consumer Psychology, 14*(1-2), 168–180. DOI: 10.1207/s15327663jcp1401&2_19

Ferraro, G. (1999). *La pubblicità nell'era di Internet*. Meltemi.

Ferraro, G. (2020). *Teorie della narrazione: Dai racconti tradizionali all'odierno storytelling*. Carocci.

Floch, J. M. (1990). *Semiotique, marketing et communication. Sous les signes, les stratégies*. PUF.

Floch, J. M. (1995). *Identités visuelles*. Presses Universitaires de France.

Fontana, A. (2020). *Storytelling d'impresa: La nuova guida definitiva verso lo storymaking*. Hoepli Editore.

Ganapini, A. I., & Gonizzi, G. (1994). *Barilla: Cento anni di pubblicità e comunicazione*. Silvana Editore.

Heejin, L., & Childs, M. (2020). Visual storytelling on Instagram: Branded photo narrative and the role of telepresence. *Journal of Research in Interactive Marketing, 14*(1), 33–50. DOI: 10.1108/JRIM-09-2018-0115

Holt, D. (2004). *How brands become icons*. Harvard Business Press.

Kerpen, D. (2011). *Likeable social media: How to delight your customers, create an irresistible brand, and be generally amazing on Facebook (and other social networks)*. McGraw-Hill.

Kristensen, J., Gabrielsen, G., & Zaichkowski, L. (2012). How valuable is a well-crafted design and name brand? Recognition and willingness to pay. *Journal of Consumer Behaviour, 11*(1), 44–55. DOI: 10.1002/cb.368

Laurita, G., & Venturini, R. (2016). *Strategia digitale: Comunicare bene su internet e i social media*. Hoepli.

Lund, N. F., Cohen, S. A., & Scarles, C. (2018). The power of social media storytelling in destination branding. *Journal of Destination Marketing & Management, 8*, 271–280. DOI: 10.1016/j.jdmm.2017.05.003

Maggio, A. (2024). *Visioni future di digital marketing*. Dario Flaccovio Editore.

Manning, P. (2010). The semiotics of brand. *Annual Review of Anthropology*, *39*(1), 33–49. DOI: 10.1146/annurev.anthro.012809.104939

Marchese, A. (1983). *L'officina del racconto*. Mondadori.

Marrone, G. (2007). *Il discorso di marca: Modelli semiotici per il branding*. Laterza.

Martinus, T., & Chaniago, M. (2017). Analysis of branding strategy through Instagram with storytelling in creating brand image on proud projects. *Humaiora*, *8*(3), 201–210. DOI: 10.21512/humaniora.v8i3.3678

Mayer, P. (2015). *Dallo spot al post: La pubblicità dopo i social media*. Edizione LSWR.

Mazzoni, G. (2011). *Teoria del romanzo*. Il Mulino.

Miller, C. (2017). *Branding and communication*. Routledge.

Mohammadreza, M., Shairi, H., & Ahmadpanah, A. (2017). Social semiotic aspects of Instagram social network. *IEEE International Conference on Innovations in Intelligent Systems and Applications (INISTA)*, 460–465.

Morales, L. (2008). *Narrare con le immagini*. Dino Audino.

Orzati, G. (2019). *Visual storytelling: Quando il racconto si fa immagine*. Einaudi.

Oswald, G. (2011). Brand communication in social media. *Journal of Advertising*, *48*(1), 14–26.

Pezzini, M. (2008). *Immagini quotidiane: Sociosemiotica visuale*. Laterza.

Polidoro, P. (2008). *Che cos'è la semiotica visiva*. Carocci.

Poulsen, S. V., & Kvale, G. (2018). Studying social media as semiotic technology: A social semiotic multimodal framework. *Social Semiotics*, *28*(5), 700–717. DOI: 10.1080/10350330.2018.1505689

Pozzato, F. (2001). *Semiotica del testo: Metodi, autori, esempi*. Carocci.

Quesenbery, W., & Brooks, K. (2010). *Storytelling for user experience: Crafting stories for better design*. Rosenfeld Media.

Rodriguez, A. (2020). *Brand storytelling and consumer experience*. Springer.

Seifert, C., & Chattaraman, V. (2020). A picture is worth a thousand words! How visual storytelling transforms the aesthetic experience of novel designs. *Journal of Product and Brand Management*, *29*(7), 913–926. DOI: 10.1108/JPBM-01-2019-2194

Volli, U. (2021). *Semiotica della pubblicità*. Laterza.

Wheeler, A., & Meyerson, R. (2024). *Designing brand identity: A comprehensive guide to the world of brand and branding*. Wiley.

Woodside, A. G.. (2008). Brand storytelling: Exploring narrative marketing. *The Journal of Consumer Research*, *35*(5), 445–458.

Zoe, H. (2023). Signs of #self: A Peircean semiotic framework for theorizing self-(re)presentation on Instagram. *Visual Communication*, *22*(4), 671–692. DOI: 10.1177/14703572211022400

KEY TERMS AND DEFINITIONS

Brand: A brand is the unique and distinctive identity of a company or product, built through a combination of values, emotions, experiences, and perceptions that it evokes in the public. It is not just the logo or name, but the sum of how a brand is perceived, experienced, and recognized in the hearts and minds of consumers. The brand tells a story that intertwines with that of the customer, creating a bond of trust and belonging.

Brandtelling: Brand storytelling is the authentic and engaging narrative that a brand constructs to communicate its values, mission, and vision, with the goal of creating a lasting emotional connection with the audience. It is not just about telling what the company does, but how it does it, why it does it, and the impact it has on people and the world. It is a story that goes beyond the product, making the brand part of the life and experience of those who choose it.

Digital Marketing: Digital marketing refers to the strategies and promotional actions carried out through digital channels to reach, engage, and convert the audience into customers. By leveraging technologies, online platforms, and data, digital marketing aims to create personalized experiences, optimize brand visibility, and improve commercial performance, adapting quickly to changes in consumer habits and emerging technologies. In essence, it is a dynamic and multidimensional approach to building lasting relationships between brands and consumers in the digital world.

Semiotics of Advertising: The semiotics of advertising is the study of the signs and symbols used in advertising campaigns to create meaning, influence perceptions, and motivate behaviors. It analyzes how visual, verbal, and iconic messages combine to construct persuasive narratives that speak to the subconscious of the audience. Through semiotics, advertising taps into cultural codes, shared values, and stereotypes to evoke emotions, desires, and ideologies, transforming products and services into symbols of status, belonging, or aspiration. Essentially, the semiotics of advertising explores how signs are manipulated to guide consumer choices and actions in an increasingly stimulus-saturated environment.

Social Media: Social media refers to digital platforms that allow people to connect, interact, and share content in real time, creating online communities around shared interests, identities, and experiences. These are dynamic spaces where individuals, companies, and organizations can exchange information, ideas, and creativity through text, images, videos, and other forms of visual communication. Social media not only facilitates communication between individuals but also amplifies the power of collective narratives, influencing opinions, behaviors, and social trends. In this context, social media becomes a kind of "digital marketplace" where everyone can simultaneously be both a producer and consumer of content, contributing to a more interactive and participatory form of communication.

Storytelling Advertising: Storytelling advertising is a marketing strategy that uses narrative to emotionally engage the audience, building a deep connection with the brand through authentic and meaningful stories. Instead of focusing solely on a direct promotional message, storytelling advertising transforms the product or service into a protagonist in a story that reflects shared values, experiences, or aspirations. The stories told in this way are not merely a means of selling, but of creating a lasting emotional bond, leveraging the power of emotions, conflicts, and narrative resolutions. In this process, the consumer is not just a recipient of a message but becomes an integral part of a narrative that can be experienced, shared, and remembered.

Visual Storytelling: Visual storytelling is the art of telling stories through images and visual elements, using photographs, videos, illustrations, or graphics to evoke emotions, communicate concepts, and engage the audience. Instead of merely narrating a fact or message with words, visual storytelling creates a narrative that unfolds visually, where each image, color, and composition contributes to building a plot, atmosphere, and meaning. This approach harnesses the power of images to transcend linguistic and cultural barriers, connecting with the audience on an emotional and intuitive level. In summary, visual storytelling is a universal language that transforms seeing into a rich and immersive narrative experience.

Compilation of References

Adeoye-Olatunde, O. A., & Olenik, N. L. (2021). Research and scholarly methods: Semi-structured interviews. [purdue.edu]. *Journal of the American College of Clinical Pharmacy: JAACP*, *4*(10), 1358–1367. DOI: 10.1002/jac5.1441

Agnello, M. (2013). *Semiotica dei colori*. Carocci.

Ahmad, F., Guzmán, F., & Al-Emran, M. (2024). Brand activism and the consequence of woke washing. *Journal of Business Research*, *170*, 114362. DOI: 10.1016/j.jbusres.2023.114362

Ahmed, K. M. (2020). Effect of design elements for social media ads on consumer's purchasing decision. *Global Media Journal*, *18*(34), 1–12.

Aiello, G. (2020). Visual semiotics: Key concepts and new directions. *The SAGE handbook of visual research methods*. academia.edu

Aiello, G. (2020). *Visual Semiotics: Key Concepts and New Directions*. The SAGE Handbook of Visual Research Methods SAGE Publications.

Aimé, I. (2021). The dynamic construction of brand storytelling. *Journal of Strategic Marketing*, *31*(7), 1243–1262. DOI: 10.1080/0965254X.2021.1908404

Akestam, N., Rosengren, S., & Dahlen, M. (2017). Advertising 'Like a Girl': Toward a Better Understanding of 'Femvertising' and Its Effects. *Psychology and Marketing*, *34*(8), 795–806. DOI: 10.1002/mar.21023

Akkaya, M. (2021). Understanding the impacts of lifestyle segmentation & perceived value on brand purchase intention: An empirical study in different product categories. [sciencedirect.com]. *European Research on Management and Business Economics*, *27*(3), 100155. DOI: 10.1016/j.iedeen.2021.100155

Alcindor, M., Jackson, D., & Alcindor-Huelva, P. (2022). Heritage places as the settings for virtual playgrounds: Perceived realism in video games, as a tool for the re-localisation of physical places. *International Journal of Heritage Studies*, *28*(7), 865–883. DOI: 10.1080/13527258.2022.2091638

Al-Natour, S., Benbasat, I., & Cenfetelli, R. (2011). The adoption of online shopping assistants: Perceived similarity as an antecedent to evaluative beliefs. *Journal of the Association for Information Systems*, *12*(5), 347–374. DOI: 10.17705/1jais.00267

Alwan, M., & Alshurideh, M. (2022). The effect of digital marketing on purchase intention: Moderating effect of brand equity. [growingscience.com]. *International Journal of Data and Network Science*, *6*(3), 837–848. DOI: 10.5267/j.ijdns.2022.2.012

Amazon. (n.d.). Amazon Go is a new kind of corner store. *Amazon.* Retrieved December 20, 2024, from https://www.amazon.com/b?node=16008589011

Amos, O. (2020, August 26). Covid-19'un uğramadığı 10 ülke. *BBC News Türkçe.* https://www.bbc.com/turkce/haberler-dunya-53909497

Araújo, S. O., Peres, R. S., Barata, J., Lidon, F., & Ramalho, J. C. (2021). Characterising the Agriculture 4.0 Landscape—Emerging Trends, Challenges and Opportunities [MDPI.]. *Agronomy (Basel)*, *11*(11), 2206. DOI: 10.3390/agronomy11040667

Arnould, E. J., & Thompson, C. J. (2005). Consumer Culture Theory (CCT): Twenty Years of Research. *The Journal of Consumer Research*, *31*(4), 868–882. DOI: 10.1086/426626

Aw, E. C.-X., Basha, N. K., Ng, S.-I., & Ho, J.-A. (2021). Unraveling determinants of webrooming behavior: A qualitative inquiry. *International Journal of Business and Society*, *22*(3), 1550–1568. DOI: 10.33736/ijbs.4321.2021

Aw, E. C.-X., Kamal Basha, N., Ng, S. I., & Ho, J. A. (2021). Searching online and buying offline: Understanding the role of channel-, consumer-, and product-related factors in determining webrooming intention. *Journal of Retailing and Consumer Services*, *58*, 102328. DOI: 10.1016/j.jretconser.2020.102328

Azodo, I., Williams, R., Sheikh, A., & Cresswell, K. (2020). Opportunities and challenges surrounding the use of data from wearable sensor devices in health care: Qualitative interview study. [jmir.org]. *Journal of Medical Internet Research*, *22*(10), e19542. DOI: 10.2196/19542 PMID: 33090107

Badloe, T., & Rho, J. (2024). Enabling New Frontiers of Nanophotonics with Metamaterials, Photonic Crystals, and Plasmonics. *Nanophotonics*, *13*(7), 965–969. DOI: 10.1515/nanoph-2024-0100 PMID: 39634002

Bae, H., Jo, S. H., & Lee, E. (2021). Why do older consumers avoid innovative products and services? *Journal of Services Marketing*, *35*(1), 41–53. DOI: 10.1108/JSM-10-2019-0408

Baker, S., & Boyle, M. (2009). The timeless power of storytelling. *Journal of Sponsorship*, *3*(1), 11–26.

Bakshi, A., & Kaur, S. (2023). A Conceptualization of Marketing through the Perspective of Semiotics. *Academy of Marketing Studies Journal*, *27*(2), 1–15.

Ballio, L., & Zanacchi, A. (1987). *Carosello story. La via italiana alla pubblicità televisiva*. Eri.

Ball, M. (2022). *The metaverse: And how it will revolutionize everything*. Liveright.

Bankov, K. (2022). *The Digital Mind: Semiotic Explorations in Digital Culture*. Springer. DOI: 10.1007/978-3-030-92555-0

Bartosik-Purgat, M., & Filimon, N. (2022). *European consumers in the digital era: Implications of technology, media and culture on consumer behavior* (1st ed.). Routledge., DOI: 10.4324/9781003263685

Barwitz, N., & Maas, P. (2018). Understanding the omnichannel customer journey: Determinants of interaction choice. *Journal of Interactive Marketing*, *43*(1), 116–133. DOI: 10.1016/j.intmar.2018.02.001

Bashirzadeh, Y., Mai, R., & Faure, C. (2022). How rich is too rich? Visual design elements in digital marketing communications. [sciencedirect.com]. *International Journal of Research in Marketing*, *39*(1), 58–76. DOI: 10.1016/j.ijresmar.2021.06.008

Batat, W. (2019). *Experiential marketing: Consumer behavior, customer experience and the 7es*. Routledge. DOI: 10.4324/9781315232201

Batat, W. (2022). What does phygital really mean? A conceptual introduction to the phygital customer experience (PH-CX) framework. *Journal of Strategic Marketing*, *32*(8), 1220-1243. DOI: 10.1080/0965254X.2022.2059775

Batat, W., & Hammedi, W. (2023). The extended reality technology (ERT) framework for designing customer and service experiences in phygital settings: A service research agenda. *Journal of Service Management*, *34*(1), 10–33. DOI: 10.1108/JOSM-08-2022-0289

Baudrillard, J. (2016). The consumer society: Myths and structures. *Sage (Atlanta, Ga.)*.

Beaird, J., Walker, A., & George, J. (2020). *The principles of beautiful web design*. uni-osnabrueck.de

Beasley, R., & Danesi, M. (2002). *Persuasive Signs: The Semiotics of Advertising* (Vol. 4). Mouton De Gruyter. DOI: 10.1515/9783110888003

Beer, D. (2009). Power through the algorithm? Participatory web cultures and the technological unconscious. *New Media & Society*, *11*(6), 985–1002. DOI: 10.1177/1461444809336551

Belghiti, S., Ochs, A., Lemoine, J.-F., & Badot, O. (2018). The phygital shopping experience: An attempt at conceptualization and empirical investigation. In Rossi, P., & Krey, N. (Eds.), *Marketing transformation: Marketing practice in an ever-changing world* (pp. 61–74). Springer International Publishing., DOI: 10.1007/978-3-319-68750-6_18

Belova, A. (2021). Storytelling in Advertising and Branding. *Cognition, Communication, Discourse*, *19*, 5–18.

Berners-Lee, B. (2024). The Semiotics of Digital Cartography at the Geoguessr Interface: A Practice-Oriented Case Study. *New Media & Society*, *26*(12), 6881–6899. DOI: 10.1177/14614448231160132

Beverland, M. B., Eckhardt, G. M., Sands, S., & Shankar, A. (2021). How brands craft national identity. [cbs.dk]. *The Journal of Consumer Research*, *48*(4), 586–609. DOI: 10.1093/jcr/ucaa062

Bevins, C. (2014). *Get Schooled: A visual social semiotic analysis of Target's branding using Instagram*. Liberty University.

Bezemer, J., & Cowan, K. (2022). "Exploring Reading in Social Semiotics: Theory and Methods" Reading.

Bhat, S., & Reddy, S. K. (1998). Symbolic and functional positioning of brands. *Journal of Consumer Marketing*, *15*(1), 32–43. DOI: 10.1108/07363769810202664

Bianchi, C. (2020). Nuove forme di testualità nel digital marketing. *Lexia. Rivista di semiotica, 33–34*, 13–29.

Bianchi, C., & Cosenza, G. (2020) (eds.), Semiotica e digital marketing, Aracne, Rome.

Bianchi, C. (2005). *Spot. Analisi semiotica dell'audiovisivo pubblicitario*. Carocci.

Bianchi, C. (2020). *Semiotica e digital marketing*. Lexia.

Bianchi, C., Montanari, F., & Zingale, S. (Eds.). (2010). *La semiotica e il progetto 2. Spazi, oggetti, interfacce*. Franco Angeli.

Bianchi, C., & Ragonese, R. (2013). *L'annuncio stampa*. Carocci.

Bissell, K., & Rask, A. (2010). Real Women on Real Beauty: Self-Discrepancy, Internalization of the Thin Ideal, and Perceptions of Attractiveness and Thinness in Dove's Campaign for Real Beauty. *International Journal of Advertising*, *29*(4), 643–668. DOI: 10.2501/S0265048710201385

Boero, M., & Greco, M. (2023). Semiotics, artificial intelligence, and ChatGPT: Research lines, analytical perspectives and potential applications. *Filosofi(e) semiotiche*, 10(1).

Boero, M. (2018). *La famiglia della pubblicità*. Franco Angeli.

Boero, M. (2019). Il metodo etnosemiotico per lo studio delle pratiche di consumo. *E (Norwalk, Conn.)*, *C*, 25, 51–60.

Boero, M. (2022). Natura, clima, sostenibilità. Il linguaggio pubblicitario tra etica e semiotica. *Filosofi(e). Semiotiche*, *9*(1), 21–31.

Boero, M., & Greco, C. (2023). "Semiotics, Artificial Intelligence, ChatGpt. Research Lines, Analytical Perspectives and Potential Application", Filosofi(e). *Semiotiche*, *10*(1), 2023.

Bolos, C., Idemudia, E. C., Mai, P., Rasinghani, M., & Smith, S. (2016). Conceptual models on the effectiveness of e-marketing strategies in engaging consumers. *Journal of International Technology and Information Management*, *25*(4). Advance online publication. DOI: 10.58729/1941-6679.1293

Bonarou, C, (2021). "The Poetics of Travel through Unravelling Visual Representations on Postcards: A Critical Semiotics Analysis" Journal of Tourism, Heritage & Services Marketing.

Borghini, S., Diamond, N., Kozinets, R. V., McGrath, M. A., Muniz, A. M.Jr, & Sherry, J. F.Jr. (2009). Why Are Themed Brandstores So Powerful? Retail Brand Ideology at American Girl Place. *Journal of Retailing*, *85*(3), 363–375. DOI: 10.1016/j.jretai.2009.05.003

Boström, M., & Micheletti, M. (2016). Introducing the sustainability challenge of textiles and clothing. *Journal of Consumer Policy*, *39*(4), 367–375. DOI: 10.1007/s10603-016-9336-6

Branzaglia, M. (2011). *Comunicare con le immagini*. Mondadori.

Briganti, A. (2024). *Barilla. Made in Italy*. Mondadori Electa.

Brown, S. (2016). *Brands and branding*. Pearson Education.

Buyukozturk, B., Gaulden, S., & Dowd-Arrow, B. (2018). Contestation on Reddit, Gamergate, and movement barriers. *Social Movement Studies*, *17*(5), 592–609. DOI: 10.1080/14742837.2018.1483227

Çakırkaya, M., & Koçyiğit, M. (2024). Consumer involvement in augmented reality applications in the context of phygital marketing communications. *ASR: Chiang Mai University Journal of Social Sciences and Humanities*, *11*(1). Advance online publication. DOI: 10.12982/CMUJASR.2024.008

Cambier, F., & Poncin, I. (2020). Inferring brand integrity from marketing communications: The effects of brand transparency signals in a consumer empowerment context. *Journal of Business Research*. nscpolteksby.ac.id

Cammarota, A., D'Arco, M., Marino, V., & Resciniti, R. (2023). Brand activism: A literature review and future research agenda. *International Journal of Consumer Studies*, *47*(5), 1669–1691. DOI: 10.1111/ijcs.12967

Campbell, R., Freeman, O., & Gannon, V. (2021). From Overt Threat to Invisible Presence: Discursive Shifts in Representations of Gender in Menstrual Product Advertising. *Journal of Marketing Management*, *37*(3–4), 216–237. DOI: 10.1080/0267257X.2021.1876752

Cara, M. (2019). The semiotic layers of Instagram: Visual tropes and brand meaning. *American Journal of Semiotics*, *34*(3/4), 331–352.

Ceriani, G. (2001). *Marketing moving: l'approccio semiotico. Analizzare il mix di comunicazione, gestirne gli effetti di senso*. Franco Angeli Milan.

Ceriani, G. (2001). *Marketing moving: L'approccio semiotico. Analizzare il mix di comunicazione, gestirne gli effetti di senso*. Franco Angeli.

Ceriani, G. (2007). *Hot spots e sfere di cristallo. Semiotica della tendenza e ricerca strategica*. Franco Angeli.

Chae, H., Kim, S., Lee, J., & Park, K. (2020). Impact of product characteristics of limited edition shoes on perceived value, brand trust, and purchase intention; focused on the scarcity message frequency. [HTML]. *Journal of Business Research*, *120*, 398–406. DOI: 10.1016/j.jbusres.2019.11.040

Chaffey, D., & Ellis-Chadwick, F. (2019). *Digital marketing* (7th ed.)., https://books.google.com.tr/books?hl=tr&lr=&id=-1yGDwAAQBAJ&oi=fnd&pg=PT17&dq=Chaffey,+D.,+%26+Ellis-Chadwick,+F.+(2019).+Digital+Marketing.+Pearson+UK.&ots=XjQnbVnJ40&sig=pvGNpt2Btzgl9aRMbYndzvhrifk&redir_esc=y#v=onepage&q=Chaffey%2C%20D.%2C%20%26%20Ellis-Chadwick%2C%20F.%20(2019).%20Digital%20Marketing.%20Pearson%20UK.&f=false

Chaffey, D., & Smith, P. (2023). *Digital marketing excellence* (6th ed.). Routledge., DOI: 10.4324/9781003009498

Chandler, D. (2022). Semiotics: the basics. [HTML]

Chandy, R. K., Johar, G. V., & Roberts, J. H. (2021). Better Marketing for a Better World. *Journal of Marketing*, *85*(3), 1–9. DOI: 10.1177/00222429211003690

Chellappa, R. K., & Sin, R. G. (2005). Personalization versus privacy: An empirical examination of the online consumer's dilemma. *Information Technology and Management*, *6*(2–3), 181–202. DOI: 10.1007/s10799-005-5879-y

Chen, Z. T., & Cheung, M. (2022). Consumption as extended carnival on Tmall in contemporary China: a social semiotic multimodal analysis of interactive banner ads. *Social Semiotics*. arts.ac.uk

Cheng, Z., Shao, B., & Zhang, Y. (2022). Effect of product presentation videos on consumers' purchase intention: The role of perceived diagnosticity, mental imagery, and product rating. *Frontiers in Psychology*, *13*, 812579. DOI: 10.3389/fpsyg.2022.812579

Chibás Ortiz, F. (2013). Ciclo do marketing digital: Tática e estratégia blended. *Revista ENIAC Pesquisa*, *2*(1), 64. DOI: 10.22567/rep.v2i1.111

Codeluppi, V. (2020). "Semiotica e pubblicità: Il problema della marca", Filosofi(e). *Semiotiche*, *7*(1), 2020.

Cohen, S. (2020, May 30). *'For Once, Don't Do It': The Powerful Idea Behind Nike's New Anti-Racism Ad.* Retrieved from Forbes: https://www.forbes.com/sites/sethcohen/2020/05/30/for-once-dont-do-it---the-powerful-idea-behind-nikes-new-anti-racism-ad/

Cooper, A. (1999). *The inmates are running the asylum.* Sams. DOI: 10.1007/978-3-322-99786-9_1

Cooper, A., Reimann, R., & Cronin, D. (2007). *About face 3: The essentials of interaction design.* Wiley.

Cosenza, G. (2024). Semiotica per campagne di digital marketing: Alcune proposte operative. *Ocula*, 25(29).

Cosenza, G. (2014). *Introduzione alla semiotica dei nuovi media*. Laterza.

Cosenza, G. (2020). Narrative semiotics, storytelling, and User Experience Design (UXD). *Lexia*, *33*, 51–71.

Cosenza, G. (2020). Semiotic Perspectives on Digital Marketing: Tools for AI Integration in Branding. *Journal of Cultural Marketing*, *8*(3), 101–115.

Cosenza, G. (2024). Semiotica per campagne di digital marketing. Alcune proposte operative. *Ocula*, *25*, 36–58.

Cosenza, G. (2024). *Semiotica per campagne di digital marketing. Alcune proposte operative*. Ocula.

Crabtree, B. F. & Miller, W. L. (2023). *Doing qualitative research*. [HTML]

Cui, T. H., Ghose, A., Halaburda, H., Iyengar, R., Pauwels, K., Sriram, S., Tucker, C., & Venkataraman, S. (2021). Informational challenges in omnichannel marketing: Remedies and future research. *Journal of Marketing*, *85*(1), 103–120. DOI: 10.1177/0022242920968810

Dacko, S. G. (2017). Enabling smart retail settings via mobile augmented reality shopping apps. *Technological Forecasting and Social Change*, *124*, 243–256. DOI: 10.1016/j.techfore.2016.09.032

Dalamu, T. O. (2021). Social semiotic genre: Exploring the interplay of words and images in advertising. *Anuari de filologia. Llengües i literatures modernes*. ub.edu

Damayanti, N. P. W., Santika, I. D A D. M., & Eka, D. P. (2021). Semiotic Analysis of Mentos Advertisement. *Humanis*, *25*(2), 1–12.

De Fina, A. (2023). 'I especially loved the little Nana dancing on the balcony': The emergence, formation, and circulation of chronotopes in mass-mediated communication. *Language in Society*. cambridge.org

de Oca, J. M., Mason, S., & Ahn, S. (2022). Consuming for the greater good: "Woke" commercials in sports media. *Communication & Sport*, *10*(6), 1165–1187. DOI: 10.1177/2167479520949283

Deng, X. & Wang, L. (2020). The impact of semantic fluency on consumers' aesthetic evaluation in graphic designs with text. *Journal of Contemporary Marketing Science*. [HTML]

Deni, M., & Proni, G. (Eds.). (2008). *La semiotica e il progetto. Design, comunicazione, marketing*. Franco Angeli.

Dhaoui, C., & Webster, C. M. (2021). Brand and consumer engagement behaviors on Facebook brand pages: Let's have a (positive) conversation. [HTML]. *International Journal of Research in Marketing, 38*(1), 155–175. DOI: 10.1016/j.ijresmar.2020.06.005

Díaz, A., Gómez, M., & Molina, A. (2017). A comparison of online and offline consumer behaviour: An empirical study on a cinema shopping context. *Journal of Retailing and Consumer Services, 38*, 44–50. DOI: 10.1016/j.jretconser.2017.05.003

Dodd, M. D., & Supa, D. W. (2014). Conceptualizing and measuring "corporate social advocacy" communication: Examining the impact on corporate financial performance. *The Public Relations Journal, 8*(3), 2–23.

Dove (2024). *The Real State of Beauty: A Global Report.*

Dove (n.d.). *The world's largest beauty report*. Retrieved from Dove: https://www.dove.com/us/en/campaigns/purpose/global-state-of-beauty.html

Dressler, M. & Paunovic, I. (2021). The value of consistency: portfolio labeling strategies and impact on winery brand equity. *Sustainability*. mdpi.com

Dunleavy, D. (2020). "Visual Semiotics Theory: Introduction to the Science of Signs" Handbook of Visual Communication Taylor & Francis.

Dwivedi, Y. K., Ismagilova, E., Hughes, D. L., Carlson, J., Filieri, R., Jacobson, J., Jain, V., Karjaluoto, H., Kefi, H., Krishen, A. S., Kumar, V., Rahman, M. M., Raman, R., Rauschnabel, P. A., Rowley, J., Salo, J., Tran, G. A., & Wang, Y. (2021). Setting the future of digital and social media marketing research: Perspectives and research propositions. [sciencedirect.com]. *International Journal of Information Management, 59*, 102168. DOI: 10.1016/j.ijinfomgt.2020.102168

Eco, U. (1968). *La struttura assente. Introduzione alla ricerca semiologica.* Bompiani.

Eco, U. (1975). *Trattato di semiotica generale*. Bompiani.

Eco, U. (1979). *Lector in fabula. La cooperazione interpretativa nei testi narrativi*. Bompiani.

Eco, U. (1979). *Lector in fabula: La cooperazione interpretativa nei testi narrativi*. Bompiani.

Eco, U. (1979). *The role of the reader: Explorations in the semiotics of texts*. Indiana University Press. DOI: 10.2979/2846.0

Eco, U. (1994). *Sei passeggiate nei boschi narrativi.* Bompiani.

Edelman (2018, May 1). *Edelman Trust Barometer: Expectations for CEOs.* Retrieved from Edelman Trust Barometer: https://www.edelman.com/post/trust-barometer-expectations-for-ceos

Ekwall, P. E., Ädel, A., & Nyström Höög, C. (2023). Towards a unified affordance approach: searching for congruent meaning making in COVID-19 warning designs. *Social Semiotics.* tandfonline.com

El-Desouky, D. F. (2020). Visual storytelling in advertising: A study of visual storytelling as a marketing approach for creating effective ads. *International Journal of Humanities* [IJHSSE]. *Social Sciences and Education*, *7*(10), 118–127.

Elhamy H M, (2022). "Social Semiotics for Social Media Visuals: A Framework for Analysis and Interpretation" … on Advanced Research Methodologies for a Digital Age IGI Global.

Elliott, R., & Wattanasuwan, K. (1998). Brands as symbolic resources for the construction of identity. *International Journal of Advertising*, *17*(2), 131–144. DOI: 10.1080/02650487.1998.11104712

Els, D. (2021). *The role of intersemiotic translation in multimodal communication in educational textbooks.* ufs.ac.za

Engelbrecht, N. (2022). Responsible consumer behavior in the digital age: Empirical evidence on the impact of (micro-)environmental factors on consumers' socially responsible behavior [Dissertation, Georg-August-University Göttingen]. DOI: 10.53846/goediss-9428

Escalas, J. E. (2004). Narrative processing: Building consumer connections to brands. *Journal of Consumer Psychology*, *14*(1-2), 168–180. DOI: 10.1207/s15327663jcp1401&2_19

Eugeni, R. (2015). *La condizione postmediale. Media, linguaggi e narrazioni.* La scuola.

Eugeni, R. (2010). *Semiotica dei media: le forme dell'esperienza.* Carocci.

Fabris, G. (2008). *Societing: il marketing nella società postmoderna.* Egea.

Fabris, G. (2009). *Societing. Il marketing nella società postmoderna.* Egea.

Fanelli, R. M. (2021). Changes in the food-related behaviour of Italian consumers during the COVID-19 pandemic. *Foods.* mdpi.com

Ferm, L. E. C., & Thaichon, P. (2021). … pre-participatory social media drivers and their influence on attitudinal loyalty within the retail banking industry: A multi-group analysis utilizing social exchange theory. [HTML]. *Journal of Retailing and Consumer Services*.

Ferraresi, M., & Schmitt, B. H. (2006). *Marketing esperienziale. Come sviluppare l'esperienza di consumo*. FrancoAngeli.

Ferraro, G. (1999). *La pubblicità nell'era di internet*. Meltemi.

Ferraro, G. (1999). *La pubblicità nell'era di Internet*. Meltemi.

Ferraro, G. (2020). *Teorie della narrazione: Dai racconti tradizionali all'odierno storytelling*. Carocci.

Filieri, R., Alguezaui, S., & McLeay, F. (2015). Why do travelers trust TripAdvisor? Antecedents of trust towards consumer-generated media and its influence on recommendation adoption and word of mouth. *Tourism Management*, *51*, 174–185. DOI: 10.1016/j.tourman.2015.05.007

Flecha-Ortiz, J. A., Rivera-Guevarrez, R., Santos-Corrada, M., & Fonseca, M. (2024). Boycott and Buycott Intent to Actions: Unpacking the Role of Political Ideology and Advertising through The Society of the Spectacle. *Journal of Political Marketing*, •••, 1–27. DOI: 10.1080/15377857.2024.2397964

Flight, R. L., & Coker, K. (2021). Birds of a feather: Brand attachment through the lens of consumer political ideologies. *Journal of Product and Brand Management*, *31*(5), 731–743.

Floch, J. M. (1990). *Sémiotique, marketing et communication. Sous les signes, les stratégies*. Presses Universitaires de France.

Floch, J. M. (1990). *Semiotique, marketing et communication. Sous les signes, les stratégies*. PUF.

Floch, J.-M. (1992). *Semiotica, marketing e comunicazione* (Semprini, A., & Franceschetti, M., Trans.). FrancoAngeli. (Original work published 1990)

Floch, J.-M. (1995). *Identités visuelles*. PUF.

Floch, J.-M. (1997). *Identità visive* (Ranelletti, L., Trans.). FrancoAngeli. (Original work published 1995)

Floch, J.-M. (2001). *Semiotics, marketing and communication: Behind the signs, the strategies* (Bodkin, R. O., Trans.). Palgrave. (Original work published 1990)

Floch, J.-M. (2013). *Bricolage. Analizzare pubblicità, immagini e spazi*. FrancoAngeli.

Flux, n. 25, vol 29, 2024

Fontana, A. (2020). *Storytelling d'impresa: La nuova guida definitiva verso lo storymaking*. Hoepli Editore.

Fraccastoro, S., Gabrielsson, M., & Pullins, E. B. (2021). The integrated use of social media, digital, and traditional communication tools in the B2B sales process of international SMEs. *International business review*. sciencedirect.com

Gamiz Sandoval J, (2024). "Globalization of Visual Media in Marketing: The Impact of Immigration in Marketing Media in Finland".

Ganapini, A. I., & Gonizzi, G. (1994). *Barilla: Cento anni di pubblicità e comunicazione*. Silvana Editore.

Gandla, R., Vemali, L. K., Choudhary, S., Pallavi, M. S., Saurav, A., Sahoo, P., & Golla, V. (2023). Semiotics and brand perception: How symbols and signs influence consumer behavior. *Journal of Informatics Education and Research, 3*(2), 2275–2288. DOI: 10.52783/jier.v3i2.378

Garg, V., & Kaur, A. (2018). Has physical retail lost its relevance in e-commerce world? *Journal of Business Management and Information Systems, 5*(2), 1–8. DOI: 10.48001/jbmis.2018.0502001

Ge, J. (2020). The Functional Building Blocks of Emoji in Consumer Engagement: A Visual Semiotic Perspective. *International Journal of Semiotics and Visual Rhetoric, 4*(2), 16–32. DOI: 10.4018/IJSVR.2020070102

Gensler, S., Neslin, S. A., & Verhoef, P. C. (2017). The Showrooming Phenomenon: It's More than Just about Price. *Journal of Interactive Marketing, 38*(1), 29-43. DOI: 10.1016/j.intmar.2017.01.003

Ghorbani, Z., Kargaran, S., & Saberi, A. (2021). Trends and Patterns in Digital Marketing Research: Bibliometric Analysis [Springer.]. *Journal of Marketing Trends, 8*(1), 1–17.

Giaccardi, C. (1996). *I luoghi del quotidiano. Pubblicità e costruzione della realtà sociale*. FrancoAngeli.

Girginkaya Akdağ, S. (2021). *"Small Icons with Wide Borders: The Semiotics of Micro-Mobility in Urban Space" The Dialectics of Urban and Architectural*. Springer.

Grace, S. C. (2021). "The Intermingling of Meanings in Marketing: Semiology and Phenomenology in Consumer Culture Theory" AMS Review, Springer.

Gramigna R, Madisson M L, (2023). "Unravelling Semiotics in 2022: A Year in Review" Sign Systems Studies.

Greco, G., & Boero, R. (2023). Semiotics and Digital Marketing: Synergies in AI and Consumer Engagement. *Journal of Semiotics and Marketing Research, 12*(2), 123–139.

Greimas, A. J. (1966). *Sémantique structurale*. Seuil.

Greimas, A. J. (1970). *Du sens I. Essais sémiotiques*. Seuil.

Greimas, A. J. (1983). *Du sens II. Essais sémiotiques*. Seuil.

Greimas, A. J., & Courtés, J. (1979). *Sémiotique. Dictionnaire raisonné de la théorie du langage*. Hachette.

Greimas, A. J., & Courtés, J. (1979). *Sèmiotique. Dictionnaire raisonné de la théorie du langage*. Hachette.

Greimas, A. J., & Courtés, J. (2007). *Semiotica. Dizionario ragionato della teoria del linguaggio* (Fabbri, P., Trans.). Mondadori. (Original work published 1979)

Grewal D, Herhausen D, Ludwig S, Ordenes F V, (2022). "The Future of Digital Communication Research: Considering Dynamics and Multimodality" Journal of Retailing, Elsevier.

Grewal, D., Herhausen, D., Ludwig, S., & Ordenes, F. V. (2022). The future of digital communication research: Considering dynamics and multimodality. *Journal of Retailing*. sciencedirect.com

Grillo, E., & Polidoro, P. (2023). Simulacri per progettare. Un punto di vista semiotico su archetipi e personas, *Filosofi(e) Semiotiche, 10*(2), 66-75.

Guibourgé J, (2020). "Semiotics: About Logo, Identity and Brand Image" Translated from Guibourgé Jérôme, Design phase 1, hal.science.

Guibourgé, J. (2020). Semiotics: about logo, identity and brand image. *Translated from Guibourgé Jérôme, Design phase 1, améliorer sa conception, L'Harmattan, Paris, 2021*. hal.science

Gupta, N. (2020). Digital Marketing: Trends, Opportunities, and Challenges. *Asian Journal of Management, 11*(2), 53–60.

Guzzetti, A., Crespi, R., & Belvedere, V. (2024). Phygital luxury experiences: A correspondence analysis on retail technologies. *International Journal of Consumer Studies, 48*(2), e13008. DOI: 10.1111/ijcs.13008

Habes, M., Alghizzawi, M., & Ali, S., SalihAlnaser, A., & Salloum, S. A. (2020). The Relation among Marketing ads, via Digital Media and mitigate (COVID-19) pandemic in Jordan. International [researchgate.net]. *Journal of Advanced Science and Technology*, *29*(7), 12326–12348.

Haghbin, F., Nambusubramaniyan, S., & Monfared, N. (2022). The semiotics of social-distance branding during the post-coronavirus crisis. *Semiotica*. degruyter.com

Haghbin, F., Nambusubramaniyan, S., & Monfared, N. (2022). The Semiotics of Social-Distance Branding during the Post-Coronavirus Crisis. *Semiotica*, *2022*(249), 145–175. DOI: 10.1515/sem-2021-0157

Halupka, M. (2014). Clicktivism: A systematic heuristic. *Policy and Internet*, *6*(2), 115–132. DOI: 10.1002/1944-2866.POI355

Hamdy, A., & Eid, R. (2024). *COVID-19, Destination Image, and Destination Visit Intention: Unpacking the Impacts of Familiarity, Generation, and Gender Amidst COVID-19*. Consumer Behavior in Tourism and Hospitality, Emerald.

Hamzah, Z. L., Abdul Wahab, H., & Waqas, M. (2021). Unveiling drivers and brand relationship implications of consumer engagement with social media brand posts. [researchgate.net]. *Journal of Research in Interactive Marketing*, *15*(2), 336–358. DOI: 10.1108/JRIM-05-2020-0113

Hansen, N., Kupfer, A. K., & Hennig-Thurau, T. (2018). Brand crises in the digital age: The short-and long-term effects of social media firestorms on consumers and brands. *International Journal of Research in Marketing*, *35*(4), 557–574. DOI: 10.1016/j.ijresmar.2018.08.001

Hasyim, M. & Arafah, B. (2023). Semiotic multimodality communication in the age of new media. *Studies in Media and Communication*. academia.edu

Hasyim, M., & Arafah, B. (2023). *Social Media Text Meaning: Cultural Information Consumption*. Wseas Transactions on Information Science.

Hébert, L. (2020). *An introduction to applied semiotics: Tools for text and image analysis*. Routledge.

Heejin, L., & Childs, M. (2020). Visual storytelling on Instagram: Branded photo narrative and the role of telepresence. *Journal of Research in Interactive Marketing*, *14*(1), 33–50. DOI: 10.1108/JRIM-09-2018-0115

Hegy, P. M. (2023). Symbol preaching in the digital age: From symbol recognition to symbol interpretation in Facebook ads. *Religions*, *14*(2), 229. DOI: 10.3390/rel14020229

Hennig-Thurau, T., Wiertz, C., & Feldhaus, F. (2015). Does twitter matter? The impact of microblogging word of mouth on consumers' adoption of new movies. *Journal of the Academy of Marketing Science, 43*(3), 375–394. DOI: 10.1007/s11747-014-0388-3

Hesse, A., Niederle, F., Schön, L., & Stautz, D. (2021). Consumer responses to brand communications involving COVID-19. *Journal of Marketing Management, 37*(17–18), 1783–1814. DOI: 10.1080/0267257X.2021.2000008

Himmelmann N, (2024). "Creative Storytelling in IKEA Advertising: Furnishing Narratives: A Multimodal Discourse Analysis of Creative Storytelling Techniques in IKEA Advertising".

Hmidi Z, (2023). "Text and Context in Multimedia Translation" Journal of Translation and Interpretation Studies.

Holopainen, J., Mattila, O., Parvinen, P., Pöyry, E., & Seppälä, K. (2018). Employing mixed reality applications: Customer experience perspective. *Proceedings of the 51st Hawaii International Conference on System Sciences,* 1168–1176. DOI: 10.24251/HICSS.2018.145

Holt, D. (2004). *How brands become icons.* Harvard Business Press.

Holt, D. B. (2002). Why Do Brands Cause Trouble? A Dialectical Theory of Consumer Culture and Branding. *The Journal of Consumer Research, 29*(1), 70–90. DOI: 10.1086/339922

Holt, D. B. (2004). *How Brands Become Icons: The Principles of Cultural Branding*. Harvard Business Press.

Hossain, T. M. T., Akter, S., Kattiyapornpong, U., & Dwivedi, Y. (2020). Reconceptualizing integration quality dynamics for omnichannel marketing. *Industrial Marketing Management, 87*, 225–241. DOI: 10.1016/j.indmarman.2019.12.006

Huaqi Y, Meng L, (2023). "Exploring the Innovation of Calligraphy Art in Animation in the Context of Globalisation—Based on Semiotics" Frontiers in Art Research.

Hult, G. T. M., Sharma, P. N., Morgeson, F. V.III, & Zhang, Y. (2019). Antecedents and consequences of customer satisfaction: Do they differ across online and offline purchases? *Journal of Retailing, 95*(1), 10–23. DOI: 10.1016/j.jretai.2018.10.003

Hussain, W., & Panggabean, H. (2024). Language and Power Dynamics in Automobile Advertising: A Multimodal Discourse Analysis of Word Choice and Semiotics. [eltaorganization.org]. *Journal of Applied Linguistics, 4*(1), 71–81. DOI: 10.52622/joal.v4i1.242

Hydock, C., Paharia, N., & Blair, S. (2020). Should Your Brand Pick a Side? How Market Share Determines the Impact of Corporate Political Advocacy. *JMR, Journal of Marketing Research, 57*(6), 1135–1151. DOI: 10.1177/0022243720947682

Ibrahim, I., & Sulaiman, S. (2020). Semiotic communication: An approach of understanding a meaning in communication. *International Journal of Media and Communication Research, 1*(1), 22–31. uir.ac.id. DOI: 10.25299/ijmcr.v1i1.4584

Indrawati, D., & Amalia, R. R. (2020). "Semiotic Analysis of Typography in Virtual Advertisements" *Proceeding Conference.*

Jain, P., & Duggal, T. (2016). The influence of transformational leadership and emotional intelligence on organizational commitment. *Journal of Commerce and Management Thought, 7*(3), 586. DOI: 10.5958/0976-478X.2016.00033.1

Januartha, I. W. (2024). Semiotic Analysis: Decoding Signs and Messages on Grand Filano YouTube Ads. *RETORIKA: Jurnal Ilmu Bahasa, 11*(1), 1–15.

Jenkins, H. (2006). *Convergence culture: Where old and new media collide.* New York University Press.

John, S. P., & De'Villiers, R. (2020). Elaboration of marketing communication through visual media: An empirical analysis. *Journal of Retailing and Consumer Services.* nscpolteksby.ac.id

Johnson, C. D., Bauer, B. C., & Carlson, B. D. (2022). Constituency building: Determining consumers' willingness to participate in corporate political activities. *International Journal of Research in Marketing, 39*(1), 42–57. DOI: 10.1016/j.ijresmar.2021.06.004

Johnson, M., & Barlow, R. (2021). Defining the phygital marketing advantage. *Journal of Theoretical and Applied Electronic Commerce Research, 16*(6), 2365–2385. DOI: 10.3390/jtaer16060130

Johnson, M., & Barlow, R. (2024). Phygital marketing through the lens of neuroscience and phenomenology: An interpretivist account. *Qualitative Market Research, 27*(3), 471–494. DOI: 10.1108/QMR-07-2023-0098

Kalamut, A. (Southside Adguy). (2011, June 02). McDonalds "Pick N' Play" interactive - Experiential outdoor ad. Retrieved December 23, 2024, from https://www.youtube.com/watch?v=D2UkIo-0prw

Kang, H. J., Shin, J., & Ponto, K. (2020). How 3D virtual reality stores can shape consumer purchase decisions: The roles of informativeness and playfulness. [HTML]. *Journal of Interactive Marketing, 49*(1), 70–85. DOI: 10.1016/j.intmar.2019.07.002

Kannan, P. K., & Li, H. A. (2017). Digital Marketing: A Framework, Review, and Research Agenda. *International Journal of Research in Marketing, 34*(1), 22–45. DOI: 10.1016/j.ijresmar.2016.11.006

Kaplan, A., & Haenlein, M. (2019). Siri, Siri, in My Hand: Who's the Fairest in the Land? On the Interpretations, Illustrations, and Implications of Artificial Intelligence. *Business Horizons, 62*(1), 15–25. DOI: 10.1016/j.bushor.2018.08.004

Karimov, F. P., & Brengman, M. (2011). The effect of website design dimensions on initial trust: A synthesis of the empirical literature. *Journal of Electronic Commerce Research, 12*(4), 272–301.

Kartal, C., & Şentürk, E. E. (2020). Endüstri 4.0 ve pazarlamada yeni gelişmeler. In Çetinkaya, F. F., & Şener, E. (Eds.), *Endüstri 4.0 paradigması* (1st ed., pp. 259–286). Efe Akademi Yayınevi.

Karunakaran, A. (2024). Frontline Professionals in the Wake of Social Media Scrutiny: Examining the Processes of Obscured Accountability. *Administrative Science Quarterly, 69*(3), 747–790. DOI: 10.1177/00018392241256303

Kauflin, J. (2017, February 6). *Why Audi's Super Bowl Ad Failed.* Retrieved from Forbes: https://www.forbes.com/sites/jeffkauflin/2017/02/06/why-audis-super-bowl-ad-failed/

Keller, K. L. (2020). Consumer research insights on brands and branding: A JCR curation. [HTML]. *The Journal of Consumer Research, 46*(5), 995–1001. DOI: 10.1093/jcr/ucz058

Keller, K. L., & Swaminathan, V. (2019). *Strategic brand management: Building, measuring, and managing brand equity.* Pearson.

Kerpen, D. (2011). *Likeable social media: How to delight your customers, create an irresistible brand, and be generally amazing on Facebook (and other social networks).* McGraw-Hill.

Khan, A. H., Snow, S., Heiner, S., & Matthews, B. (2020). "Disconnecting: Towards a Semiotic Framework for Personal Data Trails" *Proceedings of the 2020 ACM.* DOI: 10.1145/3357236.3395580

Killen, C. P., Geraldi, J., & Kock, A. (2020). The role of decision makers' use of visualizations in project portfolio decision making. *International Journal of Project Management.* cbs.dk

Kleinlercher, K., Linzmajer, M., Verhoef, P. C., & Rudolph, T. (2020). Antecedents of webrooming in omnichannel retailing. *Frontiers in Psychology, 11*, 606798. DOI: 10.3389/fpsyg.2020.606798

Klein, N. (2001). *No Logo* (Borgo, S., Trans.). Baldini & Castoldi. (Original work published 2000)

Klostermann, J., Hydock, C., & Decker, R. (2022). The effect of corporate political advocacy on brand perception: An event study analysis. *Journal of Product and Brand Management, 31*(5), 780–797. DOI: 10.1108/JPBM-03-2021-3404

Koch, C. H. (2020). Brands as activists: The Oatly case. *Journal of Brand Management, 275*(5), 593–606. DOI: 10.1057/s41262-020-00199-2

Kothari, H., Lodha, S., Joshi, N., & Khan, S. (2021). A study of the impact of online consumer buying behaviour on offline market while purchasing white goods. *MET Management Review, 8*(2), 78–82. DOI: 10.34047/MMR.2020.8210

Kotler, P., Kartajaya, H., & Setiawan, I. (2023). *Marketing 6.0: The future is immersive.* Wiley.

Kozinets, R. V. (2019). *Netnography: The essential guide to qualitative social media research.* Sage.

Kozinets, R. V., & Nocker, M. (2018). Netnography: Online ethnography for a digital age of organization research. In Bryman, A., & Buchanan, D. A. (Eds.), *Unconventional methodology in organization and management research* (pp. 127–146). Oxford University Press.

Kozinets, R. V., & Seraj-Aksit, M. (2024). Everyday activism: An AI-assisted netnography of a digital consumer movement. *Journal of Marketing Management, 40*(3–4), 347–370. DOI: 10.1080/0267257X.2024.2307387

Kraus, S., Durst, S., Ferreira, J. J., Veiga, P., Kailer, N., & Weinmann, A. (2022). Digital transformation in business and management research: An overview of the current status quo. [sciencedirect.com]. *International Journal of Information Management, 63*, 102466. DOI: 10.1016/j.ijinfomgt.2021.102466

Kraus, S., Jones, P., Kailer, N., Weinmann, A., Chaparro-Banegas, N., & Roig-Tierno, N. (2021). Digital transformation: An overview of the current state of the art of research. [sagepub.com]. *SAGE Open, 11*(3), 21582440211047576. DOI: 10.1177/21582440211047576

Kravchenko N, Yudenko O, (2023). "Multimodal Advertising: Semiotic and Cognitive-Pragmatic Aspects" Scientific journal «International.

Kristensen, J., Gabrielsen, G., & Zaichkowski, L. (2012). How valuable is a well-crafted design and name brand? Recognition and willingness to pay. *Journal of Consumer Behaviour, 11*(1), 44–55. DOI: 10.1002/cb.368

Kuiler, E. W. (2022). *"Semiotics" Encyclopedia of Big Data Springer.*

Kumar, S., Murphy, M., Talwar, S., Kaur, P., & Dhir, A. (2021). What drives brand love and purchase intentions toward the local food distribution system? A study of social media-based REKO (fair consumption) groups. [sciencedirect.com]. *Journal of Retailing and Consumer Services, 60*, 102444. DOI: 10.1016/j.jretconser.2021.102444

Labrecque, L. I., Vor Dem Esche, J., Mathwick, C., Novak, T. P., & Hofacker, C. F. (2013). Consumer power: Evolution in the digital age. *Journal of Interactive Marketing, 27*(4), 257–269. DOI: 10.1016/j.intmar.2013.09.002

Lalaounis, S. T. (2020). Strategic brand management and development: *Creating and marketing successful brands*. [HTML]

Landowski, E. (2006). Les interactions risquées. *Nouveaux actes sémiotiques, 101-102-103.*

Landowski, E. (1989). *La société réfléchie. Essais de socio-sémiotique*. Seuil.

Lareau, A. (2021). Listening to people: *A practical guide to interviewing, participant observation, data analysis, and writing it all up*. [HTML]

Laurino, A. (2020a). Per una nuova assiologia del consumo. Una proposta di ampliamento, approfondimento e aggiornamento del modello flochiano, *Ocula*, 1-29.

Laurino, A. (2020b). Intorno al quadrato delle filosofie pubblicitarie. Per una sottoarticolazione di alcune delle categorie flochiane originarie, *Filosofi(e) Semiotiche*, *7*(1), 116-129.

Laurita, G., & Venturini, R. (2016). *Strategia digitale: Comunicare bene su internet e i social media*. Hoepli.

Lawes R, (2022). "Using Semiotics in Retail: Leverage Consumer Insight to Engage Shoppers and Boost Sales".

Lawes R, (2023). "Using Semiotics in Marketing: How to Achieve Consumer Insight for Brand Growth and Profits".

Lawes, R. (2023). Using semiotics in marketing: *How to achieve consumer insight for brand growth and profits*. [HTML]

Leal, V. C. (2021). *Rhetoric and Visual Argument: Proposition of Methodological Models Based on the Analysis of Infographics*. Revista da ABRALIN.

Lee, S., & Choi, J. (2017). Enhancing user experience with conversational agent for movie recommendation: Effects of self-disclosure and reciprocity. *International Journal of Human-Computer Studies*, *103*, 95–105. DOI: 10.1016/j.ijhcs.2017.02.005

Lee, S., & Rao, V. S. (Chino). (2010). Color and store choice in electronic commerce: The explanatory role of trust. *Journal of Electronic Commerce Research*, *11*(2), 110–127.

Lemon, K. N., & Verhoef, P. C. (2016). Understanding customer experience throughout the customer journey. *Journal of Marketing*, *80*(6), 69-96. DOI: 10.1509/jm.15.0420

Levitt, H. M. (2021). Qualitative generalization, not to the population but to the phenomenon: Reconceptualizing variation in qualitative research. [HTML]. *Qualitative Psychology*, *8*(1), 95–110. DOI: 10.1037/qup0000184

Lévy-Strauss, C. (1990). *Antropologia strutturale* (Caruso, P., Trans.). Il Saggiatore. (Original work published 1958)

Li, H., Zhang, L., & Hsu, C. H. C. (2023). "Research on User-Generated Photos in Tourism and Hospitality: A Systematic Review and Way Forward" Tourism Management, Elsevier.

Liao, C., To, P.-L., Wong, Y.-C., Palvia, P., & Kakhki, M. D. (2016). The impact of presentation mode and product type on online impulse buying decisions. *Journal of Electronic Commerce Research*, *17*(2), 153–168.

Li, H. (2023). How digital retail markets recovered China's economy and changed consumer behaviors during COVID-19. *BCP Business & Management*, *38*, 1893–1901. DOI: 10.54691/bcpbm.v38i.3999

Liu, H., Lobschat, L., & Verhoef, P. (2018). Multichannel retailing: A review and research agenda. *Foundations and Trends in Marketing*, *12*(1), 1-79. DOI: 10.1561/1700000059

Liu, W., Cao, Y., & Proctor, R. W. (2021). How do app icon color and border shape influence visual search efficiency and user experience? Evidence from an eye-tracking study. [HTML]. *International Journal of Industrial Ergonomics*, *84*, 103160. DOI: 10.1016/j.ergon.2021.103160

Li, Y., Zhang, Z., & Zhao, Y. (2016). Analysis on influencing factors of consumers' purchasing behavior online for furniture: A case study on furniture malls and business centers in Harbin. *Proceedings of the 18th Annual International Conference on Electronic Commerce E-Commerce in Smart Connected World - ICEC '16*, 1–8. DOI: 10.1145/2971603.2971606

Llorente-Barroso, C., Kolotouchkina, O., & García-García, F. (2021). The meaning of the logo from its semiotic construction and its reliance on new formats of digital communication: The case of Apple. *Revista Latina de Comunicacion Social*, (79), 333-356. researchgate.net

Logi, L., & Zappavigna, M. (2023). A Social Semiotic Perspective on Emoji: How Emoji and Language Interact to Make Meaning in Digital Messages. *New Media & Society*, *25*(12), 3222–3246. DOI: 10.1177/14614448211032965

Lombardi, M. (Ed.). (2001). *Il dolce tuono*. FrancoAngeli.

Lombardi, M. (Ed.). (2007). *La marca, una come noi. La personalità di marca nell'era post spot*. FrancoAngeli.

Lourenção, M., Giraldi, J. M. E., & de Oliveira, J. H. C. (2020). Destination advertisement semiotic signs: Analysing tourists' visual attention and perceived ad effectiveness. [HTML]. *Annals of Tourism Research*, *84*, 103001. DOI: 10.1016/j.annals.2020.103001

Lovethehstory. (2024, December 23). AI virtual hair experience. Retrieved February 1, 2025, from https://www.instagram.com/reel/DD6l6aySjkP/?igsh=dm1qMDRkcTRqbWNp

Luangrath, A. W., Peck, J., Hedgcock, W., & Xu, Y. (2022). Observing product touch: The vicarious haptic effect in digital marketing and virtual reality. [HTML]. *JMR, Journal of Marketing Research*, *59*(2), 306–326. DOI: 10.1177/00222437211059540

Lund, N. F., Cohen, S. A., & Scarles, C. (2018). The power of social media storytelling in destination branding. *Journal of Destination Marketing & Management*, *8*, 271–280. DOI: 10.1016/j.jdmm.2017.05.003

Lytvynenko A, Zavialova O, Kalashnyk M, Varadi N, (2022). "Semiotics of Advertisement".

Lytvynenko, A., Zavialova, O., Kalashnyk, M., Varadi, N., & Enska, O. (2022). Semiotics of advertisment. hnpu.edu.ua

Maggio, A. (2024). *Visioni future di digital marketing*. Dario Flaccovio Editore.

Makrides, A., Vrontis, D., & Christofi, M. (2020). The gold rush of digital marketing: Assessing prospects of building brand awareness overseas. [sagepub.com]. *Business Perspectives and Research*, *8*(1), 4–20. DOI: 10.1177/2278533719860016

Maks-Solomon, C., & Drewry, J. M. (2020). Why do corporations engage in LGBT rights activism? LGBT employee groups as internal pressure groups. *Business and Politics*, *23*(1), 124–152. DOI: 10.1017/bap.2020.5

Mandler, T., Johnen, M., & Gräve, J. F. (2020). Can't help falling in love? How brand luxury generates positive consumer affect in social media. [HTML]. *Journal of Business Research*, *120*, 330–342. DOI: 10.1016/j.jbusres.2019.10.010

Mangano, D. (2008). *Semiotica e design*. Carocci.

Manning, P. (2010). The semiotics of brand. *Annual Review of Anthropology*, *39*(1), 33–49. DOI: 10.1146/annurev.anthro.012809.104939

Marchese, A. (1983). *L'officina del racconto*. Mondadori.

Mari, A., Mandelli, A., & Algesheimer, R. (2024). Empathic voice assistants: Enhancing consumer responses in voice commerce. *Journal of Business Research*, *175*, 114566. DOI: 10.1016/j.jbusres.2024.114566

Maria-Teresa, M. T. G. R., Pineda, A. P. A., David, J. D. F. G. J., & Gómez, F. (2023). Brand Community and Symbolic Interactionism: A Literature Review. *Review of Communication Research*, 11, 01-32. rcommunicationr.org

Marrone, G. (1999). *C'era una volta il telefonino. Un'indagine sociosemiotica*. Meltemi.

Marrone, G. (2001). *Corpi sociali*. Einaudi.

Marrone, G. (2001). *Corpi sociali: processi comunicativi e semiotica del testo*. Einaudi.

Marrone, G. (2007). *Il discorso di marca. Modelli semiotici per il branding*. Laterza.

Marrone, G. (2007). *Il discorso di marca: Modelli semiotici per il branding*. Laterza.

Martínez-González, J. A., & Álvarez-Albelo, C. D. (2021). Influence of site personalization and first impression on young consumers' loyalty to tourism websites. *Sustainability (Basel)*, *13*(3), 1425. DOI: 10.3390/su13031425

Martinus, T., & Chaniago, M. (2017). Analysis of branding strategy through Instagram with storytelling in creating brand image on proud projects. *Humaiora*, *8*(3), 201–210. DOI: 10.21512/humaniora.v8i3.3678

Masuda, H., Han, S. H., & Lee, J. (2022). Impacts of influencer attributes on purchase intentions in social media influencer marketing: Mediating roles of characterizations. *Technological Forecasting and Social Change*. kyoto-u.ac.jp

Matyas, M. (2020). Opportunities and barriers to multimodal cities: Lessons learned from in-depth interviews about attitudes towards mobility as a service. *European Transport Research Review*. springer.com

Mayer, P. (2015). *Dallo spot al post: La pubblicità dopo i social media*. Edizione LSWR.

Mazzoni, G. (2011). *Teoria del romanzo*. Il Mulino.

Mehmeti-Bajrami, S., Qerimi, F., & Qerimi, A. (2022). The impact of digital marketing vs. traditional marketing on consumer buying behavior. *HighTech and Innovation Journal*, *3*(3), 326–340. DOI: 10.28991/HIJ-2022-03-03-08

Mele, C., Spena, T. R., Marzullo, M. et al. (2023). The phygital transformation: A systematic review and a research agenda. *Italian Journal of Marketing*, 323-349.

Mele, C., Di Bernardo, I., Ranieri, A., & Russo Spena, T. (2024). Phygital customer journey: A practice-based approach. *Qualitative Market Research*, *27*(3), 388–412. DOI: 10.1108/QMR-08-2023-0102

Mele, C., & Russo-Spena, T. (2022). The architecture of the phygital customer journey: A dynamic interplay between systems of insights and systems of engagement. *European Journal of Marketing*, *56*(1), 72–91. DOI: 10.1108/EJM-04-2019-0308

Menon, A. S., Pillai, R., & Pai, Y. P. (2024). Customer engagement through transformational campaigns: A netnographic exploration on the storytelling power of 'Jaago Re.'. *Journal of Creative Communications*, *09732586241276345*, 09732586241276345. Advance online publication. DOI: 10.1177/09732586241276345

Mertler, C. A., Vannatta, R. A., & LaVenia, K. N. (2021). Advanced and multivariate statistical methods: *Practical application and interpretation*. unt.edu

Miao, F., Kozlenkova, I. V., Wang, H., Xie, T., & Palmatier, R. W. (2022). An emerging theory of avatar marketing. *Journal of Marketing*, *86*(1), 67–90. DOI: 10.1177/0022242921996646

Michaelidou, N., Micevski, M., & Halkias, G. (2021). How do international advertisers use consumer culture positioning strategies? A cross-national, cross-category approach. *International Marketing Review*, *38*(2), 367–386. lboro.ac.uk. DOI: 10.1108/IMR-05-2020-0101

Michael, N., & Fusté-Forné, F. (2022). Marketing of Luxurious Gastronomic Experiences on Social Media: The Visual Storytelling of Luxury Hotels [Wiley Online Library.]. *International Journal of Tourism Research*, *24*(3), 235–248. DOI: 10.1002/jtr.2548

Mick, D. G., Burroughs, J. E., Hetzel, P., & Brannen, M. Y. (2004). Pursuing the meaning of meaning in the commercial world: An international review of marketing and consumer research founded on semiotics. *Semiotica, 2004*(152-1/4), 1–74. DOI: 10.1515/semi.2004.2004.152-1-4.1

Mick, D. G., & Buhl, C. (1992). A Meaning-Based Model of Advertising Experiences. *The Journal of Consumer Research, 19*(3), 317–338. DOI: 10.1086/209305

Mick, D. G., Burroughs, J. E., Hetzel, P., & Brannen, M. Y. (2004). Pursuing the Meaning of Meaning in the Commercial World: An International Review of Marketing and Consumer Research Founded on Semiotics. *Journal of Business Research, 57*(6), 760–768.

Miller, C. (2017). *Branding and communication*. Routledge.

Mirzaei, A., Wilkie, D. C., & Siuki, H. (2022). Woke brand activism authenticity or the lack of it. *Journal of Business Research, 139*, 1–12. DOI: 10.1016/j.jbusres.2021.09.044

Mishra, S., Malhotra, G., Chatterjee, R., & Shukla, Y. (2023). Consumer retention through phygital experience in omnichannel retailing: Role of consumer empowerment and satisfaction. *Journal of Strategic Marketing, 31*(4), 749–766. DOI: 10.1080/0965254X.2021.1985594

Mohammad Alzub, A. (2023). Navigating the disruption of digital and conventional media in changing media consumption landscape in the digital era. [JETAS]. *Journal of Engineering, Technology, and Applied Science, 5*(1), 38–48. DOI: 10.36079/lamintang.jetas-0501.517

Mohammadreza, M., Shairi, H., & Ahmadpanah, A. (2017). Social semiotic aspects of Instagram social network. *IEEE International Conference on Innovations in Intelligent Systems and Applications (INISTA)*, 460–465.

Moinuddin, S., & Moinuddin, S. (2021). *Geographies of Semiotics in Social Mediasphere in India*. Digital Shutdowns and Social Media Springer. DOI: 10.1007/978-3-030-67888-3_5

Moisander, J., Närvänen, E., & Valtonen, A. (2020). Interpretive marketing research: Using ethnography in strategic market development. *Marketing management*. tuni.fi

Moore, G. A. (2014). *Crossing the chasm: Marketing and selling disruptive products to mainstream customers*. HarperCollins.

Moorman, C. (2020). Commentary: Brand activism in a political world. *Journal of Public Policy & Marketing, 39*(4), 388–392. DOI: 10.1177/0743915620945260

Morales, L. (2008). *Narrare con le immagini*. Dino Audino.

Moschini, I. (2018). Social semiotics and platform studies: An integrated perspective for the study of social media platforms. *Social Semiotics*, *28*(5), 623–640. DOI: 10.1080/10350330.2018.1504714

Musso, P. (2005). *I nuovi territori della marca. Percorsi di senso, discorsi, azioni*. Franco Angeli.

Nam, H. & Kannan, P. K. (2020). Digital environment in global markets: Cross-cultural implications for evolving customer journeys. *Journal of International Marketing*. sagepub.com

Neureiter, M., & Bhattacharya, C. B. (2021). Why do boycotts sometimes increase sales? Consumer activism in the age of political polarization. *Business Horizons*, *64*(5), 611–620. DOI: 10.1016/j.bushor.2021.02.025

Niranjini, N., & Sridevi, J. (2023). Covid-19—Pushes marketers to sell differently to global millennials in emerging markets. *Journal of Pharmaceutical Negative Results*, *13*(Special issue 7), 6993–7003. DOI: 10.47750/pnr.2022.13.S07.847

Nosi, C., Pucci, T., Melanthiou, Y., & Zanni, L. (2022). The influence of online and offline brand trust on consumer buying intention. *EuroMed Journal of Business*, *17*(4), 550–567. DOI: 10.1108/EMJB-01-2021-0002

O'Brien, S. A. (2020, August 18). *Glossier, a billion-dollar beauty brand, apologizes to former retail workers after racism allegations*. Retrieved from CNN: https://edition.cnn.com/2020/08/18/tech/glossier-apology-retail-workers/index.html

O'Halloran, K. L. (2023). Matter, Meaning and Semiotics. *Visual Communication*, *22*(1), 174–201. DOI: 10.1177/14703572221128881

Odoardi, P. (2020). Search Engine Optimization (SEO) e semiotica: Come lavorare efficacemente sulle keyword. *Lexia*, *33-34*, 73–88.

Odoardi, P. (2024). Critica (semiotica) della ragion (algoritmica) d'Instagram. *Versus*, *2*, 355–376.

Oja, M. (2023). Semiotic Mode and Sensory Modality in Multimodal Semiotics: Recognizing Difference and Building Complementarity Between the Terms. *Sign Systems Studies*, *51*(3-4), 604–637. DOI: 10.12697/SSS.2023.51.3-4.05

Orzati, G. (2019). *Visual storytelling: Quando il racconto si fa immagine*. Einaudi.

Osmanova, I., Ozerden, S., Dalal, B., & Ibrahim, B. (2023). Examining the relationship between brand symbolism and brand evangelism through consumer brand identification: Evidence from Starbucks coffee brand. *Sustainability (Basel)*, *15*(2), 1684. DOI: 10.3390/su15021684

Østergaard, P., Hermansen, J., & Fitchett, J. (2015). Structures of brand and anti-brand meaning: A semiotic square analysis of reflexive consumption. *Journal of Brand Management*, *22*(1), 60–77. DOI: 10.1057/bm.2015.4

Oswald, L. R. (2020). Doing semiotics: *A research guide for marketers at the edge of culture*. [HTML]

Oswald, L. R. (2020). What do affluent Chinese consumers want?: A semiotic approach to building brand literacy in developing markets. *Marketing Management*. researchgate.net

Oswald, G. (2011). Brand communication in social media. *Journal of Advertising*, *48*(1), 14–26.

Oswald, L. (2011). *Marketing Semiotics: Signs*. Strategies, and Brand Value.

Oswald, L. R. (2015). Developing Brand Literacy among Consumers. *Journal of Business Research*, *68*(8), 1634–1642.

Özbölük, T., & Kurtoğlu, R. (2019). *The role of language and symbols in promotional strategies and marketing schemes* (Epure, M., & Mihăeş, L. C., Eds.). IGI Global., DOI: 10.4018/978-1-5225-5778-4

Pantano, E., Rese, A., & Baier, D. (2017). Enhancing the online decision-making process by using augmented reality: A two-country comparison of youth markets. *Journal of Retailing and Consumer Services*, *38*, 81–95. DOI: 10.1016/j.jretconser.2017.05.011

Pappas, I. O. (2018). User experience in personalized online shopping: A fuzzy-set analysis. *European Journal of Marketing*, *52*(7/8), 1679–1703. DOI: 10.1108/EJM-10-2017-0707

Paraskevaidis, P., & Weidenfeld, A. (2021). Perceived and projected authenticity of visitor attractions as signs: A Peircean semiotic analysis. [HTML]. *Journal of Destination Marketing & Management*, *19*, 100515. DOI: 10.1016/j.jdmm.2020.100515

Paris, O. (2020). "Costruire un mito: Marche, prodotti e la rappresentazione dell'italianità nel mondo", Filosofi(e). *Semiotiche*, *7*(1), 2020.

Pasirayi, S., Fennell, P. B., & Follmer, K. B. (2023). #Activism: Investor reactions to corporate sociopolitical activism. *Business & Society*, *62*(4), 704–744. DOI: 10.1177/00076503221110457

Paton, E., Friedman, V., & Testa, J. (2022, November 29). *When High Fashion and QAnon Collide*. Retrieved from The New York Times: https://www.nytimes.com/2022/11/28/style/balenciaga-campaign-controversy.html

Paul, J. & Criado, A. R. (2020). The art of writing literature review: What do we know and what do we need to know?. *International business review*. drjustinpaul.com

Paul, J., Lim, W. M., O'Cass, A., Hao, A. W., & Bresciani, S. (2021). Scientific procedures and rationales for systematic literature reviews (SPAR-4-SLR). [researchgate.net]. *International Journal of Consumer Studies*, *45*(4), O1–O16. DOI: 10.1111/ijcs.12695

Peho C, (2020). "Storytelling as a Means of Brand Building-Building Authenticity and Emotions through Brand Stories".

Pengnate, S., & Sarathy, R. (2017). An experimental investigation of the influence of website emotional design features on trust in unfamiliar online vendors. *Computers in Human Behavior*, *67*, 49–60. DOI: 10.1016/j.chb.2016.10.018

Perrino, S. & Kohler, G. (2020). Chronotopic identities: Narrating Made in Italy across spatiotemporal scales. *Language & Communication*. sciencedirect.com

Pezzini, M. (2008). *Immagini quotidiane: Sociosemiotica visuale*. Laterza.

Pfeffer, J., Zorbach, T., & Carley, K. M. (2014). Understanding online firestorms: Negative word-of-mouth dynamics in social media networks. *Journal of Marketing Communications*, *20*(2), 117–128. DOI: 10.1080/13527266.2013.797778

Pieters, R., & Wedel, M. (2007). Goal Control of Attention to Advertising: The Yarbus Implication. *The Journal of Consumer Research*, *34*(2), 224–233. DOI: 10.1086/519150

Pimentel, P. C., Bassi-Suter, M., & Didonet, S. R. (2024). Brand activism as a marketing strategy: An integrative framework and research agenda. *Journal of Brand Management*, *31*(2), 212–234. DOI: 10.1057/s41262-023-00335-8

Pine, J. B., & Gilmore, J. H. (2000). *L'economia delle esperienze. Oltre il servizio* (Monkhouse, A. S., Trans.). Etas. (Original work published 1999)

Plakoyiannaki, E., Stavraki, G., & Tsapi, V. (2022). The artist and the photograph: A semiotic analysis of consumers' experiences with photographs. *Qualitative Market Research*, *25*(2), 256–271. surrey.ac.uk. DOI: 10.1108/QMR-09-2021-0119

Polat E, Çelik F, Ibrahim B, (2023). "Unpacking the Power of User-Generated Videos in Hospitality and Tourism: A Systematic Literature Review and Future Direction" Journal of Travel & Tourism Marketing, Taylor & Francis.

Polesana, M. A. (2019). *Pubblicità e valori. Nuovi consumi e nuovi messaggi per una società che cambia*. FrancoAngeli.

Polidoro, P. (2008). *Che cos'è la semiotica visiva*. Carocci.

Poulsen, S. V., & Kvale, G. (2018). Studying social media as semiotic technology: A social semiotic multimodal framework. *Social Semiotics*, *28*(5), 700–717. DOI: 10.1080/10350330.2018.1505689

Pöyry, E., & Laaksonen, S. M. (2022). Opposing brand activism: Triggers and strategies of consumers' antibrand actions. *European Journal of Marketing*, *56*(13), 261–284. DOI: 10.1108/EJM-12-2020-0901

Pozzato, F. (2001). *Semiotica del testo: Metodi, autori, esempi*. Carocci.

Pozzato, M. P. (2001). *Semiotica del testo. Metodi, autori, esempi*. Carocci.

Priya, A. (2021). Case study methodology of qualitative research: Key attributes and navigating the conundrums in its application. *Sociological Bulletin*. sagepub.com

Pusceddu, G., Moi, L., & Cabiddu, F. (2023). Do they see eye to eye? Managing customer experience in phygital high-tech retail. *Management Decision*. Advance online publication. DOI: 10.1108/MD-05-2022-0673

Qualizza, G. (2006). *I nuovi luoghi del consumo: percorsi, esplorazioni, progetti*. Edizioni Goliardiche.

Quesenbery, W., & Brooks, K. (2010). *Storytelling for user experience: Crafting stories for better design*. Rosenfeld Media.

Rahman, M. (2023). The impact of Covid-19 (coronavirus) on consumers' behavior towards e-commerce. *Canadian Journal of Business and Information Studies*, *5*(4), 81–91. DOI: 10.34104/cjbis.023.081091

Rane, N., Choudhary, S., & Rane, J. (2023). Metaverse for enhancing customer loyalty: Effective strategies to improve customer relationship, service, engagement, satisfaction and experience. SSRN *Electronic Journal*. DOI: 10.2139/ssrn.4624197

Ransbotham, S., Kiron, D., Gerbert, P., & Reeves, M. (2017). Reshaping Business with Artificial Intelligence. *MIT Sloan Management Review*, *59*(1), 1–17.

Rathi R, Garg R, Kataria A, (2022). "Evolution of Luxury Marketing Landscape: A Bibliometric Analysis and Future Directions" Journal of Brand.

Rauschnabel, P. A., Kammerlander, N., & Ivens, B. S. (2016). Collaborative brand attacks in social media: Exploring the antecedents, characteristics, and consequences of a new form of brand crises. *Journal of Marketing Theory and Practice*, *24*(4), 381–410. DOI: 10.1080/10696679.2016.1205452

Rigby, D. (2014, September 1). Digital-physical mashups. *Harvard Business Review*. https://hbr.org/2014/09/digital-physical-mashups

Rindell, A. & Santos, F. P. (2021). What makes a corporate heritage brand authentic for consumers? A semiotic approach. *Journal of Brand Management*. springer.com

Rodriguez, A. (2020). *Brand storytelling and consumer experience*. Springer.

Roggeveen, A. L., Grewal, D., Karsberg, J., Noble, S. M., Nordfält, J., Patrick, V. M., Schweiger, E., Soysal, G., Dillard, A., Cooper, N., & Olson, R. (2021). Forging meaningful consumer-brand relationships through creative merchandise offerings and innovative merchandising strategies. [sciencedirect.com]. *Journal of Retailing*, *97*(1), 81–98. DOI: 10.1016/j.jretai.2020.11.006

Rokka J, (2021). "Consumer Culture Theory's Future in Marketing" Journal of Marketing Theory and Practice, Taylor & Francis.

Rolle, L. (2014). *Semiotica in pratica*. FrancoAngeli.

Rolle, L. (2014). *Semiotica in pratica. Strumenti per governare le strategie di brand*. Franco Angeli.

Rosch, E., & Lloyd, B. B. (Eds.). (1978). *Cognition and Categorization*. Erlbaum Associates.

Rossolatos G, (2023). "Advances in Brand Semiotics & Discourse Analysis".

Rossolatos, G. (2012). Applications, implications and limitations of the semiotic square for analyzing advertising discourse and discerning alternative brand futures. *Signs - International Journal of Semiotics, 6*, 1-47.

Rossolatos, G. (2015). *Handbook of brand semiotics*. Kassel University Press.

Rossolatos, G. (2021). The Depth of Brand Engagement Funnel: Dimensionalizing Interaction in Social Media Brand Communities. *Qualitative Market Research*, *24*(2), 200–220. DOI: 10.1108/QMR-03-2019-0041

Rust, R. T., & Huang, M.-H. (2021). The AI Revolution in Marketing. *Journal of the Academy of Marketing Science*, *49*(1), 24–42.

Saba, C. (2006). *Lo sguardo che insegue. Strumenti per l'analisi delle forme audiovisive pubblicitarie (spot, trailer, videoclip e rich media)*. Lupetti.

Sağtaş, S. (2022). Dijital pazarlamanın değişen yüzü: Fijital pazarlama ve uygulamaları üzerine bir araştırma. *Social Sciences Studies Journal, 8*(95), 629–637. DOI: 10.26449/sssj.3866

Sandra, N. P. A. A., & Noina, N. M. K. (2024). Semiotic analysis of tourism soft-selling: Decoding short films as persuasive narratives. *Ultimart: Jurnal Komunikasi Visual,* 49–63. DOI: 10.31937/ultimart.v17i1.3547

Sang, S. (2021). Reconstructing the place branding model from the perspective of Peircean semiotics. [HTML]. *Annals of Tourism Research, 89*, 103209. DOI: 10.1016/j.annals.2021.103209

Sargın, S. (2024). Dijital reklamcılığın tüketiciler üzerindeki izleri. In Kartal, C., Şentürk, E. E., & Durukan, T. (Eds.), *Teknolojik tüketiciler çağı* (pp. 39–58). Nobel Akademik Yayıncılık.

Sarkar, C., & Kotler, P. (2018). *Brand Activism: From Purpose to Action*. Idea Bite Press.

Sauerbrei, W., Perperoglou, A., Schmid, M., Abrahamowicz, M., Becher, H., Binder, H., Dunkler, D., Harrell, F. E.Jr, Royston, P., & Heinze, G. (2020). State of the art in selection of variables and functional forms in multivariable analysis—Outstanding issues. [springer.com]. *Diagnostic and Prognostic Research, 4*(1), 1–18. DOI: 10.1186/s41512-020-00074-3 PMID: 32266321

Schmidt, H. J., Ind, N., Guzmán, F., & Kennedy, E. (2021). Sociopolitical activist brands. *Journal of Product and Brand Management, 31*(1), 40–55. DOI: 10.1108/JPBM-03-2020-2805

Schmitt, B. H. (1999). *Experiential marketing: How to get customers to sense, feel, think, act, relate to your company and brands*. The Free Press.

Schreiber, J. B. (2021). Issues and recommendations for exploratory factor analysis and principal component analysis. *Research in Social and Administrative Pharmacy*. academia.edu

Schroeder, J. E. (2017). Corporate branding in perspective: A typology. *European Journal of Marketing, 51*(9/10), 1522–1529. DOI: 10.1108/EJM-07-2017-0450

Schultz, D. E. (2020). From advertising to integrated marketing communications. *A reader in marketing communications*. [HTML]

Sechi, G., Šķilters, J., Selecka, M., Kalnača, L., & Leškēviča, K. (2023). Knowledge exchange and growth in a hybrid community–a social-capital-based approach: Evidence from Latvia. [sagepub.com]. *IFLA Journal, 49*(1), 87–98. DOI: 10.1177/03400352221089673

Seifert, C., & Chattaraman, V. (2020). A picture is worth a thousand words! How visual storytelling transforms the aesthetic experience of novel designs. *Journal of Product and Brand Management, 29*(7), 913–926. DOI: 10.1108/JPBM-01-2019-2194

Semprini, A. (1993). *Marche e mondi possibili. Un approccio semiotico al marketing della marca.* Franco Angeli.

Semprini, A. (2003). *Lo sguardo sociosemiotico. Comunicazione, marche, media, pubblicità.* FrancoAngeli.

Senivongse, C., & Bennet, A. (2022, September). Semiotic inception, attitude altering, and behavioral expression: Understanding the foundation of organizational knowledge construction. *In 23rd European Conference on Knowledge Management Vol* 2. Academic Conferences and publishing limited. academic-conferences.org DOI: 10.34190/eckm.23.2.465

Şenses, S. (2024, April 23). Patiswiss krizinden neler öğrendik? *MediaCat.* https://mediacat.com/patiswiss-krizinden-neler-ogrendik/

Sergio, F. (2020). "Storytelling in the Luxury Industry: Narratives as a Tool for Experiential Branding-The Case of Christian Dior Couture" dspace.unive.it

Serkan Akturk, M., Ketzenberg, M., & Heim, G. R. (2018). Assessing impacts of introducing ship-to-store service on sales and returns in omnichannel retailing: A data analytics study. *Journal of Operations Management, 61*(1), 15–45. DOI: 10.1016/j.jom.2018.06.004

Shahzadi, M. & Maqbool, A. (2024). Semiotic Analysis of Pakistani Clothing Brands Advertisements using Barthes' Theory. *Competitive Linguistic Research Journal.* clrjournal.com

Shankar, V. (2018). How Artificial Intelligence (AI) is Reshaping Retailing. *Journal of Retailing, 94*(4), 6–11. DOI: 10.1016/S0022-4359(18)30076-9

Shankar, V., Grewal, D., Sunder, S., Fossen, B., Peters, K., & Agarwal, A. (2022). Digital marketing communication in global marketplaces: A review of extant research, future directions, and potential approaches. [google.com]. *International Journal of Research in Marketing, 39*(2), 541–565. DOI: 10.1016/j.ijresmar.2021.09.005

Shanmugavel, N. & Micheal, M. (2022). Exploring the marketing related stimuli and personal innovativeness on the purchase intention of electric vehicles through Technology Acceptance Model. *Cleaner Logistics and Supply Chain*. sciencedirect.com

Sherry, J. F.Jr. (2020). *The soul of the company store: Nike Town Chicago and the emplaced brandscape*. The Retailing Reader. [HTML]

Shi, D. (2021). Exploring Digital Interactivity: A Multimodal and Social Semiotic Approach to Intersemiotic Construction in COVID China Website. *Multimodal Communication, 10*(3), 311–327. DOI: 10.1515/mc-2021-0010

Shoenberger, H., Kim, E. A., & Sun, Y. (2021). Advertising during COVID-19: Exploring perceived brand message authenticity and potential psychological reactance. *Journal of Advertising*, *50*(3), 253–261. DOI: 10.1080/00913367.2021.1927914

Shukla, M., Misra, R., & Singh, D. (2023). Exploring relationship among semiotic product packaging, brand experience dimensions, brand trust and purchase intentions in an Asian emerging market. [HTML]. *Asia Pacific Journal of Marketing and Logistics*, *35*(2), 249–265. DOI: 10.1108/APJML-10-2021-0718

Sibai, O., Mimoun, L., & Boukis, A. (2021). Authenticating brand activism: Negotiating the boundaries of free speech to make a change. *Psychology and Marketing*, *38*(10), 1651–1669. DOI: 10.1002/mar.21477

Simakova, S. (2020). *Media Aesthetic Component of Communication and its Manifestation in Infographic Content*. Lumina. DOI: 10.34019/1981-4070.2020.v14.30188

Simões, C., & Sebastiani, R. (2017). The nature of the relationship between corporate identity and corporate sustainability: Evidence from the retail industry. *Business Ethics Quarterly*, *27*(3), 423–453. DOI: 10.1017/beq.2017.15

Singla V, Ongsakul V, Raj S, (2021). “Investigating the Relationship of Semiotics Associated with Colour and Font of Google Logo with Brand Perception” Journal for Global.

Sitanggang, A. O. (2020). The meaning of advertising'Aqua life'in the semiotic perspective of roland barthes. *International journal of multi science*. multiscience-journal.com

Slater, J. (2018, August 28). Let’s get phigital. *The Marketing Sage*. https://www.themarketingsage.com/lets-get-phigital/

Smink, A. R., Frowijn, S., Van Reijmersdal, E. A., Van Noort, G., & Neijens, P. C. (2019). Try online before you buy: How does shopping with augmented reality affect brand responses and personal data disclosure. *Electronic Commerce Research and Applications*, *35*, 100854. DOI: 10.1016/j.elerap.2019.100854

Smith, A. (2017, April 5). *Pepsi Pulls Controversial Kendall Jenner Ad After Outcry*. Retrieved from NBC News: https://www.nbcnews.com/news/nbcblk/pepsi-ad-kendall-jenner-echoes-black- lives-matter-sparks-anger-n742811

Sobande, F. (2019). Woke-washing: "Intersectional" femvertising and branding "woke" bravery. *European Journal of Marketing*, *54*(11), 2723–2745. DOI: 10.1108/EJM-02-2019-0134

Solano-Flores, G. (2021). The semiotics of test design: Conceptual framework on optimal item features in educational assessment across cultural groups, countries, and languages. *Frontiers in Education*. frontiersin.org

Sommer, V. (2021). Multimodal Analysis in Qualitative Research: Extending Grounded Theory Through the Lens of Social Semiotics. *Qualitative Inquiry*, *27*(8-9), 1102–1113. DOI: 10.1177/1077800420978746

Sridhar, S., & Srinivasan, R. (2012). Social influence effects in online product ratings. *Journal of Marketing*, *76*(5), 70–88. DOI: 10.1509/jm.10.0377

Sterbenk, Y. M., Ward, J., Luttrell, W. R., & Summer Shelton, S. (2022). Silence has no place: A framing analysis of corporate statements about racial inequity, immigration policy and LGBTQ rights. *Corporate Communications*, *27*(2), 404–421. DOI: 10.1108/CCIJ-09-2021-0106

Stigliano, G., & Kotler, P. (2018). *Retail 4.0. 10 regole per l'era digitale*. Mondadori.

Suhaimi, S. N., & Fauzi, T. A. (2021). Visual semiotics: identity reflection in personal symbol creation. *KUPAS SENI*. upsi.edu.my

Sultan, J. K. (2021). The War-Zone Consequences of the Deformed Linguistic Image: Iraqi Simultaneous Interpreters during the US-led Invasion.. *Journal of College of Education/Wasit*. iasj.net

Swaminathan, V., Sorescu, A. S., O'Guinn, T. C., & Schmitt, B. H. (2020). Branding in a hyperconnected world: Refocusing theories and rethinking boundaries. *Journal of Marketing*, *84*(2), 24–46. DOI: 10.1177/0022242919899905

Swani, K., & Labrecque, L. I. (2020). Like, Comment, or Share? Self-presentation vs. brand relationships as drivers of social media engagement choices. [HTML]. *Marketing Letters*, *31*(2-3), 279–298. DOI: 10.1007/s11002-020-09518-8

Szwajca, D. (2022). The use of digital communication channels by Polish consumers – Changes caused by the pandemic. *Foundations of Management, 14*(1), 37–50. DOI: 10.2478/fman-2022-0003

Tang, P., Chen, J., & Raghunathan, S. (2023). Physical stores as warehouses for online channels: Implications for channel choices under competition. *Information Systems Research, 34*(4), 1554–1581. DOI: 10.1287/isre.2023.1198

Tan, T., & Ming, M. (2003). Leveraging on symbolic values and meanings in branding. *Journal of Brand Management, 10*(3), 208–218. DOI: 10.1057/palgrave.bm.2540117

Taylor, J., Johnston, J., & Whitehead, K. (2016). A Corporation in Feminist Clothing? Young Women Discuss the Dove 'Real Beauty' Campaign. *Critical Sociology, 42*(1), 123–144. DOI: 10.1177/0896920513501355

Teltzrow, M., Meyer, B., & Lenz, H.-J. (2007). Multi-channel consumer perceptions. DOI: 10.5167/UZH-65987

Terho, H., Mero, J., Siutla, L., & Jaakkola, E. (2022). Digital content marketing in business markets: Activities, consequences, and contingencies along the customer journey. *Industrial Marketing Management.* sciencedirect.com

The New York Times. (2023, October 27). *Kanye and Adidas: Money, Misconduct and the Price of Appeasement.* Retrieved from The New York Times: https://www.nytimes.com/2023/10/27/business/kanye-west-adidas-yeezy.html

Tirpude, R. (2022). Study of impact of digital marketing on consumer buying behaviour for electronic goods. *International Journal for Research in Applied Science and Engineering Technology, 10*(2), 905–909. DOI: 10.22214/ijraset.2022.40348

Traini, S. (2018), "The slow pace of change in advertising New family types in advertisements for people carriers", Ocula, www.ocula.it

Traini, S. (2020). Comunicazioni emotive dei media nell'epoca della «post-verità»: le isole di plastica negli oceani raccontate da la Repubblica. *Rivista Italiana di Filosofia del Linguaggio*, 188–202.

Tran, A. T. N., Nguyen, U. H. D., Ngo, V. M., & Nguyen, H. H. (2023). Explaining consumers' channel-switching behavior in the post-COVID-19 pandemic era. *Cogent Business & Management, 10*(1), 2198068. DOI: 10.1080/23311975.2023.2198068

Travere, A. (2023). The Interplay of Signs and Visuals: Unveiling the Symbiotic Relationship Between Semiotics and Visual Communication [Pioneer Publisher.]. *Journal of Linguistics and Communication Studies, 5*(1), 1–12.

Travere, A. (2023). The Interplay of Signs and Visuals: Unveiling the Symbiotic Relationship Between Semiotics and Visual Communication. [pioneerpublisher.com]. *Journal of Linguistics and Communication Studies*, *2*(3), 28–40.

Tsiotsou, R. H. & Diehl, S. (2022). Delineating transformative value creation through service communications: an integrative framework. *Journal of Service Management*. uom.gr

Tsiotsou, R. H. (2021). Introducing relational dialectics on actor engagement in the social media ecosystem. *Journal of Services Marketing*. uom.gr

Turban, E., Strauss, J., & Lai, L. (2012). *Social commerce*. Prentice Hall.

Tyrer, C. (2021). "The Voice, Text, and the Visual as Semiotic Companions: An Analysis of the Materiality and Meaning Potential of Multimodal Screen Feedback" Education and Information Technologies, Springer.

Tyrväinen, O., Karjaluoto, H., & Saarijärvi, H. (2020). Personalization and hedonic motivation in creating customer experiences and loyalty in omnichannel retail. *Journal of Retailing and Consumer Services*, *57*, 102233. DOI: 10.1016/j.jretconser.2020.102233

Udris-Borodavko, N., Oliinyk, V., & Bozhko, T. (2023). *Aesthetics and Semiotics in 21st Century Visual Communications: Pedagogical and Sociocultural Aspects*. Research Journal in Advanced Humanities.

Uğurlu, Ö. (2014). Encoding the daily life through social networks "Binboa – A social night" analysis of advertising in accordance with the new media symbols. *Journal of Media Critiques*, *1*(1), 177–194. DOI: 10.17349/jmc114111

Unilever (2024, April 23). *20 years on: Dove and the future of Real Beauty*. Retrieved from Unilever: https://www.unilever.com/news/news-search/2024/20-years-on-dove-and-the-future-of-real-beauty/

Valdivieso Benavente, D. J. (2023). "Homogenized Branding: A Semiotic and Cultural Inquiry into Visual Identity" politesi.polimi.it

Van den Broeck, E., & Pauwels, K. (2021). Visual Storytelling and AI in Marketing: Enhancing the Consumer-Brand Relationship. *Journal of Interactive Marketing*, *55*(2), 134–149.

Vanninen, H., Mero, J., & Kantamaa, E. (2023). Social media influencers as mediators of commercial messages. *Journal of Internet Commerce*. lut.fi

Varghese, N., & Kumar, N. (2020). Feminism in advertising: Irony or revolution? A critical review of femvertising. *Feminist Media Studies*, *22*(2), 441–459. DOI: 10.1080/14680777.2020.1825510

Varma, A., Varde, Y., & Ray, S. (2024). Reinventing the retail experience: The case of Amazon GO. *World Journal of Advanced Research and Reviews*, *21*(03), 1123–1133. DOI: 10.30574/wjarr.2024.21.3.0779

Vaughan, A. (2014, October 9). *Lego ends Shell partnership following Greenpeace campaign*. Retrieved from The Guardian: https://www.theguardian.com/environment/2014/oct/09/lego-ends-shell-partnership-following-greenpeace-campaign#:~:text=Lego%20will%20not%20renew%20its,that%20dates%20to%20the%201960s

Ventalon, G., Erjavec, G., & Tijus, C. (2020). Processing visual metaphors in advertising: An exploratory study of cognitive abilities. [HTML]. *Journal of Cognitive Psychology*, *32*(8), 816–826. DOI: 10.1080/20445911.2020.1817038

Ventura Bordenca, I. (2022). *Food packaging. Narrazioni semiotiche e branding alimentare*. Franco Angeli.

Ventura, I. (2005). Di che packaging sei? Generi discorsivi e confezioni dei prodotti, sulla scia di J.-M. Floch. *E|C*, 1-23.

Verhagen, T., Van Nes, J., Feldberg, F., & Van Dolen, W. (2014). Virtual customer service agents: Using social presence and personalization to shape online service encounters. *Journal of Computer-Mediated Communication*, *19*(3), 529–545. DOI: 10.1111/jcc4.12066

Vimeo. (n.d.). The World's First Digital Mirror on Vimeo. Retrieved December 23, 2024, from https://vimeo.com/116120605

Vincent Jaiwant, S. (2023). Changing structure of consumer buying behaviour and expectation in the digital era. In Singh, G., Goel, R., & Garg, V. (Eds.), *Industry 4.0 and the digital transformation of international business* (pp. 207–215). Springer Nature Singapore., DOI: 10.1007/978-981-19-7880-7_12

Volli, U. (2003). *Semiotica della pubblicità*. Laterza.

Vredenburg, J., Kapitan, S., Spry, A., & Kemper, J. A. (2020). Brands taking a stand: Authentic brand activism or woke washing? *Journal of Public Policy & Marketing*, *39*(4), 444–460. DOI: 10.1177/0743915620947359

Wang, J., & Li, M. (2024). *Brand transcreation as multimodal configuration: The (re) making of text, context, and meaning in brand semiotics*. Babel. [HTML] DOI: 10.1075/babel.00370.wan

Wang, W., Chen, C. H. S., Nguyen, B., & Shukla, P. (2020). Collaboration between East and West: Influence of consumer dialectical self on attitude towards co-brand personality traits. [HTML]. *International Marketing Review, 37*(6), 1155–1180. DOI: 10.1108/IMR-01-2019-0012

Wang, Y., & Qiao, F. (2020). The symbolic meaning of luxury-lite fashion brands among younger Chinese consumers. [HTML]. *Journal of Fashion Marketing and Management, 24*(1), 83–98. DOI: 10.1108/JFMM-09-2019-0204

Ward, E., Yang, S., Romaniuk, J., & Beal, V. (2020). Building a unique brand identity: Measuring the relative ownership potential of brand identity element types. *Journal of Brand Management, 27*(4), 393–407. DOI: 10.1057/s41262-020-00187-6

Warren, N. L. (2021). Boycott or Buycott: The aftermath of corporate activism. *NIM Marketing Intelligence Review, 13*(2), 32–37. DOI: 10.2478/nimmir-2021-0014

Wedel, M., Bigné, E., & Zhang, J. (2020). Virtual and augmented reality: Advancing research in consumer marketing. *International Journal of Research in Marketing, 37*(3), 443–465. DOI: 10.1016/j.ijresmar.2020.04.004

Weinzimmer, L. G., & Esken, C. A. (2016). Risky business: Taking a stand on social issues. *Business Horizons, 59*(3), 331–337. DOI: 10.1016/j.bushor.2016.01.007

Welch, D. (2020). Consumption and teleoaffective formations: Consumer culture and commercial communications. *Journal of Consumer Culture*. sagepub.com

West, D. E. (2021). *Between two minds: The work of Peirce's energetic interpretant*. Contemporary Pragmatism. [HTML]

Wheeler, A., & Meyerson, R. (2024). *Designing brand identity: A comprehensive guide to the world of brand and branding*. Wiley.

Widaman, K. F. & Helm, J. L. (2023). Exploratory factor analysis and confirmatory factor analysis.. [HTML]

Wiggins R J, (2022). "Semiotic Analysis for More Thoughtful Marketing Mix Decision-Making in the Age of Online Consumer Discourse".

Wind, J., & Mahajan, V. (2000). Digital marketing. *European Business Forum*. https://faculty.wharton.upenn.edu/wp-content/uploads/2012/04/0004_The_Challenge_of_Digital_Marketing.pdf

Wolk, A., & Ebling, C. (2010). Multi-channel price differentiation: An empirical investigation of existence and causes. *International Journal of Research in Marketing, 27*(2), 142–150. DOI: 10.1016/j.ijresmar.2010.01.004

Woodside, A. G.. (2008). Brand storytelling: Exploring narrative marketing. *The Journal of Consumer Research, 35*(5), 445–458.

Worakittikul, W., Saenwerm, C., & Naruetharadhol, P. (2024). Unlocking the secrets of green semiotics: The revolutionary power of eco-symbols in transforming consumer perceptions and catalyzing behavioral shifts in emerging .... *PloS one*. plos.org

Xi, N. & Hamari, J. (2021). Shopping in virtual reality: A literature review and future agenda. *Journal of Business Research*. sciencedirect.com

Xiao, H., & Li, L. (2023). A Bibliometric and Visual Analysis of Social Semiotics: Development, Hotspots, and Trend Directions. *Semiotica, 2023*(251), 193–213. DOI: 10.1515/sem-2021-0089

Xu, Y., Liu, X., Cao, X., Huang, C., Liu, E., Qian, S., Liu, X., Wu, Y., Dong, F., Qiu, C.-W., Qiu, J., Hua, K., Su, W., Wu, J., Xu, H., Han, Y., Fu, C., Yin, Z., Liu, M., & Zhang, J. (2021). Artificial intelligence: A powerful paradigm for scientific research. *Innovation (Cambridge (Mass.)), 2*(4), 1–20. DOI: 10.1016/j.xinn.2021.100179

Yao, A., Chan, N., & Yao, N. (2024). Understanding consumer behavior in phygital environments: An interpretivist methodological framework. *Qualitative Market Research, 27*(3), 449–470. DOI: 10.1108/QMR-08-2023-0100

Yezhova, O., Pashkevych, K., & Bezuhla, R. (2024). *Semiotics and Cognitive Dimensions in the Design of Corporate Visual Identity for Chemical Enterprises*. Linguistic and Philosophical Studies.

Yin, W., & Xu, B. (2021). Effect of online shopping experience on customer loyalty in apparel business-to-consumer ecommerce. *Textile Research Journal, 91*(23–24), 2882–2895. DOI: 10.1177/00405175211016559

Yu, J., Dickinger, A., & Egger, R. (2024). Leveraging emojis as visual semiotics for enhanced engagement in destination marketing. [researchgate.net]. *Journal of Destination Marketing & Management, 33*, 100925. DOI: 10.1016/j.jdmm.2024.100925

Zannin, A. (2009). *Analisi, progettazione e valutazione dell'efficacia dello spot pubblicitario. Una semiotica per la ricerca di mercato*. [Unpublished doctoral dissertation]. Università di Bologna - Alma Mater Studiorum, Bologna, Italia.

Zeghdani M B, (2023). "A Semiotic Analysis of the 'Reflect Your Respect' Infographic Poster for the World Cup Qatar 2022".

Zhang, K. (2020). The effect of para-social interaction in endorsement advertising: SEM studies based on consumers' exposure to celebrity symbols. *Language and Semiotic Studies*. degruyter.com

Zhang, T., Ge, L., Gou, Q., & Chen, L. (2018). Consumer showrooming, the sunk cost effect and online-offline competition. *Journal of Electronic Commerce Research, 19*(1), 55–74.

Zhang, W., & Wang, Y. (2023). Not just apologizing: The impact of complaint handling on sustained participation behavior in live-streaming shopping. *Journal of Consumer Behaviour, 22*(3), 688–700. DOI: 10.1002/cb.2154

Zhou, S., Barnes, L., McCormick, H., & Cano, M. B. (2021). Social Media Influencers' Narrative Strategies to Create eWOM: A Theoretical Contribution [Elsevier.]. *International Journal of Information Management, 56*, 102245. DOI: 10.1016/j.ijinfomgt.2020.102293

Zingale, S. (2009). *Gioco, dialogo, design. Una ricerca semiotica.* ATì.

Zingale, S. (2012). *Interpretazione e progetto. Semiotica dell'inventiva.* Franco Angeli.

Zingale, S. (2020). Design o progettualità? Il progetto come trasformazione inventiva. *Ocula, 24*, 51-72.

Zinna, A. (2004). *Le interfacce degli oggetti di scrittura: teoria del linguaggio e ipertesti*. Meltemi.

Zoe, H. (2023). Signs of #self: A Peircean semiotic framework for theorizing self-(re)presentation on Instagram. *Visual Communication, 22*(4), 671–692. DOI: 10.1177/14703572211022400

Zotova, A. S. (2021). Semiotics of advertising communication in WEB 2.0 network social services. *RUDN Journal of Language Studies. Semiotics and Semantics, 12*(4), 1285–1298. DOI: 10.22363/2313-2299-2021-12-4-1285-1298

About the Contributors

Marianna Boero, PhD, is Associate Professor of Philosophy and Language Theory at the University of Teramo (Italy), Department of Communication Sciences, where she teaches Semiotics, New Media Semiotics and Semiotics of Advertising and Consumption. She mainly deals with text semiotics, semiotics of advertising and consumption, semiotics of culture, socialsemiotics and communication studies, and has published several articles and three scientific monographs on these topics.

Rossana Piccolo is a researcher at the University of Teramo (Italy), Department of Communication Sciences, where she teaches Retail Marketing and Brand Management. She holds a European PhD in Entrepreneurship and Innovation. During PhD, she studied at the University of the West of Scotland (UWS), UK. She conducts research on technological innovation, knowledge management, corporate social responsibility, healthcare management and digital marketing. She is involved in several Peer Review processes for international journals and has participated in numerous international conferences as Key Speaker and Chair.

***

Nilesh Anute is an Associate Professor at Sri Balaji University, Pune. With a strong academic background, he specializes in his field of expertise, contributing significantly to both teaching and research. Dr. Anute is known for his dedication to student development and academic excellence, combining theoretical knowledge with practical insights. His experience in academia has established him as a respected figure in his department, guiding students toward their professional goals while also contributing to scholarly research and publications.

Prashant Kalshetti is a Professor and Head of the Department of BBA at Dr. D.Y. Patil Vidyapeeth, Global Business School and Research Centre, Pune. With extensive experience in business education, he is committed to academic excellence, research, and student mentorship. His expertise spans various aspects of management and business studies, contributing to the growth and development of future business leaders.

Sarvesh Khaitan is a Bachelor of Business Administration (BBA) student at Christ University. He is passionate about business and management studies, with a particular interest in research and academic writing. This book chapter showcases his commitment to learning and his aspiration to contribute valuable insights to the field of business.

Antonio Laurino received a bachelor's degree in Communication Sciences from the Suor Orsola Benincasa University of Naples and a master's degree in Semiotics from the University of Bologna - Alma Mater Studiorum, both with honors. He is currently an adjunct professor at the University of Bologna, the University of San Marino and the International Telematic University Uninettuno, where he holds courses related to functional writing and business communication. His scholarly articles in the field of applied semiotics have appeared in Ocula, Filosofi(e)Semiotiche and in the International Journal of Marketing Semiotics & Discourse Studies.

Paolo Odoardi is a Marketing professional and communications analyst; in his career he combines an important academic background with twenty years of work experience in the design and management of digital strategies, for Italian and international brands. PhD in Semiotics, in 2009, at SUM Italia (Scuola Normale Superiore - Scuola Superiore di Studi Umanistici), chaired by Umberto Eco. In 2008 he was Research Scholar in the Department of Cognitive Science of Case Western Reserve University in Cleveland, Ohio. Today he is Digital Marketing Manager in Euris, a leading technology company, in the Top 100 of software and services companies in Italy. Since 2009 he has been working as a contract professor in various universities: University of Bologna, IAAD, Uninettuno University, University of San Marino, where he is Adjunct Professor in Digital Marketing. His publications are mainly dedicated to the study of the intersection areas between semiotic and digital skills.

P. Selvakumar is currently an Associate Professor in the Department of Science and Humanities at Nehru Institute of Technology, Coimbatore, Tamil Nadu, India. Since 2023, he has served as the Department IQAC Coordinator at the institute. Prior to joining Nehru Institute of Technology, he held positions as an Assistant Professor in the Department of Science and Humanities various engineering colleges in Coimbatore, Tamil Nadu, India, spanning from 2011 to 2023. Dr.P. Selvakumar's academic and research interests lie primarily in the field of phytochemistry. He has made significant contributions to his field, with an impressive record that includes 30 journal publications, 12 patents, and 20 conference papers. Additionally, he has organized 5 seminars and conferences, further demonstrating his commitment to academic and scientific exchange. Throughout his career, Dr. P.Selvakumar has been recognized for his dedication and excellence in teaching, having been honored with several awards, including the Best Teacher Awards. He holds a prominent position in the academic community, contributing actively to research.

Naga Palakurti is a seasoned Solution Architect with over 23 years of expertise in the IT industry, specializing in the Financial and Insurance domains. Naga Palakurti is a highly accomplished and results-driven Solution architect with a proven track record in business analysis, solution architecture, and driving business and technical transformations. With extensive experience in advanced software solutions and products, as well as leading prestigious organizations' Centers of Excellence, Naga has consistently delivered outstanding outcomes. In his current role as a Solution Architect at TCS/Bank of America, Naga leads the charge in designing, implementing, and enhancing cutting-edge algorithms utilizing AI/ML with Business Rules Management systems (Risk Management applications/Data Manipulations), predictive analytics, and adaptive analytics. His expertise enables the creation of contextual, relevant, and personalized customer experiences across TCS's Banking applications and Check deposit and credit card business units, resulting in increased profitability, customer loyalty, and sustained growth. Naga's past accomplishments include spearheading the design, development,

Jayashree Patole is an Associate Professor at Ramachandran International Institute of Management (RIIM), Pune. With a strong academic background and extensive experience in management education, she has contributed significantly to the field through teaching, research, and mentoring students. Dr. Patole has been actively involved in academic research and industry collaborations.

Priyanka Pawar is an Associate Professor at Indira College of Engineering and Management, Pune. With extensive experience in academia, Dr. Pawar is dedicated to research, teaching, and mentoring students, contributing significantly to her field.

Esma Ebru Şentürk received her bachelor's degree from Gazi University in 2006, master's degree in 2014 and PhD degree from Kırıkkale University in 2020. She worked in the sector between 2006-2013 and has been working as a lecturer at Hitit University Osmancık Ömer Derindere Vocational School since 2013. She is working in the fields of consumer behavior, digital marketing, marketing communication, product and brand management, entrepreneurship and marketing, marketing research. In these fields, she has carried out various studies such as projects, research articles, papers, book editing and book chapter authorship. She has also served on the organizing committees of various scientific congresses and is currently working as a journal editor.

Mohit Sharma is a research scholar at the Institute of Management Studies and Research, Maharshi Dayanand University, Rohtak, Haryana, India. His research focuses on the dynamic relationship between brand image and purchase intentions, particularly in the context of brand extensions within the FMCG sector. Mohit actively engages in bibliometric research, analyzing publication trends and identifying research gaps in his area of interest. He has co-authored several scholarly works and continues to contribute to the academic community. Mohit can be reached at mohitattri.rs.imsar@mdurohtak.ac.in

Kartikeya Singh is an Assistant Professor of BBA in Christ University and is taking care of subjects like basic management papers, Research Methodology and International Business his top skills include MySQL and Python (Programing language). His vision us to inspire and guide the next generation of business leaders.

Alice Venturini holds a PhD in Marketing from IULM University in Milan and is currently a research fellow in Semiotics of Advertising at the University of Modena and Reggio Emilia. Her research interests focus on the contemporary advertising scenario, particularly the co-construction processes of brand image and brand meaning. She has written for several national and international journals, including Ocula, Filosofi(e) Semiotiche, and the Journal of Global Fashion Marketing.

Index

A

B

C

D

V

W

www.ingramcontent.com/pod-product-compliance
Lightning Source LLC
LaVergne TN
LVHW080859300926
849162LV00003B/481